India's First

BOLTI KITAAB

15 Years

Chapter-wise Solved Question Bank

PHYSICS

for NEET

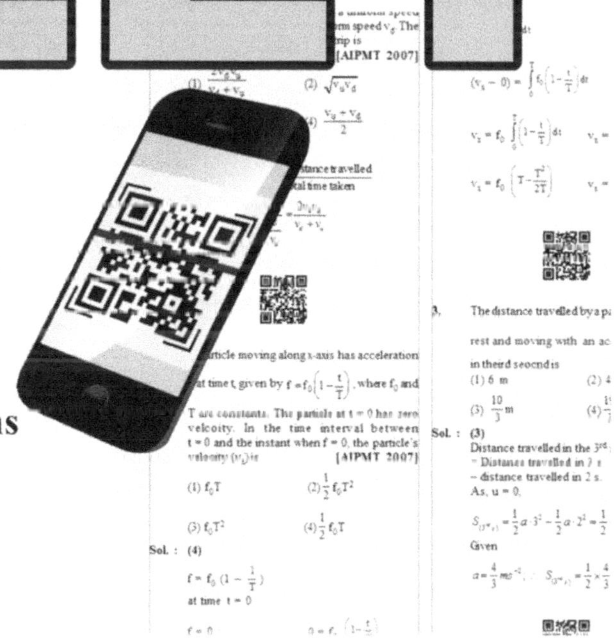

Special Features

- Errorless
- Compiled by Ex. Allen Faculty Kota
- Chapter wise solutions
- NCERT Sequence
- Audio-Video explanation of questions
- Unique method of learning

Dedicated to

"OUR INDIAN SOLDIERS"

Preface

As a next step in the continuance of our tradition, where we strive to develop innovative tools and techniques to push the concurrent learning pattern to a bigger next level we have evolved a series of new books, one of their kind by amalgamating current standards with a new angle of innovation. We have christened these books as "***Speaking Book***", as the name suggests by the help of some basic technological tools this book is capable to narrate and elaborate the key concepts through audio-visual techniques whenever and wherever needed. The first three books of this series are NEET PREVIOUS YEAR QUESTION BANK from past 15 years. It has been composed by Kota's best faculties under the guidance of Mr. Amit Dixit, he is a great visionary and an entrepreneur who has put immense toil in the educational field for its upliftment. It was him who conceived the core idea and numerous teachers, subject experts, and various tech experts put their efforts to develop this series, without whom it would have been impossible to develop it.

FEATURES OF THIS BOOK

Previous year questions have been incorporated into this book with maximum accuracy. A step ahead of the other "PREVIOUS YEAR QUESTION BANK" available in the market place. It is a perfect combination of regular paperback book and the concurrent technologies being used by the masses. The solutions of each question are given next to them. Along with this QR codes have been incorporated into entire solutions of all questions. After scanning it with any regular QR code scanner, it will lead you to a perfect audio-visual solution thus making the key concepts of problem-solving crystal clear. In this book, previous year questions have been grouped and tagged in both chapter-wise as well as the year-wise manner and available for all three subjects (viz. physics, chemistry, and biology) separately, which is hard to find in the marketplace. Multiple revisions have been done to make it errorless. The book is designed strictly in accordance with the concurrent relevancy which will provide a deep insight of the past as well as the present trend of questions being asked in actual test papers.

About the Author

"AMIT KUMAR DIXIT"

After the acquisition of certificate course from Kanpur I.I.T. in Foreign Language, he handled the medical aspirants in various branches of Delhi Public School in India and also monitored an online project in GYAN SEVA TRUST Chandigarh. Taken satellite classes in entire regions of Punjab for PUNJAB EDU BOARD. Has experience of many years in botany teaching at Aakash Institute New Delhi. Taught Botany to medical aspirants in Career Point Kota. Has been Founder biology faculty in the Pre-medical division of Bansal classes. Authored many books of biology for NEET for international Cengage publication. He has acquired teaching experience of more than 16 years while serving at ***ALLEN (Kota)***, ***Aakash Institute (New Delhi), Bansal classes (Kota)***, Resonance (Kota), Career point (Kota).

Contributors

Technical & Sales Support: Mr. Shabbir Ahmed Qureshi (Head), Mr. Harish Bhojwani, Mr. Sunil Shukla

Solution Preparation: Mr. Nirmal Gupta, Mr. Rahul Virash, Mr. Nitesh, Mr.Ravindra, Mr. Dharmendra Singh

DTP Support: Mr. Inayat Ahmed, Mr. Rakesh Mahawar, Mr. Manoj Purohit, Mr. Anil Bhola

Editorial Support: Mr. Kishlay Kumar, Mr. Jitendra Saini

CONTENTS

How to fill error free NEET online form?

(Scan the QR code for details)

ISBN: 9781977063014

01 Physical World, Units & Measurement

Note: Scan QR code with your mobile camera or QR scanner for video solutions.

1. Dimensions of resistance in an electrical circuit, in terms of dimension of mass M, of length L, of time T and of current I, would be **[AIPMT 2007]**

(1) $[ML^2T^{-3}I^{-1}]$ (2) $[ML^2T^{-2}]$

(3) $[ML^2T^{-1}I^{-1}]$ (4) $[ML^2T^{-3}I^{-2}]$

Sol. : (4) According to Ohm's law,

$$V=RI \text{ or } R=\frac{V}{I}$$

Dimensions of $V=\frac{W}{q}=\frac{[ML^2T^{-2}]}{[IT]}$

$$\therefore R=\frac{[ML^2T^{-2}/IT]}{[I]}=[ML^2T^{-3}/I^{-2}].$$

2. If the error in the measurement of radius of a sphere is 2%, then the error in the determination of volume of the sphere will be **[AIPMT 2008]**

(1) 4% (2) 6%

(3) 8% (4) 2%

Sol. : (2) $V=\frac{4}{3}\pi R^3;\ \text{In } V=\text{In}\left(\frac{4}{3}\pi\right)+\text{In } R^3$

Differentiating, $\frac{dV}{V}=3\frac{dR}{R}$

Error in the determination of the volume

= 3 × 2% = 6%

3. Which two of the following five physical parameters have the same dimensions

(a) energy density (b) refractive index

(c) dielectric constant (d) Young's modulus

(e) magnetic field **[AIPMT 2008]**

(1) b and d (2) c and e

(3) a and d (4) a and e

Sol. : (3)

$$[\text{Energy density}]=\left[\frac{\text{Work done}}{\text{Volume}}\right]=\frac{MLT^{-2}.L}{L^3}$$

$$=[ML^{-1}T^{-2}]$$

$$[\text{Young's modulus}]=[Y]\left[\frac{\text{Force}}{\text{Area}}\right]\times\frac{[l]}{[\Delta l]}$$

$$=\frac{MLT^{-2}}{L^2}\cdot\frac{L}{L}=[ML^{-1}T^{-2}]$$

The dimension of 1 and 4 are the same.

4. If the dimensions of a physical quantity are given by $M^aL^bT^c$, then the physical quantity will be **[AIPMT 2009]**

(1) pressure if a = 1, b = –1, c = –2

(2) velocity if a = 1, b = 0, c = –1

(3) acceleration if a = 1, b = 1, c = –2

(4) force if a = 0, b = –1, c = –2

Sol. : (1) Pressure, $P=\frac{\text{foce}}{\text{area}}=\frac{\text{mass}\times\text{acceleration}}{\text{area}}$

$$\therefore [P]=\frac{M^1LT^{-2}}{L^2}=[M^1L^{-1}T^{-2}]=M^aL^bT^c.$$

$$\therefore a=1, b=-1, c=-2.$$

5. The dimension of $\frac{1}{2}\ {}_0E^2$, where ε_0 is permitivity of free space and E is electric field, is **[AIPMT 2016]**

(1) $[ML^2T^{-2}]$ (2) $[ML^{-1}T^{-2}]$
(3) $[ML^2T^{-1}]$ (4) $[MLT^{-1}]$

Sol. : (2) Energy density of an electric field E is

$$u_E = \frac{1}{2}\varepsilon_0 E^2$$

Where ε_0 is permittivity of free space

$$u_E = \frac{\text{Energy}}{\text{Volume}} = \frac{ML^2T^{-2}}{L^3} = ML^{-1}T^{-2}$$

Hence the dimension of $\frac{1}{2}\varepsilon_0 E^2$ is $ML^{-1}T^{-2}$

6. The dimensions of $(\mu_0\varepsilon_0)^{-1/2}$ are **[AIPMT 2011]**

(1) $[L^{-1}T]$ (2) $[LT^{-1}]$
(3) $[L^{-1/2}T^{1/2}]$ (4) $[L^{1/2}T^{-1/2}]$

Sol. $C = \frac{1}{\sqrt{\mu_0 \in_0}}$, $(\mu_0, \in_0)^{-1/2}$

$[C] = LT^{-1}$

7. The density of material in CGS system of units is 4 g/cm³. In a system of units in which unit of lengths is 10 cm and unit of mass is 100 g, the value of density of material will be **[AIPMT 2011]**

(1) 0.4 (2) 40
(3) 400 (4) 0.04

Sol. : (2) As $n_1u_1 = n_2u_2$

$$4\frac{g}{cm^3} = n_2\frac{100g}{(10cm)^3} \Rightarrow n_2 = 40$$

8. In an experiment four quantities a, b, c and d are measured with percentage error 1%, 2%, 3% and 4% respectively. Quantity P is calculated as follows : **[AIPMT 2013]**

$P = \frac{a^3b^2}{ca}$ % error in P is

(1) 14% (2) 10%
(3) 7% (4) 4%

Sol. : (1) As $P = \frac{a^3b^2}{cd}$ % error in P is

$$\frac{\Delta P}{P}\times 100 = \left[3\left(\frac{\Delta a}{a}\right) + 2\left(\frac{\Delta b}{b}\right) + \frac{\Delta c}{c} + \frac{\Delta d}{d}\right]\times 100$$

$$= [3\times 1\% + 2\times 2\% + 3\% + 4\%]$$

$$= 14\%$$

9. If force (F), velcoity (V) and time (T) are taken as fundamental units, then the dimensions of mass are **[AIPMT 2014]**

(1) $[FVT^{-1}]$ (2) $[FVT^{-2}]$
(3) $[FV^{-1}T^{-1}]$ (4) $[FV^{-1}T]$

Sol. : **(4)** Let mass $m \propto F^aV^bT^c$ or $m = kF^aV^bT^c$

where k is a dimensionless constant and a,b and c are the exponents.

Writing dimensions on both sides, we get

$[ML^0T^0] = [MLT^{-2}]^a[LT^{-1}]^b[T]^c$

$[ML^0T^0] = [M^aL^{a+b}T^{-2a-b+c}]$

Applying the principle of homogeneity of dimensins, we get

$a = 1$ ....(ii)

$a + b = 0$ ....(iii)

$-2a - b + c = 1$ ....(iv)

Solving eqns. (ii), (iii) and (iv), we get

$a = 1, b = -1, c = 1$

From eqn. (i), $[m] = [FV^{-1}T]$

10. If energy (E), velocity (V) and time (T) are chosen as the fundamental quantities, the dimensional formula of surface tension will be **[AIPMT 2015]**

(1) $[EV^{-2}T^{-1}]$ (2) $[EV^{-1}T^{-2}]$

(3) $[EV^{-2}T^{-2}]$ (4) $[E^{-2}V^{-1}T^{-3}]$

Sol. : **(3)** Lets S.T. $S \propto E^aV^bT^c$

$S = K\left[E^a\right]\left[V\right]^b\left[T\right]^c$

$\left[MT^{-2}\right] = \left[ML^2T^{-2}\right]^a\left[LT^{-1}\right]^b\left[T^c\right]$

$\left[M^1L^oT^{-2}\right] = \left[M^aL^{2a+b}T^{-2a-b+c}\right]$

a = 1 .....(i)

2a + b = 0 .....(ii)

− 2a − b + c = −2 .....(iii)

by (i), (ii) & (iii)

a = 1, b = −2, c = −2

$\therefore$ S.T. $S = \left[EV^{-2}T^{-2}\right]$.

11. In dimension of cirtical velocity v_c, of liquid following through a tube are expressed as (η^x, ρ^y, r^x) where η, ρ and rare the coefficient of viscosity of liquid, density of liquid and radius of the tube respectively, then the values of x, y and z are given by **[AIPMT 2015 Re]**

(1) 1, 1, 1 (2) 1, −1, −1

(3) −1, −1, 1 (4) −1, −1, −1

Sol. : **(2)** $v_c \propto [\eta^x\rho^yr^z]$

$[L^1T^{-1}] \propto [M^1L^{-1}T^{-1}]^x[M^1L^{-3}]^y[L^1]^z$

$[L^1T^{-1}] \propto [M^{x+y}][L^{-x-3y+z}][T^{-x}]$

Talking comparision on both size

$x + y = 0, -x - 3y + z = 1, -x = -1$

$\Rightarrow x = 1, y = -1, z = -1.$

12. A physical quantity of the dimensions of length that can be formed out of c, G and $\frac{e^2}{4\pi\epsilon_0}$ is [c is velocity of light, G is universal constant of gravitation and e is charge] : **[NEET - 2017]**

(1) $\frac{1}{c^2}\left[G\frac{e^2}{4\pi\epsilon_0}\right]^{1/2}$ (2) $c^2\left[G\frac{e^2}{4\pi\epsilon_0}\right]^{1/2}$

(3) $\frac{1}{c^2}\left[\frac{e^2}{G4\pi\epsilon_0}\right]^{1/2}$ (4) $\frac{1}{c}G\frac{e^2}{4\pi\epsilon_0}$

Sol. $\ell = C^x G^y (A)^z$

$[M^oL^1T^o] = (LT^{-1})^x [M^{-1}L^3T^{-2}][ML^3T^{-2}]^z$

$M^oL^1T^o = M^{-y+z} L^{x+3y+3z} T^{-x-2y-2z}$

$M : 0 = -y + z$

$y = 3$ ....(1)

$T : 0 = -x - 2y - 2z$

$x = -2y - 2(y) = -4y$

$x = -4y$ ....(2)

$L : 1 = x + 3y + 3z$ ....(3)

From equation (1), (2) & (3)

$$1 = x + 3\left(\frac{-x}{4}\right) + 3\left(\frac{-x}{4}\right)$$

$$1 = x - \frac{3x}{2}, \frac{2x - 3x}{2} = \frac{-x}{2}$$

$x = -2$

$+4y = -2$

$$y = \frac{1}{2}$$

$$z = y = \frac{1}{2}$$

13. A student measured the diameter of a small steel ball using a screw gauge of least count 0.001 cm. The main scale reading is 5 mm and zero of circular scale division coincides with 25 division above the reference level. If screw gauge has zero error of -0.004 cm, the correct diameter of the ball is **[NEET-2018]**

(1) 0.053 cm (2) 0.525 cm

(3) 0.521 cm (4) 0.529 cm

Ans. **(4)**

02 Motion in a Straight Line

Note: Scan QR code with your mobile camera or QR scanner for video solutions.

1. A car moves from X to Y with a uniform speed v_u and returns to Y with a uniform speed v_d. The average speed for this round trip is **[AIPMT 2007]**

(1) $\frac{2v_d v_u}{v_d \quad v_u}$ (2) $\sqrt{v_u v_d}$

(3) $\frac{v_d v_u}{v_d \quad v_u}$ (4) $\frac{v_u \quad v_d}{2}$

Sol. : (1) Average speed $= \frac{\text{total distance travelled}}{\text{total time taken}}$

$$= \frac{s+s}{t_1+t_2} = \frac{2s}{\frac{s}{v_u}+\frac{s}{v_d}} = \frac{2v_u v_d}{v_d+v_u}$$

2. A particle moving along x-axis has acceleration f, at time t, given by $f \quad f_0 \; 1 \quad \frac{t}{T}$, where f_0 and T are constants. The particle at t = 0 has zero velcoity. In the time interval between t = 0 and the instant when f = 0, the particle's velocity (v_x) is **[AIPMT 2007]**

(1) $f_0 T$ (2) $\frac{1}{2} f_0 T^2$

(3) $f_0 T^2$ (4) $\frac{1}{2} f_0 T$

Sol. : (4)

$f = f_0 \left(1 - \frac{1}{T}\right)$

at time t = 0

f = 0 ; $0 = f_0\left(1-\frac{t}{T}\right)$

t = T $f = \left(\frac{dv}{dt}\right)$

$$\int_0^v dv = \int_{t=0}^{t=T} f\,dt$$

$$(v_x - 0) = \int_0^T f_0\left(1-\frac{t}{T}\right)dt$$

$$v_x = f_0 \int_0^T \left(1-\frac{t}{T}\right)dt \qquad v_x = f_0\left(t-\frac{t^2}{2T}\right)\Bigg|_0^T$$

$$v_x = f_0\left(T-\frac{T^2}{2T}\right) \qquad v_x = \frac{f_0 T}{2}$$

3. The distance travelled by a particle starting from rest and moving with an acceleration $\frac{4}{3}\text{ms}^{\;2}$, in theird seocnd is **[AIPMT 2008]**

(1) 6 m (2) 4 m (3) $\frac{10}{3}$m (4) $\frac{19}{3}$m

Sol. : (3)

Distance travelled in the 3rd second
= Distance travelled in 3 s
– distance travelled in 2 s.
As, u = 0,

$$S_{(3^{rd}s)} = \frac{1}{2}a\cdot 3^2 - \frac{1}{2}a\cdot 2^2 = \frac{1}{2}\cdot a\cdot 5$$

Given

$$a = \frac{4}{3}ms^{-2};\ \therefore\ S_{(3^{rd}s)} = \frac{1}{2}\times\frac{4}{3}\times 5 = \frac{10}{3}m.$$

4. A particle shows distance-time curve as given in this figure. The maximum instantaneous velocity of the particle is around the point **[AIPMT 2008]**

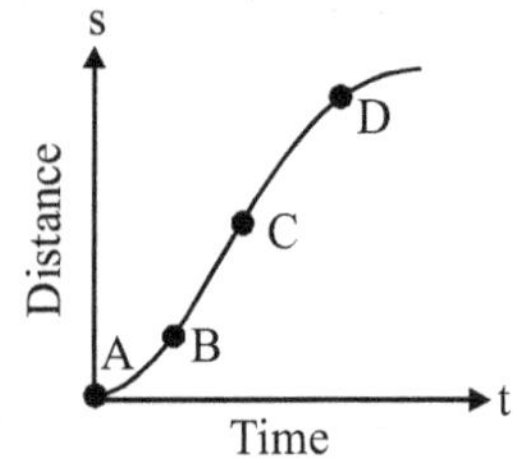

(1) B (2) C
(3) D (4) A

Sol. : (2)

In distance - time graph, the speed at instant is expressed by slope at that instant. The slope is maximum at C.

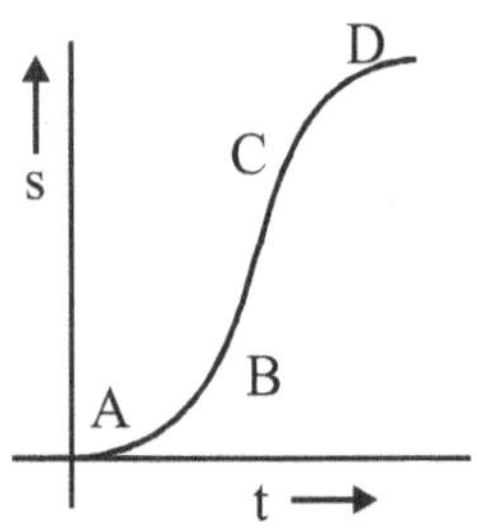

5. A particle moves in a straight line with a constant acceleration. It changes its velocity from $10ms^{-1}$ to $20\ ms^{-2}$ while passing through a distance 135 m in t second. The value of t is **[AIPMT 2008]**

(1) 10 (2) 1.8 (3) 12 (4) 9

Sol. : (4)

$v^2 - u^2 = 2as$

Given v $=20\ ms^{-1}$, u = $10\ ms^{-1}$, s = 135m

$$\therefore\ a = \frac{400-1001}{2\times 135} = \frac{300}{270} = \frac{10}{9}\text{m/s}^2$$

$$v = u + at \Rightarrow t = \frac{v-u}{a} = \frac{10m/s}{\frac{10}{9}m/s^2} = 9s$$

6. A bus is moving with a speed of $10ms^{-1}$ on a straight road. A scooterist wishes to overtake the bus in 100.s If the bus is at a distance of 1 km from the scooterist with what speed should the scooterist chase the bus ? **[AIPMT 2009]**

(1) $20\ ms^{-1}$ (2) $40\ ms^{-1}$
(3) $25\ ms^{-1}$ (4) $10\ ms^{-1}$

Sol. : (1)

Let v_s be the velocity of the scooter, the distance between the scooter and the bus = 1000m,

The velocity of the bus = $10\ ms^{-1}$

Time taken to overtake = 100 s

Relative velocity of the scooter with respect to the bus = $(v_s - 10)$

$$\therefore\ \frac{1000}{(v_s - 10)} = 100s \Rightarrow v_s = 20ms^{-1}$$

7. A particle starts its motion from rest under the action of a constant force. If the distance convered in first 10 s is s_1 and that converd in the first 20 s is s_2, then **[AIPMT 2009]**

(1) $s_2 = 2s_1$ (2) $s_2 = 3s_1$
(3) $s_2 = 4s_1$ (4) $s_2 = s_1$

Sol. : (3) Given u = 0.

Distance travelled in 10 s,

$$S_1 = \frac{1}{2}a\cdot 10^2 = 50a$$

Distance travelled in 20 s,

$$S_2 = \frac{1}{2}a\cdot 20^2 = 200a$$

$$\therefore S_2 = 4S_1.$$

8. A ball is dropped from a high rise platfrom at t = 0 staring from rest. After 6 s antoher ball is thrown dowenwards from the same platform withs a spped v. The two balls meet at t = 18's What is the value of v?

(take g = 10ms^{-2}) **[AIPMT 2010]**

(1) 75 ms^{-1} (2) 55 ms^{-1}

(3) 40 ms^{-1} (4) 60 ms^{-1}

Sol. : **(3)** Let the two balls meet after t s at distance x from the platform.

For the first ball

u = 0, t =18s, g = 10 m/s^2

Using $h = ut + \frac{1}{2}gt^2$

$\therefore \quad x = \frac{1}{2} \times 10 \times 18^2$ ....(i)

For the second ball

u = v, t =12s, g = 10 m/s^2

Using $h = ut + \frac{1}{2}gt^2$

$\therefore \quad x = v \times 12 + \frac{1}{2} \times 10 \times 12^2$

from the equation (i) and (ii), we get

$$\frac{1}{2} \times 10 \times 18^2 = 12v + \frac{1}{2} \times 10 \times 12^2$$

or $12v = \frac{1}{2} \times 10 \times [(18^2 - (12)^2]$

$= \frac{1}{2} \times 10 \times [(18+12)(18-12)]$

$12v - \frac{1}{2} \times 10 \times 30 \times 6$

or $v = \frac{1 \times 10 \times 30 \times 6}{2 \times 12} = 75$ m/s

9. A particle has initial velocity $3\hat{i} + 4\hat{j}$ and has acceleration $(0.4\hat{i} + 0.3\hat{j})$. Its speed after 10 s is **[AIPMT 2010]**

(1) 7 unit (2) $7\sqrt{2}$

(3) 8.5 unit (4) 10 unit

Sol. : **(2)** $\vec{v} = (3\hat{i} + 4\hat{j})$

$\vec{v} = (0.4\hat{i} + 0.3\hat{j})$ t = 10 second

$\vec{v} = \vec{v} + \vec{d}t$

$\vec{v} = 7\hat{i} + 7\hat{j}$

$|\vec{v}| = 7\sqrt{2}$ m/s

10. A particle moves a distance x in time t according to equation x = (t +5)$^{-1}$. The acceleration of particle is proportional to **[AIPMT 2010]**

(1) (velocity)$^{3/2}$ (2) (distance)^2

(3) (distance)$^{-2}$ (4) (velocity)$^{2/3}$

Sol : **(1)**

$x = (t + 5)^{-1}$

$v = \left(\frac{dx}{dt}\right) = -1\,(t + 5)^{-2}$

$a = \frac{dv}{dt} = +2(t + 5)^{-3}$

$a = 2\left(\frac{1}{t+5}\right)^3$

$a = (v)^{3/2}$

$a \propto v^{3/2}$

11. A boy standing at the top of a tower of 20 m height drops a stone. Assuming g = 10 ms^{-2}, the velocity with which it hits the ground is **[AIPMT 2011]**

(1) 20 m/s (2) 40 m/s

(3) 5 m/s (4) 1 m/s

Sol. : (1)

$$v = \sqrt{2gh} = \sqrt{2 \times 10 \times 20} = 20\,\text{m/sec}.$$

12. A body is moving with velocity 30 m/s towards east. After 10 s its velocity becomes 40 m/s towards north. The average acceleration of the body is **[AIPMT 2011]**

(1) 7 m/s^2 (2) $\sqrt{7}\,m/s^2$

(3) 5 m/s^2 (4) 1 m/s^2

Sol. : (3) Average acceleration

$$\vec{A}_{avg} = \frac{\vec{v}_f - \vec{v}_i}{t} = \frac{40\hat{j} - 30\hat{i}}{10}$$

$$\vec{A}_{avg} = \frac{\sqrt{40^2 + 30^2}}{10} = 5\,\text{m/sec}^2$$

13. A particle covers half of its total distance with speed v_1 and the rest half distance with speed v_2, Its average speed during the complete journery is **[AIPMT 2011]**

(1) $\frac{v_1 v_2}{v_1 + v_2}$ (2) $\frac{2v_1 v_2}{v_1 + v_2}$

(3) $\frac{2v_1^2 v_2^2}{v_1^2 + v_2^2}$ (4) $\frac{v_1 + v_2}{2}$

Sol : (3)

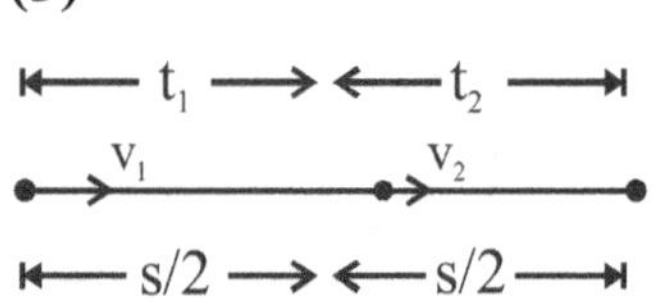

$$t_1 = \frac{(s/2)}{v_1}, \frac{S}{2N_1}$$

$$t_2 = \frac{S}{2V_2}$$

$$\text{Average speed} = \frac{\text{Total Distance}}{\text{Total time}}$$

$$v_{avg} = \frac{\left(\frac{3}{2}\right) + \left(\frac{5}{2}\right)}{(t_1 + t_2)}$$

$$v_{avg} = \frac{s}{\left(\frac{s}{2v_1} + \frac{s}{2v_2}\right)}, \frac{2v_1 v_2}{v_1 + v_2}$$

14. The motion of a particle along a staight line is described by equation :

x =8 + 12t +3 where x is in meter ant t in second. The retardation of the particle when its velocity becomes zero is **[AIPMT 2012]**

(1) 12 ms^{-1} (2) 24 ms^{-2}

(3) zero (4) 6 ms^{-1}

Sol : (1)

$x = 8 + 12t - t^3$

velocity, $v = \left(\frac{dx}{dt}\right) = 0 + 12 - 3t^2$

velocity = v = 0

$= = 12 - 3t^2$

$t^2 = 4$

t = 2 second

$a = \left(\frac{dv}{dt}\right) = -6t$

at t = 2 second

$a = 6(2) = 12\ m/s^2$

15. A stone falls freely under gravity. It covers distance h_1,h_2 and h_3 in the first 5 seconds, the next 5 seconds and the next 5 seconds rspectively. The relation between h_1, h_2 and h_3 is :

(1) $h_1 = 2h_2 = 3h_3$ **[AIPMT 2013]**

(2) $h_1 = \frac{h_2}{3} = \frac{h_3}{5}$

(3) $h_2 = 3h_1$ and $h_3 = 3h_2$

(4) $h_1 = h_2 = h_3$

Sol : (2)

Distance covered by the stone in first

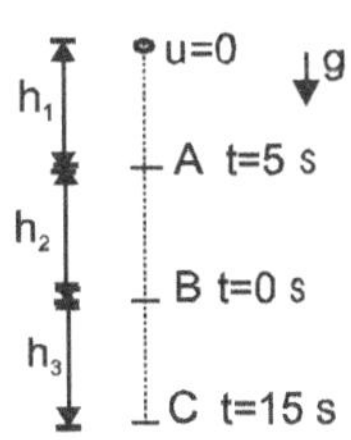

5 secound (i.e. t = 5 s) is

$$h_1 = \frac{1}{2}g(5)^2 = \frac{25}{2}g \quad ...(i)$$

Distance covered by the stone in first 5 secound (i.e. $t = 5$ s) is

$$h_1 + h_2 = \frac{1}{2}g(10)^2 = \frac{100}{2}g \quad ...(ii)$$

Distance travelled by the stone in first 5 second (i.e. t = 15 s) is

$$h_1 + h_2 + h_3 = \frac{1}{22}g(15)^2 = \frac{225}{2}g \quad ...(iii)$$

Subtract (ii) from (iii), we get

$$(h_1 + h_2) - h_1 - \frac{100}{2}g - \frac{25}{2}g - \frac{75}{2}g$$

$$h_2 = \frac{75}{2}g = 3h_1 \quad ...(iv)$$

Subtract (ii) from (iii), we get

$$(h_1 + h_2 + h_3)\ (h_2 + h_1) = \frac{225}{2}g - \frac{100}{2}g$$

$$h_3 = \frac{125}{2}g = 5h_1 \quad ....(v)$$

From (i), (iv) and (v), we get

$$h_1 = \frac{h_2}{3} = \frac{h_3}{5}$$

16. The displacement 'x' (in meter) of a particle of mass 'm' (in kg) moving in one dimension under the action of a force is released to time 't' (in sec) by $t = \sqrt{x} + 3$. The displacment of the particle when its velocity is zero will be **[AIPMT 2013]**

(1) 2 m (2) 4 m

(3) zero (4) 6m

Sol : (3)

$t = \sqrt{x} + 3$

$x = (t - 3)^2$

$v = \frac{dx}{dt} = 2(t - 3)$

velocity (v) = 0

$v = 2(t - 3) = 0$

t = 3 second

at t = 3 second

$x = (t - 3)^2$

$x = (3 - 3)^2 = 0$ m

17. A particle of unit mass undergoes one- dimesional motion such that its velocity varies according to $\upsilon(x) = \beta x^{-2n}$

where β and n are constants and x is the position of the particle. The acceleration of the particle. as a function of x is given by **[AIPMT 2015]**

(1) $-2n\beta^2 x^{-2n-1}$ (2) $-2n\beta^2 x^{-4n-1}$

(3) $-2n\beta^2 x^{-2n+1}$ (4) $-2n\beta^2 e^{-4n+1}$

Sol. : (2)

$$a = \frac{dv}{dx} \times \frac{dx}{dt}$$

$$\left(\beta(-2n) \times x^{-2n-1}\right) \times \left(\beta x^{-2n}\right)$$

so, $-2n\beta^2 x^{-4n-1}$.

18. If the velocity of a particle is $v = At + Bt^2$, where A and B are constants, then the distane travelled by it between 1s and 2s is :- **[AIPMT 2016]**

(1) $\frac{3}{2}A + 4B$ (2) 3A+7B

(3) $\frac{3}{2}A + \frac{7}{3}B$ (4) $\frac{A}{2} + \frac{B}{3}$

Sol. : (3)

$v = At + 8t^2$ $v = \frac{dx}{dt}$

$$\int_{x_1}^{x_2} dx = \int_{1s}^{2s} v\,dt \qquad (x_2 - x_1) = \int_{1s}^{2s} \left(At + Bt^2\right) dt$$

$$x_2 - x_1 = \left|\frac{At^2}{2} + \frac{Bt^3}{3}\right|_1^2$$

$$x_2 - x_1 \left[\left(2A + \frac{8B}{3}\right) - \left(\frac{A}{2} + \frac{B}{3}\right)\right]$$

$$= \left(\frac{6A + 8B}{3}\right) - \left(\frac{3A + 2B}{6}\right)$$

$$= \frac{12A + 16B - 3A - 2B}{6}$$

$$x_2 - x_2 = \frac{9A + 14B}{6}$$

$$\Delta x = \left(\frac{3A}{2} + \frac{7B}{3}\right)$$

19. Preeti reached the metro station and found that the escalator was not working. She walked up the stationary escalator in time t_1. On other days, if she remains stationary on the moving escalator, then the escalator takes her up in time t_2. The time taken by her to walk up on the moving escalator will be : **[NEET - 2017]**

(1) $\frac{t_1 + t_2}{2}$ (2) $\frac{t_1 t_2}{t_2 - t_1}$

(3) $\frac{t_1 t_2}{t_2 + t_1}$ (4) $t_1 - t_2$

Sol. : (3)

Velocity of girl w.r.t. elevator $= \frac{d}{t_1} = v_{ge}$

Velocity of elevator w.r.t. ground $v_{eg} = \frac{d}{t_2}$ then velocity of girl w.r.t. ground

$$\vec{V}_{gG} = \vec{V}_{ge} + \vec{V}_{eG}$$

i.e, $V_{gG} = V_{ge} + V_{eG}$

$$\frac{d}{t} = \frac{d}{t_1} + \frac{d}{t_2}$$

$$\frac{1}{t} = \frac{1}{t_1} + \frac{1}{t_2}$$

$$t = \frac{t_1 t_2}{(t_1 + t_2)}$$

03 Motion in a Plane

Note: Scan QR code with your mobile camera or QR scanner for video solutions.

1. A particle starting from the origin (0,0) moves in a straight line in the (x,y) plane. Its cordinates at a later time are $\sqrt{3},3$. The path of the particle makes with the x-axis an angle of : **[AIPMT 2007]**

(1) 30° (2) 45°

(3) 60° (4) 0°

Sol : **(3)**

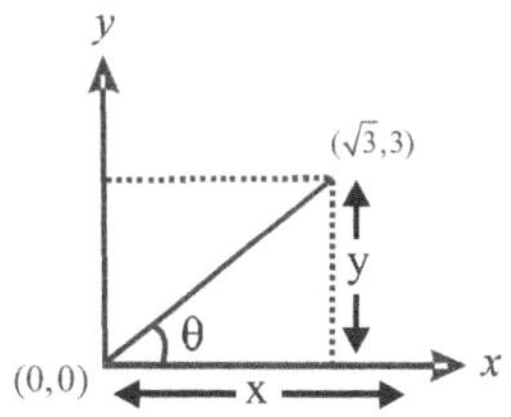

$\tan\theta = \left(\frac{y}{x}\right) = \frac{3}{\sqrt{3}}$

$\tan\theta = \sqrt{3}$

$\theta = 60°$

2. $\vec{A}$ and $\vec{B}$ are two vectors and θ is the angle between them, if $|\vec{A}\times\vec{B}| = \sqrt{3}\ \vec{A}.\vec{B}$ The value of θ is **[AIPMT 2007]**

(1) 60° (2) 45°

(3) 30° (4) 90°

Sol : **(1)** $\left|\vec{A}\times\vec{B}\right| = \sqrt{3}\left(\vec{A}\,.\,\vec{B}\right)$

$\therefore AB\sin\theta = \sqrt{3}AB\cos\theta$

or, $\tan\theta = \sqrt{3}$ or, $\theta = \tan^{-1}\sqrt{3} = 60^o$

3. The position x of a particle with respect to time t along x–axis is given by $x = 9t^2 - t^3$, when x is in metres and t in second, which will be the position of this particle when it achieves maxium speed along +x direction **[AIPMT 2007]**

(1) 24 m (2) 32 m (3) 54 m (4) 81 m

Sol : **(3)** $x = 9t^2 - t^3 \left[\because \frac{dx}{dt} = v\right]$ $\therefore v = 18t - 3t^2$

$\Rightarrow \frac{dV}{dt} = 18 - 6t$

for maximum speed $\frac{dV}{dt} = 0$, and $\frac{d^2V}{dt^2}$ negative

so $18 - 6t = 0 \Rightarrow t = 3s$

at $t = 3s, x = 9(3)^2 - (3)^3 = 81 - 27 = 54\,m$.

4. Three forces acting on body are shown in the figure. To have the resultant force only along the y-direction, the magnitude of the minimum additional force needed is : **[AIPMT 2008]**

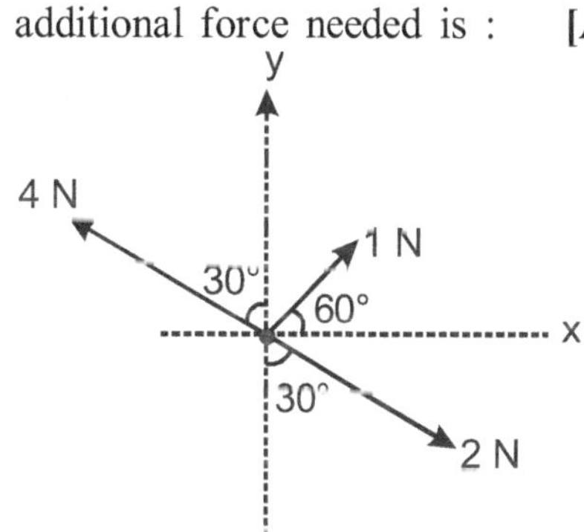

(1) 0.5 N (2) 1.5 N

(3) $\frac{\sqrt{3}}{4}$N (4) $\sqrt{3}$N

Sol. : **(1)** 4N and 2N are opposite

So net = 4 – 2 = 2N

Now figure becomes

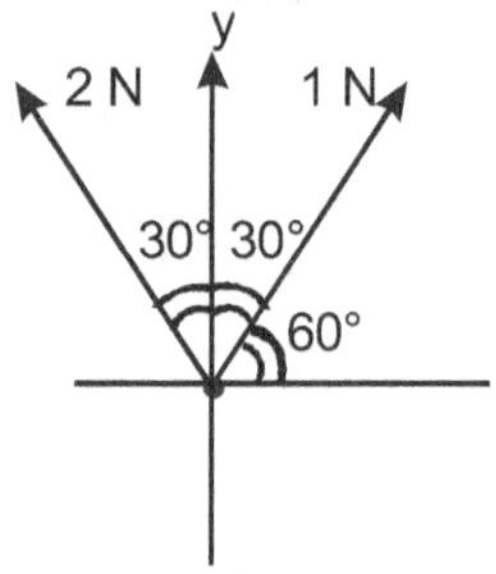

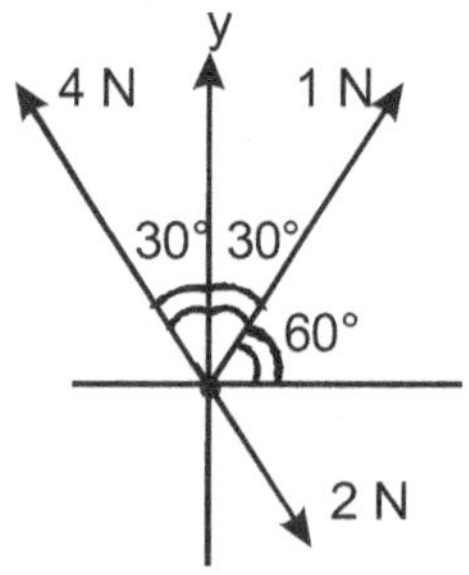

Horizontal component of 2N along –ve x-direction is $x_1 = 2 \sin 30° = 1$ N Horizontal component of 1 N along +ve

x-direction is $x_2 = 1 \cos 60° = \frac{1}{2}$N

So, net horizontal force is $\frac{1}{2}$N along –ve x-direction,

hence $\frac{1}{2}$N is required in +ve x-direction.

5. A particle of mass m is projected with velocity v making an agnle of 45° with the horizontal When the particle lands on the level ground the magnitude of the change in is momentum will be : **[AIPMT 2008]**

(1) 2 mv (2) $mv/\sqrt{2}$

(3) $mv\sqrt{2}$ (4) zero

Sol : **(3)**

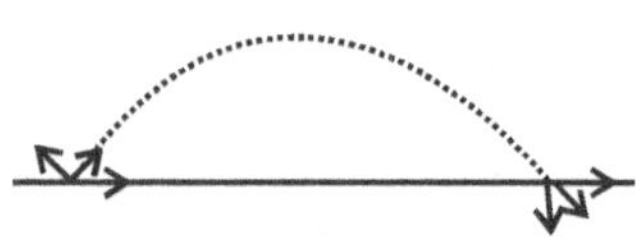

The horizontal momentum does not change. The change in vertical momentum is

$$mv\sin\theta - (-mv\sin\theta) = 2mv\frac{1}{\sqrt{2}} = \sqrt{2}mv$$

6. Six vectors $\vec{a}$ through $\vec{f}$ have the magnitudes and directions indicated in the figure. Which of the following statements is ture ? **[AIPMT 2010]**

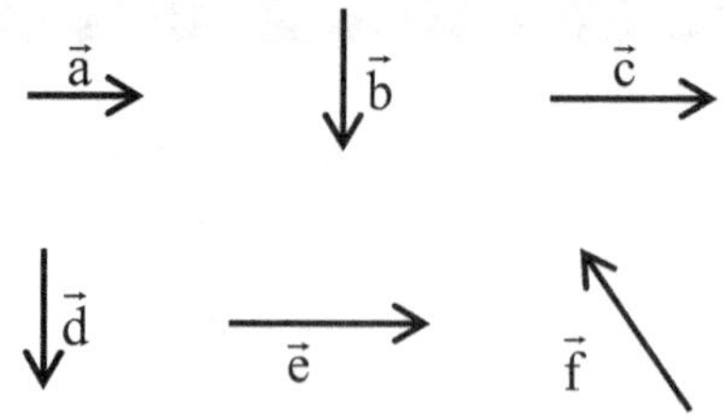

(1) $\vec{b}$ $\vec{c}$ $\vec{f}$ (2) $\vec{d}$ $\vec{c}$ $\vec{f}$

(3) $\vec{d}$ $\vec{e}$ $\vec{f}$ (4) $\vec{b}$ $\vec{e}$ $\vec{f}$

Sol : **(4)** For option (1)

$\vec{b} + \vec{c} = \vec{f}$

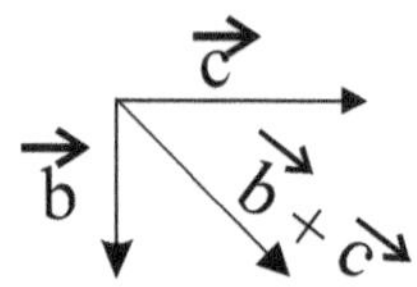

from fig. $|\vec{b} + \vec{c}| \neq |\vec{f}|$

For option (2)

$\vec{b} + \vec{c} = \vec{f}$

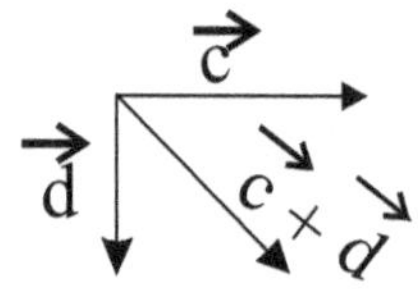

$|\vec{c} + \vec{d}| \neq |\vec{f}|$

For option (3)

$\vec{d} + \vec{e} = \vec{f}$

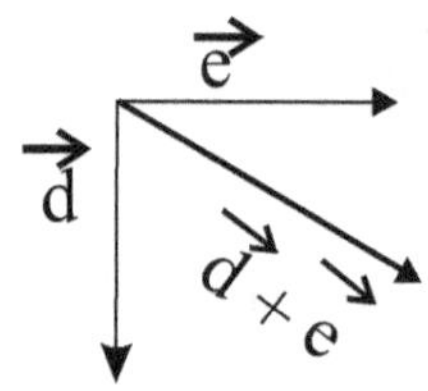

$|\vec{d} + \vec{e}| \neq |\vec{f}|$

For option (4)

$\vec{d} + \vec{e} = \vec{f}$

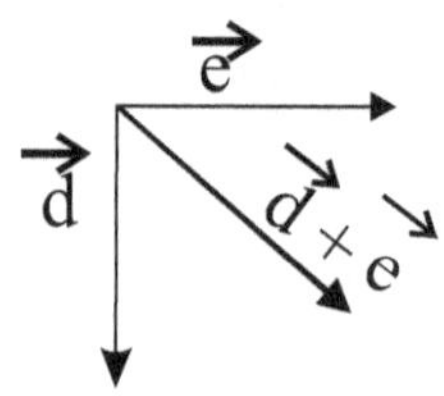

Form figer, $|\vec{d} + \vec{e}| = |\vec{f}|$

7. A particle moves in a circle of radius 5 cm with constant speed and time period 0.2 πs. The acceleration of the particle is **[AIPMT 2011]**

(1) 25 m/s² (2) 36 m/s²

(3) 5 m/s² (4) 15 m/s²

Sol : **(3)** Here, Radius, $R = 5\text{ cm} = 5\times10^{-2}\text{ m}$

Time period, $T = 0.2\pi$ s

Conripental acceleration

$$a_C = \omega^2 R = \left(\frac{2\pi}{T}\right)^2 R = \left(\frac{2\pi}{0.2\pi}\right)\left(5\times10^{-2}\right) = 5\text{ m/s}^2$$

As particle moves with constant speed, therefore its tangential acceleration is zero. So, $a_t = 0$

The acceleration of the particle is

$$a = \sqrt{a_c^2 + a_t^2} = a_c = 5\text{ m/s}^2$$

It acts towards the centre of the circle.

8. A missile is fired for maximum range with an initial velocity of 20 m/s. If g = 10 m/s², the range of the missile is **[AIPMT 2011]**

(1) 50 m (2) 60 m

(3) 20 m (4) 40 m

Sol : **(4)** Here, $u = 20\text{ m/s}, g = 10\text{ m/s}^2$

For maximum range, angle of projection is

$\theta = 45^0$

$$\therefore R_{max} = \frac{u^2 \sin 90^0}{g} = \frac{u^2}{g} \qquad \left(\because R = \frac{u^2 \sin 2\theta}{g}\right)$$

$$= \frac{(20m/s)^2}{(10m/s^2)} = 40\text{ m}$$

9. A projectile is fired at an angle of 45° with th horizontal. Elevation angle of the projectile at its highest point as seen form the point of projection is **[AIPMT 2011]**

(1) 60° (2) $\tan^{-1}\frac{1}{2}$ (3) $\tan^{-1}\frac{\sqrt{3}}{2}$ (4) 45°

Sol : **(2)**

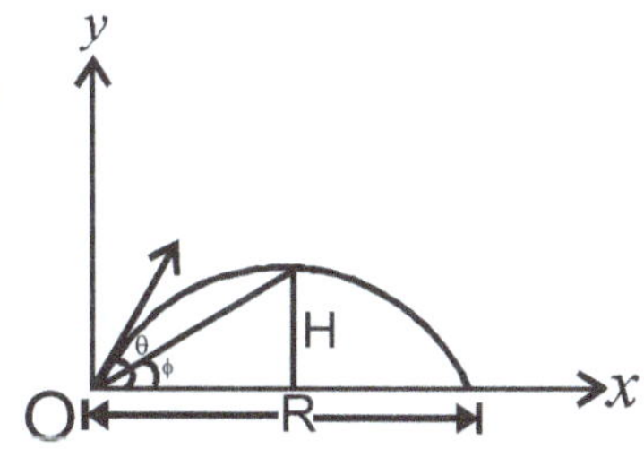

Let ϕ be elevation of the projectile at its highest point as seen from the point of projection O and θ be angle of projection with the horizontal.

From figure, $\tan\phi = \dfrac{H}{R/2}$ ....(i)

In case of projectile motion

Maximum height, $H = \dfrac{u^2\sin^2\theta}{2g}$

Horizontal range, $R = \dfrac{u^2\sin 2\theta}{g}$ Substituting these values of H and R in (i), we get

$$\tan\phi = \frac{\dfrac{u^2\sin^2\theta}{2g}}{\dfrac{u^2\sin 2\theta}{2g}}$$

$$\tan\phi = \frac{\sin^2\theta}{\sin 2\theta} = \frac{\sin^2\theta}{2\sin\theta\cos\theta} = \frac{1}{2}\tan\theta$$

$$\tan\phi = \frac{1}{2}\tan 45^0 = \frac{1}{2}$$

Here, θ = 45° $\therefore \tan\phi = \frac{1}{2}\tan 45^0 = \frac{1}{2}$

$(\because \tan 45^0 = 1)$ $\phi = \tan^{-1}\left(\frac{1}{2}\right)$.

10. The horizontal range and the maximum height of a projectile are equal. The angle of projection of the projectile is **[AIPMT 2012]**

(1) $\theta = 45°$ (2) $\tan^{-1}\frac{1}{4}$

(3) $\theta = \tan^{-1}(4)$ (4) $\theta = \tan^{-1}(2)$

Sol : **(3)** Horizontal range, $R = \frac{u^2 \sin 2\theta}{g}$

Where u is the velocity of projection and θ is the angle of projection

Maximum height, $H = \frac{u^2 \sin^2 \theta}{2g}$

According to question $R = H$

$\therefore \frac{u^2 \sin 2\theta}{g} = \frac{u^2 \sin^2 \theta}{2g}$

$\frac{2u^2 \sin\theta \cos\theta}{g} = \frac{u^2 \sin^2 \theta}{2g}$

$\tan\theta = 4$ or $\theta \tan^{-1}(4)$

11. A particle has initial velocity $2\hat{i}+3\hat{j}$ and acceleration $0.3\hat{i}+0.2\hat{j}$. The magnitude of velocity after 10 seconds will be **[AIPMT 2012]**

(1) 9 units (2) $9\sqrt{2}$ units

(3) $5\sqrt{2}$ units (4) 5 units

Sol : **(3)**

$\vec{V} = \bar{x} + \bar{a}t$

$\vec{V} = (2\hat{i}+3\hat{i}) + (0.3\hat{i}+0.2\hat{i})(10)$

$= (2\hat{i}+3\hat{j}) + (3\hat{i}+2\hat{j}) = 5\hat{i}+5\hat{j}$

$\vec{V} = 5(\hat{i}+\hat{j})$

$|\vec{V}| = 5\sqrt{2}$

12. The velocity of a projectile at the initial point A is $2\hat{i}+3\hat{j}$ m/s. Its velocity (in m/s) at point B is **[AIPMT 2013]**

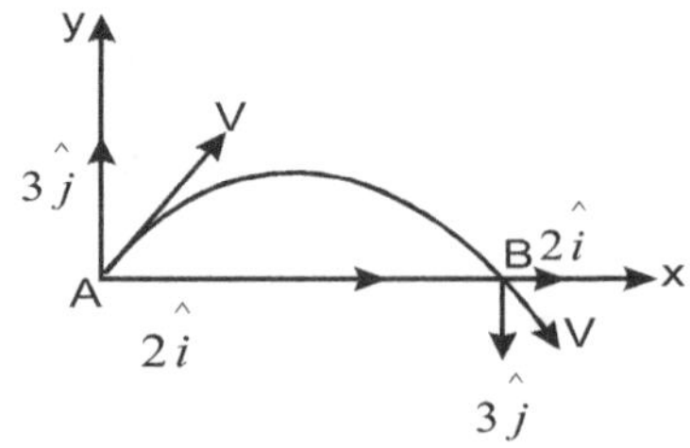

(1) $-2\hat{i}-3\hat{j}$ (2) $-2\hat{i}+3\hat{j}$

(3) $2\hat{i}-3\hat{j}$ (4) $2\hat{i}+3\hat{j}$

sol : **(3)**

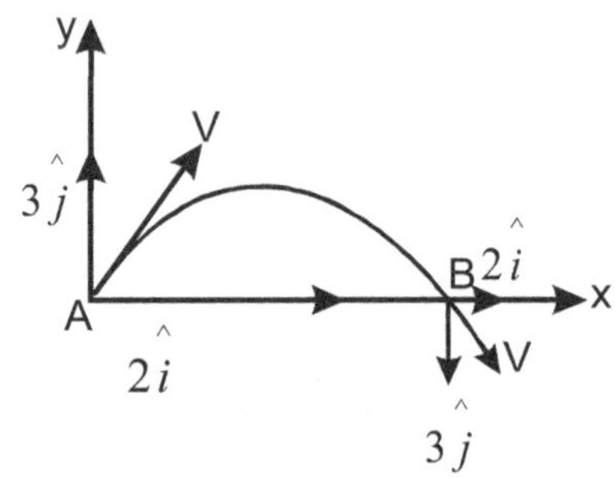

At point B X component of velocity remains unchanged while Y compoment reverses its direction.

$\therefore$ The velocity of the projectile at point B is $2\hat{i}-3\hat{j}\ m/s$.

13. A particle is moving such that its position coordinates (x, y) are (2 m , 3 m) at time t = 0, (6 m, 7 m) at time t = 2 s and (13 m, 14 m) at time t = 5 s

Average velocity vector $\vec{V}_a$ from t = 0 to t = 5 s is **[AIPMT 2014]**

(1) $\frac{1}{5}\ 13\hat{i}\ \ 14\hat{j}$ (2) $\frac{7}{3}\ \hat{i}\ \ \hat{j}$

(3) $2\ \hat{i}\ \ \hat{j}$ (4) $\frac{11}{5}\ \hat{i}\ \ \hat{j}$

Sol. : **4**

$$\vec{V}ang = \frac{\Delta s}{\Delta t}, \frac{(13-2, 11-3.)}{5-0},$$

$$\frac{(11,11)}{5}, \frac{11(\hat{i})+11\hat{j}}{5}$$

$$\vec{V}ang = \frac{11}{5}\ \hat{i}\ \hat{j}$$

14. A ship A is moving Westwards with a speed of 10 km h^{-1} and a ship B 100 km South of A is moving northwards with a speed of 10 km h^{-1} The time after which the distance between them becomes shortest is **[AIPMT 2015]**

(1) 0 h (2) 5 h

(3) $5\sqrt{2}$ h (4) $10\sqrt{2}$ h

Sol. : **(2)** $t = \frac{100}{\sqrt{2}} \times \frac{1}{10\sqrt{2}} = 5h$.

15. If vectors $\vec{A}\ \cos\ t\hat{i}\ \sin\ t\hat{j}$ and $\vec{B}\ \cos\frac{t}{2}t\ \ \sin\frac{t}{2}\hat{j}$ are functions of time, then the value of t at which they are orthogonal to each other is : **[AIPMT 2015]**

(1) t = 0 (2) t $\frac{}{4}$

(3) $t = \frac{\pi}{2\omega}$ (4) t —

Sol. : **(4)** For orthogonal to vector each other : –

$$\vec{A} . \vec{B} = 0$$

$$\cos(\omega t)\cos\left(\frac{\omega t}{2}\right) + \cos(\omega t).\ \sin\left(\frac{\omega t}{2}\right) = 0$$

$$\cos\left(\omega t - \frac{cot}{2}\right) = 0$$

$$\cos\left(\frac{\omega t}{2}\right) = 0$$

$$\frac{\omega t}{2} = \frac{\pi}{2} \Rightarrow t = \left(\frac{\pi}{\omega}\right)$$

16. The position vector of a particle $\vec{R}$ as a function of time is given by :

$$\vec{R}\ \ 4\sin(2\ \ t)\hat{i}\ \ 4\cos\ 2\ \ t\ \hat{j}$$

$\hat{j}$ denote unit vectors, t is in seconds and $\hat{i}$ denote unit vectors along x-and y- directions respecively. Which one of the following statements is wrong for the motion of particle ? **[AIPMT 2015 Re]**

(1) Path of the particle is a circle of radius 4 meter

(2) Acceleration vectors is along $-\vec{R}$

(3) Magnitude of acceleration vector is $\frac{v^2}{R}$ where v is the velocity of particle

(4) Magnitude of the velocity of particle is 8 meter/second

Sol. : **(4)** $\vec{R} - 4\sin(2\pi t)\hat{i} + 4\cos 2\pi t\,\hat{j}$

$$\vec{v} = \frac{d\vec{R}}{dt} = 8\pi\cos 2\pi t\ \hat{i} - 8\pi\sin 2\pi t\ \hat{j}$$

$$|\vec{v}| = 8\pi\sqrt{2}.$$

17. A particle moves so that its position vector is given by $\vec{r} = \cos\omega t\,\hat{x} + \sin\omega t\,\hat{y}$. Where ω is a constant. Which of the following is true ?

[AIPMT 2016]

(1) Velocity and acceleration both are perpendicular to $\vec{r}$

(2) Velocity and acceleration both are parallel to $\vec{r}$

(3) Velocity is perpendicular to $\vec{r}$ and acceleration is directed towards the origin

(4) Velocity is perpendicular to $\vec{r}$ and acceleration is directed away from the origin

Sol. : (3) $\vec{V} = \cos\omega t\hat{i} + \sin\omega t\hat{j}$

$$\vec{V} = \frac{d\vec{r}}{dt} = -\omega\sin\omega t\hat{i} + \omega\cos\omega t\hat{j}$$

$$\vec{a} = \frac{d\vec{V}}{dt} = -\omega^2\cos\omega t\hat{i} - \omega^2\sin\omega t\hat{j}$$

since $\vec{r}.\vec{V} = 0\, so\, \vec{r} \perp_r \vec{V}$ and $\vec{a} = -\omega^2\vec{r}$

So $\vec{a}$ will be always aiming towards the origin.

18. If the magnitude of sum of two vectors is equal to the magnitude of difference of the two vectors, the angle between these vectors is :-

[AIPMT 2016]

(1) 0° (2) 90°

(3) 45° (4) 180°

Sol. : (2) 90°

$$|\vec{a} + \vec{b}| = |\vec{a} - \vec{b}|$$

$$|\vec{a} + \vec{b}|^2 = |\vec{a} - \vec{b}|^2$$

$$|a|^2 + |b|^2 + |a||b|\cos\theta = |a|^2 + |b|^2 - 2|a||b|\cos\theta$$

$$2|a||b|\cos\theta = -2|a||b|\cos\theta$$

$2\cos\theta = 0$, $\cos\theta = 0$

$\theta = 90°$

19. The x and y coordinates of the particle at any time are $x = 5t - 2t^2$ and $y = 10t$ respectively, where x and y are in meters and t in seconds. The acceleration of the particle at t = 2s is :

[NEET – 2017]

(1) 0 (2) 5 m/s^2

(3) – 4 m/s^2 (4) – 8 m/s^2

Sol. : (3)

$$v_x = \frac{dx}{dt}, 5 - 4t$$

$$a_x = \frac{dv_x}{dt} = -4$$

$$v_y = \frac{dy}{dt} = 10$$

$a_y = 0$

$a = -4\ m/s^2$

04 Laws of Motion

Note: Scan QR code with your mobile camera or QR scanner for video solutions.

1. Two masses of 5 kg and 10 kg are connected to a pulley as shown. What will be the acceleration if the pulley is set free.
(g = acceleration due to gravity)
[RPMT 1992, AIPMT 2000]

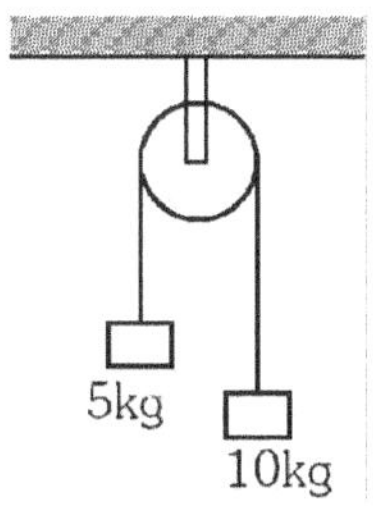

(1) g (2) g/2
(3) g/3 (4) g/4

Sol.: **(3)**

$10g - T = 10a$

$T - 5g = 5a$

$5g = 15a$

$a = \frac{5g}{15}$

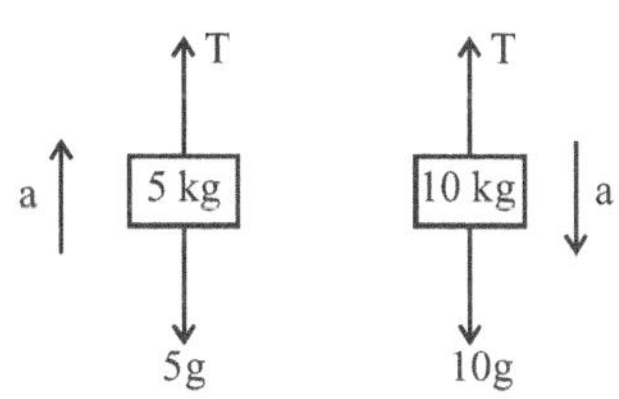

2. A cylinder of mass 10 kg is rolling in a plane with an initial velocity of 10m/s. If the coefficient of friction between the surface and the cylinder is 0.5, the before stopping, it will travelled the distance ($g = 10 m/s^2$) **[AIPMT 2000]**

(1) 10 m (2) 7.5 m
(3) 5 m (4) 2.5 m

Sol.: **(1)**

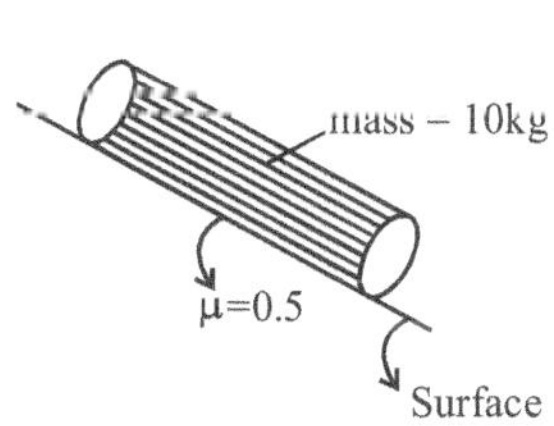

$\mu = 10$ m/s

Final velocity of cylinder when it

Stopped $(\overline{v}) = 0$

fr = ma

$(\mu\, mg) = ma$

$a = \mu g = 0.5\, g = 5$ m10

$v^2 = \mu^2 + 2as$

$0 = (10)^2 + 2(5)5$

$S = \frac{100}{10} = 10$ m

3. On the horizontal surface of a truck a block of mass 1 kg. is placed ($\mu = 0.6$) and truck is moving with acceleration 5 m/s^2 then the frictional force on block will be :– **[AIPMT-2001]**

(1) 5N (2) 6N
(3) 5.88N (4) 8N

Sol. : **(1)**

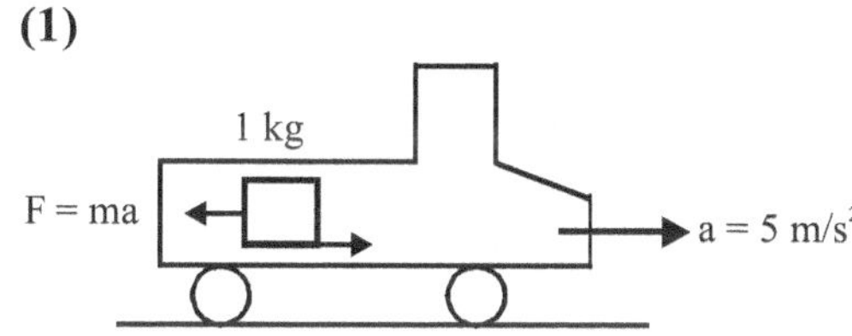

$f_r L = \mu_s N = \mu_s \times mg = 0.6 \times 1 \times 10 = 6N.$

Where $f_r L$ is the force of limiting friction.

Pseudo force = ma =1 × 5 ; F = 5 N

If $F < f_r L$ block does not move. So static friction is present.

Static friction = applied force.

$\therefore\ f_r L = 5N$

4. A monkey of mass 20 kg. is holding a vertical rope. The rope will not break when a mass of 25 kg. is suspended from it but will break if the mass exceeds 25 kg. What is the maximum acceleration with which the monkey can climb up along the rope ? (g = 10 m/s²) **[AIPMT 2003]**

(1) 5 m/s^2 (2) 10 m/s^2

(3) 25 m/s^2 (4) 2.5 m/s^2

Sol. : (4)

T – mg = ma

when T is maximum

⇒ a is also maximum

$T_{maximum} = 25\ g$

25g – 20 g = 20a

$a = \frac{5g}{20} = \frac{50}{20} = 2.5\ m/s^2$

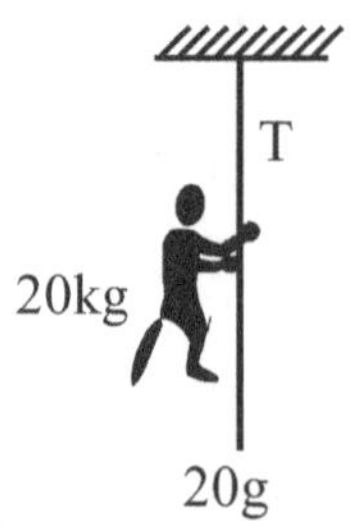

5. A man weighs 80 kg. He stands on a weighing scale in a lift which is moving upwards with a uniform acceleration of 5m/s² . What would be the reading on the scale ? (g = 10 m/s²)

[AIPMT 2003]

(1) Zero (2) 400N

(3) 800N (4)1200N

Sol. : (4)

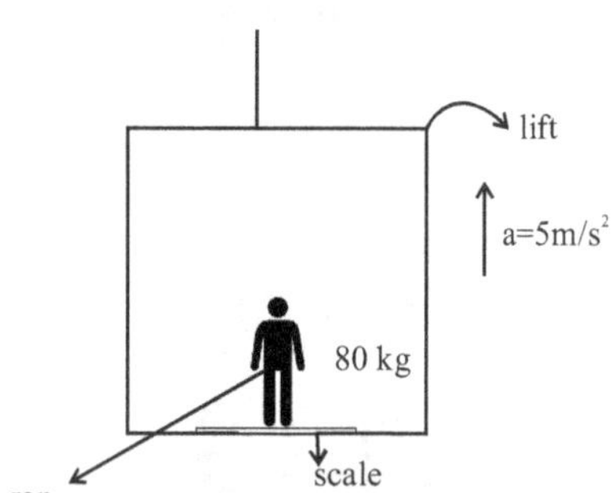

FBD of man : –

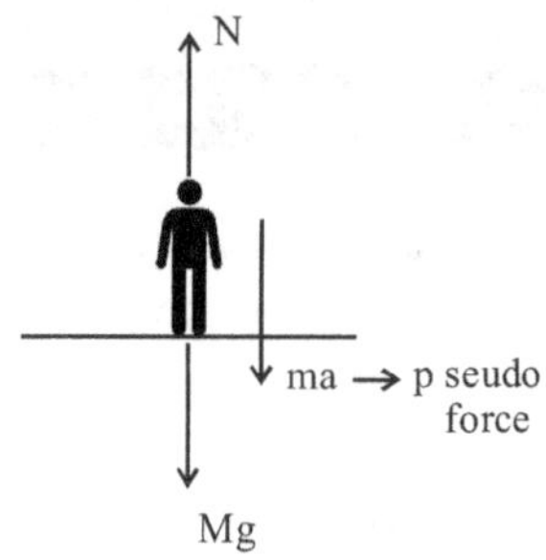

N = mg + ma, m (g + a)

= 80 (10 + 5) = 1200 N

The reading on the the scale = 1200 N

6. A block of mass m is placed on a smooth wedge of inclination θ. The whole system is accelerated horizontally so that the block does not slip on the wedge. The force exerted by the wedge on the block (g is acceleration due to gravity) will be :–

[AIPMT 2004]

(1) mg sinθ (2) mg

(3) mg/cosθ (4) mg cosθ

Sol. : (3)

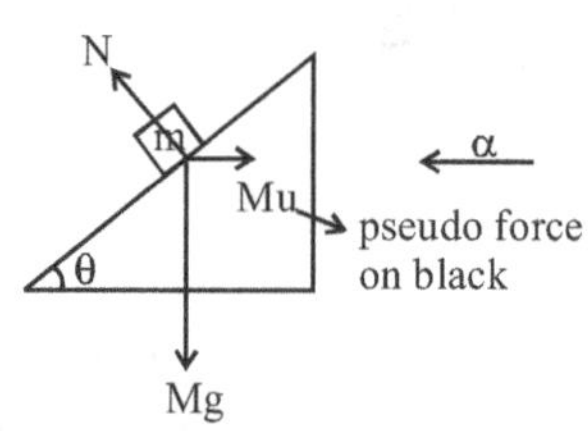

Free body diagram of black mass 'm' :–

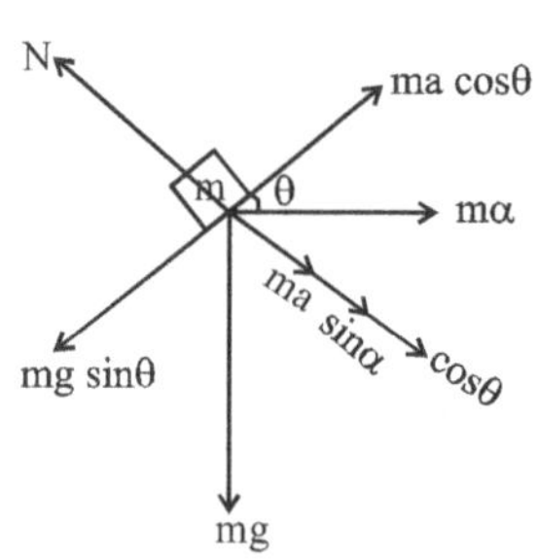

mg sinθ = mα cos θ

$$a = g\frac{\sin\theta}{\cos\theta}$$

Total reaction of the wedge on block is

N = mg cosθ + ma sin θ

N = m (g cosθ + a sin θ)

$$N = m\left(g\cos\theta + g\frac{\sin^2\theta}{\cos\theta}\right)$$

$$N = mg\frac{\left(\cos^2\theta+\sin^2\theta\right)}{\cos\theta}$$

$$N = \frac{mg}{\cos\theta} \qquad \left[\because \sin^2\theta+\cos^2\theta = 2\right]$$

7. The coefficient of static friction, μ_s, between block A of mass 2 kg. and the table as shown in the figure is 0.2. What would be the maximum mass value of block B so that the two blocks do not move ? The string and the pulley are assumed to be smooth and massless. (g = 10 m/s²) **[AIPMT-2004]**

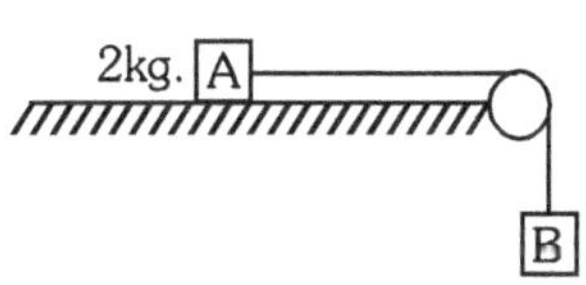

(1) 4.0 kg. (2) 0.2 kg.
(3) 0.4 kg. (4) 2.0 kg

Sol. : **(3)**

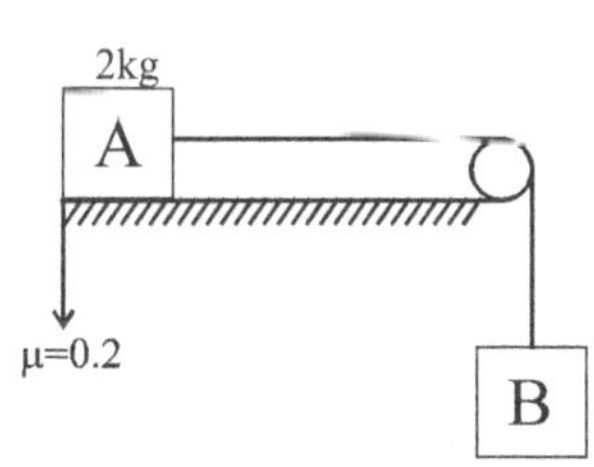

Free body diagram of system

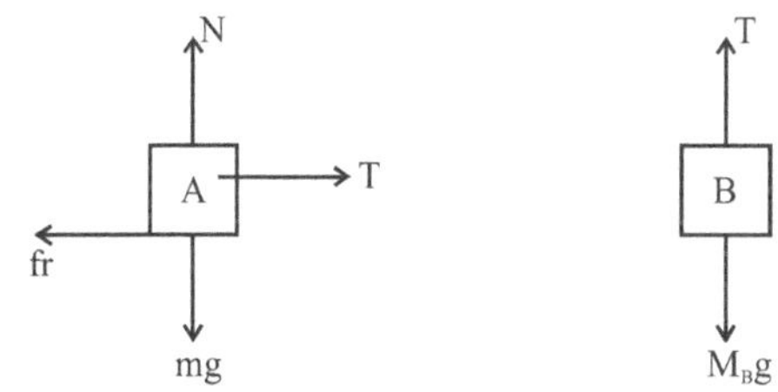

N = mg, T = fr

$T = \mu m_A g$, (0.2) (2) (10) , 4 N

$T = M_B g$, $T = M_B$ (10), $M_B = 0.4$ Kg

8. In the figure given below, the position–time graph of a particle of mass 0·1 kg is shown. The impulse at t = 2 sec is – **[2005]**

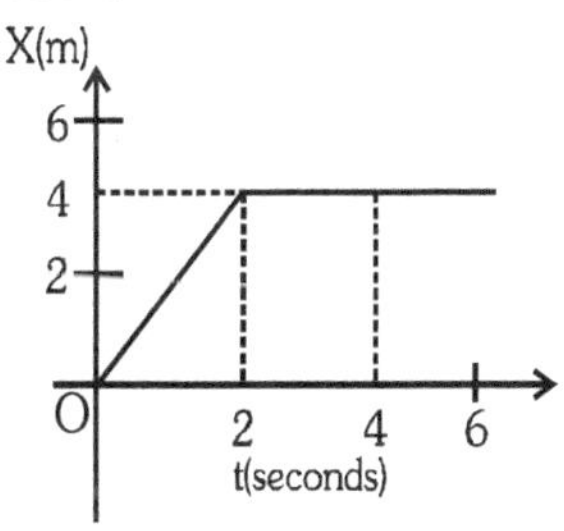

(1) 0·2 kgms⁻¹ (2) –0·2 kgms⁻¹
(3) 0·1 kgms⁻¹ (4) –0·4 kgms⁻¹

Sol. : **(2)** The Area of position time graph = $\int r\,dt$

$$\int v\,dt = \frac{1}{2} \times 2 \times 4.\ 4$$

$(V_1 - V_2)$ (2) = 4

$(V_1 - V_2)$ = 2 m/s

Impulse of 2 second

$-m\,(V_2 - V_1)$, – (0.01) (2)

= –0.2 kg m/s

9. A person is standing in an elevator. In which situation he finds his weight less :–

(1) when the elevator moves upward with constant acceleration

(2) when the elevator moves downward with constant acceleration

(3) when the elevator moves upward with uniform velocity

(4) when the elevator moves downward with uniform velocity **[2005]**

Sol. : **(2)** As same case of life

When the elevator moves downwave with cousfour acceleration.

10. A 0.5 kg ball moving with a speed of 12 m/s strikes a hard wall at an angle of 30° with the wall. It is reflected with the same speed and at the same angle. If the ball is in contact with the wall for 0.25 seconds, the average force acting on the wall is

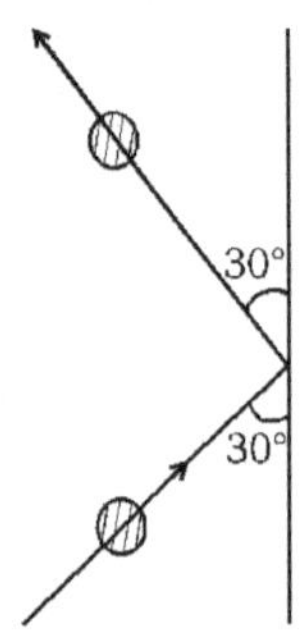

[AIPMT 2006]

(1) 48 N (2) 24 N (3) 12 N (4) 96 N

Sol. : **(2)**

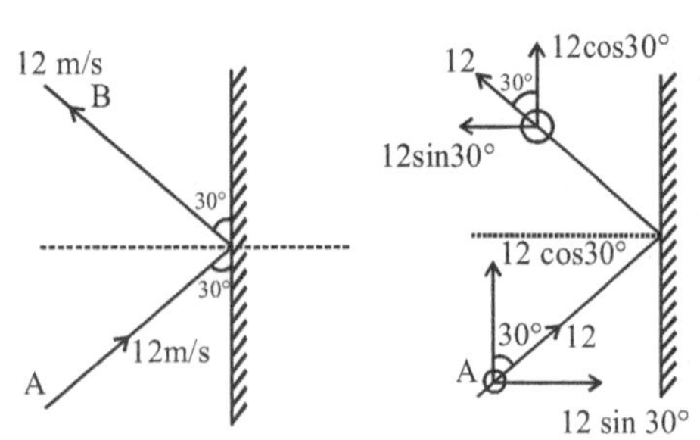

momentum change in x – axis

m (12 sin 30°) – (–12 sin 30°)

= 2m (12 sin 30°)

$= 24(0.5)\left(\frac{1}{2}\right) + 12 \times \frac{1}{2} = 6$

momentum change in y-axis

= m (12 cos 30°) – m(12 cos 30°) = 0

Change in momentum = Ft

6 = (F) = (0.25) F = 6 × 4, 24 N

11. A man of mass 90 kg is standing in an elevator whose cable broke suddenly. If the elevator falls, apparent weight of the man is : **[2009]**

(1) 90N (2) 90g N

(3) 0 N (4) any negative value

Sol. : **(3)**

When elevator falls then a mass and elevator confact break mean :

Normal force on man and normal force on elevator = 0 N

12. A body, under the action of a force $\vec{F}\ \ 6\hat{i}\ \ 8\hat{j}\ \ 10\hat{k}$, acquires an acceleration of 1m/s^2. The mass of this body must be **[AIPMT-2009]**

(1) $10\sqrt{2}$ kg (2) $2\sqrt{10}$ kg (3) 10 kg (4) 20 kg

Sol. : **(1)**

$\vec{F}\ \ 6\hat{i}\ \ 8\hat{j}\ \ 10\hat{k}$

$|\vec{F}| = \sqrt{(6)^2 + (-8)^2 + (10)^2} = 10\sqrt{2}$ N

a = 1 m/s^2 F = ma

$10\sqrt{2}$ m (1) m = $10\sqrt{2}$ kg

13. A block of mass m is in contact with the cart C as shown in the figure. The coefficient of static friction between the block and the cart is μ. The acceleration α of the cart that will prevent the block from falling statisfies :- **[AIPMT-2010]**

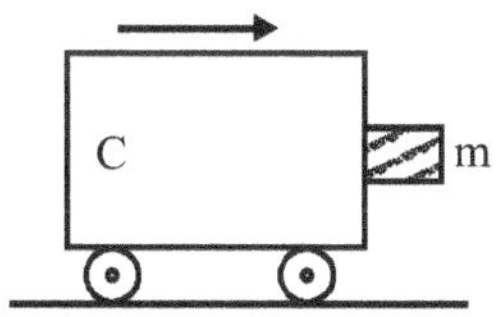

(1) $\alpha < \frac{g}{}$

(2) $\alpha > \frac{mg}{}$

(3) $\alpha > \frac{g}{m}$ (4) $\alpha \geq \frac{g}{}$

Sol. : (4)

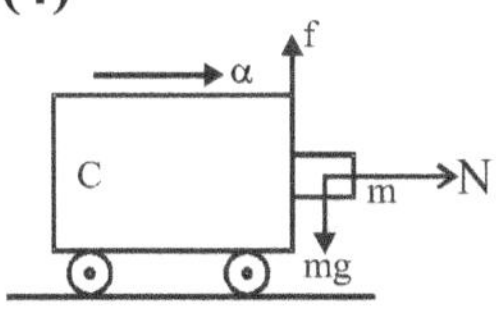

Free body diagram of a block mass 'm'

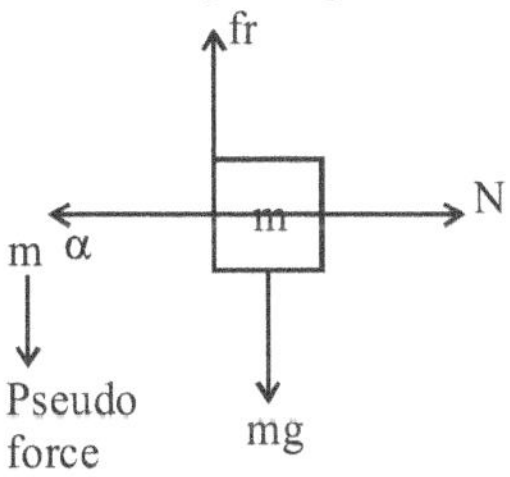

fr = μ N, (μ mα)

The block of mass m cart not fail as long as

fr $\geq$ mg

$(\mu/\alpha) \geq mg$ $\qquad \alpha \geq \left(\frac{g}{m}\right)$

14. A gramophone record is revolving with an angular velocity ω. A coin is placed at a distance r from the centre of the record. The static coefficient of friction is μ. The coin will revolve with the record if :- **[AIPMT-2010]**

(1) r $\frac{g}{2}$ (2) r g ^{2}

(3) $r < \frac{2}{g}$ (4) r $\frac{g}{2}$

Sol. : (4)

Here friction force provides centripetal force so

$f = m\omega^2 r$ but $f \leq \mu mg$

So, $m\omega^2 r \leq \mu mg \Rightarrow r \leq \frac{\mu g}{\omega^2}$.

15. A person of mass 60 kg is inside a lift of mass 940 kg and presses the button on control panel. Then lift starts moving upwards with an acceleration $1.0 m/s^2$. If $g = 10 ms^{-2}$, the tension in the supporting cable is : **[AIPMT-2011]**

(1) 8600 N (2) 9680 N

(3) 11000 N (4) 1200 N

Sol. : (3)

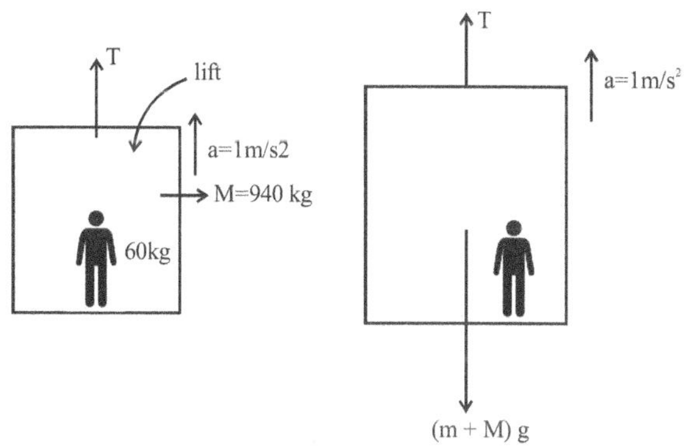

T = (m + M) g = (m + M)

T = (m + M) (g + a)

T = (60 + 940) (10 + 1)

T = 1000 (11)

T = 11000 N

16. A body of mass M hits normally a rigid will with velocity V and bounces back with the same velocity. The impulse experienced by the body is : **[AIPMT-2011]**

(1) MV (2) 1.5 MV

(3) 2 MV (4) Zero

Sol. : (3)

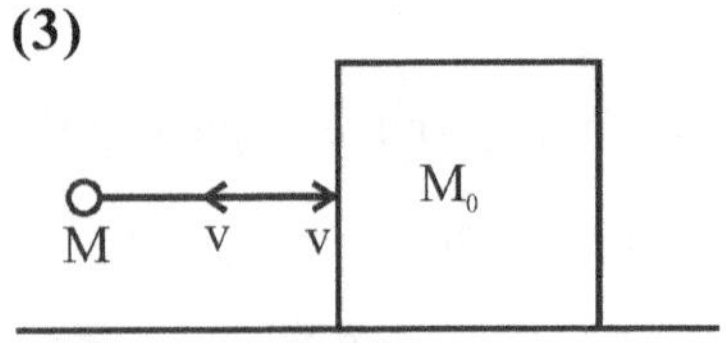

Impulse = Change in linear momentum
= MV – (– MV) = 2MV.

17. A car of mass 1000 kg negotiates a banked curve of radius 90m on a frictionless road. If the banking angle is 45°, the speed of the car is :

[AIPMT Pre.-2012]

(1) $5ms^{-1}$ (2) $10ms^{-1}$ (3) $20ms^{-1}$ (4) $30ms^{-1}$

Sol. : (4) $v = \sqrt{rg\tan\theta}$

$\Rightarrow v = \sqrt{90 \times 10 \times \tan 45^\circ} = 30\,m/s$.

18. One end of string of length l is connected to a small peg on a smooth horizontal table. If the particle moves in circle with speed $\underleftarrow{speed'\upsilon'}$, the net force on the particle (directed towards center) will be (T represents the tension in the string) :

[NEET-2017]

(1) T (2) $T + \frac{m\upsilon^2}{l}$

(3) $T - \frac{m\upsilon^2}{l}$ (4) Zero

Sol. : (1)

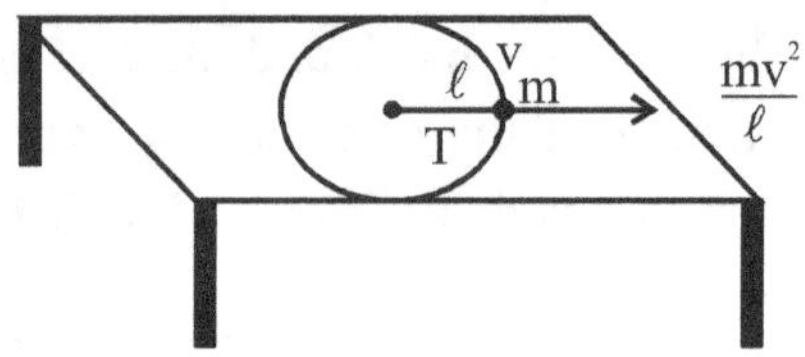

$T = \frac{mv^2}{\ell}$

19. A spring of force constant k is cut into lengths o ratio 1 : 2 : 3. They are connected in series and the new force constant is 'k'. Then they are connected in parallel and force constant is k". Then k' : k" is : **[NEET-2017]**

(1) 1 : 6 (2) 1 : 9

(3) 1 :11 (4) 1 : 14

Sol. : (3) Spring constant $\propto \frac{1}{\text{length}}$

$$K \propto \frac{1l}{l}$$

$i.e,\ k_1 = 6k;\quad k_2 = 3k;\quad k_3 = 2k$

In series $\frac{1}{k'} = \frac{1}{6k} + \frac{1}{3k} + \frac{1}{2k} = \frac{1}{k'} = \frac{6}{6k}$

$k' = k$

$k'' = 6k + 3k + 2k$

$k'' = 11k$

$\frac{k'}{k''} = \frac{1}{11}$ $i.e\ k' : k'' = 1:11$.

20. Two blocks A and B of masses 3m and m respectively are connected by a massless and inextensible string. The whole system is suspended by a massless spring as shown in figure. The magnitudes of acceleration of A and B immediately after the string is cut, are respectively : **[NEET-2017]**

(1) $g, \frac{g}{3}$

(2) $\frac{g}{3}, g$

(3) g, g

(4) $\frac{g}{3}, \frac{g}{3}$

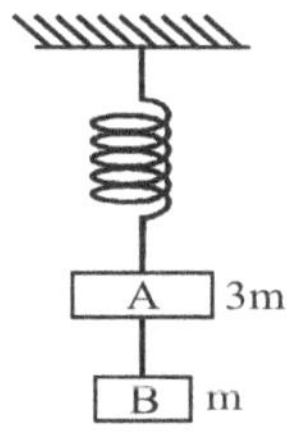

Sol. : **(2)**

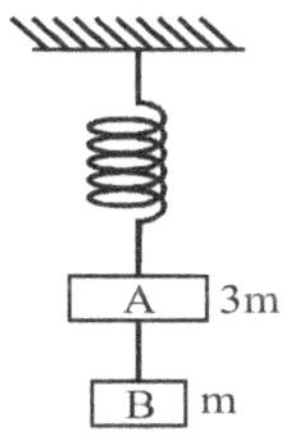

Before the spring is cut : –

fere body diagram

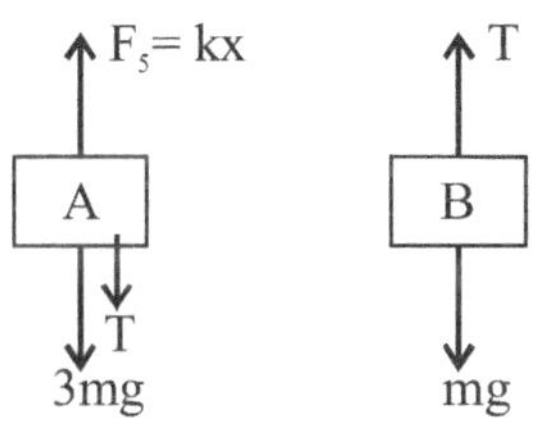

kx = 3mg + T

kx = 3mg + mg = 4mg

kx = 4mg

After the spring is cut,

T = 0

Free body diagram

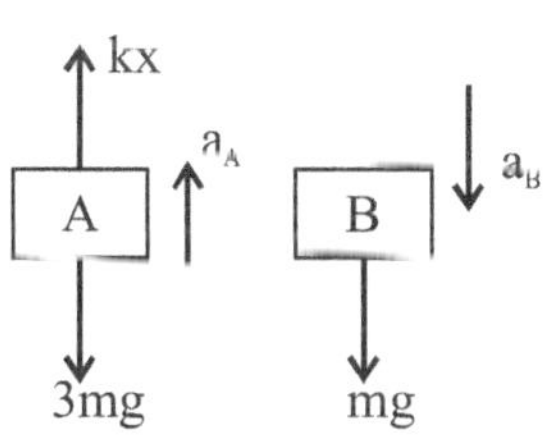

for Block 'A'

$kx - 3mg = 3ma_A$

$4mg - 3mg = 3ma_A$

$a_A = g/3$

for Block 'B' : –

$mg = ma_A$

$a_A = g$

21. A block of mass m is placed on a smooth inclined wedge ABC of inclination as shown in the figure. The wedge is given acceleration 'a' towards the right. The relation between a and the wedge is **[NEET-2018]**

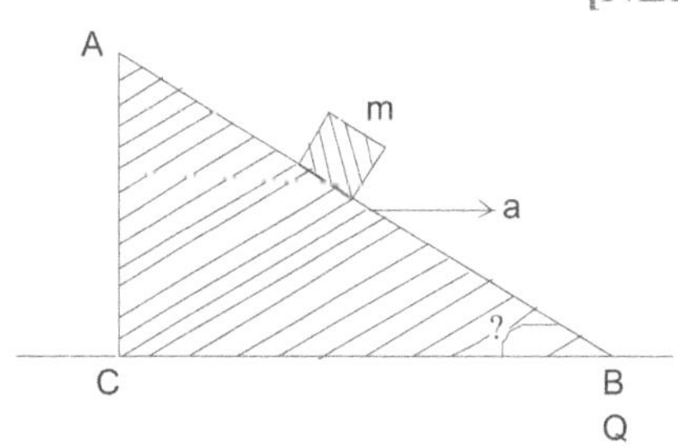

(1) $a = g\cos\theta$

(2) $a = \frac{g}{\sin\theta}$

(3) $a = \frac{g}{\operatorname{cosec}\theta}$

(4) $a = g\tan\theta$

Ans. **(4)**

05 Work, Energy and Power

Note: Scan QR code with your mobile camera or QR scanner for video solutions.

1. A bomb of mass m = 1 kg thrown vertically upwards with a speed u = 100 m/s explodes into two parts after t = 5s. A fragment of mass m_1 = 400 g moves downwards with a speed v_1 = 25 m/s, then speed v_2 and direction of another mass m_2 will be :– **[AIPMT–2000]**

(1) 40 m/s downwards (2) 40 m/s upwards
(3) 60 m/s upwards (4) 100 m/s upwards

Sol. : (4)

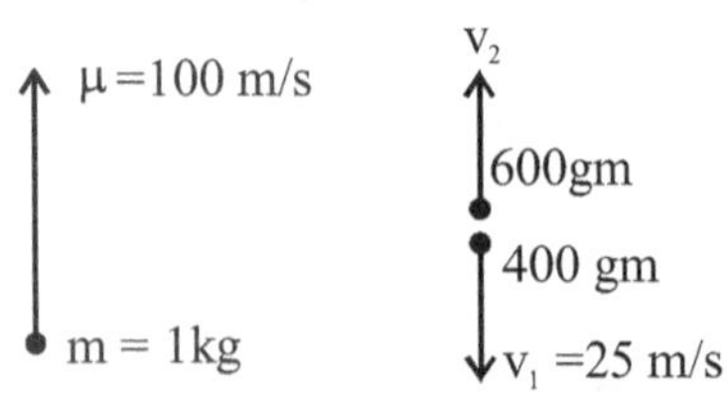

2. A suspended simple pendulum of length ℓ is making an angle θ with the vertical. On releasing, its velocity at lowest point will be :- **[AIPMT–2000]**

(1) $\sqrt{2g\ell(1+\cos\theta)}$ (2) $\sqrt{2g\ell\sin\theta}$

(3) $\sqrt{2g\ell(1-\cos\theta)}$ (4) $\sqrt{2g\ell}$

Sol. : (3)

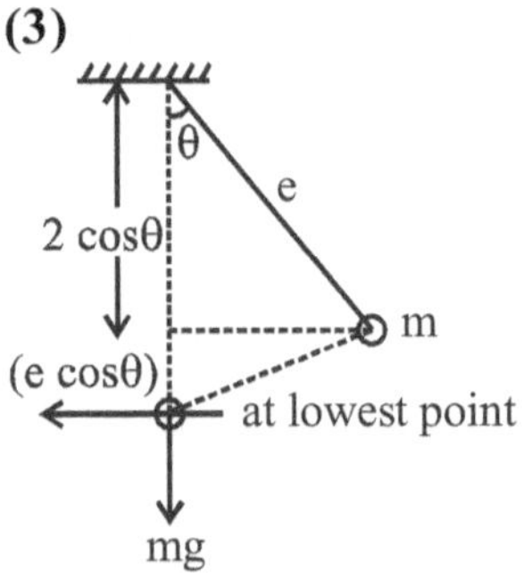

mg (e – e cosθ) = $\frac{1}{2}$ mv² = 0

Avg. (1 – cosθ) = $\frac{1}{2}$ mv²

∴ $V = \sqrt{2gl(1-\cos\theta)}$

3. A 1 kg stationary bomb is exploded in three parts having mass ratio 1 : 1 : 3. Parts having same mass move in perpendicular directions with velocity 30 m/s, then the velocity of bigger part will be : – **[AIPMT 2000]**

(1) $10\sqrt{2}$ m/s (2) $\frac{10}{\sqrt{2}}$ m/s

(3) $15\sqrt{2}$ m/s (4) $\frac{15}{\sqrt{2}}$ m/s

Sol. : (1)

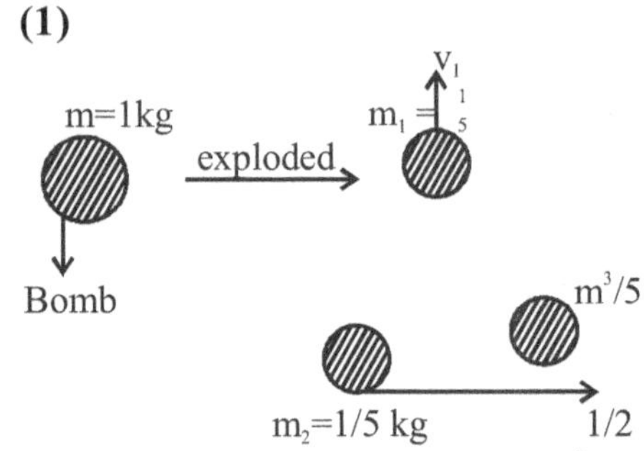

mometum conseuation

$m(0) = m_1v_1 + m_2v_2 + m_3v_3$

$m_3v_3 = -(m_1v_1 + m_2v_2)$

$\frac{3}{5}v_3 = \left(\frac{v_1}{5}+\frac{v_2}{5}\right)$

$3v_3 = -\left(30\hat{i}+30\hat{j}\right)$

$3v_3 = 30\sqrt{2}$

$v_3 = 10\sqrt{2}$,s

4. A body of mass 5 kg has momentum of 10 kg m/s. When a force of 0.2 N is applied on it for 10 seconds, what is the change in its kinetic energy :- **[AIIMS 2000]**

(1) 1.1J (2) 2.2J
(3) 3.3J (4) 4.4J

Sol. : **(4)**

Ft = change in mometum

$(0.2)(10) = P_2 - P_1 = (P_2 - 10)$

$P_2 = 12$ kg m/s

$$k = \frac{1}{2}mv^2 = \left(\frac{P^2}{2m}\right)$$

$$\Delta k = \frac{1}{2m}\left(p_2^2 - p_1^2\right)$$

$$\Delta k = \frac{1}{2\times 5}\left((12)^2 - (10)^2\right)$$

$$\Delta k = \frac{1}{10}(144 - 100),\ \frac{44}{10}$$

Δk_3 4.4 joule

5. A stationary particle explodes into two particles of masses m_1 and m_2 which move in opposite directions with velocities v_1 and v_2. The ratio of their kinetic energies E_1/E_2 is :– **[AIPMT 2003]**

(1) m_2/m_1 (2) m_1/m_2

(3) 1 (4) m_1v_2/m_2v_1

Sol. : **(1)** $m_1v_1 = m_2v_2$ (conservation of linear momentum)

$$\frac{E_1}{E_2} = \frac{(1/2)m_1v_1^2}{(1/2)m_2v_2^2} = \frac{m_1^2v_1^2}{m_2^2v_2^2}\cdot\frac{m_2}{m_1} = \frac{m_2}{m_1}.$$

6. A ball of mass 2 kg and another of mass 4 kg are dropped together from a 60 feet tall building. After a fall of 30 feet each towards earth, their respective kinetic energies will be in the ratio of : – **[AIPMT 2004]**

(1) 1 : 4 (2) 1 : 2

(3) 1 : $\sqrt{2}$ (4) $\sqrt{2}$: 1

Sol. : **(2)** Ratio of their kinetic energy is given as

$$\frac{KE_1}{KE_2} = \frac{(1/2)m_1v_1^2}{(1/2)m_2v_2^2}$$

$\Rightarrow v^2 = 2gs$ (zero initial velocity)

which is same for both

$$\therefore\ \frac{KE_1}{KE_2} = \frac{m_1}{m_2} = \frac{2}{4} = \frac{1}{2}.$$

7. A bomb of mass 3.0 kg explodes in air into two pieces of masses 2.0 kg and 1.0 kg. The smaller mass goes at a speed of 80 m/s. The total energy imparted to the two fragments is – **[2004]**

(1) 1.07 kJ (2) 2.14 kJ

(3) 2.4 kJ (4) 4.8 kJ

Sol. : **(4)**

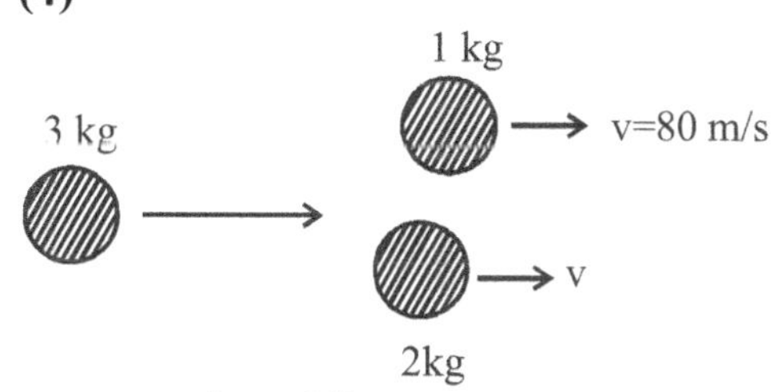

concentration of linear momentum : –

$3(0) = (1)(80) + 2(r)$; $v = 40$ m/s

$$\text{Energy impevted} = \frac{1}{2}m_1v_1^2 + \frac{1}{2}m_2v_2^2$$

$$= \frac{1}{2}(1)(80^2)^2 + \frac{1}{2}(2)(40)^2 = \frac{6400}{2} + 1600$$

$= 3200 + 1600 = 4800$ Joule $= 4.8$ kJ

8. A bomb of mass 30Kg at rest explodes into two pieces of masses 18 kg and 12 kg. The velocity of 18kg mass is $6ms^{-1}$. The kinetic energy of the other mass is **[AIPMT 2005]**

(1) 524 J (2) 256 J

(3) 486J (4) 324J

Sol. : **(3)**

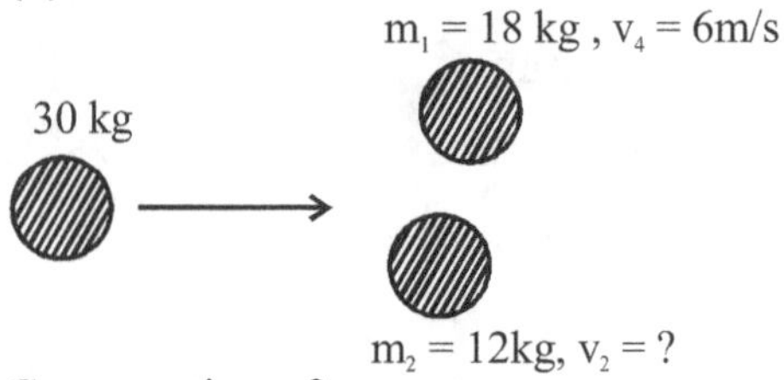

Conservation of mometum

$30(0) = 18(6) + 12\ v_2$

$v_2 = \frac{18\times6}{12} = -9$m/s

Negative sign indicates

That both tragments move in opposite direction

$(K.E.)_{12kg} = \frac{1}{2}mv^2$

$+\frac{1}{2}(12)(9)^2 = 6 \times 81 = 486$ joule.

9. A force F acting on an object varies with distance x as shown here.

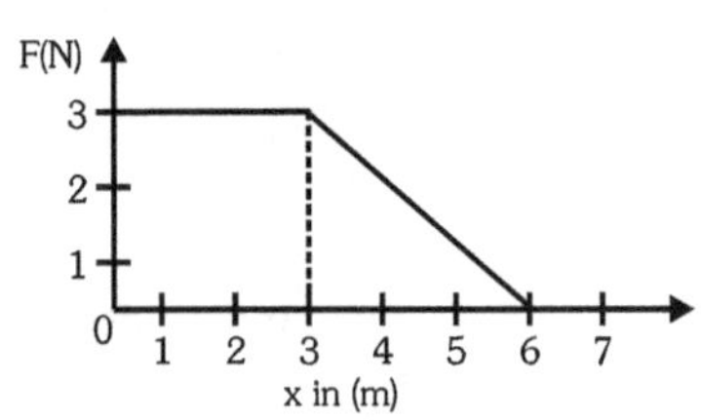

The force is in N and x in m. The work done by the force in moving the object from x = 0 to x = 6m is **[AIPMT 2005]**

(1) 18.0 J (2) 13.5 J

(3) 4.5 J (4) 9.0 J

Sol. : **(2)**

Work done = Area under (f – x) curve

= Area of square + Area of Triangle

$= (3 \times 3) + \frac{1}{2} \times (6 - 3 \times 3$

$= 9 + \frac{9}{2}, \frac{27}{2} = 13.5$ joule

10. A block of mass 10 kg. is moving in x–direction with a constant speed of 10m/sec. It is subjected to a force F = –0·1 x joules/meter during its travel from x = 20 meters to x = 30 meters. Its final kinetic energy will be **[2005]**

(1) 475 joules (2) 450 joules

(3) 275 joules (4) 250 joules

Sol. : **(1)**

F = 0.1x , m = 10 kg

v = 10 m/s

$x_1 = 20$ m

$x_2 = 80$m

$\Delta K = F.dx, (-0.1\ x)\ dx$

$k_f - k_1 = -0.1\int_{x_1}^{x_2} xdx, \frac{-0.1}{2}x^2\Big|_{x1}^{x_2}$

$k_f - \frac{1}{2}(10)(10)^2 = -\frac{0.1}{2}\left(x_2^2 - x_1^2\right)$

$k_f = 500 - \frac{1}{20}(900 - 400)$

$= 500 - \frac{1}{20} \times 500 = 500 - 25$

$k_f = 475$ joule

11. A body of mass 3 kg is under a constant force which causes a displacement s in metres in it, given by the relation $s = \frac{1}{3}t^2$, where t is in seconds. Work done by the force in 2 seconds is :- **[AIPMT 2006]**

(1) $\frac{5}{19}$ J (2) $\frac{3}{8}$ J

(3) $\frac{8}{3}$ J (4) $\frac{19}{5}$ J

Sol. : **(3)**

$S = \frac{t^2}{3}$

$\frac{ds}{dt} = \left(\frac{2t}{3}\right)$ $\qquad ds = \frac{2t}{3}\,dt$

$v = \frac{ds}{dt} = \frac{2t}{3}$ $\qquad \frac{dv}{dt} = a = \left(\frac{2}{3}\right)$

F = ma, 3 (2/3) $\qquad$ F = 2N

work done, $w = \int F.ds$

$w = \int_{t_1}^{t_2} 2\left(\frac{2t}{3}\right)dt \qquad = \frac{4}{3}\int_0^2 t\,dt,\ \frac{4}{3}\left(\frac{t^2}{2}\right)_0^2$

$= \frac{2}{3}(4), \left(\frac{8}{3}\right)$ joule

12. 300 J of work is done in sliding a 2 kg block up an inclined plane of height 10 m. Taking g = 10 m/s^2, work done against friction is :- **[AIPMT 2006]**

(1) 200 J $\qquad$ (2) 100 J

(3) Zero $\qquad$ (4) 1000 J

Sol. : **(2)** Loss in potential energy = mgh

$= 2 \times 10 \times 10 = 200$ J

Gain in kinetic energy = work done = 300 J

$\therefore$ Work done against friction = 300 – 200 = 100J.

13. A vertical spring with force constant k is fixed on a table. A ball of mass m at a height h above the free upper end of the spring falls vertically on the spring, so that the spring is compressed by a distance d. The net work done in the process is : **[2008]**

(1) $mg(h+d)+\frac{1}{2}kd^2$

(2) $mg(h+d)-\frac{1}{2}kd^2$

(3) $mg(h-d)-\frac{1}{2}kd^2$

(4) $mg(h-d)+\frac{1}{2}kd^2$

Sol. : **(3)**

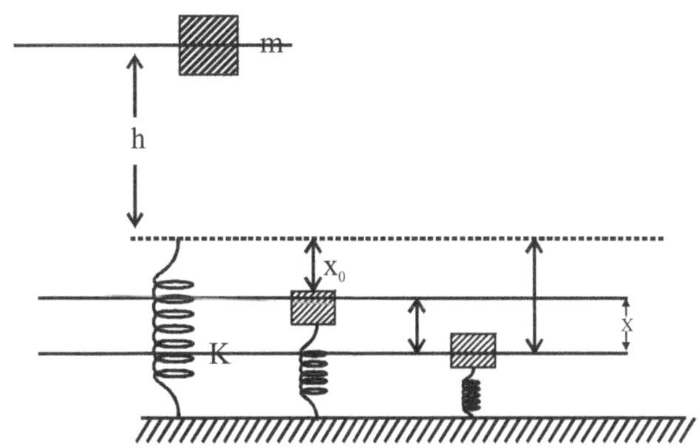

$(mg) = Kx_0$ $\qquad d = (x_0 + x^1)$

$x_0 = \left(\frac{mg}{k}\right)$

14. An explosion blows a rock into three parts. Two parts go off at right angles to each other. These two are, 1 kg first part moving with a velocity of 12 ms^{-1} and 2 kg second part moving with a velocity of 8 ms^{-1}. If the third part flies off with a velocity of 4ms^{-1}, its mass would be :- **[AIPMT 2009]**

(1) 3kg $\qquad$ (2) 5 kg

(3) 7 kg $\qquad$ (4) 17 kg

Sol. : **(2)** When an explosion breaks a rock, by the law of conservation of momentum, initial momentum is zero and for the three pieces,

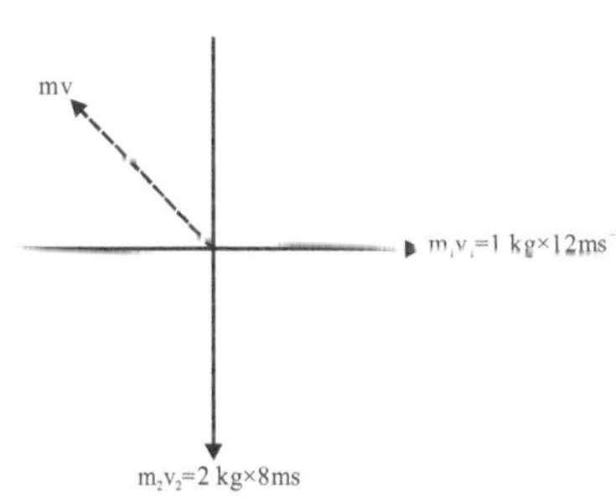

Total momentum of the two pieces 1 kg and 2 kg

$=\sqrt{12^2+16^2}=20\,kg\,ms^{-1}$

The third pieces has the same momentum and in the direction opposite to the resultantof these two momenta.

$\therefore$ Momentum of the third piece = 20 kg ms^{-1}

Velocity = 4 ms^{-1}

$\therefore$ Mass of the 3rd Piece $=\frac{mv}{v}=\frac{20}{4}=5\,kg$.

15. A block of mass M is attached to the lower end of a vertical spring. The spring is hung from a ceiling and has force constant value k. The mass is released from rest with the spring initially unstretched. the maximum extension produced in the length of the spring will be :- **[AIPMT 2009]**

(1) Mg/2k (2) Mg/k

(3) 2 Mg/k (4) 4 Mg/k

Sol. : **(3)** When the mass attached to a spring fixed at the other end is allowed to fall suddenly, it extends the spring by x. potential energy lost by the mass is gained by the spring.

$$Mgx\frac{1}{2}kx^2 \Rightarrow x=\frac{2Mg}{k}.$$

16. An engine pumps water continuously through a hose. Water leaves the hose with a velocity v and m is the mass per unit length of the water jet. What is the rate at which kinetic energy is imparted to water :- **[AIPMT 2009]**

(1) $\frac{1}{2}m^2v^2$ (2) $\frac{1}{2}mv^3$

(3) mv^3 (4) $\frac{1}{2}mv^2$

Sol. : **(2)** Velocity of water is v, mass flowing per unit lengths is m.

$\therefore$ Mass flowing per second = mv

$\therefore$ Rate of kinetic energy or K.E. per second

$$=\frac{1}{2}(mv)v^2=\frac{1}{2}mv^3.$$

17. A body of mass 1 kg is thrown upwards with a velocity 20 m/s. It momentarily comes to rest after attaining a height of 18 m. How much energy is lost due to air friction ? ($g = 10\ m/s^2$):- **[AIPMT 2009]**

(1) 10 J (2) 20 J

(3) 30 J (4) 40 J

Sol. : **(2)** Initial velocity u = 20 m/s; m = 1 kg

Kinetic energy = maximum potential energy

Initial Kinetic energy $=\frac{1}{2}\times1\times20^2=200\,J$

$Mgh(max)=200\,J.$

$\therefore h=20\,m.$

The height travelled by the body, h' = 18m

$\therefore$ Loss of energy due to air friction = mgh – mgh'

$\Rightarrow$ Energy lost $=200\,J-1\times10\times18\,J=20\,J.$

18. An engine pumps water through a hose pipe. Water passes through the pipe and leaves it with a velocity of 2 m/s. The mass per unit length of water in the pipe is 100 kg/m. What is the power of the engine ? **[AIPMT 2010]**

(1) 800 W (2) 400 W

(3) 200 W (4) 100 W

Sol. : **(1)** Here,

Mass per unit length of water, μ = 100 kg/m

Velocity of water, v = 2 m/s

Power of the engine, $P=\mu v^3$

$=(100\ kg/m)(2m/s)^3$

= 800 W

19. A ball moving with velocity 2 m/s collides head on with another stationary ball of double the mass. If the coefficient of restitution is 0.5, then their velocities (in m/s) after collision will be : **[AIPMT 2010]**

(1) 0, 2 (2) 0, 1

(3) 1, 1 (4) 1, 0.5

Sol. : **(2)** Here, $m_1 = m, m_2 = 2m$

$u_1 = 2m/s, u_2 = 0$

Coefficient of restitution, e = 0.5

Let v_1 and v_2 be their respective velocities after collision.

Applying the law of conservation of linear momentum, we get

$$m_1u_1 + m_2u_2 = m_1v_1 + m_2v_2$$

$$\therefore\ m\times 2 + 2m\times 0 = m\times v_1 + 2m\times v_2$$

or $2m = mv_1 + 2mv_2$

or $2 = (v_1 + 2v_2)$ ....(i)

By definition of coefficient of restitution,

$$e = \frac{v_2 - v_1}{u_1 - u_2} \quad \text{or} \quad e = (u_1 - u_2) = v_2 - v_1$$

$0.5(2-0) = v_2 - v_1$ ....(ii)

$1 = v_2 - v_1$

Solving equations (i) and (ii), we get

$v_1 = 0m/s, v_2 = 1m/s$.

20. The potential energy of a system increases if work is done :- **[AIPMT 2011]**

(1) Upon the system by a nonconservative force

(2) By the system against a conservative force

(3) By the system against a nonconservative force

(4) Upon the system by a conservative force

Sol. : **(2)** By the system against a conservative force.

21. A body projected vertically from the earth reaches a height equal to earth's radius before returning to the earth. The power exerted by the gravitational force is greatest : – **[AIPMT 2011]**

(1) At the highest position of the body

(2) At the instant just before the body hits the earth

(3) It remains constant all through

(4) At the instant just after the body is projected

Sol. : **(2)** Power, $P = \vec{F}\cdot\vec{v} = Fv\cos\theta$

Just before hitting the earth $\theta = 0°$. Hence, the power exerted by the gravitational force is greatest at the instant just before the body hits the earth.

22. Force F on a particle moving in a straight line varies with distance d as shown in the figure. The work done on the particle during its displacement of 12m is : **[AIPMT 2011]**

(1) 18 J

(2) 21 J

(3) 26 J

(4) 13 J

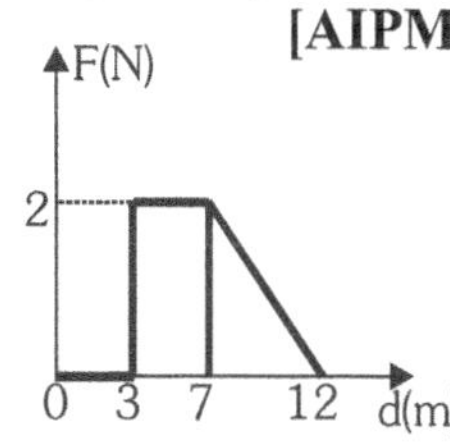

Sol. : **(4)**

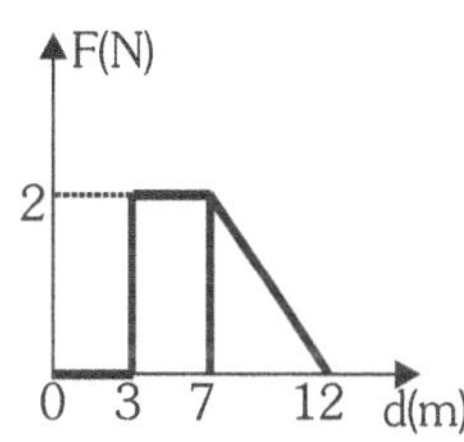

Work done = Area under (F-d) graph

= Area of rectangle ABCD + Area of triangle DCE

$$=2\times(7-3)+\frac{1}{2}\times 2\times(12-7) = 8+5 = 13J.$$

23. The potential energy of a particle in a force field is : $U = \frac{A}{r^2} \quad \frac{B}{r}$

where A and B are positive constants and r is the distance of particle from the centre of the field. For stable equilibrium, the distance of the particle is : **[AIPMT Pre. 2012]**

(1) A/B (2) B/A

(3) B/2A (4) 2A/B

Sol. : **(4)** Here, $U = \frac{A}{r^2} - \frac{B}{r}$

For equilibrium, $\frac{dU}{dr} = 0$

$$\therefore -\frac{2A}{r^3} + \frac{B}{r^2} = 0 \; or \; \frac{2A}{r^3} = \frac{B}{r^2} \; or \; r = \frac{2A}{B}$$

For stable equilibrium, $\frac{d^2U}{dr^2} > 0$

$$\frac{d^2U}{dr^2} = \frac{6A}{r^4} - \frac{2B}{r^3}$$

$$\left.\frac{d^2U}{dr^2}\right|_{r=(2A/B)} = \frac{6AB^4}{16A^4} - \frac{2B^4}{8A^3} = \frac{B^4}{8A^3} > 0$$

So for stable equilibrium, the distance of the particle is $\frac{2A}{B}$.

24. Two spheres A and B of masses m_1 and m_2 respectively collide. A is at rest initially and B is moving with velocity v along x-axis. After collision B has a velocity $\frac{v}{2}$ in a direction perpendicular to the original direction. The mass A moves after collision in the direction. **[AIPMT Pre. 2012]**

(1) $\theta = \tan^{-1}(1/2)$ to the x-axis

(2) $\theta = \tan^{-1}(-1/2)$ to the x-axis

(3) same as that of B

(4) opposite to that of B

Sol. : **(2)**

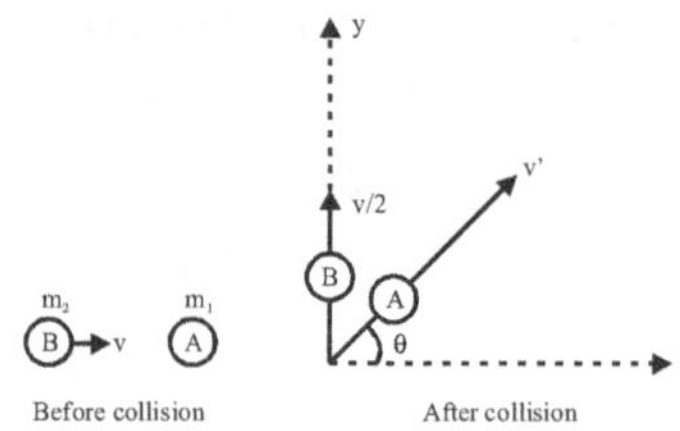

According to law of conservation of linear momentum along x-axis, we get

$$m_1 \times 0 + m_2 \times v = m_1 v' \cos\theta$$

$$m_2 v = m_1 v' \cos\theta \quad or \quad \cos\theta = \frac{m_2 v}{m_1 v'}$$

According to law of conservation of linear momentum along y-axis, we get

$$m_1 \times 0 + m_2 \times 0 = m_1 v' \sin\theta + m_2 \frac{v}{2}$$

$$-m_2 \frac{v}{2} = m_1 v' \sin\theta$$

$$\sin\theta = -\frac{m_2 v}{2 m_1 v'}$$

Divide (ii) by (i), we get

$$\tan\theta = -\frac{1}{2} \quad or \quad \theta = \tan^{-1}\left(-\frac{1}{2}\right) \text{to the x-axis}.$$

25. A car of mass m starts from rest and accelerates so that the instantaneous power delivered to the car has a constant magnitude P_0. The instantaneous velocity of this car is proportional to : **[AIPMT 2012]**

(1) $t^{-1/2}$ (2) $t/\sqrt{m}$

(3) t^2P_0 (4) $t^{1/2}$

Sol. : **(4)** $P_0 = Fv$

$\because F = ma = m\frac{dv}{dt}$

$\therefore P_0 = mv\frac{dv}{dt}$ or $P_0 dt = mvdv$

Integrating both sides, we get

$$\int_0^t P_0 dt = m\int_0^v vdv$$

$$P_0 t = \frac{mv^2}{2}; \qquad v = \left(\frac{2P_0 t}{m}\right)^{1/2} \quad or \quad v \propto \sqrt{t}.$$

26. A stone is dropped from a height h. It hits the ground with a certain momentum P. If the same stone is dropped from a height 100% more than the previous height, the momentum when it hits the ground will change by **[AIPMT 2012]**

(1) 200 % (2) 100 %

(3) 68% (4) 41%

Sol. : **(4)**

Velocity $v = \sqrt{2gh}$ ....(i)

and momentum p = mv .....(ii)

From (eqn.) (i) and (ii), we have

$p \propto \sqrt{h}$

Here, $\frac{p_2}{p_1} = \sqrt{\frac{h_2}{h_1}}$

$\therefore \frac{p_2}{p_1} = \sqrt{\frac{2h}{h}} = \sqrt{2}$

$p_2 = 1.414\, p_1$

%change = $\frac{p_2 - p_1}{p_1} \times 100 = 41\%$

27. Consider a drop of rain water having mass 1 g falling from a height of 1 km. It hits the ground with a speed of 50 m/s. Take 'g' constant with a value 10 m/s^2. The work done by the (i) gravitational force and the (ii) resistive force of air is : **[NEET - 2017]**

(1) (i) – 10 J (ii) – 8.25 J

(2) (i) 1.25 J (ii) – 8.25 J

(3) (i) 100 J (ii) 8.75 J

(4) (i) 10 J (ii) – 8.75 J

Sol. : **(4)** $w_g + w_a = K_f - K_i$

$mgh + w_a = \frac{1}{2}mv^2 - 0$

$10^{-3} \times 10 \times 10^3 + w_a = \frac{1}{2} \times 10^{-3} \times (50)^2$.

$w_a = -8.75$ J i.e. work done due to air resistance and work done due to gravity $= 10$ J.

28. A moving block having mass m, collides with another stationary block having mass 4m. The lighter block comes to rest after collision. The lighter block comes to rest after collision. When the initial velocity of the lighter block is v, then the value of coefficient of restitution (e) will be

[NEET-2018]

(1) 0.8 (2) 0.25

(3) 0.5 (4) 0.4

Ans. **(2)**

06 Systems of Particles and Rotational Motion

Note: Scan QR code with your mobile camera or QR scanner for video solutions.

1. A wheel has angular acceleration of 3.0 rad/s^2 and an initial angular speed of 2.00 rad/s. In a tine of 2 s it has rotated through an angle (in radian) of **[AIPMT 2007]**

(1) 6 (2) 10

(3) 12 (4) 4

Sol. : (2)

Given : Angular acceleration, $\alpha = 3$ rad/sec^2

Initial angular velocity $\omega_i = 2$ rad/sec

$Time\, t = 2\,\text{sec}$

Using, $\theta = \omega_i t + \frac{1}{2}\alpha t^2$

$\therefore \theta = 2\times2+\frac{1}{2}\times3\times4 = 4+6 = 10$ *radian.*

2. A uniform rod AB of length l and mass m is free to rotate about point A. The rod is released from rest in the horizontal position. Given that the moment o inertia of the rod about A is $\frac{ml^2}{3}$ the Initial angular acceleration of the rod will be : **[AIPMT 2007]**

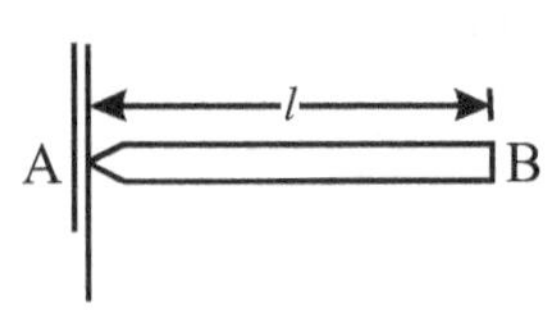

(1) $\frac{2g}{3l}$ (2) $mg\frac{1}{2}$

(3) $\frac{3}{2}gl$ (4) $\frac{3g}{2l}$

Sol. : (4)

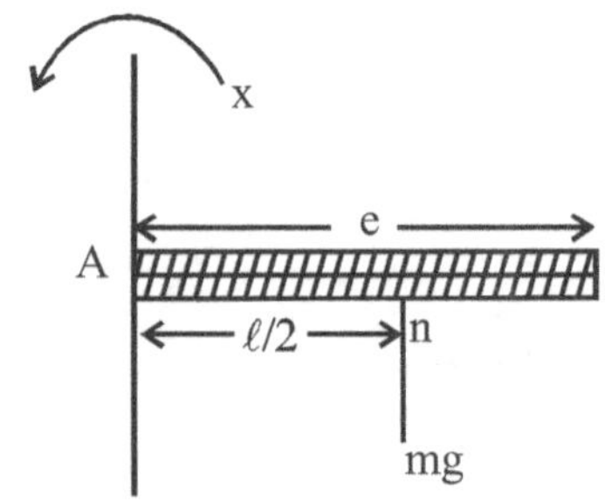

Torgue about 'A'

$\tau = (mg)(\ell/2)$

$\tau = mg\ell/2$

$\tau = I\alpha$ [$\because \alpha$ = Angular aceteration]

$\alpha = \left(\frac{\tau}{I}\right)$

$\alpha = \frac{(mg\ell/2)}{(m\ell^2 3)} = \left(\frac{3g}{2\ell}\right)$

3. A particle of mass m moves in the XY plane with a velocity v along the straight line AB. If the angular momentum of the particle with respect to origion O is L_A when it is at A and L_B when it is at B, then **[AIPMT 2007]**

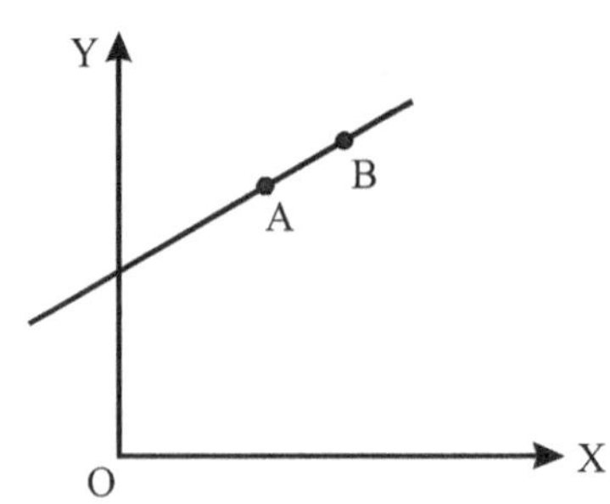

(1) $L_A > L_B$

(2) $L_A = L_B$

(3) the relationship between L_A and L_B depends upon the slope of the line AB

(4) $L_A < L_B$

Sol. : (2)

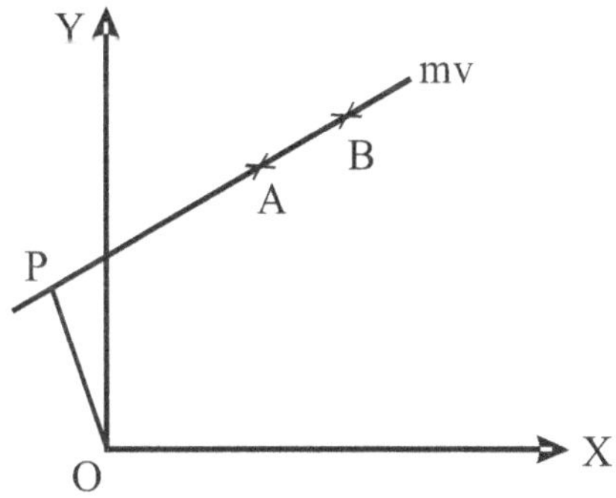

Momentum of momentum is angular momentum. OP is the same whether the mass is at A or B.

$\therefore L_A = L_B$.

4. The ratio of the radii of gyration of a circular disc to that of a circular ring. each of same mass and radius, around their respective axes is **[AIPMT 2008]**

(1) $\sqrt{3}:\sqrt{2}$ (2) $1:\sqrt{2}$

(3) $\sqrt{2}:1$ (4) $\sqrt{2}:\sqrt{3}$

Sol. : (2)

Mometum inertia (I) of a circular

disc ; (1) = $\frac{MR^2}{2}$

radius of gyration of circular disc

$mK_1^2 = \frac{MR^2}{2}$

$K_1 = \frac{R}{\sqrt{3}}$

momentum inertia (I) of circular disc (I) = MR^2

radius of gyration of circular ring (k_2)

$mK_2^2 = mR^2$

$k_2 = 2$

$$\frac{K_1}{K_2} = \frac{\left(\frac{R}{\sqrt{2}}\right)}{R} = \frac{1}{\sqrt{2}}$$

5. A thin rod of length L and mass M is bent at its midpoint into two halves so that the angle between them is 90°. The moment of inertia of the bent rod about an axis passing through the bending point and perpendicular to the plane defined by the two halves of the rod is **[AIPMT 2008]**

(1) $\frac{ML^2}{24}$ (2) $\frac{ML^2}{12}$

(3) $\frac{ML^2}{6}$ (4) $\frac{\sqrt{2}ML^2}{24}$

Sol. : (2)

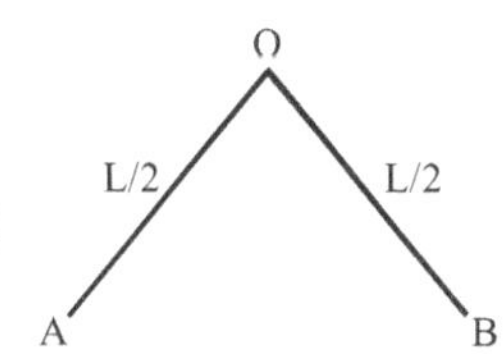

Total mass = M, total length = L

Moment of Inertia of OA about O = Moment of inertial of OB about O.

$$\Rightarrow M.I.total = 2\times\left(\frac{M}{2}\right)\left(\frac{L}{2}\right)^2\cdot\frac{1}{3} = \frac{ML^2}{12}.$$

6. A thin circular ring of mass M and radius R is rotating in a horizontal plane about an axis vertical to its plane with a constant angular velocity ω. If two objects each of mass m be attached gently to the opposite ends of a diameter of the ring, the ring will then rotate with an angular velocity. **[AIPMT 2009]**

(1) $\frac{\omega\ M-2m}{M+2m}$ (2) $\frac{\omega M}{M+2m}$

(3) $\frac{\omega\ M+2m}{M}$ (4) $\frac{\omega M}{M+m}$

Sol. : **(2)** As the masses are added to the ring gently, there is no torque and angular momentum is conserved.

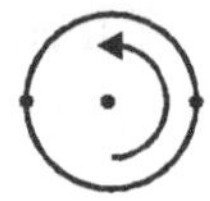

$$I_1\omega_1 = I'\omega'$$

$$\Rightarrow MR^2\omega = (MR^2 + 2mR^2)\omega'$$

$$\Rightarrow \omega' = \frac{MR^2\omega}{(M+2m)R^2} \Rightarrow \omega' = \frac{M\omega}{M+2m}.$$

7. If $\vec{F}$ is the force acting on a particle having position vector $\vec{r}$ and $\vec{\ }$ be the torque of this force about the origin, then **[AIPMT 2009]**

(1) $\vec{r}\,.\,\vec{\ } \neq 0$ and $\vec{F}\,.\,\vec{\ } = 0$

(2) $\vec{r}\,.\,\vec{\ } \neq 0$ and $\vec{F}\,.\,\vec{\ } < 0$

(3) $\vec{r}\,.\,\vec{\ } \neq 0$ and $\vec{F}\,.\,\vec{\ } = 0$

(4) $\vec{r}\,.\,\vec{\ } = 0$ and $\vec{F}\,.\,\vec{\ } \neq 0$

Sol. : **(2)** Torque is always perpendicular to $\vec{F}$ as well as $\vec{r}$.

$\therefore \vec{r}\,.\,\vec{\ } = 0$ as well as $\vec{F}\,.\,\vec{\ } = 0$.

8. Four identical thin road each of mass M and length l form a sequare frame. Moment of inertia of this frame about an axis through the centre of the square and perpendicular to its plane is **[AIPMT 2009]**

(1) $\frac{2}{3}Ml^2$ (2) $\frac{4}{3}Ml^2$ (3) $\frac{13}{3}Ml^2$ (4) $\frac{1}{3}Ml^2$

Sol. : **(2)**

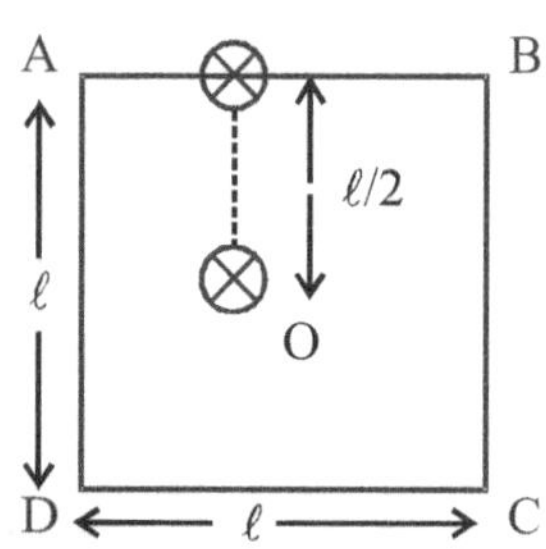

$$I_D = \frac{m\ell^2}{12}$$

I_0 at centre of square of one rod $= I_0 = I_D + md^2$

$$= M\frac{\ell^2}{12} + \frac{m\ell^2}{4}$$

$$= \frac{M\ell^2}{3}$$

For all the form rods

$$I = \frac{4}{3}m\ell^2$$

9. Two bodies of mass 1 kg and 3 kg have position vectors $\hat{i}\ \ 2\hat{j}\ \ \hat{k}$ and $-3\hat{i}-2\hat{j}\ \ \hat{k}$, respectively. The centre of mass of this system has a position vector **[AIPMT 2009]**

(1) $-2\hat{i}\ \ 2\hat{k}$ (2) $-2\hat{i}-\hat{j}\ \ \hat{k}$

(3) $2\hat{i}-\hat{j}\ \ 2\hat{k}$ (4) $-\hat{i}\ \ \hat{j}\ \ \hat{k}$

Sol. : **(2)** $\vec{r_1} = \hat{i}\ \ 2\hat{j}\ \ \hat{k}$ for $M_1 = 1kg$

$\vec{r_2} = -3\hat{i} - 2\hat{j} + \hat{k}$ for $M_2 = 3kg$

$$r_{C.M.} = \frac{\sum m_i r_i}{\sum m_i}$$

$$\Rightarrow r_{C.M.} = \frac{(1\hat{i}+2\hat{j}+1\hat{k})\times 1 + (-3\hat{i}-2\hat{j}+\hat{k})\times 3}{4}$$

$$\Rightarrow r_{C.M.} = \frac{(1\hat{i}+2\hat{j}+1\hat{k})\times 1 + (-9\hat{i}-6\hat{j}+3\hat{k})}{4}$$

$$\Rightarrow r_{C.M.} = \frac{-81\hat{i}-4\hat{j}+4\hat{k}}{4} = -2\hat{i}-\hat{j}+\hat{k}.$$

10. A circular disk of moment of inerita I_1 is rotating in a horizontal plane, about its symmetry axis, with a constant angular speed ω_1. Another disk of moment of inertia I_b is dropped coaxially onto the rotating disk. Initially the second disk has zero angular speed. Eventually both the disks rotate with a constant anguar speed ω_f. The energy lost by the initially rotating disc due to friction is : **[AIPMT 2010]**

(1) $\frac{1}{2}\frac{I_b^2}{I_t \quad I_b}\ {}^{2}_{1}$ (2) $\frac{1}{2}\frac{I_t^2}{I_t \quad I_b}\ {}^{2}_{1}$

(3) $\frac{1}{2}\frac{I_b - I_t}{I_t \quad I_b}\ {}^{2}_{1}$ (4) $\frac{1}{2}\frac{I_b\ I_t}{I_t \quad I_b}\ {}^{2}_{1}$

Sol. : **(4)** As no external torque is applied to the system, the angular momentum of the system remains conserved.

$\therefore L_i = L_f$

According to given problem,

$I_t\omega_i = (I_t + I_b)\omega_f$

or $\omega_f = \dfrac{I_t\omega_i}{I_t + I_b}$ ....(i)

Initial energy, $E_i = \frac{1}{2}I_t\omega_i^2$ ....(ii)

Final energy, $E_f = \frac{1}{2}(I_t + I_b)\omega_f^2$ ....(iii)

Substituting the value of ω_f from equation (i) in equation (iii), we get

Final energy, $E_f = \frac{1}{2}(I_t + I_b)\left(\dfrac{I_t\omega_i}{I_t + I_b}\right)^2$

$= \dfrac{1}{2}\dfrac{I_t^2\omega_i^2}{(I_t + I_b)}$ ....(iv)

Loss of energy, $\Delta E = E_i - E_f$

$= \frac{1}{2}I_t\omega_i^2 - \dfrac{1}{2}\dfrac{I_t^2\omega_i^2}{(I_t + I_b)}$ (Using (ii) and (iv))

$= \dfrac{\omega_i^2}{2}\left(I_t - \dfrac{I_t^2}{(I_t + I_b)}\right) = \dfrac{\omega_i^2}{2}\left(\dfrac{I_t^2 + I_bI_t - I_t^2}{(I_t + I_b)}\right)$

$= \dfrac{1}{2}\dfrac{I_bI_t}{(I_t + I_b)}\omega_i^2$.

11. Two particles which are initially at rest move towards each other under the action of their internal attraction. If their speeds are v and 2v at any instant, then the speed of centre of mass of the system will be **[AIPMT 2010]**

(1) 2 v (2) 0 (3) 1.5 v (4) v

Sol. : **(2)** As no external force is acting on the system, the centre of mass must be at rest i.e. $v_{CM} = 0$.

12. A man of 50 kg mass is standing in a gravity free space at a height of 10 m above the floor. He throws a stone of 0.5 kg mass downwards with a speed $2ms^{-1}$. When the stone reaches the floor, the distance of the man above the floor will be **[AIPMT 2010]**

(1) 9.9 m (2) 10.1 m

(3) 10 m (4) 20 m

Sol. : **(2)** Let distance of man from the floor be (10 + x)m. As centre of mass of system remains at 10m above the floor.

So $50(x) = 0.5(10) \Rightarrow x = 0.1m$

$\Rightarrow$ distance of the man above the floor

$= 10 + 0.1 = 10.1$ m.

13. The instantaneous angular position of a point on a rotating wheel is given by the equation $\theta(t) = 2t^3 - 6t^2$ **[AIPMT 2011]**

The torque on the wheel becomes zero at

(1) t = 0.5 s (2) t = 0.25 s

(3) t = 2s (4) t = 1 s

Sol. : **(4)**

given by :

$\theta = 2t^3 - 6t^2$

$$w = \left(\frac{d\theta}{dt}\right) = 6t^2 - 12t$$

$$\alpha = \left(\frac{dw}{d\theta}\right) = 12t - 12$$

torque (t) = $I\alpha$

$0 = I\alpha$

$\alpha = 0$

$12t - 12 = 0$

t = 1 second

14. The moment of inertia of a thin uniform rod of mass M and length L about an axis passing through its mid-point and perpendicular to its length is I_0. Its moment of inertia about an axis passing through one of its ends and perpendicular to its length is **[AIPMT 2011]**

(1) $I_0 + ML^2/4$ (2) $I_0 + 2ML^2$

(3) $I_0 + ML^2$ (4) $I_0 + ML^2/2$

Sol. : **(1)** According to the theorem of parallel axes, the moment of inertia of the thin rod of mass M and length L about an axis passing through one of the ends is

$$I = I_{CM} + Md^2$$

Where I_{CM} is the moment of inertia of the given rod about an axis passing through its centre of mass and perpendicular to its length and d is the distance between two parallel axes.

Here, $I_{CM} = I_0$, $d = \frac{L}{2}$

$$\therefore I = I_0 + M\left(\frac{L}{2}\right)^2 = I_0 + \frac{ML^2}{4}$$

15. A small mass attached to a string rotates on frictionless table top as shown. If the tension of the string is increased by pulling the string causing the radius of the circular motion to decrease by a factor of 2, the kinetic energy of the mass will be. **[AIPMT 2011]**

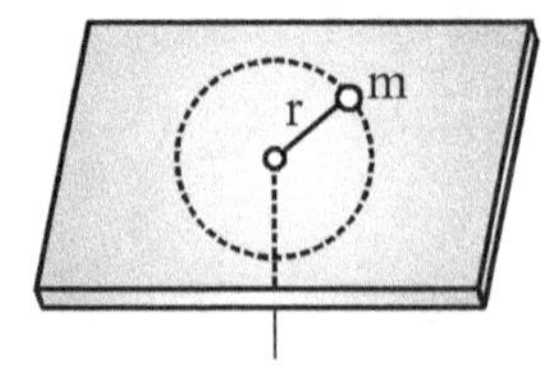

(1) remain constant

(2) increase by a factor of 2

(3) increase by a factor of 4

(4) decrease by a factor of 2

Sol. : **(3)** According to law of conservation of angular momentum

$$mvr = mv'r'$$

$$vr = v'\left(\frac{r}{2}\right)$$

$$v' = 2v \quad \text{...............(i)}$$

$$\therefore \frac{K}{K'} = \frac{\frac{1}{2}mv^2}{\frac{1}{2}mv'^2} = \left(\frac{v}{v'}\right)^2$$

$$\text{or } \therefore \frac{K'}{K} = \left(\frac{v'}{v}\right)^2 = (2)^2 \quad \text{(Using (i))}$$

$$K' = 4K$$

16. When a mass is rotating in a plane about a fixed point, its angular momentum is directed along

(1) the tangent to the orbit

(2) a line perpendicular to the plane of rotation

(3) the line making an angle of 45° to the plane of rotation

(4) the radius **[AIPMT 2012]**

Sol. : (2) 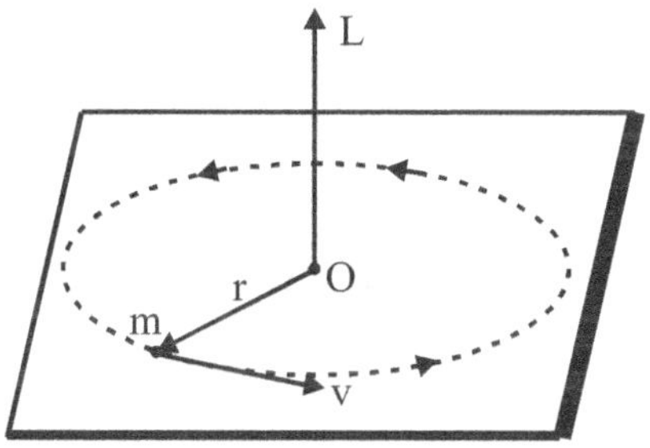

When a mass is rotating in a plane about a fixed point its angular momentum is directed along a line perpendicular to the plane of rotation.

17. Two persons of masses 55 kg and 65 kg respectively are at the opposite ends of a boat. The length of the boat is 3.0 m and weight 100 kg The 55 kg man walks up to the 65 kg man and sits with him. If the boat is in still water the centre of mass of the system shifts by **[AIPMT 2012]**

(1) 0.75 m (2) 3.0 m

(3) 2.3 m (4) zero

Sol. : **(4)** As no external force acts on the system therefore centre of mass will not shift.

18. ABC is an equilateral triangle with O as the centre. $\vec{F}_1$, $\vec{F}_2$ and $\vec{F}_3$ represent three forces acting along the sides AB,BC and AC respectively. If the total torque about O is zero then the magnitude of $\vec{F}_3$ is **[AIPMT 2012]**

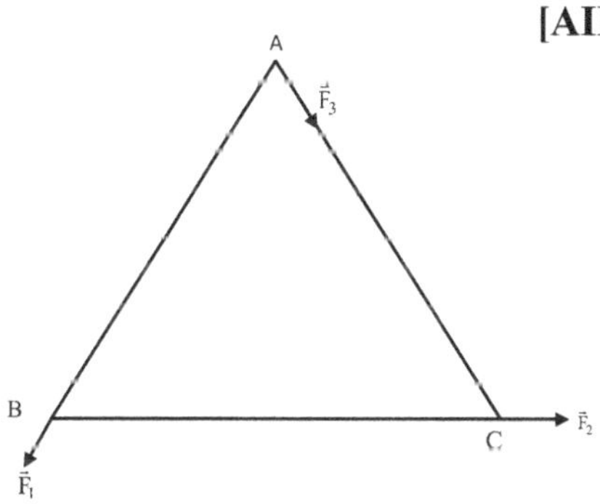

(1) $2(F_1, F_2)$ (2) $F_1 + F_2$

(3) $F_1 - F_2$ (4) $\frac{F_1 - F_2}{2}$

Sol. : **(2)** Let x be the distance of centre O of equilateral triangle from each side.

Total torque about O = 0

$\Rightarrow F_1x + F_2x - F_3x = 0 \text{ or } F_3 = F_1 + F_2$.

19. A circular platform is mounted on a friction less vericles axle. Its radius R = 2 m and its moment of inertia about the axle is 200 kg m^2 It is initially at rest. A 50 kg man, stands on the edge of the platform and begins to walk along the edge at the speed of 1 ms^{-1} relative to the ground. Time taken by the man to complete one revolution is: **[AIPMT 2012]**

(1) π sec (2) $\frac{3\pi}{2}$sec

(3) 2π sec (4) $\frac{\pi}{2}$sec

Sol. : **(3)** As the system is initially at rest, therefore, initial angular momentum $L_i = 0$.

According to the principle of conservation of angular momentum, final angular momentum, $L_f = 0$.

∴ Angular momentum = Angular momentum of i.e., $mvR = I\omega$

$$or\ \omega = \frac{mvR}{I} = \frac{50 \times 1 \times 2}{200} = \frac{1}{2} rad\ S^{-1}$$

Angular velocity of man relative to platform is

$$\omega_r = \omega + \frac{v}{R} = \frac{1}{2} + \frac{1}{2} = 1\ rad\ s^{-1}$$

Time taken by the man to complete one revolution is

$$T = \frac{2\pi}{\omega_r} = \frac{2\pi}{1} = 2\pi\ s.$$

20. The moment of inetria of a uniform circular disc is maximum about an axis perpendiculr to the disc and passing through **[AIPMT 2012]**

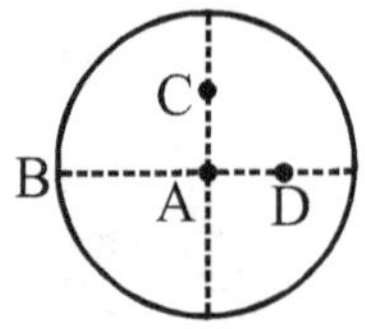

(1) B (2) C
(3) D (4) A

Sol. : **(1)** According to the theorem of parallel axes,

$I = I_{CM} + Ma^2$

As a is maximum for point B.

Therefore I is maximum about B.

21. Three masses are placed on the x- axis : 300 g at origin, 500 g at x = 40 cm and 400 g at x = 70 cm. The distance of the centre of mass from the origin is **[AIPMT 2012]**

(1) 40 cm (2) 45 cm
(3) 50 cm (4) 30 cm

Sol. : **(1)**

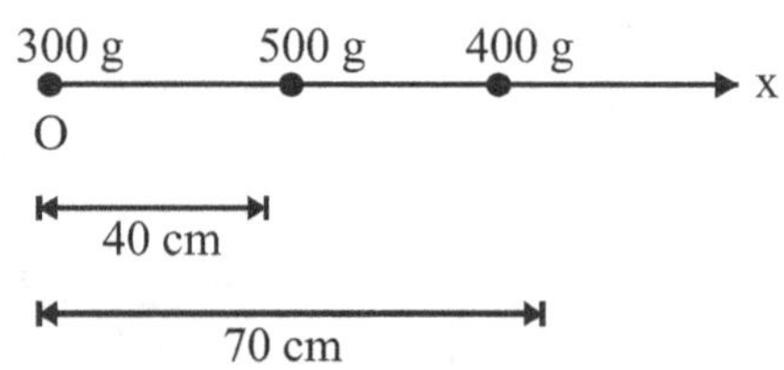

The distance of the centre of mass of the system of three masses from the origin O is

$$X_{CM} = \frac{m_1x_1 + m_2x_2 + m_3x_3}{m_1 + m_2 + m_3}$$

$$= \frac{300\times0 + 500\times40 + 400\times70}{300+500+400}$$

$$= \frac{500\times40 + 400\times70}{1200} = \frac{400[50+70]}{1200}$$

$$= \frac{50+70}{3} = \frac{120}{3} = 40\,cm.$$

22. A solid cylinder of mass 3 kg is rolling on a horizontal surface with velocity $4ms^{-1}$, It collides with a horizontal spring of force constant 200 Nm^{-1}.The maximum compression produced in the spring will be **[AIPMT 2012]**

(1) 0.2 m (2) 0.5 m
(3) 0.6 m (4) 0.7 m

Sol. : **(3)** $\frac{1}{2}mv^2\left[1+\frac{K^2}{R^2}\right] = \frac{1}{2}kx^2_{max}$

Putting $m=3kg, v = 4m/s, \frac{K^2}{R^2} = 1/2$ (for solid cylinder), $k = 200\,Nm^{-1}$ we get $x_{max} = 0.6\,m$.

23. A small object of uniform density rolls up a curved surface with an intitial velocity v. It reaches up to a maximum height of $\frac{3v^2}{4g}$ with respect to the initial position. The object is **[AIPMT 2013]**

(1) Ring (2) Solid sphere
(3) Hollow sphere (4) Disc

Sol. : **(4)** The kinetic energy of the rolling object is converted into potential energy at height

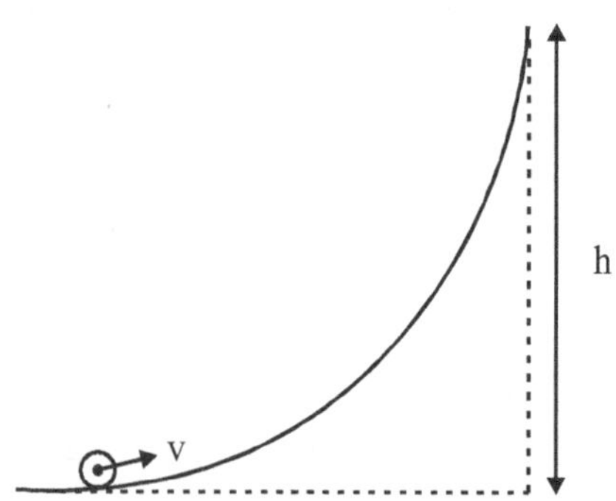

$$h\left(=\frac{3v^2}{4g}\right)$$

So by the law of conservation of mechanical energy, we have

$$\frac{1}{2}mv^2+\frac{1}{2}I\omega^2=Mgh \qquad \left(\because \omega\frac{v}{R}\right)$$

$$\frac{1}{2}mv^2+\frac{1}{2}I\omega\left(\frac{v}{R}\right)^2=Mg\left(\frac{3v^2}{4g}\right)$$

$$\frac{1}{2}I\frac{v^2}{R^2}=\frac{3}{4}Mv^2-\frac{1}{2}Mv^2$$

$$\frac{1}{2}I\frac{v^2}{R^2}=\frac{1}{4}Mv^2 \quad or \quad I=\frac{1}{2}MR^2$$

Hence, the object is disc.

24. A rod PQ of mass M and length L is hinged at end P. The rod is kept horizontal by a massless string tied to point Q as shown in the figure When string is cut, the initial angular acceleration of the rod is **[AIPMT 2013]**

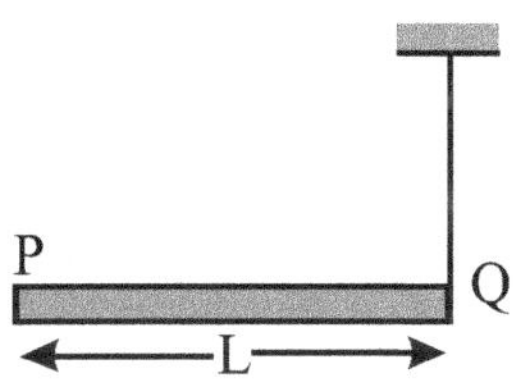

(1) $\frac{3g}{2L}$ (2) $\frac{g}{L}$

(3) $\frac{2g}{L}$ (4) $\frac{2g}{2L}$

Sol. : (1)

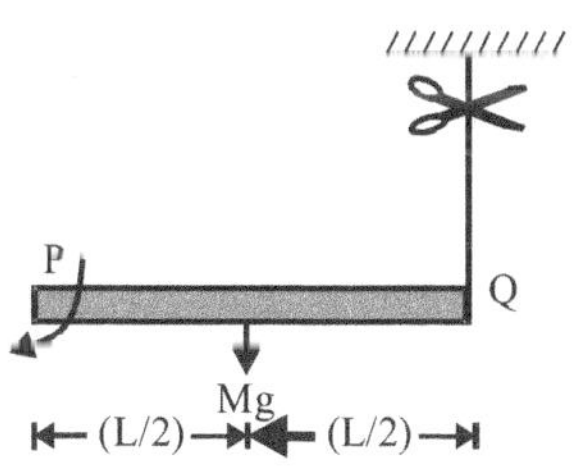

When the string is cut, the rod will rotate about P.

Let α be initial angular acceleration of the rod. Then

Torque, $\tau=I\alpha=\frac{ML^2}{3}\alpha$ ....(i)

(Moment of inertial of the rod about one end $=\frac{ML^2}{3}$)

Also, $\tau=Mg\frac{L}{2}$ ....(ii)

Equation (i) and (ii), we get

$$Mg\frac{L}{2}=\frac{ML^2}{3}\alpha \quad or \quad \alpha=\frac{3g}{2L}.$$

25. A solid cylinder of mass 50 kg and radius 0.5 m is free to rotate about the horizontal axis. A massless string is wound round the cylinder with one end attached to it and other hanging freely. Tension in the string required to produce an angular acceleration of 2 revolutions s^{-2} is

[AIPMT 2014]

(1) 25 N (2) 50 N

(3) 78.5 N (4) 157 N

Sol. : (4)

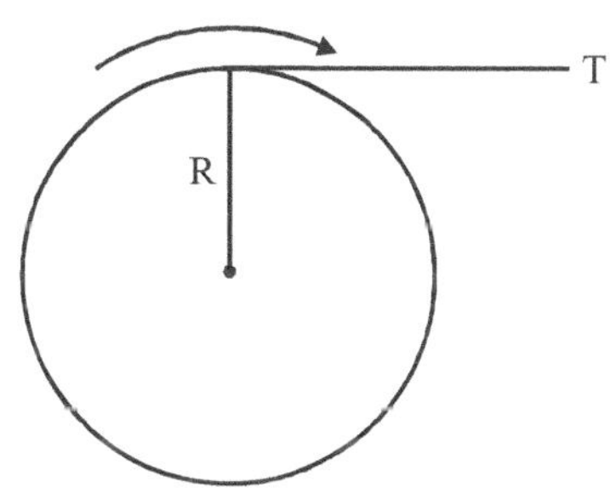

Here mass of the cylinder, M = 50 kg

Radius of the cylinder, R = 0.5 m

Angular acceleration, $\alpha=2\,rev\,s^{-2}$

$=2\times2\pi\,rad\,s^{-2}=4\pi\,rad\,s^{-2}$

Torque, $\tau = TR$

Moment of inertia of the solid cylinder about its axis, $I = \frac{1}{2}MR^2$

$\therefore$ Angular acceleration of the cylinder

$$\alpha = \frac{\tau}{I} = \frac{TR}{\frac{1}{2}MR^2}$$

$$T = \frac{MR\alpha}{2} = \frac{50 \times 0.5 \times 4\pi}{2} = 157\,N$$

26. The ratio of the acceleration for a solid sphere (mass m and radius R) rolling down an incline of angle 'θ' without slipping and spipping down the incline without rolling is **[AIPMT 2014]**

(1) 5 : 7 (2) 2 : 3

(3) 2 : 5 (4) 7 : 5

Sol. : **(1)** Acceleration of the solid sphere slipping down the incline without rolling is

$$a_{slipping} = g\sin\theta \quad ....(i)$$

Acceleration of the solid sphere rolling down the incline without slipping is

$$a_{rolling} = \frac{g\sin\theta}{1+\frac{k^2}{R^2}} = \frac{g\sin\theta}{1+\frac{2}{5}}$$

$$\left(\because For\ solid\ sphere, \frac{k^2}{R^2} = \frac{2}{5}\right). \quad ....(ii)$$

$$= \frac{5}{7}g\sin\theta$$

Divide eqn. (ii) by eqn. (i), we get

$$\frac{a_{rolling}}{a_{slipping}} = \frac{5}{7}.$$

27. A mass m moves in a circle on a smooth horizontal plane with velocity v_0 at a radius R_0. The mass is attached to a string which passes through a smooth hole in the plane as shown. **[AIPMT 2015]**

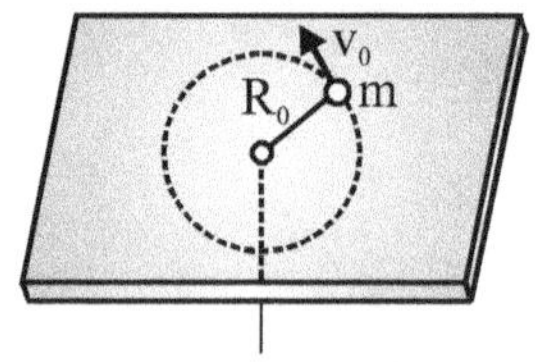

The tension in the string is increased gradually and finally m move in a circle of radius $\frac{R_0}{2}$

The final value of the kintic energy is

(1) mv_0^2 (2) $\frac{1}{4}mv_0^2$ (3) $2mv_0^2$ (4) $\frac{1}{2}mv_0^2$

Sol. : **(3)** Apply conservation of angular momentum

$$mv_0R_0 = mv_2\frac{R_0}{2}$$

$$v_2 = 2v_0 = \frac{1}{2}m(2v_0)^2 = 2mv_0^2$$

28. A rod of weight W is supported by two parallel knife edges A and B and is equilibrium in a horizontal position. The knives are at a distance d form each other. The centre of mass of the rod is at distance x from A. The normal reaction on A is **[AIPMT 2015]**

(1) $\frac{Wx}{d}$ (2) $\frac{Wd}{x}$

(3) $\frac{W\ d-x}{x}$ (4) $\frac{W\ d-x}{d}$

Sol. : **(4)** $N_1 + N_2 = W$

so, torque about 'B' is 0

$$N_1 d = W(d-x)$$

$$N_1 = W\left(\frac{d-x}{d}\right).$$

29. Three identical spherical shells, each of mass m and radius r are placed as shown in the figure. Consider an axis XX' which is touching to two shells and passing through diameter to third shell. Moment of inertia of the system consisting of these three spherical shells about XX' axis is

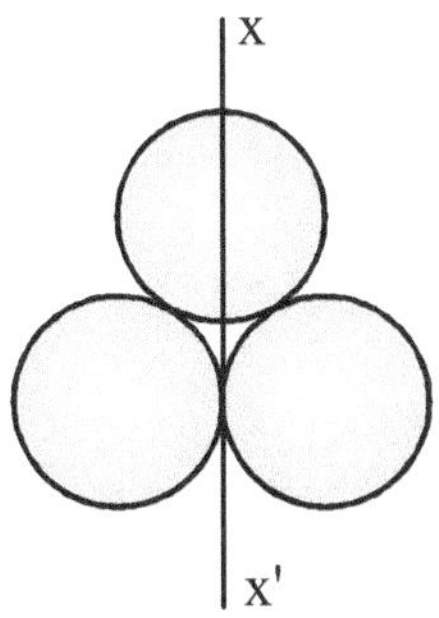

[AIPMT 2015]

(1) $\frac{11}{5}mr^2$ (2) $\frac{16}{5}mr^2$

(3) 3 mr (4) 4 mr^2

Sol. : **(4)** $I_1 = \frac{2}{3}mr^2$

$$I_2 = \frac{2}{3}mr^2 + mr^2 = \frac{5}{3}mr^2$$

$$I_3 = \frac{2}{3}mr^2 + mr^2 = \frac{5}{3}mr^2$$

$$I = I_1 + I_2 + I_3 = \frac{12}{3}mr^2 = 4mr^2.$$

30. An automobile moves on a road with a speed of 54 km h^{-1}. The radius of its wheels is 0.45 m and the moment of inertia of the wheel about its axis of rational is 3 kg m^2. If the vehicle is brough to rest in 15 s, the magnitude of average torque transmitted by its brakes to the wheel is

[AIPMT 2015]

(1) 2.86 kg m^2s^{-2} (2) 6.66 kg m^2s^{-2}

(3) 8.58 kg m^2s^{-2} (4) 10.86 kg m^2s^{-2}

Sol. : **(2)** Velocity of the mobile

$$v = 54 \times \frac{5}{18} = 15\,m/s$$

$$\omega_0 = \frac{v}{R} = \frac{15}{0.45} = \frac{100}{3}\,rad/s$$

So angular acceleration

$$\alpha = \frac{\Delta\omega}{t} == \frac{\omega_f - \omega_0}{t} = \frac{100}{45}\ rad/s^2$$

$$= I\alpha = 3 \times \frac{100}{45} = 6.66\,kg - m^2s^{-2}.$$

31. Point masses m_1 and m_2 are placed at the opposite ends of a rigid rod of length L, and negligible mass. The rod is to be set rotating about an axis perpendicular to it. The position of point P on this rod through which the axis should pass so that the work required to set the rod rotating with angular velocity w_0 is minimum is given by

[AIPMT 2015Re]

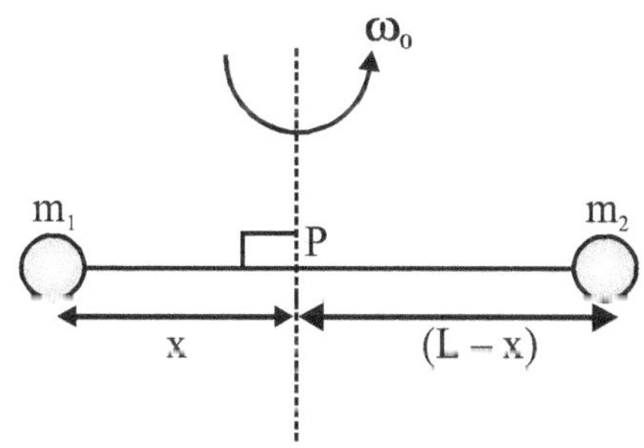

(1) $x \frac{m_2L}{m_1 \quad m_2}$ (2) $x = \frac{m_2L}{m_1 + m_2}$

(3) $x = \frac{m_1}{m_2}L$ (4) $x = \frac{m_2}{m_1}L$

Sol. : **(1)** 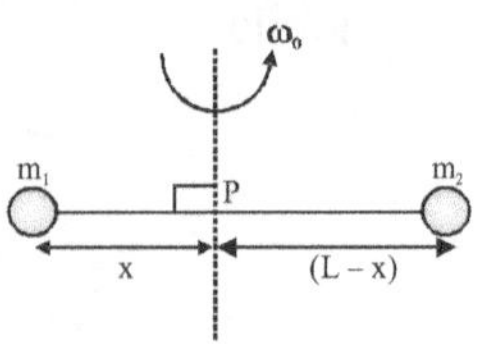

The position of point P on rod through which the axis should pass so that the work required to set the rod rotating with minimum angular velocity ω_0 is their centre of mass

So $m_1 x = m_2(L-x) \Rightarrow x = \dfrac{m_2 L}{m_1 + m_2}$.

32. A force $\vec{F}\ \hat{i}\ 3\hat{j}\ 6\hat{k}$ is acting at a point $\vec{r}\ 2\hat{i}-6\hat{j}-12\hat{k}$. The value of a for conseved angular momentum about origin is conserved is **[AIPMT 2015 Re]**

(1) 1 (2) –1 (3) 2 (4) zero

Sol. : **(2)**

$\vec{F} = \alpha\hat{i} + 3\hat{j} + 6\hat{k}$

$\vec{r} = 2\hat{i} - 6\hat{j} - 12\hat{k}$

For conservation of angular momentum about origin

$\Sigma 6_{net} = 0 = \vec{r} \times \vec{t}$

$$\vec{r}\times\vec{t} = \begin{vmatrix} \hat{i} & \hat{j} & \hat{k} \\ \alpha & 3 & 6 \\ 2 & -6 & -12 \end{vmatrix}$$

$i(-36+36) - \hat{j}\,(-12\alpha - 12)\,n + \hat{k}\,(-6\alpha - 6) = 0$

$(12\alpha + 12)\,\hat{j} - (6\alpha + 6)\,\hat{k} = 0$

$12\alpha + 12 = 0$

$\alpha = -\dfrac{12}{12} = -1$

33. A disk and a sphere of same radius but different masses roll off on two inclined planes of the same altitude and length. Which one of the two objects gets to the bottom of the plane first ?

(1) Disk **[AIPMT 2016]**

(2) Sphere

(3) Both reach at the same time

(4) Depends on their masses

Sol. : **(2)** Time does not depend on mass, else

$$t \propto \sqrt{\left(1 + \frac{k^2}{R^2}\right)}$$

$\dfrac{k^2}{R^2}$ is least for sphere and hence least time is taken by sphere.

34. From a disc of radius R and mass M, a circular hole of diameter R, whose rim passes through the centre is cut. What is the moment of inertia of the remaining part of the disc about a perpendicular axis, passing through the centre ?

[AIPMT 2016]

(1) $15\ MR^2/32$ (2) $13\ MR^2/32$

(3) $11\ MR^2/32$ (4) $9\ MR^2/32$

Sol. : **(2)**

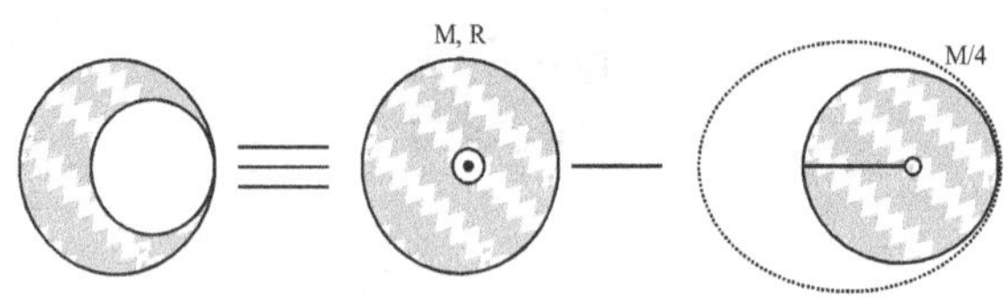

$$I_1 = \frac{MR^2}{2}$$

$$I_2 = \frac{\left(\frac{M}{4}\right)\left(\frac{R}{2}\right)^2}{2} + \left(\frac{M}{4}\right)\left(\frac{R}{2}\right)^2 = \frac{3MR^2}{32}$$

$$I_{net} = I_1 - I_2 = \frac{MR^2}{2} - \frac{3MR^2}{32} = \frac{13MR^2}{32}$$

So answer is 2.

35. Which of the following statements are correct ? **[NEET – 2017]**

(a) Centre of mass of a body always coincides with the centre of gravity of the body.

(b) Centre of mass of a body is the point at which the total gravitational torque on the body is zero.

(c) A couple on a body produce both translational and rotational motion in a body.

(d) Mechanical advantage greater than one means that small effort can be used to lift a large load.

(1) (b) and (d) (2) (a) and (b)

(3) (b) and (c) (4) (c) and (d)

Sol. : **(1)** Centre of mass may or may not coincide with centre of gravity.

36. Two discs of same moment of inertia rotating about their regular axis passing through centre and perpendicular to the plane of disc with angular velocities ω_1 and ω_2. They are brought into contact face to face coinciding the axis of rotation. The expression for loss of energy during this process is : **[NEET – 2017]**

(1) $\frac{1}{2}I(\omega_1+\omega_2)^2$ (2) $\frac{1}{4}I(\omega_1-\omega_2)^2$

(3) $I(\omega_1-\omega_2)^2$ (4) $\frac{1}{8}(\omega_1-\omega_2)^2$

Sol. : **(2)** $\Delta KE = \frac{1}{2}\frac{I_1 I_2}{I_1+I_2}(\omega_1-\omega_2)^2$

$$= \frac{1}{2}\frac{I^2}{(2I)}(\omega_1-\omega_2)^2 = \frac{1}{4}I(\omega_1-\omega_2)^2.$$

37. A rope is wound around a hollow cylinder of mass 3 kg and radius 40 cm. What is the angular acceleration of the cylinder if the rope is pulled with a force of 30 N ? **[NEET – 2017]**

(1) 25 m/s² (2) 0.25 rad/s²

(3) 25 rad/s² (4) 5 m/s²

Sol. : **(3)**

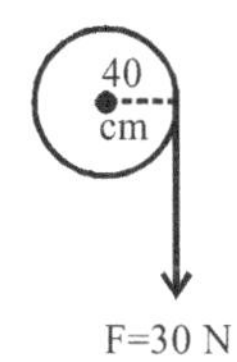

$\tau = I\alpha$

$F \times R = MR^2\alpha \Rightarrow 30 \times 0.4 = 3 \times (0.4)^2\alpha$

$12 = 3 \times 0.16\alpha \Rightarrow 400 = 16\alpha$

$\alpha = 25\,\text{rad/s}^2$.

38. A solid sphere is in rolling motion. In rolling motion a body possesses translational kinetic energy (K_t) as well as rotational kinetic energy (K_r) simultaneously. The ratio $K_t : (K_t + K_r)$ the sphere is **[NEET-2018]**

(1) 10 : 7 (2) 5 : 7

(3) 7 : 10 (4) 2 : 5

Ans. **(2)**

39. A solid sphere is rotating freely about its symmetry axis in free space. The radius of the sphere is increased keeping its mass same. Which of the following physical quantities would remain constant for the sphere ? **[NEET-2018]**

(1) Rotational kinetic energy

(2) Moment of inertia

(3) Angular velocity

(4) Angular momentum

Ans. **(4)**

40. A body initially at reset and sliding along a frictionless track from a height h (as shown in the figure) just completes a vertical circle of diameter AB = D. The height h is equal to **[NEET-2018]**

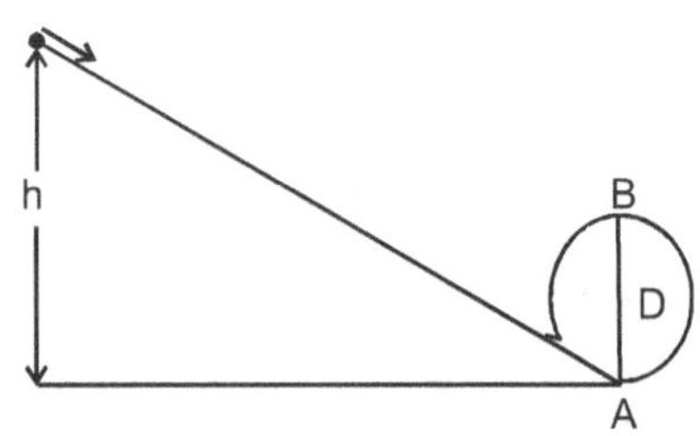

(1) $\frac{7}{5}D$ (2) D

(3) $\frac{3}{2}D$ (4) $\frac{5}{4}D$

Ans. **(4)**

41. Three objects, A : (a solid sphere), B : (a thin circular disk) and C : (a circular ring), each have the same mass M and radius R. They all spin with the same angular speed about their own symmetry axes. The amounts of work. (W) required to bring them to rest, would satisfy the relation **[NEET-2018]**

(1) $W_B > W_A > W_C$ (2) $W_A > W_B > W_C$

(3*) $W_C > W_B > W_A$ (4) $W_A > W_C > W_B$

Ans. **(3)**

42. Which one of the following statements is incorrect ? **[NEET-2018]**

(1) Frictional force opposes the relative motion.

(2) Limiting value of static friction is directly proportional to normal reaction.

(3) Rolling friction is smaller then sliding friction.

(4) Coefficient of sliding friction has dimensions of length

Ans. **(4)**

43. The moment of the force, $\vec{F} = 4\hat{i} + 5\hat{j} - 6\hat{k}$ at (2, 0, –3), about the point (2, –2, –2), is given by **[NEET-2018]**

(1) $-7\hat{i} - 8\hat{j} - 8\hat{k}$ (2) $-4\hat{i} - \hat{j} - 8\hat{k}$

(3) $-8\hat{i} - 4\hat{j} - 7\hat{k}$ (4) $-7\hat{i} - 4\hat{j} - 8\hat{k}$

Ans. **(4)**

07 Gravitation

Note: Scan QR code with your mobile camera or QR scanner for video solutions.

1. Escape velocity from earth is 11.2 km/sec. Another planet of same mass has radius $\frac{1}{4}$ times that of earth. What is the escape velocity from this planet ? **[AIPMT 2000]**

(1) 11.2 km/sec (2) 44.8 km/sec

(3) 22.4 km/sec (4) 5.6 km/sec

Sol. : (3)

2. A body attains a height equal to the radius of the earth when projected from earth' surface. The velocity of the body with which it was projected is : **[AIPMT 2001]**

(1) $\sqrt{\frac{GM}{R}}$ (2) $\sqrt{\frac{2GM}{R}}$

(3) $\sqrt{\frac{5}{4}\frac{GM}{R}}$ (4) $\sqrt{\frac{3GM}{R}}$

Sol. : (1)

3. Imagine a new planet having the same density as that of earth but it is 3 times bigger than the earth in size. If the acceleration due to gravity on the surface of earth is g and that on the surface of the new planet is g', then : **[AIPMT- 2005]**

(1) g' = 3g (2) g' = g/9

(3) g' = 9g (4) g'=27 g

Sol. : (1) $g=\frac{GM}{r^2}$ and $g'=\frac{GM'}{r^2}$ $[M'-3M]$

$$\frac{g'}{g}=\frac{3M}{M}\Rightarrow g'=3g.$$

4. Escape velocity for a projectile at earth's surface is V_e. A body is projected form earth's surface with velocity 2 V_e. The velocity of the body when it is at infinite distance from the centre of the earth is **[AIPMT- 2005]**

(1) V_e (2) $2V_e$

(3) $\sqrt{2}\,V_e$ (4) $\sqrt{3}\,V_e$

Sol. : (4)

5. For a satellite moving in an orbit around the earth, the ratio of kinetic energy to potential energy is **[AIPMT- 2005]**

(1) 2 (2) 1/2

(3) $\frac{1}{\sqrt{2}}$ (4) $\sqrt{2}$

Sol. : (2) $-\frac{GMm}{R^2}+m\omega^2R=0$

$$\therefore \frac{GMm}{R^2}=m\omega^2R$$

$$K.E.=\frac{1}{2}I\omega^2=\frac{1}{2}mR^2\omega^2=\frac{GMm}{2R}$$

$$P.E.=-\frac{GMm}{R}.$$

$$\therefore K.E.=\frac{|P.E.|}{2}$$

$$\therefore \frac{K.E.}{|P.E.|}=\frac{1}{2}.$$

6. Two satellites of earth, S_1 and S_2, are moving in the same orbit. The mass of S_1 is four times the mass of S_2. Which one of the following statements is true ? **[AIPMT- 2007]**

(1) The kinetic energies of t he two satellites are equal
(2) The time period of S_1 is four times that of S_2
(3) The potential energies of earth and satellite in the two cases are equal
(4) S_1 and S_2 are moving with the same speed

Sol. : **(4)** The satellite of mass m is moving in a circular orbit of radius r.

$\therefore$ Kinetic energy of the satellite, $K = \dfrac{GMm}{2r}$ ....(i)

Potential energy of the satellite, $U = \dfrac{-GMm}{r}$ ....(ii)

Orbital speed of satellite, $v = \sqrt{\dfrac{GM}{r}}$ .....(iii)

Time-period of satellite,

$$T = \left[\left(\frac{4\pi^2}{GM}\right)r^3\right]^{1/2} \quad ....(iv)$$

Given $m_{s_1} = 4m_{s_2}$

Since M, r is same for both the satellites S_1 and S_2

$\therefore$ From equation (ii), we get $U \propto m$

$$\therefore \frac{U_{s_1}}{U_{s_2}} = \frac{m_{s_1}}{m_{s_2}} = 4 \; or, \; U_{s_1} = 4U_{s_2}$$

Option (a) is wrong.
From (iii), since v is independent of the mass of a satellite, the orbital speed is same for both satellites S_1 and S_2. Hence option (b) is correct. From (i), we get $K \propto m$

$$\therefore \frac{K_{s_1}}{K_{s_2}} = \frac{m_{s_1}}{m_{s_2}} = 4 \; or, \; K_{s_1} = 4K_{s_2}.$$

Hence option (c) is wrong.
From (iv), since T is independent of the mass of a satellite, time period is same for both the satellite S_1 and S_2. Hence option (d) is wrong.

7. The figure shows elliptical orbit of a planet m about the sun S. The shaded area SCD is twice the shaded area SAB. If t_1 is the time for the planet to move from C to D and t_2 is the time to move from A to B then :- **[AIPMT- 2009]**

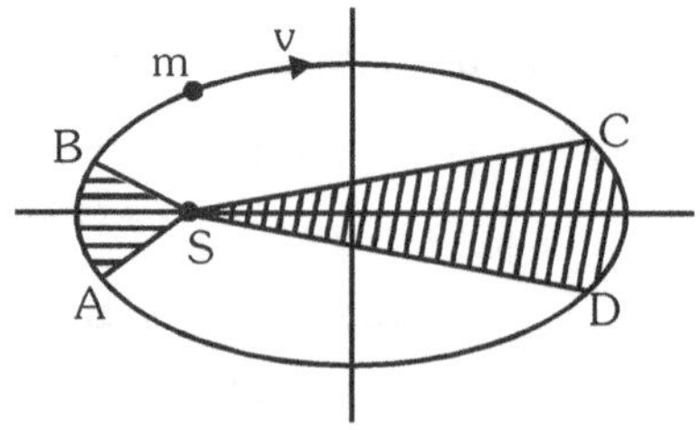

(1) $t_1 = t_2$ (2) $t_1 > t_2$
(3) $t_1 = 4t_2$ (4) $t_1 = 2t_2$

Sol. : **(4)** Equal areas are swept in equal time.
t_1, the time taken to go from C to D = 2 t_2
Where t_2 is the time taken to go from A to B.
As it is given that area SCD = 2SAB.

8. The radii of circular orbits of two satellites A and B of the earth, are 4R and R, respectively. If the speed of satellite A is 3V, then the speed of satellite B will be :- **[AIPMT- 2010]**

(1) 3V/2 (2) 3V/4
(3) 6V (4) 12V

Sol. : **(3)** Orbit speed of the satellite around the earth is

$$v = \sqrt{\frac{GM}{r}}.$$

Where, G = Universal gravitational constant
M = Mass of earth
r = Radius of the orbit of the satellite

For satellite A

$r_A = 4R, v_A = 3V$; $v_A = \sqrt{\dfrac{GM}{r_A}}$

For satellite B

$r_B = R, v_B = ?$

$v_B = \sqrt{\dfrac{GM}{r_B}}$

Dividing equation (ii) by equation (i), we get

$\therefore \dfrac{v_B}{v_A} = \sqrt{\dfrac{r_A}{r_B}}$ or $v_B = v_A\sqrt{\dfrac{r_A}{r_B}}$

Substituting the given values, we get

$v_B = 3V\sqrt{\dfrac{4R}{R}}$ or $v_B = 6V$.

9. A particle of mass M is situated at the centre of a spherical shell of same mass and radius a. The magnitude of the gravitational potential at a point situated at $\frac{a}{2}$ distance from the centre, will be :- **[AIPMT- 2010]**

(1) $\dfrac{4GM}{a}$ (2) $\dfrac{3GM}{a}$ (3) $\dfrac{2GM}{a}$ (4) $\dfrac{GM}{a}$

Sol. : **(2)** Here,
Mass of a particle = M
Mass of a spherical shell = M
Radius of a spherrical shell = a
Let O be centre of a spherical shell.
Gravitational potential at point P due to particle at O is $V_1 = -\dfrac{GM}{a/2}$ Gravitational potential at point P due to spherical shell is $V_2 = -\dfrac{GM}{a}$ Hence, total gravitational potential at point P is $V = V_1 + V_2$

$= -\dfrac{GM}{a/2} + \left(-\dfrac{GM}{a}\right) = -\dfrac{2GM}{a} - \dfrac{GM}{a} = -\dfrac{3GM}{a}$

$|V| = \dfrac{3GM}{a}$.

10. The dependence of acceleration due to gravity 'g' on the distance 'r' from the centre of the earth, assumed to be a sphere of radius R of uniform density, is as shown in figure below :- **[AIPMT- 2010]**

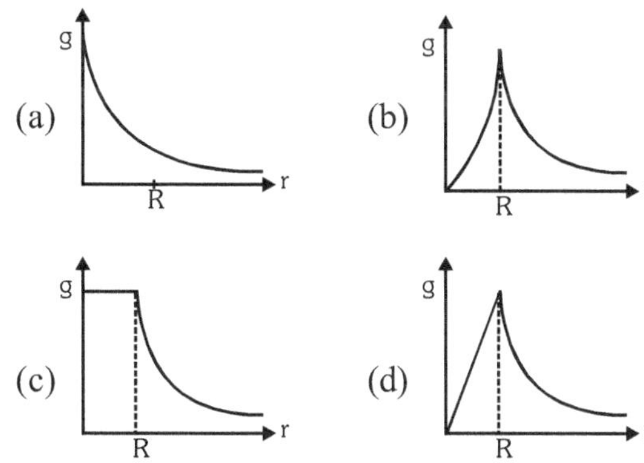

The correct figure is :-
(1) (a) (2) (b) (3) (c) (4) (d)

Sol. : **(1)** The acceleration due to gravity at a depth d below surface of earth is

$$g'\frac{GM}{R_2}\left(1-\frac{d}{R}\right) = g\left(1-\frac{d}{R}\right)$$

$g' = 0$ at $d = R.$

i.e., acceleration due to gravity is zero at the centre of earth.

Thus, the variation in value g with r is

For, r > R, $g' = \dfrac{g}{\left(1+\dfrac{h}{R}\right)^2} = \dfrac{gR^2}{r^2} \Rightarrow g' \propto \dfrac{1}{r^2}$

Here, R + h = r

For $r < R$, $g' = g\left(1-\dfrac{d}{R}\right) = \dfrac{gr}{R}$

Here, $R - d = r \Rightarrow g' \propto r$

Therefore, the variation of g with distance from centre of the earth will be as shown in the figure.

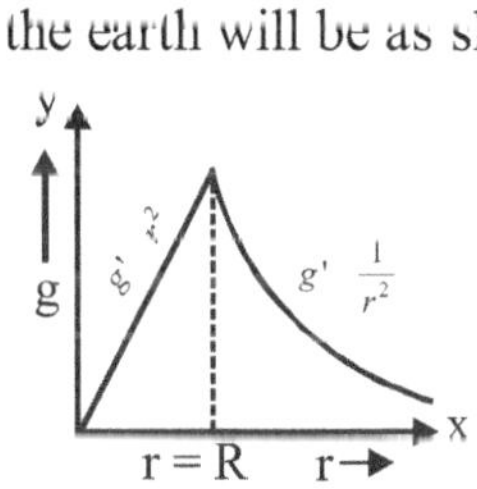

11. The additional kinetic energy to be provided to a satellite of mass m revolving around a planet of mass M, to transfer it from a circular orbit of radius R_1 to another of radius $R_2 (R_2 > R_1)$ is :-

[AIPMT- 2010]

(1) $GmM \; \frac{1}{R_1} \; \frac{1}{R_2}$ (2) $2GmM \; \frac{1}{R_1} \; \frac{1}{R_2}$

(3) $\frac{1}{2}GmM \; \frac{1}{R_1} \; \frac{1}{R_2}$ (4) $GmM \; \frac{1}{R_1^2} \; \frac{1}{R_2^2}$

Sol. : **(3)** $\frac{1}{2}GmM \; \frac{1}{R_1} \; \frac{1}{R_2}$

12. A planet moving along an elliptical orbit is closest to the sun at a distance r_1 and farthest away at a distance of r_2. If v_1 and v_2 are the linear velocities at these points respectively, then the ratio $\frac{v_1}{v_2}$ is :-

[AIPMT- 2011]

(1) $(r_1/r_2)^2$ (2) r_2/r_1

(3) $(r_2/r_1)^2$ (4) r_1/r_2

Sol. : **(2)** According to the law of conservation of angular momentum

$$L_1 = L_2$$

$$mv_1r_1 = mv_2r_2 \Rightarrow v_1r_1 = v_2r_2 \text{ or } \frac{v_1}{v_2} = \frac{r_2}{r_1}.$$

13. A spherical planet has a mass M_p and diameter D_p. A particle of mass m falling freely near the surface of this planet will experience an aceleration due to gravity, equal to :-

[AIPMT Pre.-2012]

(1) GM_p/D_p^2 (2) $4GM_pm/D_p^2$

(3) $4GM_p/D_p^2$ (4) GM_pm/D_p^2

Sol. : **(3)** Gravitational force acting on particle of mass m is

$$F = \frac{GM_pm}{(D_p/2)^2}$$

Acceleration due to gravity experience by the particle is

$$g = \frac{F}{m} = \frac{GM_p}{(D_p/2)^2} = \frac{4GM_p}{D_p^2}.$$

14. A geostationary satellite is orbiting the earth at a height of 5R above that surface of the earth, R being the radius of the earth. The time period of another satellite in hours at a height of 2R from the surface of the earth is :-

[AIPMT Pre.-2012]

(1) $6\sqrt{2}$ (2) $6/\sqrt{2}$

(3) 5 (4) 10

Sol. : **(1)** According to Kelper's third law $T \propto r^{3/2}$

$$\therefore \frac{T_2}{T_1} = \left(\frac{r_2}{r_1}\right)^{3/2} = \left(\frac{R+2R}{R+5R}\right)^{3/2} = \frac{1}{2^{3/2}}$$

Since $T_1 = 24$ hours

So, $\frac{T_2}{24} = \frac{1}{2^{3/2}}$

$$\frac{T_2}{24} = \left(\frac{r_2}{r_1}\right)^{3/2} \text{ or } T_2 = \frac{24}{2^{3/2}} = \frac{24}{2\sqrt{2}} = 6\sqrt{2} \text{ hours}$$

15. The height at which the weight of a body becomes $1/16^{th}$, its weight on the surface of earth (radius R), is :- **[AIPMT Pre.-2012]**

(1) 3R (2) 4R

(3) 5R (4) 15R

Sol. : **(1)** Acceleration due to gravity at a height h from the surface of earth is

$$g' = \frac{g}{\left(1+\frac{h}{R}\right)^2} \quad \text{.............(i)}$$

Where g is the acceleration due to gravity at the surface of earth and R is the radius of earth.

Multiplying by m (mass of the body) on both sides in (i), we get

$$mg' = \frac{mg}{\left(1+\frac{h}{R}\right)^2}$$

$\therefore$ Weight of body at height h, $W' = mg'$ Weight of body at surface of earth, $W = mg$

According to question, $W' = \frac{1}{16}W$

$$\therefore \quad \frac{1}{16} = \frac{1}{\left(1+\frac{h}{R}\right)^2}$$

$$\frac{1}{\left(1+\frac{h}{R}\right)^2} = \frac{1}{16} \quad or \quad 1+\frac{h}{R} = 4$$

or $\frac{h}{R} = 3 \quad or \quad h = 3R$.

16. Which one of the following plots represents the variation of gravitational field on a particle with distance r due to a thin spherical shell of radius R? (r is measured from the centre of the spherical shell) **[AIPMT Mains-2012]**

(1) 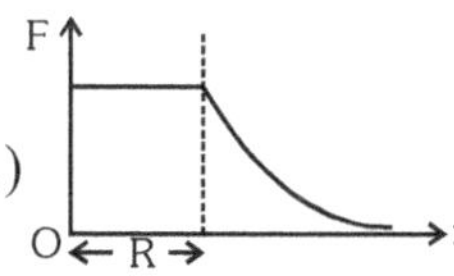

(2) 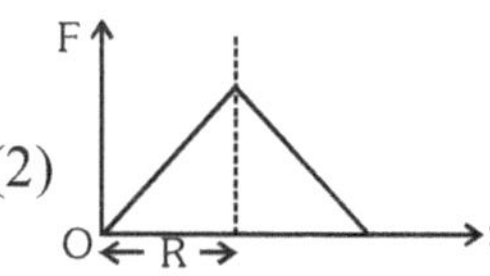

(3) 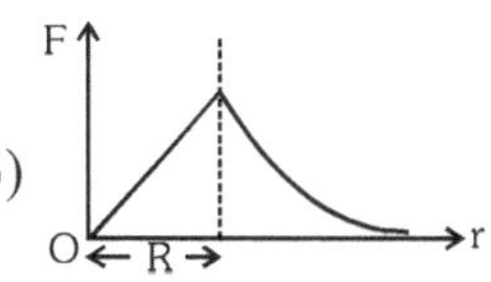

(4) 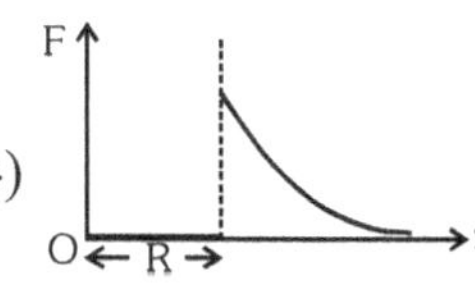

Sol. : **(4)**

Gravitaitonal field due to the thin spherical shell

Inside the shell, i.e. (For r < R)

F = 0

On the surface of the shell, i.e.(For r = R)

$$F = \frac{GM}{R^2}$$

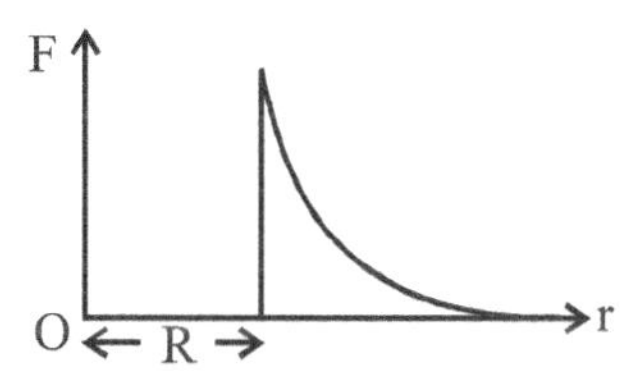

The variation of F with distance r from the centre is as shown in the adjacent figure.

17. If v_e is escape velocity and v_0 is orbital velocity of a satellite for orbit close to the earth's surface, then these are related by : **[AIPMT Mains-2012]**

(1) $v_e = \sqrt{2v_0}$ (2) $v_e = \sqrt{2}v_0$

(3) $v_0 = \sqrt{2}v_e$ (4) $v_0 = v_e$

Sol. : **(2)** Escape velocity, $v_e = \sqrt{\frac{2GM}{R}}$ ....(i)

where M and R be the mass and radius of the earth respectively.

The orbital velocity of a satellite close to the earth's surface is

$$v_0 = \sqrt{\frac{GM}{R}} \quad ....(ii)$$

From (i) and (ii), we get

$$v_e = \sqrt{2} v_0 .$$

18. The acceleration due to gravity at a height 1km above the earth is the same as at a depth d below the surface of earth. Then : **[NEET - 2017]**

(1) $d = \frac{1}{2} km$ (2) d = 1 km

(3) $d = \frac{3}{2} km$ (4) d = 2 km

Sol. : **(4)**

Above earth surface	Below earth surface
$g' = g\left(1 - \frac{2h}{R_e}\right)$	$g' = g\left(1 - \frac{d}{R_e}\right)$
$\Delta g' = g\frac{2h}{R_e}$ ......(1)	$\Delta g = g\frac{d}{R_e}$ ......(2)
From (1) & (2)	

$d = 2h$

$d = 2 \times 1 km$.

19. Two astronauts are floating in gravitaional free space after having lost contact with their spaceship. The two will : **[NEET - 2017]**

(1) Keep floating at the same distance between them.

(2) move towards each other.

(3) move away from each other.

(4) will become stationary.

Sol. : **(2)** Both the astronauts are in the condition of weightness. Gravitational force between them pulls towards each other.

20. The kinetic energies of a planet in an elliptical orbit about the Sun, at positions A, B and C are KA, KB and KC, respectively. AC is the major axis and SB is perpendicular to AC at the position of the Sun S as shown in the figure. Then **[NEET-2018]**

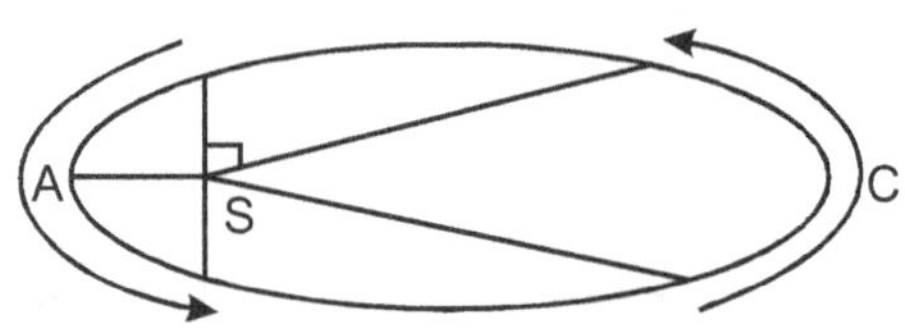

(1) $K_B < K_A < K_C$ (2) $K_A > K_B > K_C$

(3) $K_A < K_B < K_C$ (4) $K_B > K_A > K_C$

Ans. **(2)**

21. If the mass of the Sun were ten times smaller and the universal gravitational constant were ten times large in magnitude, which of the following is not correct ? **[NEET-2018]**

(1) Time period of a simple pendulum on the Earth would decrease.

(2) Walking on the ground would become more difficult.

(3) Raindrops will fall faster.

(4) 'g' on the Earth will not change.

Ans. **(4)**

08 Mechanical Properties of Solids

Note: Scan QR code with your mobile camera or QR scanner for video solutions.

1. The following four wires are made of the same material. Which of these will have the largest extension when the same tension is applied ? **[AIPMT 2013]**

(1) Length = 50cm, diameter = 0.5 mm

(2) Length = 100cm, diameter = 1 mm

(3) Length = 200cm, diameter = 2 mm

(4) Length = 300cm, diameter = 3 mm

Sol. : **(1)** Young's modulus, $Y = \frac{FL}{A\Delta L} = \frac{4FL}{\pi D^2 \Delta L}$

or, $\Delta L = \frac{4FL}{\pi D^2 Y}$

Where F is the force applied, L is the length, D is the diameter and ΔL is the extension of the wire respectively.

As each wire made up of same material therefore their Young's modulus is same for each wire.

For all the four wire,Y, F(= tension) are the same.

$\therefore \ \Delta L \propto \frac{L}{D^2}$

In (a) $\frac{L}{D^2} = \frac{200cm}{(0.2cm)^2} = 5 \times 10^3 \ cm^{-1}$

In (b) $\frac{L}{D^2} = \frac{300 \text{ cm}}{(0.3 \text{ cm})^2} = 3.3 \times 10^3 \ cm^{-1}$

In (c) $\frac{L}{D^2} = \frac{50 \text{ cm}}{(0.05 \text{ cm})^2} = 20 \times 10^3 \ cm^{-1}$

In (d) $\frac{L}{D^2} = \frac{100 \text{ cm}}{(0.1 \text{ cm})^2} = 10 \times 10^3 \ cm^{-1}$

2. Copper of fixed volume V is drawn into wire of length l. When this wire is subjected to a constant force F, the extension produced in the wire is Δl. which of the following graphs is a straight line ? **[AIPMT 2014]**

(1) Δl versus $\frac{1}{l}$ (2) Δl versus l^2

(3) Δl versus $\frac{1}{l^2}$ (2) Δl versus l

Sol. : **(2)** As $V = Al$ ...(i)

Where A is the area of cross-section of the wire.

Young's modulus, $Y = \frac{(F/A)}{(\Delta l / l)} = \frac{Fl}{A\Delta l}$

$\Delta l = \frac{Fl}{YA} = \frac{Fl^2}{YV}$ ...(Using (i))

$\Delta l \propto l^2$

Heans, the graph between Δl and l^2 is a straight line.

3. A wind with speed 40m/s blows parallel to the roof of a house. The area of rhe roof is 250 m^2 Assuming that the pressure inside the house is atmospheric pressure, the force exerted by the wind on the roof and the direction of the force will be

(P_{air} = 1.2 kg/m^3) **[AIPMT 2015]**

(1) 4.8 × 10^5 N, downwards

(2) 4.8 × 10^5 N, upwards

(3) 2.4 × 10^5 N, upwards

(4) 2.4 × 10^5 N, downwards

Sol. (3) : $P_1 + \frac{1}{2}\rho v^2 = P_2$ (By bernoullis theorem)

$$\Delta P = \frac{1}{2}\rho v^2$$

$$F = \Delta P.A = \frac{1}{2}\rho v^2.A$$

$$F = \frac{1}{2\times1.2\times(40)^2} \times 250 = 2.4 \times 10^5 N$$

Since on the roof velocity is more so K.E. is more therefore pressure is less. Hence the force is upward.

4 . The Young's modulus of steel is twice that of brass. Two wires of the same length and of the same area of cross section, one of steel and another of brass are suspended from the same roof If we want the lower ends of the wires to be at the same level, then the weights added to the steel and brass wires must be in the ratio of **[AIPMT 2015]**

(1) 1 : 1 (2) 1 : 2
(3) 2 : 1 (4) 4 : 1

Sol. **: (3)** $Y = \frac{F\ell}{A\Delta\ell} \Rightarrow \Delta\ell = \frac{F\ell}{AY}$

$$(\Delta\ell)_{steel} = (\Delta\ell)_{sBrans}$$

$$\Rightarrow \frac{W_s\ell}{AY_s} = \frac{W_B\ell}{AY_B}$$

$$\Rightarrow \frac{W_s}{W_B} = \frac{Y_s}{Y_B} = 2.$$

09 Mechanical Properties of Fluids

Note: Scan QR code with your mobile camera or QR scanner for video solutions.

1. The wetttabilty of a surface by a liquid depends primarily on **[AIPMT 2013]**

(1) Viscosity

(2) Surface tension

(3) Denstiy

(4) Angle of contact beteween the surface and the liquid

Sol. : **(4)** The wettability of a surface by a liquid depends primarily on angle of contact between the surface and the liquid.

2. A certain number of spherical drops of a liquid of radius r coalesce to form a single drop of radius R and volume V. If T is the surface tension of the liquid, then : **[AIPMT 2014]**

(1) Energy $=4VT \ \frac{1}{r}-\frac{1}{R}$ is released

(2) Energy $=3VT \ \frac{1}{r}+\frac{1}{R}$ is abosrbed

(3) Energy $=3VT \ \frac{1}{r}-\frac{1}{R}$ is released

(4) Energy is neither relesed nor absorbed

Sol. : **(3)** Let n droplets each of radius r coalesce to form a big drop of radius R.

$\therefore$ Volume of n droplets = Volume of big drop

$$n\times\frac{4}{3}\pi r^3 = \frac{4}{3}\pi R^3$$

$$n=\frac{R^3}{r^3} \qquad \text{...........(i)}$$

Volume of big drop, $V=\frac{4}{3}\pi R^3$ ....(ii)

Initial surface area of n droplets,

$$A_i = n\times 4\pi r^2 = \frac{R^3}{r^3}\times 4\pi r^2 \qquad \text{(Using (i))}$$

$$=4\pi\frac{R^3}{r}=\left(\frac{4}{3}\pi R^3\right)\frac{3}{r}$$

$$=\frac{3V}{r} \qquad \text{(Using (ii))}$$

Final surface area of big drop

$$A_f = 4\pi r^2 = \left(\frac{4}{3}\pi r^3\right)\frac{3}{R}=\frac{3V}{R} \qquad \text{(Using (ii))}$$

Decrease in surface area

$$\Delta A = A_i - A_f = \frac{3V}{r}-\frac{3V}{R}=3V\left(\frac{1}{r}-\frac{1}{R}\right)$$

$\therefore$ Energy released = Surface tension × Decrease in surface area

$$=T\times\Delta A$$

$$=3VT\left(\frac{1}{r}-\frac{1}{R}\right).$$

3. The approximate depth of an ocean is 2700 m. The compressibility of water is 45.4×10^{-11} Pa^{-1} and density of watrisn10^3 kg/m^3. What fractional compression of water will be obtained at the bottom of the ocean ? **[AIPMT 2015]**

(1) 0.8×10^{-2} (2) 1.0×10^{-2}

(3) 1.2×10^{-2} (4) 1.4×10^{-2}

Sol. : (3) $B = \dfrac{v\Delta P}{\Delta v}$

$$k = \frac{\Delta v}{v\Delta P}$$

$$\frac{\Delta v}{v} = k\Delta P$$

$$= 45.4 \times 10^{-11} \times 10^{3} \times 10 \times 2700$$

$$= 45.4 \times 27 \times 10^{-5}$$

$$= 1.2258 \times 10^{-2}$$

4. The cylindrical tube of a spray pump has radius R, one end of which has n fine holes, each of radius r. If the speed of the liquid in the tube is V, the speed of the ejection of the liquid through the holes is : **[AIPMT 2015]**

(1) $\dfrac{V^2R}{nr}$ (2) $\dfrac{VR^2}{n^2r^2}$ (3) $\dfrac{VR^2}{nr^2}$ (4) $\dfrac{VR^2}{n^3r^2}$

Sol. : (1)

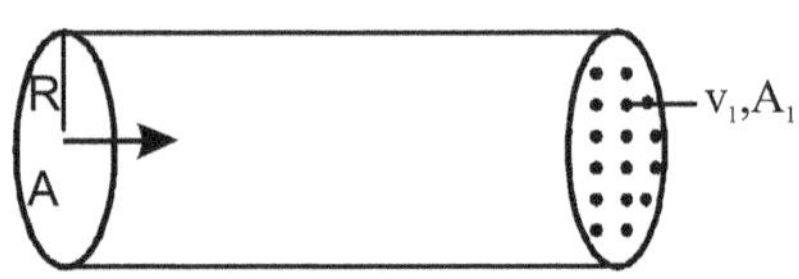

$$Av = \text{constant}$$

$$\pi R^2 V = n\pi r^2 v_1$$

$$\Rightarrow v_1 = \frac{VR^2}{nr^2}$$

5. Water rises to height 'h' in capillary tube. If the length of capillary tube above the surface of water is made less than 'h', then **[AIPMT 2015]**

(1) water does not rise at all.

(2) water rises up to the tip of capillary tube and then starts overflowing like a fountain.

(3) water rises up to the top of capillary tube and stays there without overflowing

(4) water rises up to a point a little below the top and stays there.

Sol. : (3) water rises up to the top of capillary tube and stays there without overflowing

6. Two non- mixing liquids of densities ρ and nρ (n > 1) are put in a container. the height of each liquid is h. A solid cylinder of length L and density d is put in this container. The cylinder floats with its axis vertical and length pL (P < L) in the denser liquid. The density d is equal to : **[AIPMT 2016]**

(1) {1 + (n +1)ρ}ρ (2) {2 + (n+1)ρ}ρ

(3) {2 +(n –1)ρ}ρ (4) {1 + (n –1)ρ}ρ

Sol. : (1)

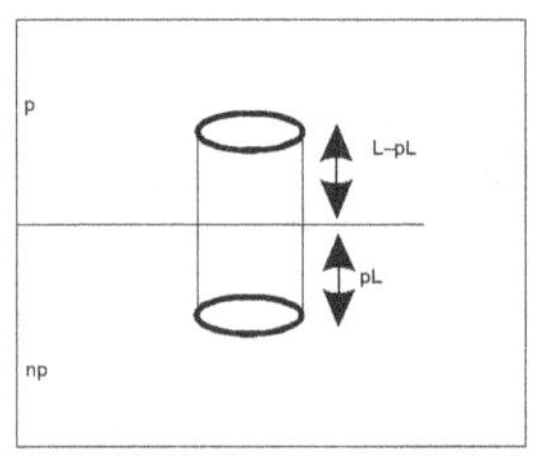

wt of body = upthrust by the two liquids

If A=Area of section then

$$(d\,A.L)g = [pA(L\text{-}pL) + np\,ApL]g$$

On solving

$$\Rightarrow d = [1 + (n-1)p]p\,.$$

7. Three liquids of densities ρ_1, ρ_2 and ρ_3 (with $\rho_1 > \rho_2 > \rho_3$), having the same value of surface tension T, rise to the same height in three identical capillaries. The angles of contact θ_1, θ_2 and θ_3 obey :- **NEET-II(2016)**

(1) $\frac{}{2}$ $_1$ $_2$ $_3$

(2) $_1$ $_2$ $_3$ $\frac{}{2}$

(3) $\frac{}{2}$ $_1$ $_2$ $_3$ 0

(4) 0 $_1$ $_2$ $_3$ $\frac{}{2}$

Sol. : **(4)** $h=\dfrac{2T\cos\theta}{\rho g r}$ $\qquad \dfrac{\cos\theta_1}{\rho_1}=\dfrac{\cos\theta_2}{\rho_2}=\dfrac{\cos\theta_3}{\rho_3}$

$\cos\theta_1 > \cos\theta_2 > \cos\theta_3$ as $\rho_1 > \rho_2 > \rho_3$

$0 \le \theta_1 < \theta_2 < \theta_3 < \dfrac{\pi}{2}$.

8. A U tube with both ends open to the atmosphere, is partially filled with water, Oil , which is immiscible with water, is poured into one side until it stands at a distance of 10 mm above the water level on the other side. Meanwhile the water rised by 65 mm from its original level (see diagram). The density of the oil is : **[NEET – 2017]**

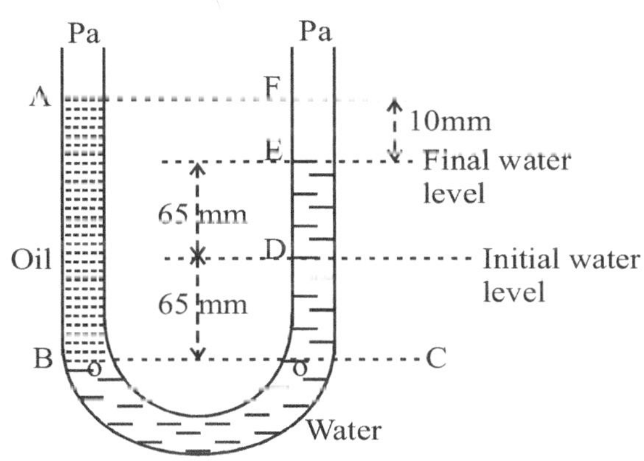

(1) 650 kg m^{-3} (2) 425 kg m^{-3}

(3) 800 kg m^{-3} (4) 928 kg m^{-3}

Sol. : **(4)** $h_{oil}\rho_{oil}\,g = h_{water}\rho_{water}g$

$140\times\rho_{oil} = 130\times\rho_{water}$

$\rho_{oil} = \dfrac{13}{14}\times1000\text{ kg/m}^3$; $\rho_{oil} = 928\text{ kg m}^{-3}$

9. A small sphere of radius 'r' falls from rest in a viscous liquid. As a result, heat is produced due to viscous force. The rate of production of heat when the sphere attains its terminal velocity, is proportional to **[NEET-2018]**

(1) r^5 (2) r^2

(3) r^3 (4) r^4

Ans. **(1)**

10 Thermal Properties of Matter

Note: Scan QR code with your mobile camera or QR scanner for video solutions.

1. A black body is at 727° C. It emits energy at a rate which is proportional to **[AIPMT 2007]**

(1) $(727)^2$ (2) $(1000)^4$

(3) $(1000)^2$ (4) $(727)^2$

Sol. : **(2)** According to Stefan's law,

rate of energy radiated $E \propto T^4$

Where T is the absolute temperature of a black body.

$\therefore\ E \propto (727+273)^4\ or\ E \propto [1000]^4.$

2. If the cold junction of thermocouple is kept at 0°C and the hot junction is kept at T°C, then the relation between neutral temperature (T_n) and temperature of inversion (T_i) is **[AIPMT 2007]**

(1) $T_n = \frac{T_i}{2}$ (2) $T_n = 2T_i$

(3) $T_n = T_i - T$ (4) $T_n = T_i + T$

Sol. : **(1)** $\because T_n = \frac{T_c + T_i}{2}\ \&\ T_c = 0°C\ \therefore T_n = \frac{T_i}{2}$

3. On a new scale of temperature (which of linear) and called the W scale, the freezing and boiling points of water are 39°W and 239°W respectively. What will be the temperature on the new scale, correspoinding to a temperature of 39°C on the Celsius scale ? **[AIPMT 2008]**

(1) 78°C (2) 117°C

(3) 200°C (4) 139°C

Sol. : **(2)**

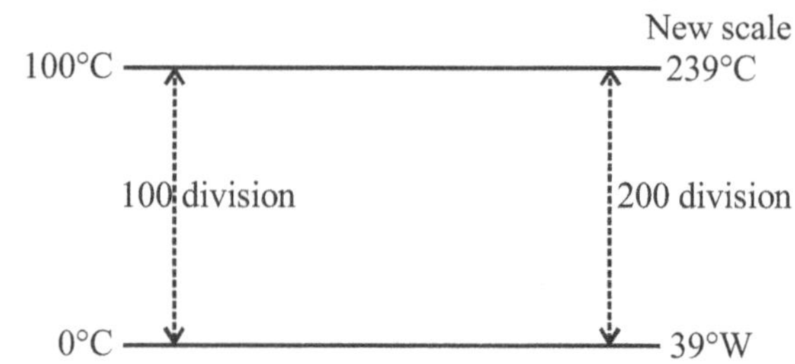

$\therefore\ 39°C = 39 \times 2 + 39 = (78+39)°W = 117°W.$

4. An electric kettle takes 4 A current at 220 V. How much time will it take to boil 1 kg of water from temperature 20°C ? The temperature of boiling water is 100°C **[AIPMT 2008]**

(1) 6.3 min (2) 8.4 min

(3) 12.6 min (4) 4.2 min

Sol. : **(2)** Heat required to boil water

$Q = mc\Delta T$

$= 1 \times 1 \times (100-20) = 80\,\text{kcal}$

Heat given by supply

$H = V.i.t = 220 \times 4 \times t$ $H = Q$

$\Rightarrow 220 \times 4 \times t = 80{,}000$

$$t = \frac{80{,}000}{220 \times 4} = \frac{1000}{11}\text{sec}$$

$$= \frac{1000}{11 \times 60} = 1.5\,\text{min}.$$

5. The two ends of a rod of length L and a uniform corss-sectional area A are kept at two termperatures T_1 and T_2 ($T_1 > T_2$). The rate of heat transfer, $\frac{dQ}{dt}$, through the rod in a steady state is given by **[AIPMT 2009]**

(1) $\frac{dQ}{dt}=\frac{KL\ T_1-T_2}{A}$ (2) $\frac{dQ}{dt}=\frac{K\ T_1-T_2}{L\ A}$

(3) $\frac{dQ}{dt}=KLA\ (T_1-T_2)$ (4) $\frac{dQ}{dt}=\frac{KA(T_1-T_2)}{L}$

Sol. : (4)

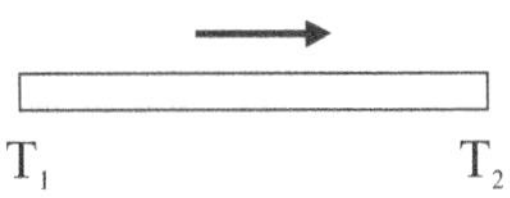

Similar to $I = V/R$

$$\frac{dQ}{dt}=\frac{kA}{L}(T_1-T_2)$$

k = conductivity of the rod.

6. A black body at 227°C radiates heat at the rate of 7cal $cm^{-2}\ s^{-1}$. At a temperature of 727°C, the rate of heat radiated in the same units will be **[AIPMT 2009]**

(1) 60 (2) 50

(3) 112 (4) 80

Sol. : (3) Rate of heat radiated at (227+273) K =7 cals/(cm^2s)

Let rate of heat radiated at (723+273)K = xcals/(cm^2s)

By stfan's law, $7 \propto (500)^4$ and $x \propto (1000)^4$

$$\therefore \frac{x}{7}=2^4 \Rightarrow x = 7\times 2^4 = 112\, cals/(cm^2 s).$$

7. A cylindrical metallic arod in thermal contact with two resevoirs of heat at its two ends conducts an amount of heat Q in time t, The metallic rod is half the radius of the original rod. What is the amount of heat conducted by the new rod when placed in thermal contact with the two reservoirs in time t ? **[AIPMT 2010]**

(1) Q/4 (2) Q/16

(3) 2Q (4) Q/2

Sol. : (2) The amount of heat flows in time t through a cylindrical metalic rod of length L and uniform area of cross - section $A(=\pi R^2)$ with its ends maintained at temperatures T_1 and T_2 ($T_1 > T_2$) is given by

$$Q=\frac{KA(T_1-T_2)t}{L} \quad \text{............(i)}$$

Where K is the thermal conductivity of the material of the rod.

Area of cross-section of new rod

$$A'=\pi\left(\frac{R}{2}\right)^2=\frac{\pi R^2}{4}=\frac{A}{4} \quad \text{...........(ii)}$$

As the volume of the rod remains unchanged

$\therefore AL = A'L'$

Where L' is the length the new rod

$$\text{or} \quad L'=\frac{L}{A'} \quad \text{............(iii)}$$

$$=4L \quad \text{(Using (ii))}$$

Now, the amount of heat flows in same time t in the new rod with its ends maintained at the same temperatures T_1 and T_2 is given by

$$Q'=\frac{KA'(T_1-T_2)t}{L'} \quad \text{..........(iv)}$$

Substituting the values of A' and L' from equations (ii) and (iii) in the above equation, we get

$$Q'=\frac{K(A/4)(T_1-T_2)t}{4L}=\frac{1}{16}\frac{KA(T_1-T_2)t}{L}$$

$$=\frac{1}{16}Q \quad \text{(Using (i)).}$$

8. The total radiant energy per unit area, normal to the direction of incidence, received at a distance R from the centre of a star of radius R, whose outer surface radiates as a black body at a temperature T K is given by **[AIPMT 2010]**

(1) $\sigma r^2T^4 / R^2$ (2) $\sigma r^2T^4/4\pi r^2$

(3) $\sigma r^4T^4/r^4$ (4) $4\pi\sigma r^2T^4/R^2$(Where σ is Sefan's constant)

Sol. : (1) According to the Stefan Boltzmann law, the power radiated by the star whose outer surface radiates as a black body at temperature T K is given by $P = \sigma 4\pi r^2 T^4$

Where, r = radius of the star

σ = Stefan's constant

The radiant power per unit area received at a distance R from the centre of a star is

$$S = \frac{P}{4\pi r^2} = \frac{\sigma 4\pi r^2 T^4}{4\pi r^2} = \frac{\sigma r^2 T^4}{R^2}.$$

9. If the radius of a stat is R and it acts as a black body, what would be the temperature of the star, in which the rate of energy production is Q ? **[AIPMT 2012]**

(1) $\frac{Q}{4\ R^2}^{1/4}$ (2) $\frac{Q}{4\ R^2}$

(3) $\frac{Q}{4\ R^2}$ (4) $(4\pi R^2Q/\sigma)^{1/4}$

(σ stands for Stefan's constant)

Sol. : (1) According to Stefan's law, $Q = \sigma AT^4$

or $T = \left(\frac{Q}{\sigma A}\right)^{1/4} = \left(\frac{Q}{\sigma 4\pi R^2}\right)^{1/4}$

10. Liquid oxygen at 50 K is heated to 300 K at constant pressure of 1 atm. The rate of heating is constant. Which one of the following graphs repersents the variation of temperature with time ? **[AIPMT 2012]**

(1) 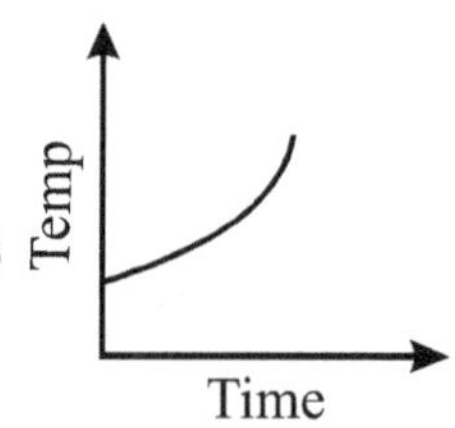

(2) 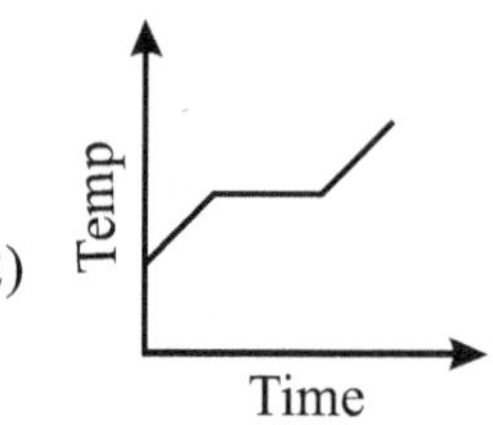

(3) 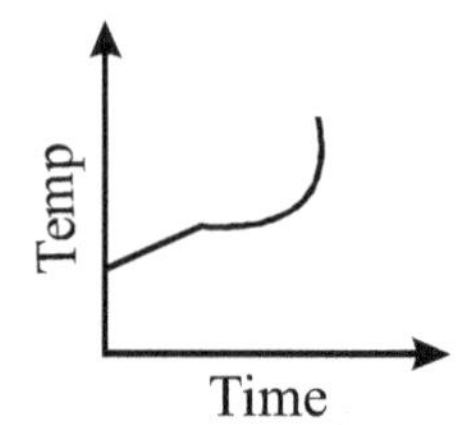

(4) 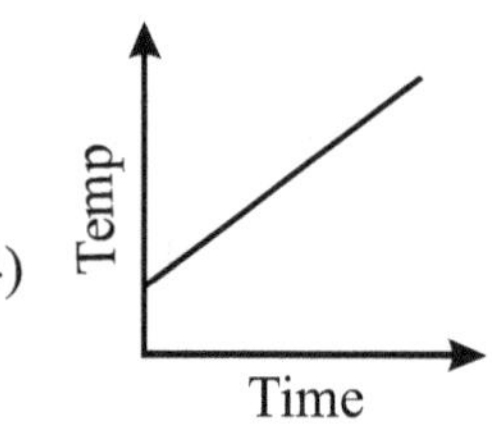

Sol. : (2) Temperature of liquid oxygen will first increase in the same phase. Then, the liquid oxygen will change to gaseous phase during which temperature will remain constant. After that temperature of oxygen in gaseous state will increase. Hence option (a) represents corresponding temperature-time graph.

11. A slab of stone of area of 0.36 m^2 and thinckness 0.1 mm is expose on thlower surface to steam 100°C. A blockof ice at 0°C rests on the upper surface of the slab. In one hour 4.8 kgo ice is melted. The thermal conductivity of slab is (Given latent heat of fusion of ice = 3.36 $\times 10^5$ j kg^{-1}) **[AIPMT 2012]**

(1) 1.24 J/m/s°C (2) 1.29 J/m/s°C

(3) 2.05 J/m/s°C (4) 1.02 J/m/s°C

Sol. : **(2)**

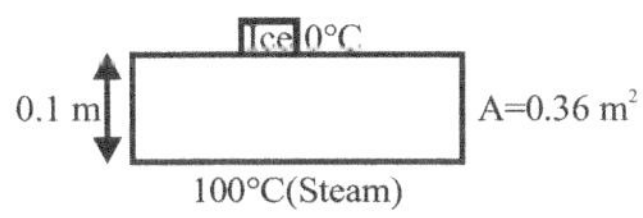

Heat flows through the slab in t s is

$$Q=\frac{KA(T_1-T_2)t}{L}=\frac{K\times0.36\times(100-0)\times3600}{0.1}$$

$$=\frac{K\times0.36\times100\times3600}{0.1} \quad ....(i)$$

so ice melted by this heat is

$$m_{ice}=\frac{Q}{L_f} \quad ....(ii)$$

or $Q=m_{ice}L_f=4.8\times3.36\times10^5$

From (i) and (ii), we get

$$=\frac{K\times0.36\times(100-0)\times3600}{0.1}=4.8\times3.36\times10^5$$

$$K=\frac{4.8\times3.36\times10^5\times0.1}{0.36\times100\times3600}=1.24J/m/s/°C$$

12. A piece of iron is heated in a flame. It first becomes dull red then becomes reddish yellow and finally turns to white hot. The correctly explanation for the above observation is possible by using. **[AIPMT 2013]**

(1) Stefan's law

(2) Wien's displacement law

(3) Kirchoff's law

(4) Newton's low of cooling

Sol. : **(4)** According to Wien's displacement law

$\lambda_m T=$ constant

$$\lambda_m=\frac{\text{constant}}{T}$$

So when a piece of iron is heated, λ_m decreases i.e. with rise in temperature the maximum intensity of radiation emitted gets shifted towards the shorter wavelengths. So the colour of the heated object will change that of longer wavelength (red) to that of shorter (reddish yellow) and when the temperature is sufficiently high and all wavelengths are emitted, the colour will become white.

13. The molar specific heats of an ideal gas at constant pressue and volume are denoted by C_p and C_υ respectively.If $\gamma=\frac{C_p}{C_\upsilon}$ and R is the universal gas constant, then C_υ is equal to : **[AIPMT 2013]**

(1) $\frac{1}{1-}$ (2) $\frac{R}{\gamma-1}$ (3) $\frac{-1}{R}$ (4) γR

Sol. : **(2)** For an ideal gas

$$C_p-C_v=R \quad ....(i)$$

Divide C_v on both sides, we get

$$\frac{C_p}{C_v}-1=\frac{R}{C_v}$$

As $\gamma-\frac{C_p}{C_v}$ $\therefore$ $\gamma-1-\frac{R}{C_v}$

$$C_v=\frac{R}{\gamma-1}$$

14. Steam at 100°C is passed into 20 g of water at 10°C. When water acquires a temperature of 80°C, the mass of water present will be [Take specific heat of water = 1 cal g^{-1} $°C^{-1}$ and latent heat of steam = 540 cal g^{-1}] **[AIPMT 2014]**

(1) 24g (2) 31.5g (3) 42.5g (4) 22.5g

Sol. : **(4)** Here,

Specific heat of water, $S_w = 1\,cal\,g^{-1}\,°C^{-1}$

Latent heat of steam, $L_s = 540\,cal\,g^{-1}$

Heat lost by m g of steam at 100°C to change into water at 80°C is

$Q_1 = mL_s + ms_w \Delta T_w$

$= m \times 540 + m \times 1 \times (100 - 80)$

$= 540m + 20m = 560m$

Heat gained by 20 g of water to change its temperature from 10°C to 80°C is

$Q_2 = m_w s_w \Delta T_w = 20 \times 1 \times (80 - 10) = 1400$

According to principle of calorimetry

$Q_1 = Q_2$

$\therefore 560m = 1400 \text{ or } m = 2.5g$

Total mass of water present

$= (20 + m)g = (20 + 2.5)g = 22.5g$

15. Certain equanity of water cools from 70°C to 60°C in the first 5 minutes and to 54°C in the next 5 minutes. The temperature of the surrounding is **[AIPMT 2014]**

(1) 45°C (2) 20°C

(3) 42°C (4) 10°C

Sol. : **(1)** Let T_s be the temperature of the suroundings. According to Newton's law of cooling

$$\frac{T_1 - T_2}{t} = K\left(\frac{T_1 + T_2}{2} - T_s\right)$$

For first 5 minutes,

$T_1 = 70°C, T_2 = 60°C, t = 5$ minutes

$$\therefore \frac{70 - 60}{5} = K\left(\frac{70 + 60}{2} - T_s\right)$$

$$\frac{10}{5} = K(65 - T_s)$$

For next 5 minutes,

$T_1 = 60°C, T_2 = 54°C, t = 5$ minutes

$$\therefore \frac{60 - 54}{5} = K\left(\frac{60 + 54}{2} - T_s\right)$$

$$\frac{6}{5} = K(57 - T_s)$$

Divide eqn. (i) by eqn. (ii), we get

$$\frac{5}{3} = \frac{65 - T_s}{57 - T_s}$$

$285 - 5T_s = 195 - 3T_s$

$2T_s = 90 \text{ or } T_s = 45°C$.

16. On observing light from three different stars P, Q nad R, it was found that intensityof violet colour is maximum in the spectrum o P, the intensity of green colour is maxiumum in the spectrum of Q. If Tp. T_Q and T_R are the respective absoluate temperatures of P.Q and R, then it can be concluded form the above observations that **[AIPMT 2015]**

(1) $T_P > T_Q > T_R$ (2) $T_P > T_R > T_Q$

(3) $T_P > T_R > T_Q$ (4) $T_P > T_Q > T_R$

Sol. : **(2)** Apply weins displacement law

$\lambda_m.T = const$

$T_P : T_R : T_Q = \frac{1}{\lambda_P} : \frac{1}{\lambda_R} : \frac{1}{\lambda_Q}$

$= \frac{1}{\lambda_{voilet}} : \frac{1}{\lambda_{green}} : \frac{1}{\lambda_{Red}}$

$\lambda_{voilet} < \lambda_{green} < \lambda_{Red}$

$\therefore \quad T_P > T_R > T_Q$

17. The two ends of a metal rod are maintained at temperatures 100°C and 110°C. The rate of heat flow in the rod is found to be 4.0 J/s. If the ends are maintained at temperatures 200°C and 210°C, the rate of heat flow will be : **[AIPMT 2015]**

(1) 44.0 J/s (2) 16.8 J/s

(3) 8.0 J/s (4) 4.0 J/s

Sol. : **(4)** $H_1 = \frac{\Delta T_1}{R}$

$H_2 = \frac{\Delta T_2}{R}$

$\Delta T_1 = \Delta T_2$.

so, $H_1 = H_2$

18. The value of coefficient of volume expansion of glycerin is 5×10^{-4} K^{-1}. The fractional change in the density of glycerin for a rise of 40°C in its temperature is **[AIPMT 2015]**

(1) 0.010 (2) 0.015

(3) 0.020 (4) 0.025

Sol : (3) $d_f = \frac{d}{(1+\gamma\Delta T)}$

fractional change

$= \frac{d_i - d_f}{d_i} = 1 - \frac{d_f}{d_i}$

$= 1 - (1 + \gamma\Delta T)$

$= 1 - (1 - \gamma\Delta T) \qquad \because (1+x)^n \approx 1 + nx$

$= \gamma\Delta T$

$= 5 \times 10^{-4} \times 40$

$= 0.020$

19. A black body is at a temperature of 5760 K. Th energy of radiation emitted by the body at wavelength 250 nm is U_1, at wavelength 500 n is U_2 and that at 1000 nm is U_3. Wien's constant b = 2.88 × 106 nmK. Which of the following is correct ? **[AIPMT 2016]**

(1) $U_1 = 0$ (2) $U_3 = 0$

(3) $U_1 > U_2$ (4) $U_2 > U_1$

Sol. : **(3)** $\lambda_{min} T = b$

$\lambda \propto \frac{1}{T}$

$u \propto (T)^4 \propto \frac{1}{(\lambda)^4}$

So, $u_1 > u_2$.

20. Coefficient of linear expansion of brass and steel rods are α_1 and α_2. Lengths of brass and steel rods are ℓ_1 and ℓ_2 respectively. If $(\ell_2 - \ell_1)$ is maintained same at all temperatures, which one of the following relations holds good ? **[AIPMT 2016]**

(1) $\ell_2 \quad {}_2\ell_1$ (2) $\ell_2^2 \quad {}_2\ell_1^2$

(3) ${}^2_1\ell_2 \quad {}^2_2\ell_1$ (4) $\alpha_1\ell_1 = \alpha_2\ell_2$

Sol. : **(4)** $l_2' = l_2(1+\alpha_2(\Delta\theta))$

$l_1' = l_1(1+\alpha_1(\Delta\theta))$

$l_2' - l_1' = (l_2 - l_1) + (\alpha_2 l_2 - \alpha_1 l_1)\Delta\theta$

As the length difference is independent of temperature difference hence

$\alpha_1 l_2 - \alpha_2 l_1 = 0 \Rightarrow \alpha_2 l_2 = \alpha_1 l_1$.

21. A piece of ice falls from a height so that it melts completely. Only one-quarter of the heat produced is absorbed by the ice and all energy of ice gets converted into heat during its fall. The value of h is : [Latent heat of ice is 3.4×10^5J/kg and g = 10 N/ kg] **[AIPMT 2016]**

(1) 34 km (2) 544 km

(3) 136 km (4) 68 km

Sol. : **(3)** $\frac{mgh}{4} = mL \qquad h = \frac{4L}{g} = 136\ km$.

22. Two rods A and b of different materials are welded together as shown in figure. Their thermal conductivities are K_1 and K_2. The thermal condutivity of the composite rod will be : **[NEET – 2017]**

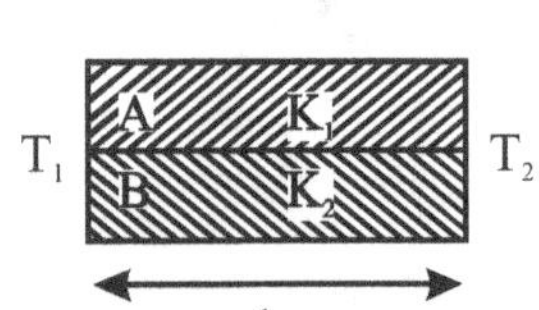

(1) $\frac{K_1+K_2}{2}$ (2) $\frac{3(K_1+K_2)}{2}$

(3) $K_1 + K_2$ (4) $2(K_1 + K_2)$

Sol. : **(1)** Thermal current

$H = H_1 + H_2$

$= \frac{K_1A(T_1-T_2)}{d} + \frac{K_2A(T_1-T_2)}{d}$

$\frac{K_{EQ}2A(T_1-T_2)}{d} = \frac{A(T_1-T_2)}{d}[K_1+K_2]$

$K_{EQ} = \left[\frac{K_1+K_2}{2}\right]$

23. A spherical black body with a radius of 12 cm radiates 450 watt power at 500 K. If the radius were halved and the temperature doubled, the power radiated in watt would be : **[NEET – 2017]**

(1) 225 (2) 450

(3) 1000 (4) 1800

Sol. : **(4)** Rate of power loss

$r \propto R^2T^4$

$\frac{r_1}{r_2} = \frac{R_1^2T_1^4}{R_2^2T_2^4}$

$= 4 \times \frac{1}{16}$

$\frac{450}{r_2} = \frac{1}{4}$

$r_2 = 1800$ watt.

11 Thermodynamics

Note: Scan QR code with your mobile camera or QR scanner for video solutions.

1. An engine has an efficiency of 1/6. When the temperature of sink is reduced by 62°C, its efficiency is doubled.Temperature of he source is : **[AIPMT 2007]**

(1) 124°C (2) 37°C (3) 62°C (4) 99°C

Sol. : **(4)** Efficiency of an engine, $\eta = 1 - \frac{T_2}{T_1}$

Where T_1 is the temperature of the source by $62^o C$ (or 62 K), efficiency becomes double. Since, the temperature of the source remain unchanged

$\therefore\ 2 \times \frac{1}{6} = 1 - \frac{(T_2 - 62)}{T_1}$ or, $\frac{1}{3} = 1 - \frac{(T_2 - 62)}{T_1}$

or, $\frac{2}{3} = \frac{T_2 - 62}{T_1}$ or, $2T_1 = 3T_2 - 186$

or, $2T_1 = 3\left[\frac{5}{6}\right]T_1 - 186$ [using(i)]

$\therefore\ \left[\frac{5}{2} - 2\right]T_1 = 186$ or, $\frac{T_1}{2} = 186$

or, $T_1 = 372$ K=$99^o C$

2. If Q, E and W denote respectively the heat added. change in internal energy and the work done in a closed cycle process, then **[AIPMT 2008]**

(1) W = 0 (2) Q = W = 0

(3) E = 0 (4) Q = 0

Sol. : **(3)** Internal energy depends only on the initial and final state of temperature and not on the path. In a cyclic process, as initial and final states are the same, the internal energy change is zero. Hence E is ΔU, the internal energy change.

3. In thermodynamic processes which of the following lowing statements is not ture ?

(1) In an adiabatic process the system is insulated form the surroundings

(2) In an isochoric process pressure remains constant

(3) In an isothermal process the temperature remains constant

(4) In an adiabatic process pV^{γ} = constant

Sol. : **(2)** In isochoric process, it is volume that is kept constant. If pressure is kept constant, it is an isobaric process.

4. The internal energy change in a system that has absorbed 2 kcal of heat and done 500 J of work is **[AIPMT 2009]**

(1) 8900 J (2) 6400 J

(3) 5400 J (4) 7900 J

Sol. : **(4)** Heat energy given $dQ = dU + dW$ Where dU is the change in internal energy and dW is the work done.

Given $dQ = 2\text{kcl} = 2000 \times 4.2\text{J}$ and $dW = 500$ J

$dQ = 2000 \times 4.2 = dU + 500 \Rightarrow dU = 7900$ J

5. If ΔU and ΔW represent the increase in internal energy and work done by the system repectively in a thermodynamical process, which of the following is true ? **[AIPMT 2010]**

(1) ΔU = –ΔW, in an adiabatic process

(2) ΔU = ΔW, in an isothermal process

(3) ΔU = ΔW, in an adiabatic process

(4) ΔU = –ΔW, in an isothermal process,

Sol. : **(1)** According to first law of the thermodynamics

$\Delta Q = \Delta U + \Delta W$ ...(i)

Where,

$\Delta Q =$ Heat supplied to the system

$\Delta U =$ Increase in internal energy of the system

$\Delta W =$ Work done by the system

For an adiabatic process

$\Delta Q = 0$

Form equation (i), we get

$\Delta u = -\Delta W$

For an isothermal process

$\Delta U = 0$

Form equation (i), we get $\Delta Q = \Delta W$

Heance, option (a) is true.

6. During an isothermal expansion, a confined ideal gas does –150 J of work against its surrounding. This implies that : **[AIPMT 2011]**

(1) 300 J of heat has been added to the gas

(2) no heat is transferred because the process is isothermal

(3) 150 J of heat has been added to the gas

(4) 150 J of heat has been removed from the gas

Sol. : **(3)**

7. A thermodynamic system is taken through the cycle ABCD as shown in the figure. Heat rejected by the gas during the cycle is **[AIPMT 2012]**

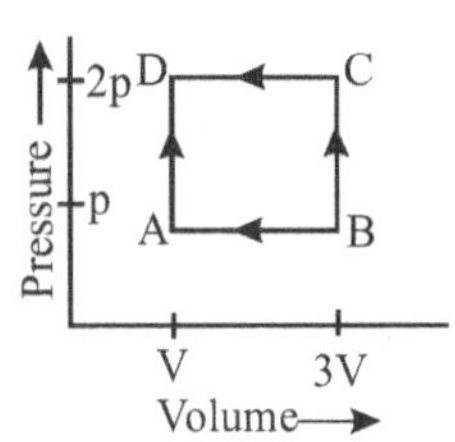

(1) PV (2) 2PV

(3) 4PV (4) 1/2PV

Sol. : **(2)** In a cyclic process, $\Delta U = 0$.

In a cyclic process work done is equal to the area under the cycle and is positive if the cycle is clockwise and negative if anticlockwise.

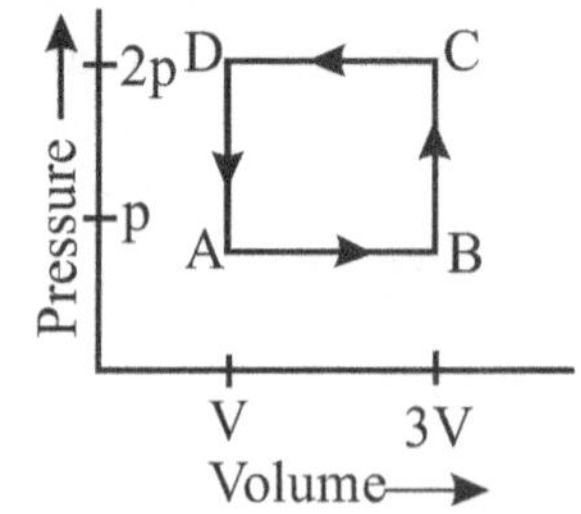

$\therefore \Delta W = -$ Area of rectangle $ABCD = -P(2V)$

$= -2PV$

According to first law of thermodynamics

$\Delta Q = \Delta U + \Delta W$ or $\Delta Q = \Delta W$ (As $\Delta U = 0$)

i.e., heat supplied to the system is equal to the work done

So heat absorbed, $\Delta Q = \Delta W = -2PV$

$\therefore$ Heat rejected by the gas = 2PV

8. An ideal gas goes from state A to state B via three dirrerent processes a indicated in the p-V diagram If Q_1, Q_2,Q_3 indicate the head absorbed by the gas along the three processes and ΔU_1,ΔU_2,ΔU_3 indicate the change in internal energy along the three processes respectively, then : **[AIPMT 2012]**

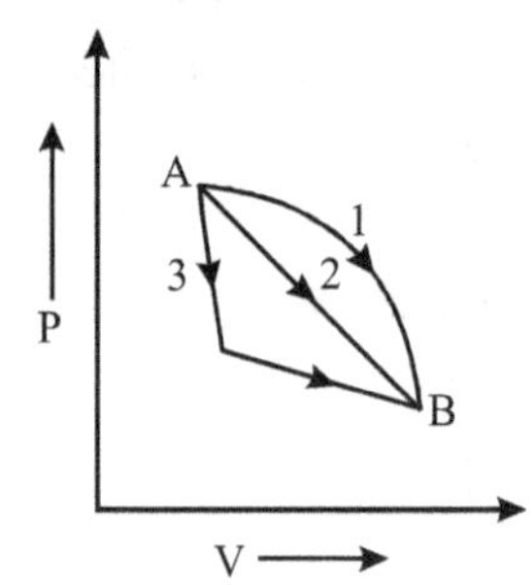

(1) $Q_1 > Q_2 > Q_3$ and $\Delta U_1 = \Delta U_2 = \Delta U_3$

(2) $Q_3 > Q_2 > Q_1$ and $\Delta U_1 = \Delta U_2 = \Delta U_3$

(3) $Q_1 = Q_2 = Q_3$ and $\Delta U_1 > \Delta U_2 > \Delta U_3$

(4) $Q_3 > Q_2 > Q_1$ and $\Delta U_1 = \Delta U_2 = \Delta U_3$

Sol. : **(1)** Change in internal energy is path independent and depends only on the initial and final states.

As the initial and final state in the three processes are same. Therefore,

$$\Delta U_1 = \Delta U_2 = \Delta U_3$$

Workdone, W = Area under P-V graph

As area under curve 1 > area under curve 2 > area under curve 3

$\therefore\ W_1 > W_2 > W_3$

According to first law of thermodynamics,

$$Q = W + \Delta U$$

As $W_1 > W_2 > W_3$ and $\Delta U_1 = \Delta U_2 = \Delta U_3$

$\therefore\ Q_1 > Q_2 > Q_3$

9. A gas is taken through the cycle A→B→ C→A, as shown. What is the net work done by the gas ? **[AIPMT 2013]**

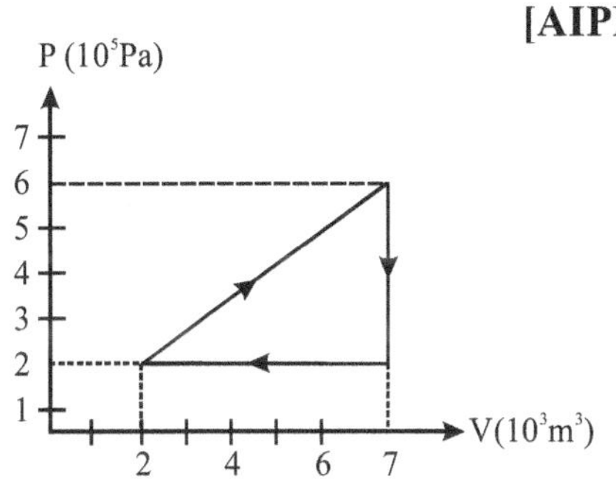

(1) 2000 J (2) 1000 J (3) Zero (4) –2000 J

Sol. : **(2)** In a cyclic process, work done is equal to the area under the cycle and is positive if the cycle is clockwise and negative if the cycle is anticlockwise.

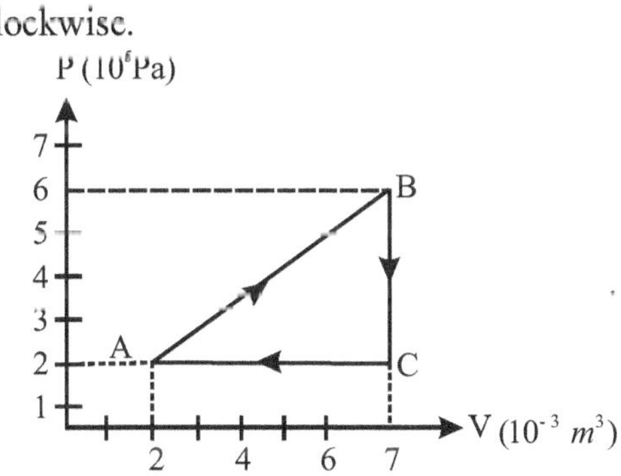

$\therefore$ The network done by the gas is

W = Area of the cycle ABCD

$$= \frac{1}{2} \times (7-2) \times 10^{-3} \times (6-2) \times 10^{5}$$

$$= \frac{1}{2} \times 5 \times 10^{-3} \times 4 \times 10^{5}$$

$$= 10 \times 10^{2}\ \text{J} = 1000\ \text{J}$$

10. A carnot engine, having an efficiency of $\eta = 1/10$ as heat engine, is used as a refrigerator. If the work done on the system 10 J the amount of energy absorbed from the reservoir at lower temperature is **[AIPMT 2015]**

(1) 100 J (2) 99 J (3) 90 J (4) 1 J

Sol. : **(3)** $\dfrac{\Delta Q_2}{\Delta Q_2 + 10} = \dfrac{T_2}{T_1} = \dfrac{9}{10}$

$10\Delta Q_2 = 9Q_2 + 90$

$Q_2 = 90$.

11. Figure below shows two paths that may be takes by a gas to go from a state A to a state C. In process. AB, 400 J of heat is added to the system and in process BC, 100 J of heat is added to the system. The heat absorbed by the system in the process AC will be **[AIPMT 2015]**

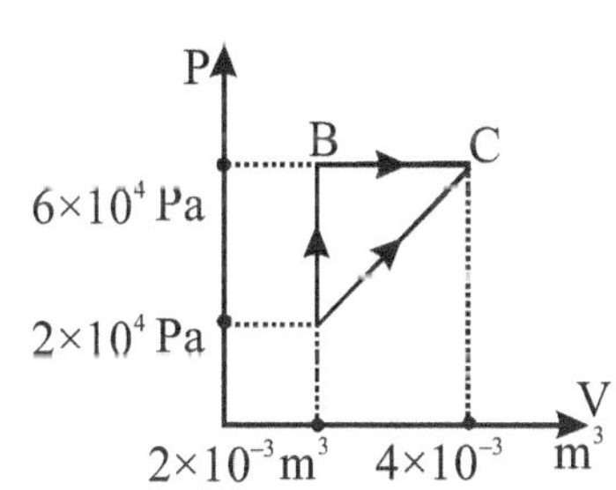

(1) 380 J (2) 500 J

(3) 460 J (4) 300 J

Sol. : **(3)** For cyclic process $\oint d\theta = \oint dw$

$$\Delta w = \frac{1}{2} \times 4 \times 10^4 \times 2 \times 10^{-3} = 40J$$

$$\Delta Q_1 + \Delta Q_2 + \Delta Q_3 = 40 \text{ for ABCA process}$$

$$\Delta Q_3 = -460J$$

hence $Q_{AC} = 460J$.

12. The coefficient of performance of a refrigerator is 5. If the temperatue inside freezeris –20°C the temperature of the surroundings to which it rejects heat is : **[AIPMT 2015]**

(1) 21°C (2) 31°C

(3) 41°C (4) 11°C

Sol. : **(2)** Coefficient of performance of refrigerator

$$COP = \frac{T_1}{T_H - T_L}$$

Where $T_L \rightarrow$ Lower Temperature &

$T_H \rightarrow$ Higher Temperature

$$So, 5 = \frac{T_1}{T_H - T_L}$$

$$\Rightarrow T_H = \frac{6}{5} T_L = \frac{6}{5}(253) = 303.6K.$$

$$T_H = (303.6 - 273)°C$$

$$= 31°C$$

13. A refrigerator works between 4°C and 30°C. It is required to remove 600 calories of heat every second in order to keep the temperature of the refrigerated space constant. The power required is: (Take 1 cal = 4.2 Joules) : **[AIPMT 2016]**

(1) 2.365 W (2) 23.65 W

(3) 236.5 W (4) 2365 W

Sol. : **(3)** $\text{C.O.P.} = \frac{\text{Heat extracted}}{\text{effort put}} = \frac{T_2}{T_1 - T_2}; (T_2 < T_1)$

For 1 secound analysis $\Rightarrow \frac{(600)(4.2)}{\text{Effort put}} = \frac{277}{26}$

$\Rightarrow$ Effort put = 236.5 J $\Rightarrow$ Power = 236.5 watt

14. A gas is compressed isothermally to half its initial volume. The same gas is compressed separately through an adiabatic process until its volume is again reduced to half. Then :- **[AIPMT 2016]**

(1) Compressing the gas isothermally will require more work to be done.

(2) Compressing the gas through adiabatic process will require more work to be done.\

(3) Compressing the gas isothermally or adiabatically will require the same amount of work.

(4) Which of the case (whether compression through isothermal or through adiabatic process) requires more work will depend upon the atomicity of the gas.

Sol. : **(3)** Directly from graph the magnitude of work done = Area under p-v plot is large for adiabatic compression

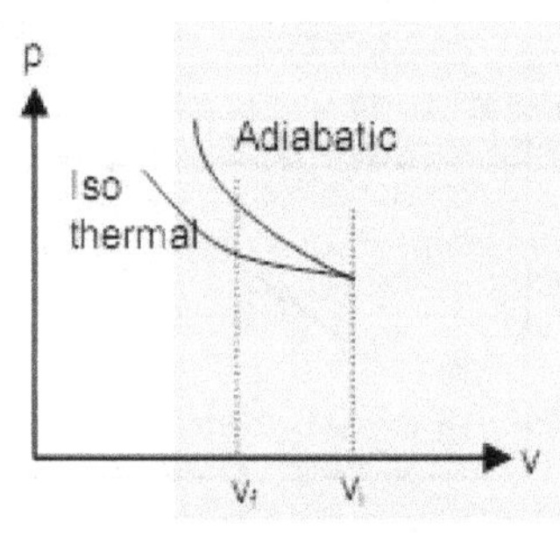

15. The temperature inside a refrigerator is t_2°C and the room temperature is t_1°C. The amount of heat delivered to the room for each joule of electrical energy consumed ideally will be : **NEET–II(2016)**

(1) $\frac{t_2 \quad 273}{t_1 - t_2}$ (2) $\frac{t_1 \quad t_2}{t_1 \quad 273}$

(3) $\frac{t_1}{t_1 - t_2}$ (4) $\frac{t_1 \quad 273}{t_1 - t_2}$

Sol. : (4) $\frac{t_1 \quad 273}{t_1 - t_2}$

16. The volume (V) of a monatomic gas varies with its temperature (T), as shown in the graph. The ratio of work done by the gas, to the heat absorbed by it, when it undergoes a change from state A to state B, is **[NEET-2018]**

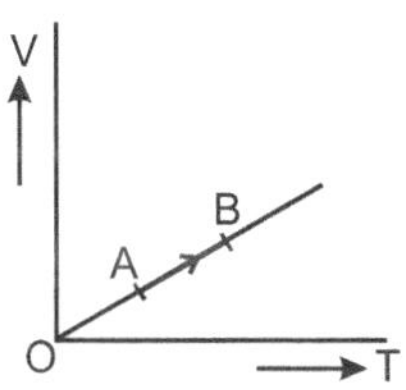

(1) $\frac{1}{3}$ (2) $\frac{2}{3}$

(3) $\frac{2}{5}$ (4) $\frac{2}{7}$

Ans. (3)

17. The efficiency of an ideal heat engine working between the freezing point and boiling point of water, is **[NEET-2018]**

(1) 6.25% (2) 20%

(3) 26.8% (4) 12.5%

Ans. (3)

18. A sample of 0.1 g of water at 100°C and normal pressure $(1.013 \times 10^5\ N\ m\ ^{2})$ requires 54 cal of heat energy to convert to steam at 100°C. If the volume of the steam produced is 167.1 cc, the change in internal energy of the sample, is **[NEET-2018]**

(1) 42.2 J (2) 208.7 J

(3) 104.3 J (4) 57.5 J

Ans. (2)

19. Two wires are made of the same material and have the same volume. The first wire has cross - sectional area A and the second wire has cross-sectional area 3A. If the length of the first wire is increased by on applying a force F, how much force is needed to stretch the second wire by the same amount ? **[NEET-2018]**

(1) 4 F (2) 6 F

(3) 9 F (4) F

Ans. (3)

Kinetic Theory of Gases

Note: Scan QR code with your mobile camera or QR scanner for video solutions.

1. At 10°C the value of the density of a fixed mass of an ideal gas divided by its pressure is x. At 110°C this ratio is **[AIPMT 2009]**

(1) x (2) $\frac{383}{283}x$

(3) $\frac{10}{110}x$ (4) $\frac{10}{110}x$

Sol. : (4)

2. A mass of diatomic gas ($\gamma = 1.4$) at a pressure of 2 atmosphere is compressed adiabatically so that its temperature rise from 27°C to 927°C. The pressure of the gas in the final state is : **[AIPMT 2011]**

(1) 28 atm (2) 68.7 atm (3) 256 atm (4) 8 atm

Sol. : (3) For an adiabatic process

$$\frac{T^{\Upsilon}}{P^{\Upsilon-1}} = \text{constant}$$

$$\therefore \left(\frac{T_i}{T_f}\right)^{\Upsilon} = \left(\frac{P_i}{P_f}\right)^{\Upsilon-1}$$

$$P_f = P_i\left(\frac{T_f}{T_i}\right)^{\frac{\Upsilon}{\Upsilon-1}} \quad \text{...(i)}$$

Here, $T_i = 27^oC = 300\text{ K}$

$T_f = 927^oC = 1200\text{ K}$

$P_i = 2$ atm

$\Upsilon = 1.4$

Substituting these value in eqn (i), we

$$P_f(2) = \left(\frac{1200}{300}\right)^{\frac{1.4}{1.4-1}}$$

$$= (2)(4)^{1.4/0.4} = (2)(2)^7 = 2^8 = 256 \text{ atm.}$$

3. One mole of an ideal gas goes from an intital state A to final state B via two processes : It first undergoes isothermal expansion from volume V to 3 V and then its volume is reduced from 3V to V at constant pressure. The correct P-V diagram representing the two processes is : **[AIPMT 2012]**

(1) 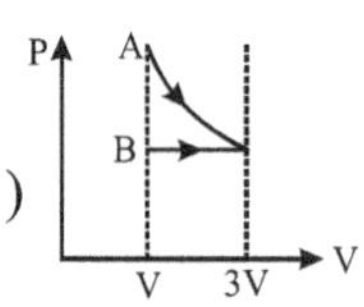

(2) 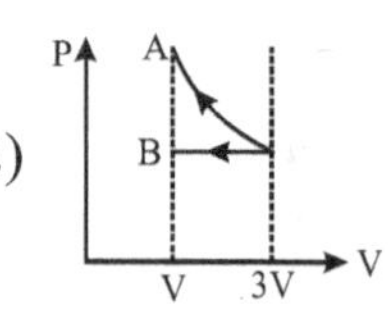

(3) 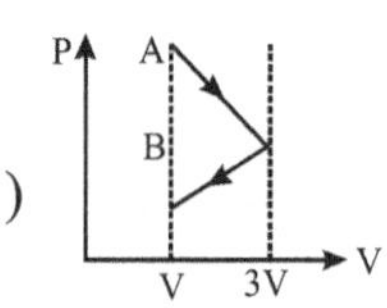

(4) 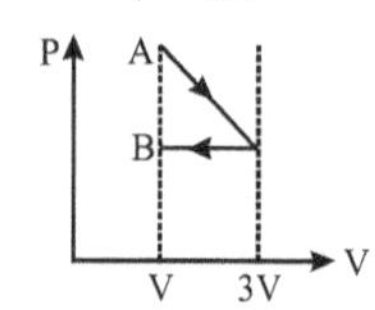

Sol. : (1)

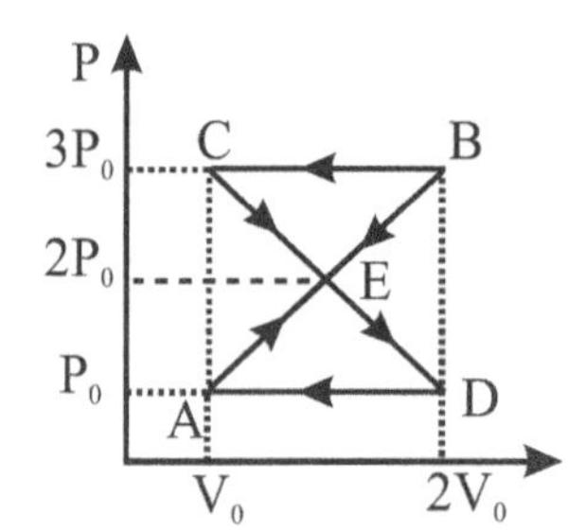

4. During an adiabatic process, the pressure of a gas is found to be proportional to the cube of its temperature. The ratio of $\frac{C_p}{C_v}$ for the gas is : **[AIPMT 2013]**

(1) $\frac{4}{3}$ (2) 2

(3) $\frac{5}{3}$ (4) $\frac{3}{2}$

Sol : **(4)** $P \propto T^{\beta}$

$PT^{-3} = \text{constant}$ ...(i)

For an adiabatic process,

$PT^{\gamma/1-\gamma} = \text{constant}$ ...(ii)

Comparing (i) and (ii), we get

$\frac{\gamma}{1-\gamma} = -3$; $\gamma = -3 + 3\gamma$

$-2\gamma = -3$ or $\gamma = \frac{3}{2}$

As $\gamma = \frac{C_p}{C_v}$ $\therefore \frac{C_p}{C_v} = \frac{3}{2}$.

5. In the given (V– T)diagram, what is the relation between pressures P_1 and P_2 **[AIPMT 2013]**

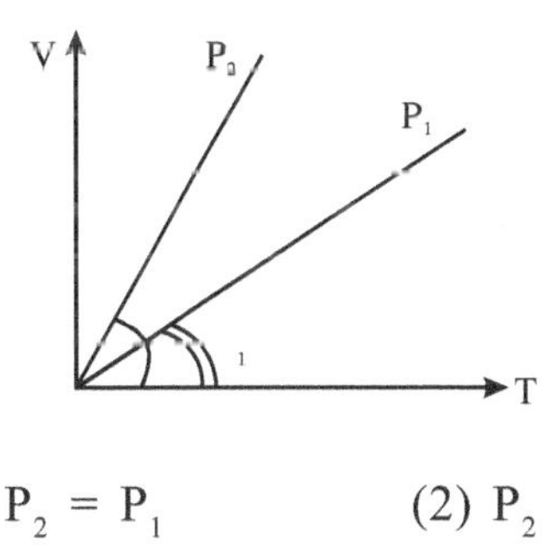

(1) $P_2 = P_1$ (2) $P_2 > P_1$

(3) $P_2 < P_1$ (4) Cannot be perdicted

Sol. : **(3)** According to ideal gas equation

$PV = nRT$ or $V = \frac{nRT}{P}$

For an isobaric process, $P = \text{constant}$ and $V \propto T$

Therefore, $V - T$ graph is a straight line passing throught origin. Slop of this line is inversely proportional to P.

In the given figure,

$(Slop)_2 > (Slop)_1$ $\therefore P_2 < P_1$

6. The amount of heat energy required to raise the temperature of 1 g of Helium at NTP, from T_1 K to T_2 K is **[AIPMT 2013]**

(1) $\frac{3}{8} N_a k_B \; T_2 - T_1$ (2) $\frac{3}{2} N_a k_B \; T_2 - T_1$

(3) $\frac{3}{4} N_a k_B \; T_2 - T_1$ (4) $\frac{3}{4} N_a k_B \; \frac{T_2}{T_1}$

Sol. : **(1)** As here volume of the gas remains constant, therefore the amount of heat energy required to raise the temperature of the gas is

$\Delta Q = nC_V \Delta T$

Here,

Number of moles, $n = \frac{1}{4}$

$C_V = \frac{3}{2}R$ ($\because$ He is a monatomic)

$\Delta T = T_2 - T_1$

$\therefore \quad \Delta Q = \frac{1}{4}\frac{3}{2}R(T_2 - T_2)$

$= \frac{3}{8} N_a k_B (T_2 - T_1) \quad \left(\because k_B = \frac{R}{N_a}\right)$

7. A thermodynamic system undergoes cyclic process ABCDA as shown in figure. The work done by the system in the cycle is **[AIPMT 2014]**

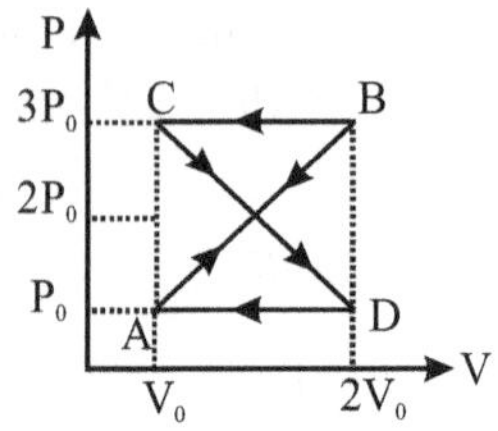

(1) P_0V_0 (2) $2P_0V_0$

(3) $\frac{P_0V_0}{2}$ (4) Zero

Sol. : **(4)** In a cyclic process work done is equal to the area under the cycle and is positive of the cycle is clockwise and negative if anticlockwise.

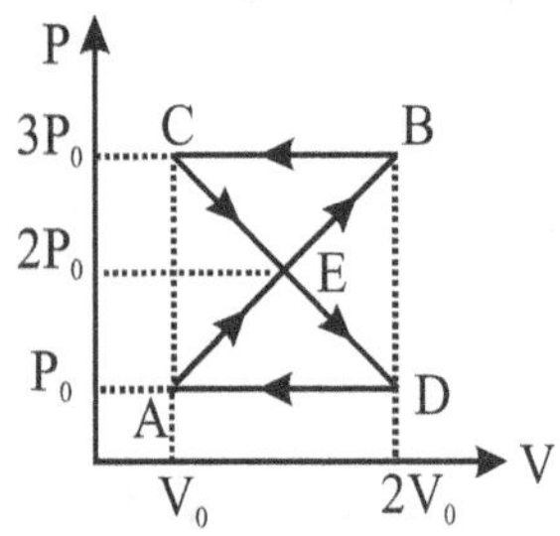

As is clear from figur,

$$W_{BCEB} = -\text{area of } \Delta BCD = -\frac{1}{2}P_0V_0$$

The net work done by the system is

$$W_{net} = W_{AEDA} + W_{BCEB}$$

$$= +\frac{1}{2}P_0V_0 - \frac{1}{2}P_0V_0 = \text{ Zero}$$

8. The mean free path of molecules of a gas (radius r) is inversely proportional to **[AIPMT 2014]**

(1) r^3 (2) r^2

(3) r (4) $\sqrt{r}$

Sol. : **(2)** Mean free path, $\lambda = \frac{1}{\sqrt{2}n\pi d^2}$

Where n is the under density and d is the diameter of the molecule.

As $d = 2r$

$$\therefore \lambda = \frac{1}{4\sqrt{2}n\pi r^2} \quad \text{or} \quad \lambda \propto \frac{1}{r^2}$$

9. One mole of an ideal diatomic gas undergoes a transition form A to B along a path AB as shown in the figure **[AIPMT 2015]**

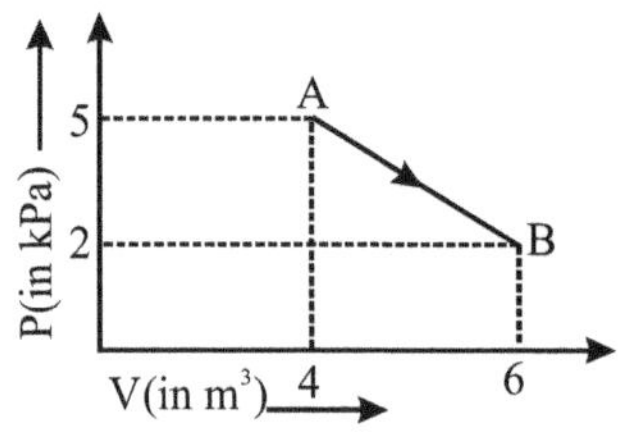

The change in internal energy of the gas during the transition is

(1) 20 kJ (2) – 20 kJ

(3) 20 J (4) – 12 kJ

Sol. : **(2)** $\Delta U = nc_v(T_2 - T_1)$

$$= nc_v\left(\frac{P_2V_2}{nR} - \frac{P_1V_1}{nR}\right)$$

$$n \times \frac{5}{2}R\left(\frac{12-20}{nR}\right) = -20.$$

10. The ratio of the specific heats $\frac{C_P}{C}$ in terms of degrees of freedom (n) is given by **[AIPMT 2015]**

(1) $1+\frac{1}{n}$ (2) $1+\frac{1}{3}$ (3) $1+\frac{2}{n}$ (4) $1+\frac{n}{2}$

Sol. : **(3)** $C_v = \frac{f}{2}R$

$$C_p = \left(\frac{f}{2}+1\right)R$$

$$\frac{C_p}{C_v} = 1+\frac{2}{f}.$$

11. Two vessels separately contain two ideal gases A and B at th same temperature, the pressure of A being twice that of B. Under such conditions, the density of A is found to be 1.5 times the density of B. The ratio of molecular weight of A and B is : **[AIPMT 2015]**

(1) $\frac{1}{2}$ (2) $\frac{2}{3}$ (3) $\frac{3}{4}$ (4) 2

Sol. : **(3)** According to ideal gas equation

$$P = \frac{\rho RT}{M} \Rightarrow M = \frac{\rho RT}{P}$$

So, $$\frac{M_A}{M_B} = \frac{\rho_A}{\rho_B}.\frac{T_A}{T_B}.\frac{P_B}{P_A} = (1.5)(1)\left(\frac{1}{2}\right)$$

$$\Rightarrow \frac{M_A}{M_B} = \frac{3}{4}$$

12. 4.0 g of a gas occupics 22.4 litrcs at NTP. Thc specific heat capacity of the gas at constant volume is 5.0 JK^{-1} mol^{-1}. If the speed of sound in this gas at NTP is 952 ms^{-1}, then the heat capacity at constant pressure is **[AIPMT 2015]**

(Take gas constant R = 8.3 JK^{-1} mol^{-1})

(1) 8.5 JK^{-1} mol^{-1} (2) 8.0 JK^{-1} mol^{-1}

(3) 7.5 JK^{-1} mol^{-1} (4) 7.0 JK^{-1} mol^{-1}

Sol. : **(2)** Molecular mass M = 4.0 g

$$v_{sound} = \sqrt{\frac{\gamma RT}{M}} \Rightarrow \gamma = \frac{Mv^2}{RT} = 1.6$$

So, $Cp = \gamma C_v = 1.6 \times 5.0 = 8.0\ JK^{-1}\ mol^{-1}$

13. An ideal gas is compressed to half its initial volume by means of several processes. Which of the process results in the maximum work done on the gas ? **[AIPMT 2015]**

(1) Isothermal (2) Adisabatic

(3) Isobaric (4) Isochoric

Sol. : **(2)**

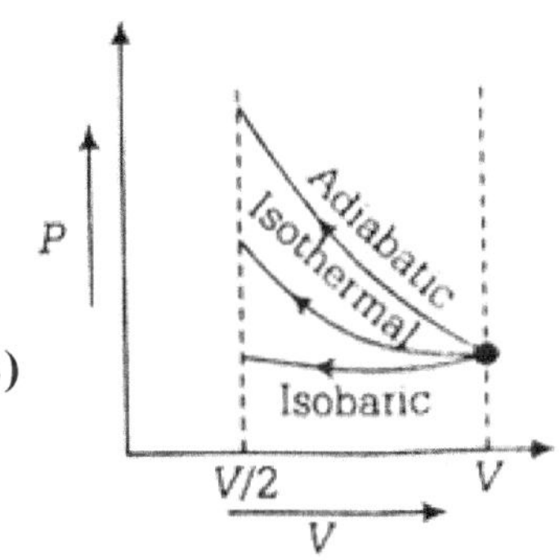

Work done on the gas

$$W_{isochoric} = 0$$

$$W_{adiabatic} > W_{Isothermal} > W_{Isobaric}$$

14. The molecules of a given mass of a gas have r.m.s. velocity of 200 ms^{-1} at 27°C and 1.0 × 105 Nm^{-2} pressure. When the temperature and pressure of the gas are respectively, 127°C and 0.05 × 105 Nm^2, the r.m.s. velocity of its molecules in ms [1] is : **[AIPMT 2016]**

(1) $100\sqrt{2}$ (2) $\frac{400}{\sqrt{3}}$

(3) $\frac{100\sqrt{2}}{3}$ (4) $\frac{100}{3}$

Sol : **(2)** $V_{RMS} = \sqrt{\frac{3RT}{Mo}}$

$$\frac{V_1}{V_2} = \sqrt{\frac{T_1}{T_2}}$$

$$\frac{200}{V_2} = \sqrt{\frac{300}{400}} \Rightarrow \quad V_2 = \frac{400}{\sqrt{3}}$$

15. One mole of an ideal monatomic gas undergoes a process described by the equation PV^3 = constant. The heat capacity of the gas during this process is **[NEET–II(2016)]**

(1) 2 R (2) R (3) $\frac{3}{2}$R (4) $\frac{5}{2}$R

Sol : **(2)** PV^3 = constant

for a polytropic process. PV^a = constant

$$C = C_V + \frac{R}{1-a} = \frac{3}{2}R + \frac{R}{1-3} = \frac{3R}{2} - \frac{R}{2} = R$$

16. A given sample of an ideal gas occupies a volume V at a pressure P and absolute temperature T. The mass of each molecule of the gas is m. Which of the following gives the density of the gas ? **[NEET–II(2016)]**

(1) P/(kTV) (2) mkT

(3) P/(kT) (4) Pm/(kT)

Sol. : **(4)** $n = \frac{PV}{RT} = \frac{\text{mass}}{\text{molar mass}} = \frac{PV}{RT}$

$$\text{density} = \frac{\text{mass}}{\text{volume}} = \frac{(\text{Molar mass})P}{RT} = \frac{(m.N_A)P}{RT} = \frac{mP}{KT}$$

17. At what temperature will the rms speed of oxygen molecules become just sufficient for escaping from the Earth's atmosphere ? **[NEET-2018]**

(Given : Mass of oxygen molecule

(m) = 2.76×10^{-26} kg

Boltzmann's constant $k_B = 1.38 \times 10^{-23}$ jK^{-1}

(1) 5.016×10^4 K (2) 8.360×10^4 K

(3) 2.508×10^4 K (4) 1.254×10^4 K

Ans. **(2)**

13 Oscillations

Note: Scan QR code with your mobile camera or QR scanner for video solutions.

1. The phase difference between the instantaneous velocity and acceleration of a particle executing simple harmonic motion is :- **[AIPMT 2007]**

(1) Zero (2) 0.5 π

(3) π (4) 0.707π

Sol. : **(2)** Let $y = A\sin\omega t$

$$\frac{dy}{dt} = A\omega\cos\omega t = A\omega\sin\left(\omega t + \frac{\pi}{2}\right)$$

Acceleration $= A\omega^2 \sin\omega t$

The phase difference between acceleration and velocity is $\pi/2$.

2. The particle executing simple harmonic motion has a kinetic energy $K_o \cos^2 \omega t$. The maximum values of the potential energy and the total energy are respectively :- **[AIPMT 2007]**

(1) K_o and K_o (2) 0 and $2K_o$

(3) $\frac{K_o}{2}$ and K_o (4) K_o and $2K_o$

Sol. : **(1)**

Kinetic energy + potential energy = total energy.

When kinetic energy is maximum, potential energy is zero and vice versa.

$\therefore$ Maximum potential energy = total energy

$0 + K_0 = K_0$

(K.E. + P.E. = total energy).

3. A mass of 2.0 kg is put on a flat pan attached to a vertical spring fixed on the ground as shown in the figure. The mass of the spring and the pan is negligible. When pressed slightly and released the mass executes a simple harmonic motion. The spring constant is 200N/m. What should be the minimum amplitude of the motion so that the mass gets detached from the pan(Take g = 10 m/s^2) **[AIPMT 2007]**

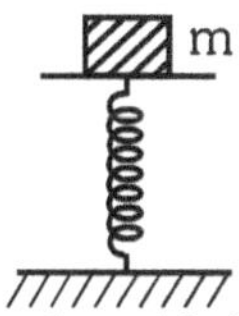

(1) 4.0 cm

(2) 8.0 cm

(3) 10.0 cm

(4) Any value less than 12.0 cm

Sol. : **(3)**

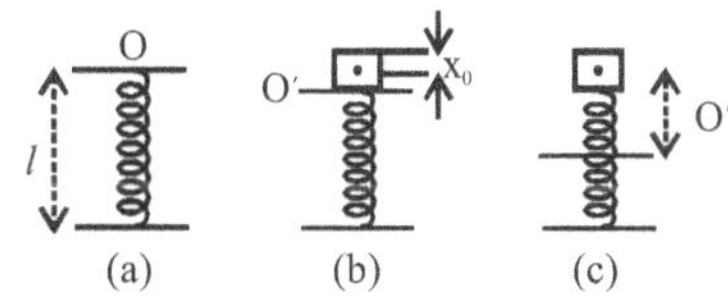

The spring has a length l. When m is placed over it, the equilibrium position becomes O'.

If it is pressed from O' (the equilibrium position) to O'', $O'O''$ is the amplitude.

$$OO' = \frac{mg}{k} = \frac{2\times 10}{200} = 0.10\ m.$$

$mg = kx_0$.

If the restoring force $mA\omega^2 > mg$, then the mass will move up with acceleration, detached from the pan.

i.e. $A > \frac{g}{k/m} \Rightarrow A > \frac{20}{200} > 0.10m.$

The amplitude > 10 cm.

i.e. the minimum is just greater than 10 cm.

(The actual compression will include x_0 also. But when talking of amplitude, it is always from the equilibrium position with respect to which the mass is oscillating.

4. A particle executes simple harmonic oscillation with an amplitude a. The period of oscillation is T. The minimum time taken by the particle to travel half of the amplitude from the equilibrium position is :- **[AIPMT 2007]**

(1) $\frac{T}{4}$ (2) $\frac{T}{8}$ (3) $\frac{T}{12}$ (4) $\frac{T}{2}$

Sol. : **(3)** $x(t) = a\sin\omega t$ (from the equilibrium position)

At x(t) = a/2

$$\therefore \ \frac{a}{2} = a\sin(\omega t)$$

$$\Rightarrow \sin\left(\frac{\pi}{6}\right) = \sin(\omega t) \ or, \ \frac{\pi}{6} = \frac{2\pi t}{T}\left[\because \omega = \frac{2\pi}{T}\right]$$

or $t = T/12.$

5. Two simple harmonic motions of angular frequency 100 and 1000 rad^{-1} have the same displacement amplitude. The ratio of their maxium acceleration is **[AIPMT 2008]**

(1) 1 : 10 (2) 1 : 10^2

(3) 1 : 10^3 (4) 1 : 10^4

Sol. : **(2)** ω_1=100 rad s^{-1}; ω_2=1000 rad s^{-1}.

Maximum acceleration of (1) $= -\omega_1^2 A$

Maximum acceleration of (2) $= -\omega_2^2 A$

$$\therefore \frac{\text{accln}(1)}{\text{accln}(2)} = \frac{\omega_1^2}{\omega_2^2} = \frac{(100)^2}{(1000)^2} = \frac{1}{100}$$

$a(1) : a(2) = 1 : 100.$

6. A point performs simple harmonic oscillation of period T and the equation of motion is given by x = a sin (ωt + π/6). After the elaphse of what fraction of the time period the velocity of the point will be equal to half of tis maximum velocity ? **[AIPMT 2008]**

(1) T (2) $T\sqrt{2}$ (3) 2 T (4) $\sqrt{2T}$

Sol. : **(4)**

x = a sin (wt + π/6)

$$V_{max} = \left(\frac{dx}{dt}\right)$$

$$V_{max} = \frac{dz}{dt} = a \cos\cos\ (wt + \frac{\pi}{6})$$

For V_{max} cos (wt + $\frac{\pi}{6}$) = 1

V_{max} = cos

$$\left(\frac{\cos}{2}\right) = \cos\cos\left(wt + \frac{\pi}{6}\right)$$

$$\cos\ (wt + \frac{\pi}{6}) = \frac{1}{2}$$

$$wt + \frac{\pi}{6} = \left(\frac{\pi}{3}\right)$$

$$\cot = \frac{\pi}{6} = t = \frac{\pi}{6w}$$

$$t = \frac{\pi}{6\times\left(\frac{2\pi}{T}\right)}, \left(\frac{T}{12}\right)$$

7. A simple pendulum performs simple harmonic motion about x = 0 with an amplitude a and time period T. The speed of the pendulum at x = a/2 will be :- **[AIPMT 2009]**

(1) $\frac{a\sqrt{3}}{T}$ (2) $\frac{a\sqrt{3}}{2T}$ (3) $\frac{a}{T}$ (4) $\frac{3\ {}^{2}a}{T}$

Sol. : **(1)** For simple harmonic motion,

$v = \omega\sqrt{a^2 - x^2}$. When $x = \frac{a}{2}$,

$$\text{When } x = \frac{a}{2}, v = \omega\sqrt{a^2 - \frac{a^2}{4}} = \omega\sqrt{\frac{3}{4}a^2}.$$

$$\text{As } \omega = \frac{2\pi}{T}, \ \therefore \ v = \frac{2\pi}{T}\cdot\frac{\sqrt{3}}{2}a \Rightarrow v = \frac{\pi\sqrt{3}a}{T}.$$

8. Which one of the following equations of motion represents simple harmonic motion :-

(1) Acceleration = kx **[AIPMT 2009]**

(2) Acceleration = $-k_0x+k_1x^2$

(3) Acceleration = $-k(x + a)$

(4) Acceleration = $k(x + a)$

Where k, k_0, k_1 and a are all positive

Sol. : **(2)** Simple harmonic motion is defined as follows

Acceleration $\frac{d^2y}{dt^2} = -\omega^2 x$

The negative sign is very important in simple harmonic motion. Acceleration is independent of any initial displacement of equilibrium position.

Then acceleration $= -\omega^2 x$.

9. A block of mass M is attached to the lower end of a vertical spring. The spring is hung from a ceiling and has force constant value k. The mass is released from rest with the spring initially unstretched. the maximum extension produced in the length of the spring will be : - **[AIPMT 2009]**

(1) Mg/k (2) 2Mg/k

(3) 4 Mg/k (4) Mg/2k

Sol. : **(2)** Loss in grav. PE = gain in spring PE

At maximum elongation

$M_{gx} = \frac{1}{2}kx^2$

$x = \frac{2Mg}{k}$.

10. The displacement of a particle along the x aixs is given by $x = a \sin^2 \omega t$. The motion of the particle corresponds to :- **[AIPMT 2010]**

(1)Simple harmonic motion of frequency $\frac{}{2}$

(2) Simple harmonic motion of frequency —

(3) Simple harmonic motion of frequency $\frac{3}{2}$

(4) Non simple harmonic motion

Sol. : **(4)**

$x = a \sin^2 (wt)$

velocity $v = \left(\frac{dx}{dt}\right)$, $2aw \sin(wt) \cos(wt)$

$v = 2aw \sin(wt) \cos(wt)$

$v = aw \sin (wt)$

acceleration = $a = \left(\frac{dx}{dt}\right)$, $2aw^2 \cos(wt)$

$a = 2aw^2 \cos(2wt)$

acce $\alpha - x$ is not satified

$T = \frac{2\pi}{2w} = \frac{\pi}{w}$

11. The period of oscillation of a mass M suspended from a spring of negligible mass is T. If along with it another mass M is also suspended, the period of oscillation will now be : **[AIPMT 2010]**

(1) $\sqrt{2}T$ (2) T (3) $\frac{T}{\sqrt{2}}$ (4) 2T

Sol. : **(1)** A mass M is suspended from a massless spring of spring constant k as shown in figure (a). Then,

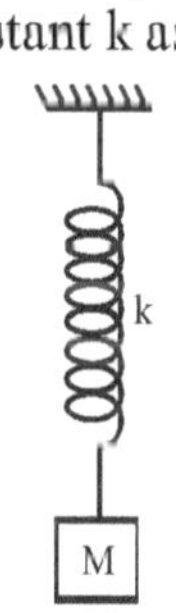

(a)

Time period of oscillation is

$$T = 2\pi\sqrt{\frac{M}{k}} \quad ....(i)$$

When a another mass M is also suspended with it as shown in figure (b).

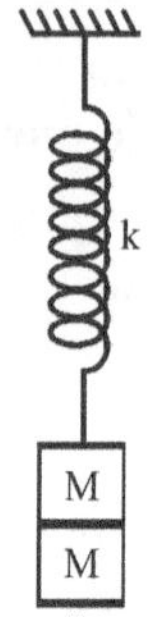

(b)

Time period of oscillation is

$$T = 2\pi\sqrt{\frac{M+M}{k}} = 2\pi\sqrt{\frac{2M}{k}}$$

$$= \sqrt{2}\left(2\pi\sqrt{\frac{M}{k}}\right) = \sqrt{2}\,T \qquad \text{(Using(i))}$$

12. A particle of mass m is releases from rest and follows a parabolic path as shown. Assuming that the displacement of the mass from the origin is small, which graph correctly depicts the position of the particle as a function of time ?

[AIPMT 2011]

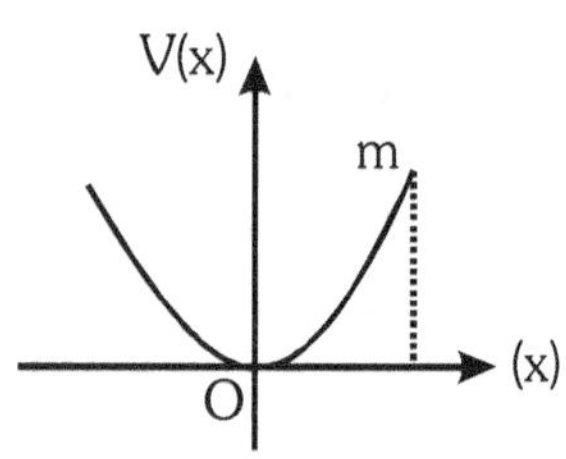

(1) 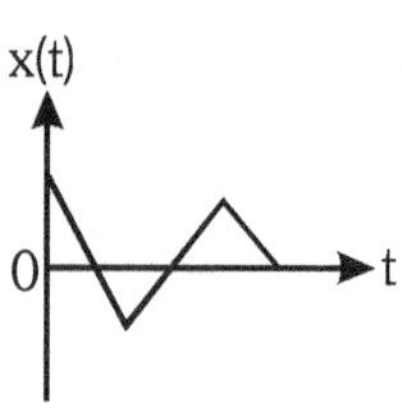

(2) 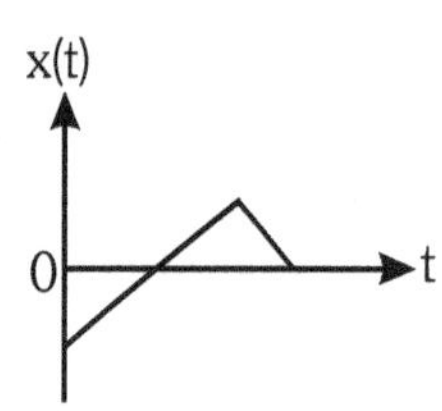

(3) 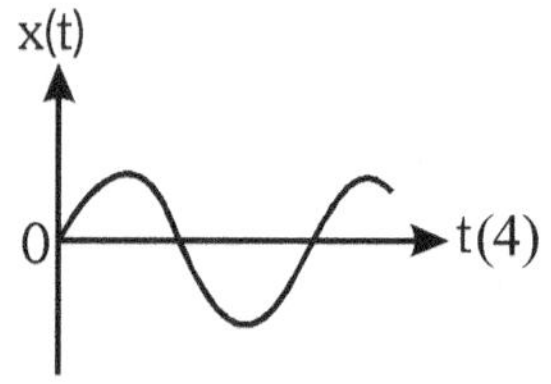

(4) 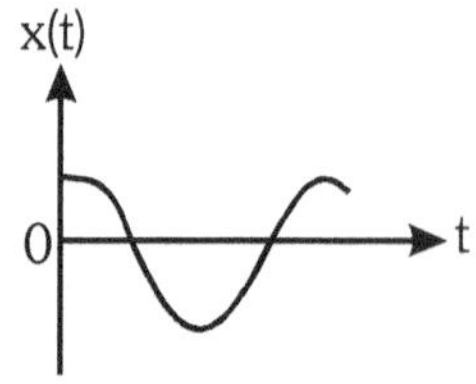

Sol. : **(4)** Motion start from extreme position and for small displacement it is SHM $y = A\cos(\omega t+\phi)$.

13. Out of the following functions representing motion of a particle which represents SHM

(I) $y = \sin \omega t - \cos \omega t$

(II) y $\sin^3\omega t$

(III) $y = 5\cos \frac{3\pi}{4} - 3\omega t$

(IV) $y = 1 + \omega t + \omega^2 t^2$ **[AIPMT 2011]**

(1) Only (IV) does not repersent SHM

(2) (I) and (III)

(3) (I) and (II)

(4) Only (I)

Sol. : **(2)** $y = \sin\omega t - \cos\omega t$

$$= \sqrt{2}\left[\frac{1}{\sqrt{2}}\sin\omega t - \frac{1}{\sqrt{2}}\cos\omega t\right] = \sqrt{2}\sin\left(\omega t - \frac{\pi}{4}\right)$$

It represents a SHM with time period, $T = \frac{2\pi}{\omega}$.

$$y = \sin^3\omega t = \frac{1}{4}[3\sin\omega t - \sin 3\omega t]$$

It represents aperiodic motion with time period $T = \frac{2\pi}{\omega}$ but not SHM.

$$y = 5\cos\left(\frac{3\pi}{4} - 3\omega t\right)$$

$$= 5\cos\left(3\omega t - \frac{3\pi}{4}\right) [\because \cos(-\theta) = \cos\theta]$$

It represents a SHM with time period, $T = \frac{2\pi}{3\omega}$.

$$y = 1 + \omega t + \omega^2 t^2$$

It represents a non-periodic motion. Also it is not physically acceptable as the $y \to \infty$ as $t \to \infty$.

14. Two particles are oscillating along two close parallel straight lines side by side, with the same frequency and amplitudes. They pass each other, moving in opposite directions when their displacement is half ofthe amplitude. The mean positons of the two particles lie on a straight line perpendicular to the paths of the two particles. The phase difference is **[AIPMT 2011]**

(1) zero (2) $\frac{\ }{3}$ (3) π (4) $\frac{\ }{6}$

Sol. : (2)

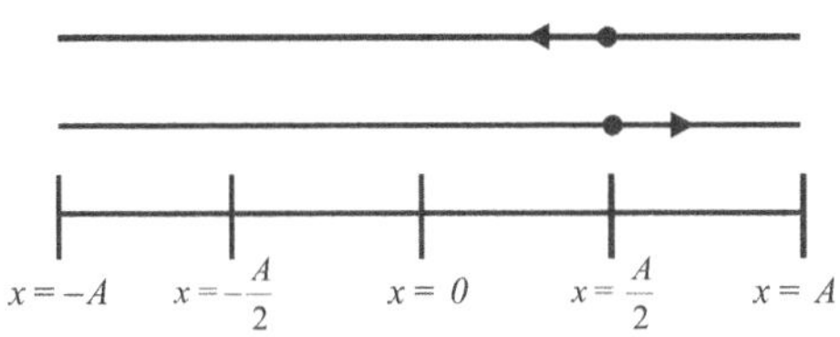

The time taken by the particle to travel from

$x = 0 \; to \; x = \frac{A}{2} \; is \; \frac{T}{12}.$

The time taken by the particle to travel from

$x = A \; to \; x = \frac{A}{2} \; is \; \frac{T}{6}.$

Time difference $= \frac{T}{6} + \frac{T}{6} = \frac{T}{3}$

Phase difference,

$\phi = \frac{2\pi}{T} \times \text{Time difference}$

$= \frac{2\pi}{T} \times \frac{T}{3} = \frac{2\pi}{3}$

15. The damping force on an oscillator is directly proportional to the velocity. The units of the constant of proportionality are **[AIPMT 2012]**

(1) kgs (2) $kgms^{-1}$ (3) $kgms^{-2}$ (4) kgs^{-1}

Sol. : (4) F = Kv

$K = \frac{F}{v}$ Unit of $K = \frac{kg\ ms^{-2}}{ms^{-1}} = kg\ s^{-1}$.

16. The equation of a simple harmonic wave is given by. **[AIPMT 2012]**

$y = 3 \sin \frac{\ }{2} (50t - x)$

where x and y are in metres and t is in seconds. The ratio of maximum particle velocity to the wave velocity is

(1) 2 π (2) $\frac{3}{2}$ (3) 3 π (4) $\frac{2}{3}$

Sol. : (2)

17. The oscillation of a boyd on a smooth horizontal surface is represented by the equation ,

X = A cos(ωt)

whrer X = displacement at time t

ω = frequence of oscillation

Which one of the following graphs shows correctly the variation a with t ? **[AIPMT 2014]**

(1)

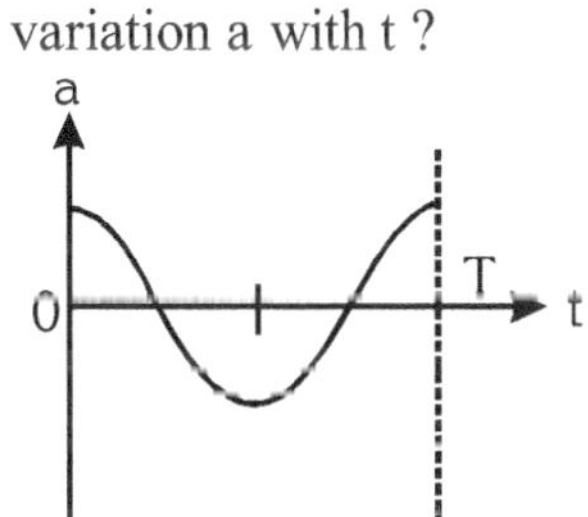

(2)

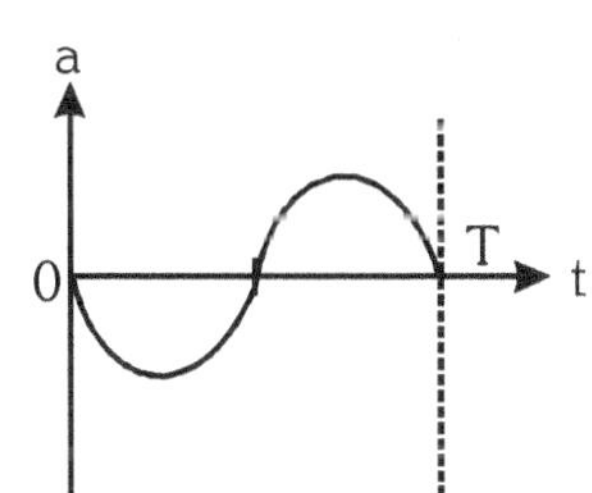

(3) 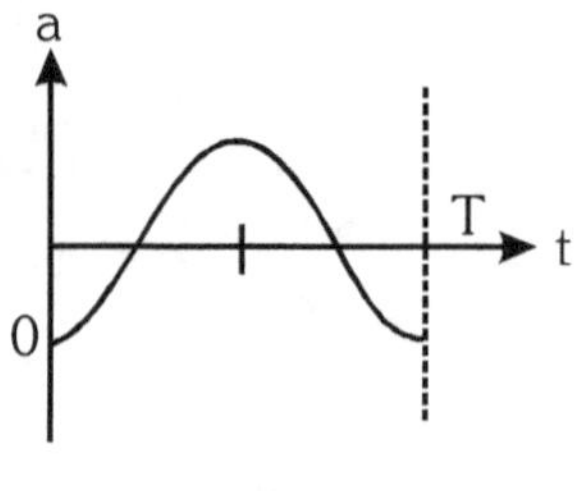

(4) 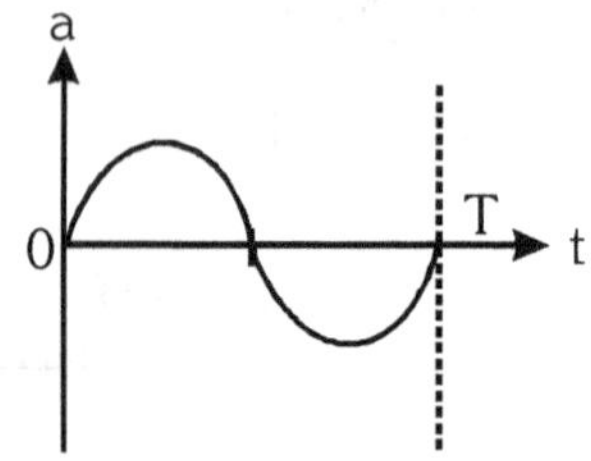

Here a = acceleration at time t

T = time peroid

Sol. : **(3)** Here, $X = A\cos\omega t$

$\therefore$ Velocity, $v = \frac{dx}{dt} = \frac{d}{dt}(A\cos\omega t)$

$= -A\omega\sin\omega t$

Acceleration, $a = \frac{dv}{dt} = \frac{d}{dt}(-A\omega\sin\omega t)$

$= -A\omega^2\cos\omega t$

Hence the variation of a with t is correctly shown by graph (c).

18. When two displacements represented by y_1=a sin(ωt) and y_2= b cos(ω_t)are superimposed the motion is **[AIPMT 2015]**

(1) Not a simple harmonic

(2) Simple harmonic with amplitude $\frac{a}{b}$

(3) Simple harmonic with amplitude $\sqrt{a^2 \; b^2}$

(4) Simple harmonic with amplitude $\frac{a \;\; b}{2}$

Sol. : **(3)** $A_R\sqrt{A_1^2+A_2^2+2A_1A_2\cos\phi}$

ϕ is the phase diff.

$\phi = 90°, A_1 = a, A_2 = b$

$\therefore A_R = \sqrt{a^2+b^2}$.

19. A particle is executing SHM along a straight line. Its velocities at distances x_1 and x_2 from the mean position are V_1 and V_2 respectively Its time period is **[AIPMT 2015]**

(1) $2\sqrt{\frac{x_1^2 \;\; x_2^2}{V_1^2 \;\; V_2^2}}$ (2) $2\sqrt{\frac{x_2^2 - x_1^2}{V_1^2 - V_2^2}}$

(3) $2\sqrt{\frac{x_2^2 \;\; V_2^2}{x_1^2 - x_2^2}}$ (4) $2\sqrt{\frac{V_1^2 - V_2^2}{x_1^2 - x_2^2}}$

Sol. : **(2)**

$V_1^2 = w^2(A^2 - x^2)$

$V_1^2 = w^2(x - x_1^2)$

$v_1^2 = w^2(A^2 - x_2^2)$

$v_1^2 - v_2^2 = w^2\left(A^2 - x_1^2 - A^2 + x_2^2\right)$

$v_1^2 - v_2^2 = w^2\left(x_1^2 - x_1^2\right)$

$w^2 = \left(\frac{v_1^2 - v_2^2}{x_2^2 - x_1^2}\right)$

$w = \sqrt{\frac{v_1^2 - v_2^2}{x_2^2 - x_1^2}}$

$T = \frac{2\pi}{w}$

$T = \frac{2\pi}{\sqrt{\frac{v_1^2 - v_2^2}{x_2^2 - x_1^2}}}, 2\pi\sqrt{\frac{x_2^2 - x_1^2}{v_1^2 - v_2^2}}$

20. A particle is executing a simple harmonis motion. Its maximum acceleration is α and maximum velocity is β. then , its time period of vibration will be : **[AIPMT 2015]**

(1) $\frac{2\pi\beta}{\alpha}$ (2) $\frac{\beta^2}{\alpha^2}$ (3) — (4) $\overset{2}{—}$

Sol. : (1) For S.H.M.

Maximum acceleration $= \omega^2 A = \alpha$

Maximum velocity $= \omega A = \beta$

$$\Rightarrow \omega = \frac{\alpha}{\beta} \Rightarrow T = \frac{2\pi}{\omega} = \frac{2\pi\beta}{\alpha}.$$

21. An air column,closed at one end and open at the other, resonates with a tuning fork when the smallest length of the column is 50 cm The next larger length of the column resonating with the same tuning fork is : **[AIPMT 2016]**

(1) 66.7 cm (2) 100 cm

(3) 150 cm (4) 200 cm

Sol. : (3)

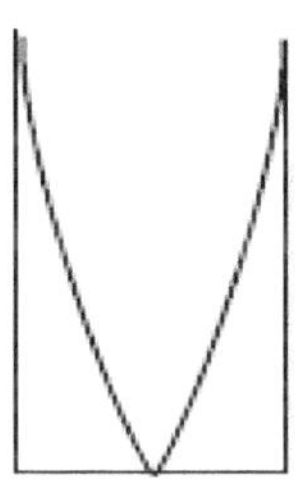

First harmonic at $\frac{\lambda}{4}$

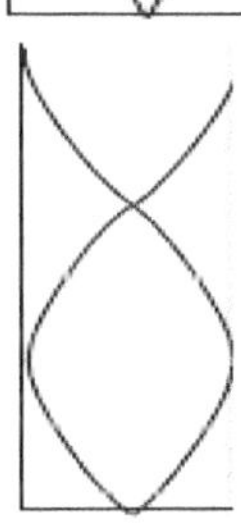

3rd harmonic $\frac{3\lambda}{4}$

1st length = 50 cm

3rd harmonic length 150 cm

22. A particle executes linear simple harmonic motion with an amplitude of 3 cm. When the particle is at 2 cm from the mean position, the magnitude of its velocity is equal to that of its acceleration. Then its time period in seconds is : **[NEET – 2017]**

(1) $\frac{\sqrt{5}}{\pi}$ (2) $\frac{\sqrt{5}}{2\pi}$

(3) $\frac{4\pi}{\sqrt{5}}$ (4) $\frac{2\pi}{\sqrt{3}}$

Sol. : (3)

A = 3 cm,

x = 2 cm

According to question

V = a

$$V = w\sqrt{A^2 - x^2}$$

$$a = xw^2$$

$$w\sqrt{A^2 - x^2} = xw^2$$

$$w = \frac{\sqrt{A^2 - x^2}}{x}$$

$$w = \frac{\sqrt{(3)^2 - (2)^2}}{2} = \frac{\sqrt{5}}{2}$$

$$T = \frac{2\pi}{w}$$

$$T = \frac{2\pi}{\left(\frac{\sqrt{5}}{2}\right)} = \frac{4\pi}{\sqrt{5}}$$

23. A pendulum is hung from the roof of a sufficiently high building and is moving freely to and fro like a simple harmonic oscillator. The acceleration of the bob of the pendulum is 20 m/s^2 at a distance of 5 m from the mean position. The time period of oscillation is **[NEET-2018]**

(1) 2s (2) πs

(3) 2π s (4) 1 s

Ans. (2)

14 Wave Motion

Note: Scan QR code with your mobile camera or QR scanner for video solutions.

1. Two vibrating tuning forks produce progressive waves given by $Y_1 = 4 \sin 500\pi t$ and $Y_2 = 2 \sin 506 \pi t$. Number of beats produced per minute is : **[AIPMT-2005]**

(1) 3 (2) 360 (3) 180 (4) 60

Sol : **(3)** $Y_1 = 4\sin 500\pi t,\ Y_2 = 2\sin 506\pi t$

$$\omega_1 = 500\pi, \omega_1 = 2\pi v, v_1 = 250, v_2 = 253$$

$$v = v_2 - v_1 = 253 - 250 = 3 \text{ beats/s.}$$

Number of beat per minute

$$= 3 \times 60 = 180.$$

2. Two sound waves with wavelengths 5.0 m and 5.5 m respectively, each propagate in a gas with velocity 330 m/s. We expect the following number of beats per second :- **[AIPMT-2006]**

(1) 12 (2) 0

(3) 1 (4) 6

Sol : **(4)** $\text{Frequency} = \dfrac{\text{velocity}}{\text{wavelength}}$

$$\therefore \quad \upsilon_1 \frac{v}{\lambda_1} = \frac{330}{5} = 66 \text{ Hz}$$

and $\upsilon = \dfrac{v}{\lambda_2} = \dfrac{330}{5.5} = 60 \text{ Hz}$

Number of beats per secound $= \upsilon_1 - \upsilon_2$

$$= 60 - 60 = 6.$$

3. A transverse wave propagating along x-axis is represented by

$$y(x, t) = 8.0 \sin (0.5\pi x - 4\pi t - \frac{\pi}{4})$$

where x is in metres and t is in seconds. The speed of the wave is :- **[AIPMT-2001, 06]**

(1) 4π m/s (2) $0.5\ \pi$ m/s

(3) $\dfrac{\pi}{4}$ m/s (4) 8 m/s

Sol : **(4)** $y(x,t) = 8.0\sin\left(0.5\pi x - 4\pi t - \dfrac{\pi}{4}\right)$

compare with a standard wave equation,

$$y = a\sin\left(\frac{2\pi x}{\lambda} - \frac{2\pi t}{T} + \phi\right)$$

we get $\dfrac{2\pi}{\lambda} = 0.5\pi$ or, $\lambda = \dfrac{2\pi}{0.5\pi} = 4$ m

$$\frac{2\pi}{T} = 4\pi \text{ or, } T = \frac{2\pi}{4\pi} = \frac{1}{2}\text{sec.}$$

$$\upsilon = \frac{1}{T} = 2\text{Hz.}$$

wave velocity, $v = \lambda\upsilon = 4 \times 2 = 8$ m/sec.

4. The time of reverberation of a room A is one second. What will be the time (in seconds) of reverberation of a room, having all the dimensions double of those of room A :- **[AIPMT-2006]**

(1) 2 (2) 4

(3) $\dfrac{1}{2}$ (4) 1

Sol : **(1)** Reveberation time, $T = \frac{0.61V}{aS}$ where V is the volume of room in cubic metres, a is the average absorption coefficien of the room, S is the totel surface area of room in square metres.

or, $T \propto \frac{V}{S}$

or, $\frac{T_1}{T_2} = \left(\frac{V_1}{V_2}\right)\left(\frac{S_2}{S_1}\right) = \left(\frac{V}{8V}\right)\left(\frac{4S}{S}\right) = \frac{1}{2}$

or, $T_2 = 2T_1 = 2 \times 1 = 2\,\text{sec}. \ (\because T_1 = 1\,\text{sec})$

5. Which one of the following statements is true:- **[AIPMT-2006]**

(1) Both light and sound waves in air are transverse

(2) The sound waves in air are longitudinal while the light waves are transverse

(3) Both light and sound waves in air are longitudinal

(4) Both light and sound waves can travel in vacuum

Sol : **(2)** Light waves are electromagnetic waves. Light waves are transverse in nature and do not require a medium to travel, hence they can travel in vacuum. Sound waves are longitudinal waves and require a medium to travel. They do not travel in vacuum.

6. A boat at anchor is rocked by waves whose crests are 100m apart and velocity is 25m/sec. The boat bounces up once in every **[2006]**

(1) 2500 s (2) 75 s

(3) 4 s (4) 0·25 s

Sol : **(3)**

$t = \frac{S}{V} = \frac{100}{25} = 4\text{ sec}$

7. For waves propagating in a medium, identify the property that is independent of the others:-

(1) Velocity **[2006]**

(2) Wavelength

(3) Frequency

(4) All these depend on each other

Sol : **(1)** Velocity

8. The driver of a car travelling with speed 30 m/sec towards a hill sounds a horn of frequency 600 Hz. If the velocity of sound in air is 330 m/s, the frequency of reflected sound as heard by driver is **[AIPMT 09]**

(1) 500 Hz (2) 550 Hz

(3) 555.5 Hz (4) 720 Hz

Sol : **(4)** Car is the source and the hill is observer.

Frequency heard at the hill, υ_1

$$\therefore \quad \upsilon_1 = \frac{\upsilon \times v}{v - V} = \frac{600 \times 330}{330 - 30}$$

Now for reflection, the hill is the source and the driver the observer.

$$\therefore \quad \upsilon_2 = \upsilon_1 \times \frac{(330 + 30)}{330}$$

$$\Rightarrow \upsilon_2 = \frac{600 \times 330}{300} \times \frac{360}{330} \Rightarrow \upsilon_2 = 720\text{ Hz.}$$

9. A wave in a string has an amplitude of 2cm. The wave travels in the + ve direction of x axis with a speed of 128 m/sec. and it is noted that 5 complete waves fit in 4 m length of the string. The equation describing the wave is :- **[AIPMT 2009]**

(1) y = (0.02) m sin (7.85x – 1005t)

(2) y = (0.02) m sin (7.85x + 1005t)

(3) y = (0.02) m sin (15.7x – 2010t)

(4) y = (0.02)m sin (15.7x + 2010t)

Sol : (1)

$$\text{Amplitute} = 2cm = 0.02m, v = 128 \text{ m/s}$$

$$\lambda = \frac{4}{5} = 0.8m;\ \upsilon = \frac{128}{0.8} = 160 \text{ Hz}$$

$$\omega = 2\pi\upsilon = 2\pi \times 160 = 1005;$$

$$K = \frac{2\pi}{\lambda} = \frac{2\pi}{0.8} = 7.85$$

$$\therefore\ y = 0.02\sin(7.85x - 1005t)$$

10. The displacement of a particle along the x axis is given by x = a sin² ωt. The motion of the particle corresponds to : **[AIPMT 2010]**

(1) simple harbmonic motion of frequency $\frac{\ }{2}$

(2) simlple harmonic motion of frequency —

(3) Simple harmonic motion of frequency $\frac{3}{2}$

(4) non simple harmonic motion

Sol. : (2) $x = a\sin^2(\omega t)$

$$[\cos 2\theta = 1 - 2\sin^2\theta]$$

$$x = \frac{a}{2}[1 - \cos(2\omega t)]$$

11. A transverse wave is represented by y = A sin (ωt – kx). For what value of the wavelength is the wave velocity equal to the maximum particle velocity ? **[AIPMT 98, 2010]**

(1) A (2) $\frac{A}{2}$

(3) πA (4) 2πA

Sol : (4) The given wave equation is

$$y = A\sin(\omega t - kx)$$

Wave velocity, $\upsilon = \frac{\omega}{k}$ ...(i)

Particle velocity,

$$\upsilon_p = \frac{dy}{dt} = A\omega\cos(\omega t - kx)$$

Maximum particle velocity,

$$(\omega_p)_{\max} = A\omega \qquad ...(ii)$$

According to the given question

$$\upsilon = (\upsilon_p)_{\max}$$

$$\frac{\omega}{k} = A\omega \qquad \{\text{Using(i) and (ii)}\}$$

$$\frac{1}{k} = A \text{ or } \frac{\lambda}{2\pi} = A \qquad \left(\because k = \frac{2\pi}{\lambda}\right)$$

$$\lambda = 2\pi A$$

12. A tuning fork of frequency 512 Hz makes 4 beats per second with the vibrating string of a piano. The beat frequency decreases to 2 beats per seconds when the tension in the piano string is slightly increased. The frequency of the piano string before increasing the tension was : **[AIPMT 2010]**

(1) 508 Hz (2) 510 Hz

(3) 514 Hz (4) 516 Hz

Sol : **(1)** Let the frequencies of tunning of tuning fork and piano string be υ_1 and υ_2 respectively.

$\therefore\ \upsilon_2 = \upsilon_1 \pm 4 = 512\ \text{Hz} \pm 4$

$= 516\ \text{Hz}$ or $508\ \text{Hz}$

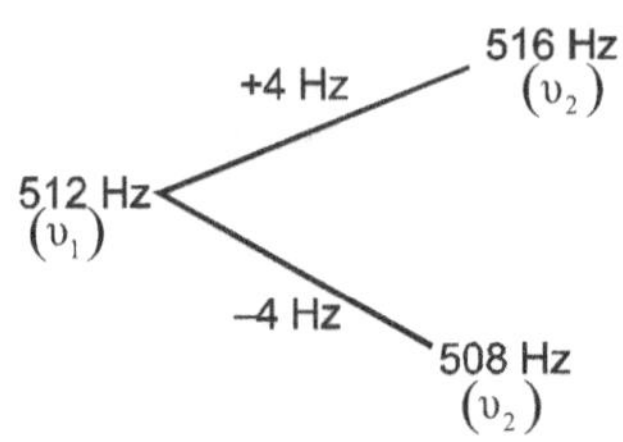

Increase in the tension of a piano string increases its frequency.

If $\upsilon_2 = 516\ \text{Hz}$, further increase in υ_2, resulted in an increase in the beat frequency. But this is not given in the question.

If $\upsilon_2 = 508\ \text{Hz}$, further increase in υ_2, resulted in decrease in the beat frequency. This is given in the question. When the frequency decreases to 2 beats per secound. Therefore, the frequency of the piano string before increasing the tension was 508 Hz.

13. Two waves are represented by the equations $y_1 = a\sin(\omega t + kx + 0.57)$ m and $y_2 = a\cos(\omega t + kx)$ m where x is in meter and t in sec. The phase difference between them is :- **[AIPMT 2004, 11]**

(1) 1.0 radian (2) 1.25 radian

(3) 1.57 radian (4) 0.57 radian

Sol : **(1)** $y_1 = a\sin\left(\omega t + kx + 0.57\right)$

$\therefore$ Phase, $\phi = \omega t + kx + 0.57$

$$y_2 = a\cos\left(\omega t + kx\right) = a\sin\left(\omega t + kx + \frac{\pi}{2}\right)$$

$\therefore$ Phase, $\phi_2 = \omega t + kx\frac{\pi}{2}$

Phase difference, $\Delta\phi = \phi_2 - \phi_1$

$$= \left(\omega t + kx + \frac{\pi}{2}\right) - \left(\omega t + kx + 0.57\right) = \frac{\pi}{2} - 0.57$$

$= \left(1.57 - 0.57\right)$ redian=1radian

14. The dimensions of $(\mu_0 \in_0)^{-\frac{1}{2}}$ are :- **[AIPMT 2011]**

(1) $[L^{\frac{1}{2}}T^{-\frac{1}{2}}]$ (2) $[L^{-1}T]$

(3) $[LT^{-1}$ (4) $[L^{-\frac{1}{2}}T^{\frac{1}{2}}]$

Sol. : **(3)**

15. Sound waves travel at 350 m/s through a warm air and at 3500 m/s through brass. The wavelength of a 700 Hz acoustic wave as it enters brass from warm air : **[AIPMT 2011]**

(1) decreases by a factor 10

(2) increases by a factor 20

(3) increases by a factor 10

(4) decreases by a factor 20

Sol. : **(3)** Here, $v_{air} = 350$ m/s, $v_{brass} = 3500$ m/s

When a sound wave travels from one medium to another its frequency remains the same

$\because$ Frequency, $\upsilon = \frac{v}{\lambda}$

Since υ remains the same in both medium

$\Rightarrow \frac{\upsilon_{air}}{\lambda_{air}} = \frac{\upsilon_{brass}}{\lambda_{brass}}$

$$\lambda_{brass} = \lambda_{air} \times \frac{v_{brass}}{v_{air}} = \lambda_{air} \times \frac{3500}{350} = 10\lambda_{air}$$

16. Two identical piano wires, kept under the same tension T have a fundamental frequency of 600 Hz. The fractional increase in the tension of one of the wires which will lead to occurrence of 6 beats/s when both the wires oscillate together would be :- **[AIPMT 2011]**

(1) 0.01 (2) 0.02 (3) 0.03 (4) 0.04

Sol. : **(2)** As $\upsilon = \frac{1}{2L}\sqrt{\frac{T}{\mu}}$. $\therefore \frac{\Delta\upsilon}{\upsilon} = \frac{1}{2}\frac{\Delta T}{T}$

$$\frac{\Delta T}{T} = 2\frac{\Delta\upsilon}{\upsilon} = 2 \times \frac{6}{600} = 0.02$$

17. A string is cut into three parts, having fundamental frquencies n_1, n_2 and n_3 respectively. Then original fundamental frequency 'n' related by the expression as (other quantities are identical) :- **[AIPMT 2000, (Pre.) 12]**

(1) $\frac{1}{n} = \frac{1}{n_1} + \frac{1}{n_2} + \frac{1}{n_3}$ (2) $n = n_1 \times n_2 \times n_3$

(3) $n = n_1 + n_2 + n_3$ (4) $n = \frac{n_1 + n_2 + n_3}{3}$

Sol. : **(1)** $\ell = \ell_1 + \ell_1 + \ell_3$

$$\frac{k}{n} = \frac{k}{n_1} + \frac{k}{n_2} + \frac{k}{n_3} \Rightarrow \frac{1}{n} = \frac{1}{n_1} + \frac{1}{n_2} + \frac{1}{n_3}.$$

18. Two sources of sound placed closed to each other, are emitting progressive waves given by

$y_1 = 4 \sin 600\pi t$ and $y_2 = 5 \sin 608\pi t$

An observer located near these two sources ratio sound will hear :- **[AIPMT (Pre.) 2012]**

(1) 8 beats per second with intensity ratio 81 : 1 between waxing and waning

(2) 4 beats per second with intensity ratio 81 : 1 between waxing and waning

(3) 4 beats per second with intensity ratio 25 : 16 between waxing and waning

(4) 8 beats per second with intensity ratio 25 : 16 between waxing and waning

Sol. : **(1)** Given : $y_1 = 4\sin 600\pi t, y_2 = 5\sin 608\pi t$

$\therefore \omega_1 = 600\pi$ or $2\pi\upsilon_1 = 600\pi$ or $\upsilon_1 = 300$

$A_1 = 4$

and $\omega_2 = 608\pi$ or $2\pi\upsilon_2 = 608\pi$ or $\upsilon_2 = 304$

$A_2 = 5$

Number of beats heard per secound

$= \upsilon_1 - \upsilon_2 = 304 - 300 = 4$

$$\frac{(I_{max})_1}{(I_{max})_2} = \frac{(A_1 + A_2)^2}{(A_1 - A_2)^2} = \frac{(4+5)^2}{(4-5)^2} = \frac{81}{1}$$

19. A train moving at a speed of 220 ms^{-1} towards a stationary object, emits a sound of frequency 1000Hz. Some of the sound reaching the object gets reflected back to the train as echo. The frequency of the echo as detected by the driver of the train is : (speed of sound in air is 330 ms^{-1}) **[AIPMT (Mains) 2012]**

(1) 5000 Hz (2) 3000 Hz

(3) 3500 Hz (4) 4000 Hz

Sol. : **(1)** Here,

Speed of the train, $\upsilon_r = 220 \text{ ms}^{-1}$

Speed of sound in air, $\upsilon = 330 \text{ ms}^{-1}$

The frequency of the echo detected by the deiver of the train is

$$\upsilon' = \upsilon_0\left(\frac{\upsilon + \upsilon_T}{\upsilon - \upsilon_T}\right) = 1000\left(\frac{330+220}{330-220}\right)$$

$$= 1000 \times \frac{550}{110} = 5000 \text{ Hz}$$

20. The two nearest harmonics of a tube closed at one end and open at other end are 220 Hz and 260 Hz. What is the fundamental frequency of the system ? **[NEET - 2017]**

(1) 10 Hz (2) 20 Hz

(3) 30 Hz (4) 40 Hz

Sol. : **(2)** Two successive frequemcies of closed pipe

$$\frac{nv}{4l} = 220 \quad ...(i)$$

$$\frac{(n+2)v}{4l} = 260 \quad ...(ii)$$

Dividing (ii) by (i), we get

$$\frac{n+2}{n} = \frac{260}{220} = \frac{13}{11}$$

$11n + 22 = 13n$; n = 11

So, $11\frac{v}{4l} = 220$; $\frac{v}{4l} = 20$

So fundamental frequency is 20 Hz.

21. Two cars moving in opposite directions approach each other with speed of 22 m/s and 16.5 m/s respectively. The driver of the first car blows a horn having a frequency 400 Hz. The frequency heard by the driver of the second car is [velocity of sound 340 m/s] : **[NEET - 2017]**

(1) 350 Hz (2) 361 Hz

(3) 411 Hz (4) 448 Hz

Sol. : **(4)** $f_A = f\left[\frac{v + v_o}{v - v_s}\right]$

$$= 400\left[\frac{340+16.5}{340-22}\right]$$

$f_A = 448$.

22. The fundamental frequency in an organ pipe is equal to the third harmonic of a closed organ pipe. If the length of the close organ pipe is 20 cm, the length of the open organ pipe is **[NEET-2018]**

(1) 12.5cm (2) 8 cm

(3) 13.2 cm (4) 16 cm

Ans. **(3)**

23. A tuning fork is used to produce resonance in a glass tube. The length of the air column in this tube can be adjusted by a variable piston. At room temperature of 27°C two successive resonances are produced at 20 cm and 73 cm of column length. If the frequency of the tuning fork is 320 Hz, the velocity of sound in air at 27°C is **[NEET-2018]**

(1) 350m/s (2) 339 m/s

(3) 330 m/s (4) 300 m/s

Ans. **(2)**

15 Electric Charges and Fields

Note: Scan QR code with your mobile camera or QR scanner for video solutions.

1. A hollow cylinder has a charge q coulomb within it. If f is the electric flux in units of voltmeter associated with the curved surface B, the flux linked with the plane surface A in units of voltmeter will be **[AIPMT 2007]**

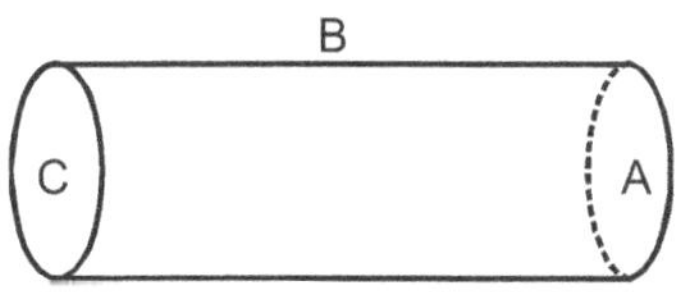

(1) $\frac{q}{\epsilon_0}-\phi$ (2) $\frac{1}{2}\left[\frac{q}{\epsilon_0}-\phi\right]$ (3) $\frac{q}{2\epsilon_0}$ (4) $\frac{\phi}{3}$

Sol. **(2) :** $\phi_{total}=\phi_{curved}+\phi_{plane\,surface}=\frac{q}{\epsilon_0}$

$\phi=2\phi_A=\frac{q}{\epsilon_0}\Rightarrow\phi_A=\frac{1}{2}\left(\frac{q}{\epsilon_0}-\phi\right).$

2. Three point charges +q, –2q and +q are placed at points (x = 0, y = a, z = 0), (x = 0, y = 0, z = 0) and (x = a, y = 0, z = 0) respectively. The magnitude and direction of the electric dipole moment vector of this charge assembly are :– **[AIPMT 2007]**

(1) $\sqrt{2}$ qa along + x direction

(2) $\sqrt{2}$ qa along + y direction

(3) $\sqrt{2}$ qa along the line joining points

(x = 0, y = 0, z = 0) and (x = a, y = a, z = 0)

(4) qa along the line joining points

(x = 0, y = 0, z = 0) and (x = a, y = a, z = 0)

Sol. **(2) :** Magnitute $=\sqrt{p^2+p^2}=\sqrt{2}p=\sqrt{2}qa$

Direction is shown in figure.

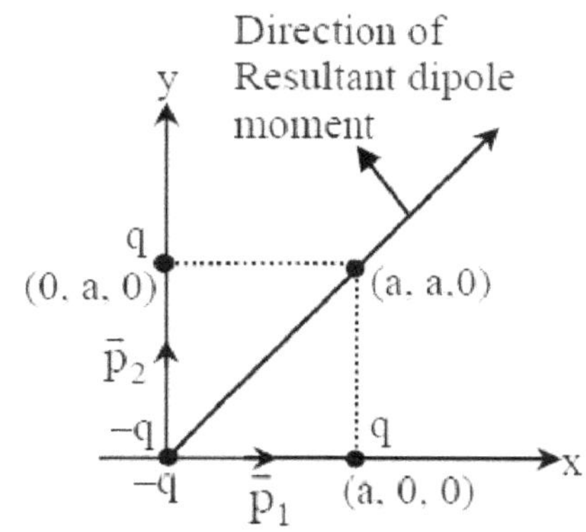

3. A thin conducing ring of radius R is given a charge +Q. The electric field at the centre O of the ring due to the charge on the part AKB of the ring is E. The electric field at the centre due to the charge on the part ACDB of the ring is **[AIPMT 2008]**

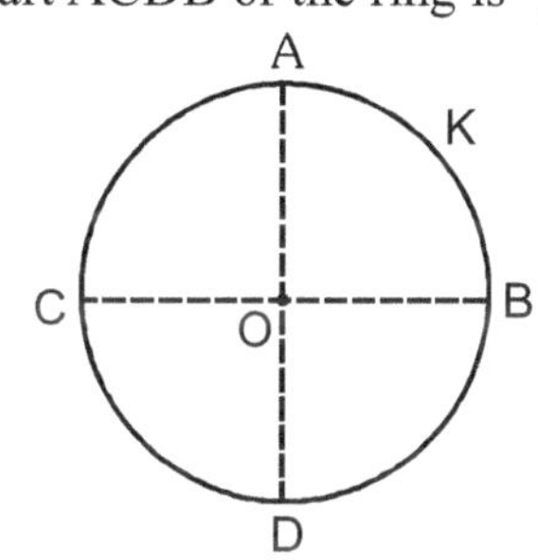

(1) 3E along KO (2) E along OK
(3) E along KO (4) 3 E along OK

Sol. **(2) :** Electric field due to the given charged ring is zero at centre *'O'*. So electric field due to *AKB* is equal and opposite to electric field due to *ACDB*, from the principle of superposition.

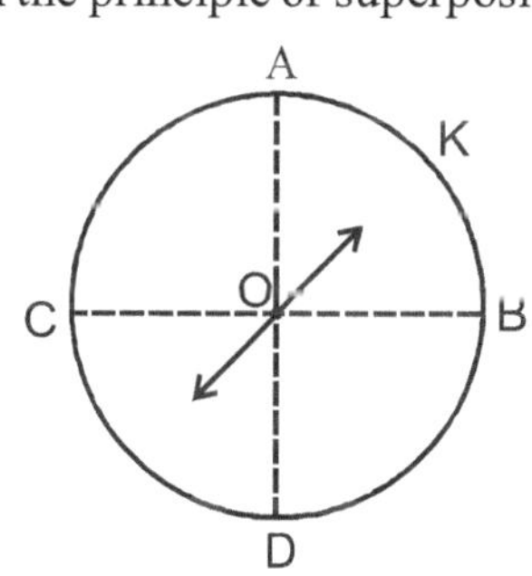

Since $\vec{E}$ is field strength of O along $\overrightarrow{KO}$ So electric field strength due to *ACDB* along $\overrightarrow{OK}$ and it is equal to E.

4. The mean free path of electrons in a metal is 4×10^{-8} m. The electric field which can give on an average 2 eV energy to an electron in the metal will be in unit of Vm^{-1} **[AIPMT 2009]**

(1) 8×10^{-7} (2) 5×10^{-11}

(3) 8×10^{-11} (4) 5×10^{7}

Sol. **(4) :** $qv = 2ev$

$$\Rightarrow 1.6 \times 10^{-19}V = 2 \times 1.6 \times 10^{-19}V$$

$$\Rightarrow \quad V^1 = 2V \ ; \qquad E = \frac{V}{d}$$

$$\Rightarrow \quad E = \frac{2V}{4 \times 10^{-8}} = 5 \times 10^7$$

5. Two positive ions each carrying a charge q, are separted by a distance d. If F is the force of repulsion between the ions, the number of electrons missing from each ion will be (e being the charge on an electron) **[AIPMT 2010]**

(1) $\frac{4\ {}_0Fd^2}{e^2}$ (2) $\sqrt{\frac{4\ {}_0Fd^2}{d^2}}$

(3) $\sqrt{\frac{4\ {}_0Fd^2}{e^2}}$ (4) $\frac{4\ {}_0Fd^2}{q^2}$

Sol. **(3) :** q• ←— d —→ •q

$$F = \frac{(ne)^2}{4\pi \in_0 d^2} \Rightarrow n = \sqrt{\frac{4\pi \in_0 Fd^2}{e^2}}.$$

6. A square surface of side L metre in the plane of the paper is placed in a uniform electric field E (volt/m) acting along the same place at an angle q with the horizontal side of the square as shown in the figure. The electric flux linked to the surface in uint of V- m is. **[AIPMT 2010]**

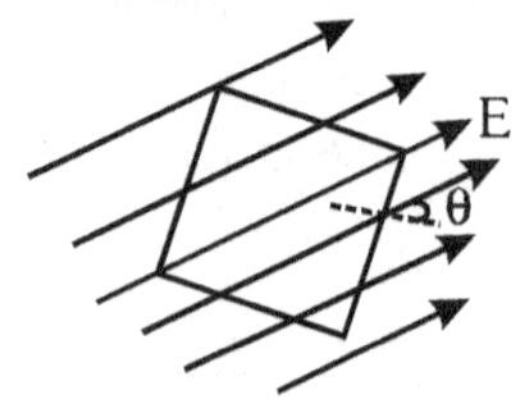

(1) EL^2 (2) $EL^2 \cos q$

(3) $EL^2 \sin q$ (4) 0

Sol. **(4) :** Here $\vec{E} \perp$ Area Vector

7. The electic filed at a distance 3R/2 from the center of a charged conducting spherical shell of radius R is E. The elecrtric field at a distance R/2 from the center of the sphere is **[AIPMT 2010]**

(1) $\frac{E}{2}$ (2) zero

(3) E (4) $\frac{E}{4}$

Sol. **(2) :** Electric field inside a charged conductor is always zero.

8. A charge Q is enclosed by a Gaussian spherical suface of radius R. If the radius is doubled, then the outward electric flux will **[AIPMT 2011]**

(1) be reduced of half

(2) remain the same

(3) be doubled

(4) increase four times

Sol. **(2) :** $\phi_{net} = \frac{\Sigma q}{\epsilon_0}$

∵ Net flux does not depend on size of Gaussian surface

⇒ Flux remains unchanged.

9. The electric potential V at any point (x,y, z), all in metres in space is given by V = $4x^2$ volt. The electric field at the point (1,0,2) in volt/ metre is **[AIPMT 2011]**

(1) 8 along positive X-axis

(2) 16 along negative X-axis

(3) 16 along positive X-axis

(4) 8 along negative X-axis

Sol. **(4) :** $\vec{E} = -\vec{\nabla} V$

$$\therefore \vec{E} = -\left[\hat{i}\frac{\partial V}{\partial x} + \hat{j}\frac{\partial V}{\partial y} + \hat{k}\frac{\partial V}{\partial z}\right]$$

Here, $V - 4x^2 \;\therefore\; \vec{E} = -8x\hat{i}$

The electric field at point (1, 0, 2) is

$$\vec{E}_{(1,0,2)} = -8\hat{i}\ \text{Vm}^{-1}$$

So electric field is along the negative X-axis.

10. Three charges each+q, are placed at the corners of an isosceles triangle ABC of sides BC and AC,2a, D and E are the mid-points of BC and CA the work done in taking a charge Q from D to E is **[AIPMT 2011]**

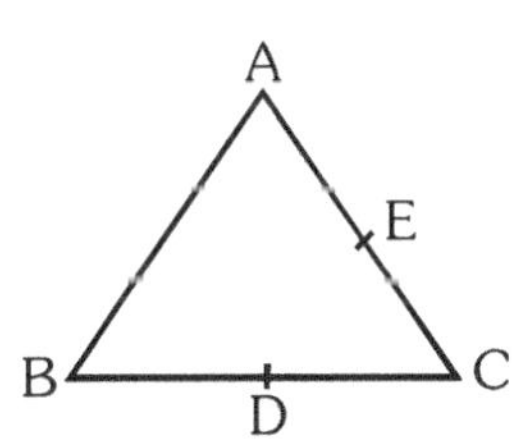

(1) $\frac{eqQ}{8\ {}_0a}$ (2) $\frac{qQ}{4\ {}_0a}$ (3) zero (4) $\frac{3qQ}{4\ {}_0a}$

Sol. (3) :

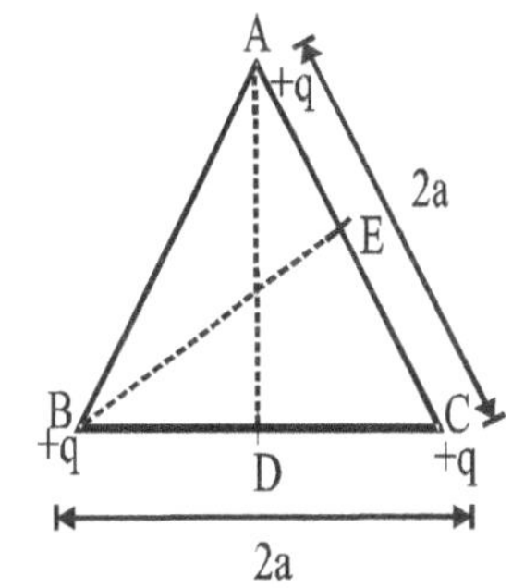

In Δ ADC, $(AD)^2 = (AC)^2 - (DC)^2$

$$= (2a)^2 - (a)^2 = 4a^2 - a^2 = 3a^2$$

$$AD = a\sqrt{3}$$

Similarly, Potential at point D due to the given charge configuration is

$$V_D = \frac{1}{4\pi\varepsilon_0}\left[\frac{q}{BD} + \frac{q}{DC} + \frac{q}{AD}\right]$$

$$= \frac{q}{4\pi\varepsilon_0}\left[\frac{1}{a} + \frac{1}{a} + \frac{1}{\sqrt{3}a}\right] = \frac{q}{4\pi\varepsilon_0 a}\left[2 + \frac{1}{\sqrt{3}}\right] \quad ...(i)$$

Potential at point E due to the given charge configuration is

$$V_E = \frac{1}{4\pi\varepsilon_0}\left[\frac{q}{AE} + \frac{q}{EC} + \frac{q}{BE}\right]$$

$$= \frac{q}{4\pi\varepsilon_0}\left[\frac{1}{a} + \frac{1}{a} + \frac{1}{\sqrt{3}a}\right] = \frac{q}{4\pi\varepsilon_0 a}\left[2 + \frac{1}{\sqrt{3}}\right] \quad ......(ii)$$

From the (i) and (ii), it is clear that

$V_D = V_E$

The work done in taking a charge Q from D to E is

$$W = Q(V_E - V_D) = 0 \qquad (\because V_D = V_E).$$

11. An electric dipole of moment 'P' is placed in an electric field of intensity 'E'. The dipole acquires a positon such that the axis of the dipole makes an angle q with the direction of the field. Assuming that the potential energy of the dipole to be zero when q = 90°, the torque and the potential energy of the dipole will respectively be **[AIPMT 2012]**

(1) pE cos θ, – pE sin q = 0

(2) pE sin θ, – pE cos q = 0

(3) pE sin θ, – 2pE cos q = 0

(4) pE sin θ, 2pE cos q = 0

Sol. **(2) :** Toque $\tau = PE\sin\theta$ and Potential energy $U = -PE\cos\theta$.

12. What is the flux through a cube of side 'a' if a point charge of q is at one of its corner ? **[AIPMT 2012]**

(1) $\frac{q}{4\ \ 0}6a^2$ (2) $\frac{2q}{0}$ (3) $\frac{q}{8\ \ 0}$ (4) $\frac{q}{0}$

Sol. **(3) :** flux $\phi = \frac{q}{8|\epsilon_0}$

13. Two metallic sphere of radii 1 cm and 3 c m are given charges of -1×10^{-2} C and respectively. If these are connected by a conducting wire, the final charge on the bigger sphere is **[AIMPT 2012]**

(1) 2×10^{-2} C (2) 3×10^{-2} C

(3) 4×10^{-2} C (4) 1×10^{-2} C

Sol. **(2) :** When the given metallic spheres are connected by a conducting wire, charge will flow till both the spheres acquire a common potential which is given by Common potential,

$$V = \frac{q_1 + q_2}{C_1 + C_2} = \frac{-1\times10^{-2} + 5\times10^{-2}}{4\pi\varepsilon_0 R_1 + 4\pi\varepsilon_0 R_1}$$

$$= \frac{4\times10^{-2}}{4\pi\varepsilon_0(1\times10^{-2} + 3\times10^{-2})}$$

$$= \frac{4\times10^{-2}}{4\pi\varepsilon_0 \times 4\times10^{-2}}$$

$\therefore$ Final charge on the bigger sphere is

$$= 4\pi\varepsilon_0 \times 3\times10^{-2} \times = \frac{4\times10^{-2}}{4\pi\varepsilon_0 \times 4\times10^{-2}} \quad \text{(Using(i))}$$

$$= 3\times10^{-2}\text{ C}.$$

14. Two pith balls carrying equal charges are suspended from a common point by stringes of equal length, the equlibrium separation between them is r. Now the strings are rigidly clamped at half the height. The equilibrium separation between the balls now become **[AIPMT 2013]**

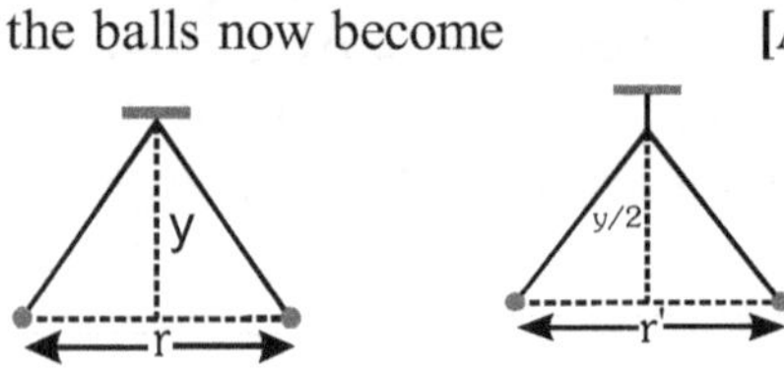

(1) $\frac{1}{\sqrt{2}}^{\,2}$ (2) $\frac{r}{\sqrt[3]{2}}$

(3) $\frac{2r}{\sqrt{3}}$ (4) $\frac{2r}{3}$

Sol. **(2) :** Let m be mass of on each ball and q be charge on each ball.

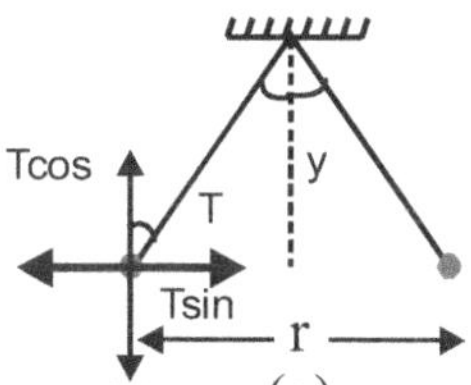

(a)

Force of repulsion,

$$F = \frac{1}{4\pi\varepsilon_0}\frac{q^2}{r^2}$$

In equilibrium

$$T\cos\theta = mg \qquad ....(i)$$

$$T\sin\theta = F \qquad ....(ii)$$

Divide (ii) by (i), we get

$$\tan\theta = \frac{F}{mg} = \frac{\frac{1}{4\pi\varepsilon_0}\frac{q}{r^2}}{mg}$$

From figure (a),

$$\frac{r/2}{y} = \frac{\frac{1}{4\pi\varepsilon_0}\frac{q}{r^2}}{mg} \qquad ....(iii)$$

$$\tan\theta' = \frac{\frac{1}{4\pi\varepsilon_0}\frac{q^2}{r'^2}}{mg}$$

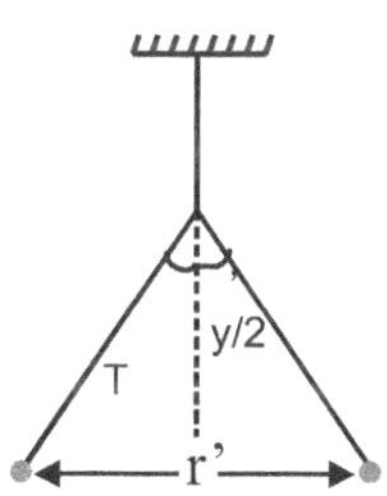

From figure (b)

$$\frac{r'/2}{y/2} = \frac{\frac{1}{4\pi\varepsilon_0}\frac{q^2}{r'^2}}{mg} \qquad ....(iv)$$

Divide (iv) by (iii), we get

$$\frac{2r'}{r} = \frac{r^2}{r'^2}$$

$$r'^3 = \frac{r^3}{2} = r' = \frac{r}{\sqrt[3]{2}}$$

15. The electric field in a certain region is acting radially outward and is given by E = Ar . A charge contained in a sphere of radius 'a' centred at the origin of the filed will be given by **[AIMPT 2015]**

(1) $4\pi\varepsilon_0 Aa^2$ (2) $4\pi\varepsilon_0 a^2$

(3) $4\pi\varepsilon_0 Aa^3$ (4) $\varepsilon_0 Aa^2$

Sol. **(3) :** $ES = \frac{Q}{\varepsilon_0}$

$$(Aa) \times 4\pi a^2 = \frac{Q}{\varepsilon_0}$$

$$Q = 4\pi\varepsilon_0 Aa^3.$$

16. Two identical charged spheres suspended from a common point by two massless strings of lengths l, are initially at a distance d (d << l) apart because of their mutual repulsion. The charges begin to leak from both the spheres at a constant rate. As a result, the spheres approach each other with avelocity v. Then v varies as a function of the distance x between the spheres, as :

[AIPMT 2016]

(1) v $x^{\frac{1}{2}}$ (2) v x

(3) v $x^{-\frac{1}{2}}$ (4) v x^{-1}

Sol. **(3) :**

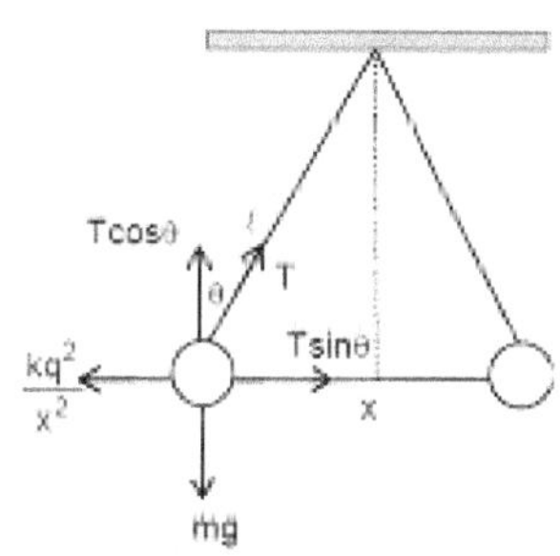

$$T\sin\theta = \frac{kq^2}{x^2}$$

$$T\cos\theta = mg$$

Dividing the equations

$$\tan\theta = \frac{kq^2}{mgx^2} \text{ here } \tan\theta \approx \sin\theta = \frac{x}{2\ell}$$

$$\Rightarrow \quad \frac{x}{2\ell} = \frac{kq^2}{x^2}$$

$$\Rightarrow \quad q \propto x^{3/2}$$

$$\Rightarrow \quad \frac{dq}{dt} \propto \frac{3}{2}x^{1/2}\left(\frac{dx}{dt}\right) \quad \Rightarrow \quad \frac{dx}{dt} \propto x^{-1/2}$$

17. An electric dipole is placed at an angle of 30° with an electric field intensity 2×10^5 N/C. It experiences a torque equal to 4 Nm. The charge on the dipole, if the dipole length is 2 cm, is :-

[NEET- II(2016)]

(1) 5 mC (2) 7 μC (3) 8 mC (4) 2 mC

Sol. **(4) :** $\tau = PE\sin\theta$

$$4 = P \times 2 \times 10^5 \times \frac{1}{2}$$

$$\Rightarrow P = 4\times10^{-5}\ \text{cm} = q \times 2 \times 10^{-2}$$

$$\text{So } q = \frac{4\times10^{-5}}{2\times10^{-2}} = 2\times10^{-3} \text{ Coulomb.}$$

18. Suppose the charge of a proton and an electron differ slightly. One of them is – e, the other is $(e+\Delta e)$. If the net of electrostatic force and gravitational force between two hydrogen atoms placed at a distance d (much greater than atomic size). Apart is zero, then Δe is of the order of [Given mass of hydrogen $m_h = 1.67 \times 10^{-27}$ kg]

(NEET - (2017)

(1) 10^{-20} C (2) 10^{-23} C

(3) 10^{-37} C (4) 10^{-47} C

Sol. **(3) :** $F_e = F_g$

$$\frac{1}{4\pi\varepsilon_0}\frac{\Delta e^2}{d^2} = \frac{Gm^2}{d^2}$$

$$9\times10^9(\Delta e^2) = 6.67\times10^{-11}\times1.67 \times10^{-27}\times1.67\times10^{-27}$$

$$\Delta e^2 = \frac{6.67\times1.67\times1.67}{9}\times10^{-74}$$

$$\Delta e \approx 10^{-37}.$$

19. A set of 'n' equal resistor, 'R' each, are connected in series to a battery of emf 'E' and internal resistance 'R'. The current drawn is I. Now, the 'n' resistors are connected in parallel to the same battery. Then the current drawn from battery becomes 10 I. The value of 'n' is **[NEET-2018]**

(1) 20 (2) 11

(3) 10 (4) 9

Ans. **(3)**

20. A toy car with charge q moves on a frictionless horizontal plane surface under the influence of a uniform electric field $\vec{E}$. Due to the force $q\vec{E}$, its velocity increases from 0 to 6 m/s in one second duration. At that instant the direction of the field is reversed. The car continues to move for two more second under the influence of this field . The average velocity and the average speed of the toy car between 0 to 3 seconds are respectively.

[NEET-2018]

(1) 1 m/s, 3.5 m/s (2) 1 m/s, 3 m/s

(3) 2 m/s, 4 m/s, (4) 1.5 m/s, 3 m/s,

Ans. **(3)**

16 Electrostatic Potential and Capacitance

Note: Scan QR code with your mobile camera or QR scanner for video solutions.

1. Charge +q and –q are placed at points A and B respectively which are a distance 2L apart, C is the midpoint between A and B. The work done in moving a charge +Q along the semicircle CRD is **[AIPMT 2007]**

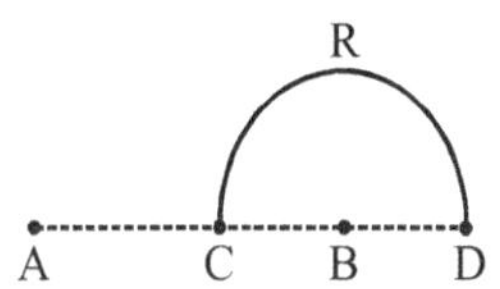

(1) $\frac{qQ}{4\pi\varepsilon_0 L}$ (2) $\frac{qQ}{2\pi\varepsilon_0 L}$

(3) $\frac{qQ}{6\pi\varepsilon_0 L}$ (4) $-\frac{qQ}{6\pi\varepsilon_0 L}$

Sol. **(4) :** $W = \Delta U = Q(V_D - V_C)$ here $V_C = 0$

$$= Q\left[\frac{q}{4\pi\in_0(3L)} - \frac{q}{4\pi\in_0(L)} - 0\right] = \frac{-Qq}{6\pi\in_0 L}.$$

2. Two condensers, one of capacity C and the other of capacity C/2, are connected to a V volt battery, as shown. **[AIPMT 2007]**

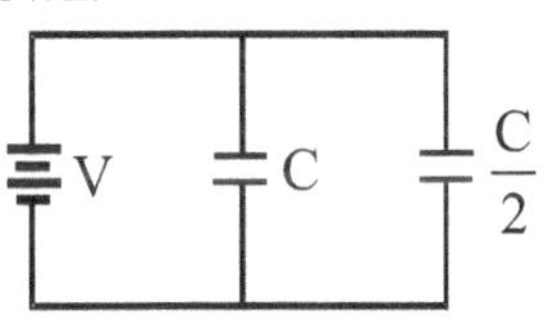

(1) $2CV^2$ (2) $\frac{1}{4}CV^2$

(3) $\frac{3}{4}CV^2$ (4) $\frac{1}{2}CV^2$

Sol. **(3) :** Work done in charging fully both the condensers $= \frac{1}{2}CV^2 + \frac{1}{2}\left(\frac{C}{2}\right)V^2 = \frac{3}{4}CV^2$.

3. The electric potential at a point in free sapce due to a charge Q coulomb is $Q \times 10^{11}$ volts. The electric field at that point is **[AIPMT 2008]**

(1) $4\pi\varepsilon_0 Q\times10^{22}$ V/m

(2) $12\pi\varepsilon_0 Q\times10^{20}$ V/m

(3) $4\pi\varepsilon_0 Q\times10^{20}$ V/m

(4) $12\pi\varepsilon_0 Q\times10^{22}$ V/m

Sol. **(3) :** Since $V = \frac{Q}{4\pi\varepsilon_0 r}$ and $E = \frac{Q}{4\pi\varepsilon_0 r^2}$;

Given $V = Q\times10^{11} = Q4\pi\varepsilon_0 r$

$\Rightarrow r = \frac{1}{4\pi\varepsilon_0\times10^{11}}$ i.e., $E = \frac{V}{r}$

$\Rightarrow E = \frac{QV}{r} = Q\times10^{11}\times4\pi\varepsilon_0\times10^{11}$

$= 4\pi\varepsilon_0 Q\times10^{22}$ volt m^{-1}

4. The energy required to charge a parallel plate condenser of plate separation d and plate area of cross-section A such that the uniform electric field between the plates is E is **[AIPMT 2008]**

(1) $\frac{1}{2}\ {}_0E^2/Ad$ (2) ε_0E^2/Ad

(3) ε_0E^2Ad (4) $\frac{1}{2}\ {}_0E^2Ad$

Sol. **(3) :** Energy stored in capacitor for field

$E = \frac{1}{2}CV^2$

$= \frac{1}{2}\left(\frac{\varepsilon_0 A}{d}\right)(E.d)^2$

$= \frac{1}{2}\varepsilon_0 AE^2d$

Energy stored in capacitor + Energy loss in the process of charging = Energy given by cell.

$$=\left(\frac{A\varepsilon_0}{d}\right)V^2$$

= 2 × Energy stored in capacitor

Since energy stored in capacitor = Energy loss in the process of storing the charge in capacitor.

5. Three concentric spherical shells have radii a, b and c (a < b < c) and have surface charge densities σ,–σ and σ respectively. If V_A, V_B and V_C denote the potentials of the three shells, then for c = a + b, we have **[AIPMT 2009]**

(1) $V_C=V_A\neq V_B$ (2) $V_C=V_B\neq V_A$

(3) $V_C\neq V_B\neq V_A$ (4) $V_C=V_B=V_A$

Sol. **(1) :** $q_A = 4\pi a^2\sigma$,

$$q_B = -4\pi b^2\sigma,$$

$$q_C = 4\pi c^2\sigma,\ c = a + b$$

$$V_A = \frac{1}{4\pi\epsilon_0}\left(\frac{q_A}{a}+\frac{q_B}{b}+\frac{q_C}{c}\right) \quad = \frac{2\sigma a}{\epsilon_0}$$

$$V_B = \frac{1}{4\pi\epsilon_0}\left(\frac{q_A}{a}+\frac{q_B}{b}+\frac{q_C}{c}\right)$$

$$=\frac{\sigma}{\epsilon_0}\left(\frac{a^2}{b}-b+c\right)$$

$$=\frac{\sigma}{\epsilon_0}\left(a+\frac{a^2}{b}\right)$$

$$V_C = \frac{1}{4\pi\epsilon_0}\left(\frac{q_A}{a}+\frac{q_B}{b}+\frac{q_C}{c}\right)$$

$$=\frac{\sigma}{\epsilon_0}\left(\frac{a^2-b}{c}+c\right)=\frac{2\sigma a}{\epsilon_0}$$

So, $V_C = V_A \neq V_B$

6. Three capacitors each of capacitance C and of breakdown voltage V are joined in series. The capacitance and breakdown voltage of the combination will be **[AIPMT 2009]**

(1) $\frac{C}{3},\frac{V}{3}$ (2) $3C,\frac{V}{3}$

(3) $\frac{C}{3},3V$ (4) $3C,3V$

Sol. **(3) :** In series, $C_{eq}=\frac{C}{3},\ \ V_{eq}=3V$.

7. The electric potential at a point (x,y,z) is given by **[AIPMT 2009]**

$$V = -x^2y - xz^3 + 4$$

The electric field $\vec{E}$ at that point is

(1) $\vec{E}=\hat{i}\ 2xy+z^3\ +\hat{j}\,x^2+\hat{k}\,3xz^2$

(2) $\vec{E}=\hat{i}\,2xy+\hat{j}\ (x^2\ \ y^2)\ \ \hat{k}\ (3xz-y^2)$

(3) $\vec{E}=\hat{i}\ z^3\ \ \hat{j}\ xyz\ \ \hat{k}\ z^2$

(4) $\vec{E}=\hat{i}\ 2xy-z^3\ +\hat{j}\ xy^2+\hat{k}\,3z^2x$

Sol. **(1) :** $V=-x^2y-xz^3+4$

$$\vec{E}=\bar{\nabla}V=-\left(\hat{i}\frac{\delta}{\delta x}+\hat{j}\frac{\delta}{\delta y}+\hat{k}\frac{\delta}{\delta z}\right)\ (-x^2-xz^3+4)$$

$$\vec{E}=\hat{i}(2xy+z^3)\hat{i}+x^2\hat{j}+3xz^2\hat{k}.$$

8. A series combination of n_1 capacitors, each of value C_1, is charged by a source of potential difference 4V. When another parallel combination of n_2 capacitors, each of value C_2, is charged by a source of potential difference V, it has the same (total) energy stored in it, as the first combination has, The value of C_2, in terms of C_1, is then **[AIPMT 2010]**

(1) $\frac{2C_1}{n_1 n_2}$ (2) $16\frac{n_2}{n_1}C_1$

(3) $2\frac{n_1}{n_1}C_1$ (4) $\frac{16C_1}{n_1 n_2}$

Sol. **(4) :** $\frac{1}{2}\left(\frac{C_1}{n_1}\right)(4V)^2 = \frac{1}{2}(n_2c_2) \Rightarrow C_2 = \frac{16C_1}{n_1n_2}$

9. A parallel plate condenser has a uniform electric field E (V/m) in the space between the plates. If the distance between the plates is d (m) and area of each plate is A(m^2) the energy (joule) stored in the condenser is **[AIPMT 2011]**

(1) $\frac{1}{2}\ {}_0E^2$ (2) $\varepsilon_0 EAd$

(3) $\frac{1}{2}\ {}_0E^2Ad$ (4) E^2Ad/ε_0

Sol. **(3) :** $U - \frac{1}{2}CV^2$

$= \frac{1}{2}\left(\frac{\epsilon_0 A}{d}\right)V^2$

$= \frac{1}{2}\epsilon_0 AD\left(\frac{V}{d}\right)^2 - \frac{1}{2}\epsilon_0 E^2AD$

10. Four electric charges +q, +q, –q are placed at the corners of a square of side 2L (see figure). The electric potential at point A, mid-way between the two charge +q and +q, is **[AIPMT 2011]**

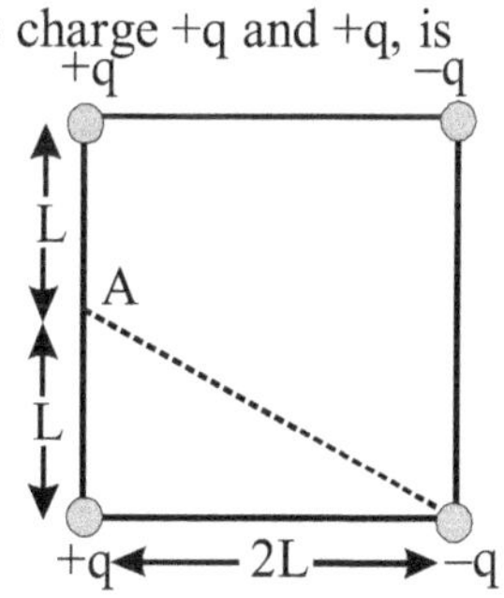

(1) $\frac{1}{4\pi\varepsilon_0}\frac{2q}{L}\ 1+\frac{1}{\sqrt{5}}$

(2) $\frac{1}{4\pi\varepsilon_0}\frac{2q}{L}\ 1-\frac{1}{\sqrt{5}}$

(3) Zero

(4) $\frac{1}{4\pi\varepsilon_0}\frac{2q}{L}\ 1+\sqrt{5}$

Sol. **(2) :** $V_A = \frac{kq}{L} + \frac{kq}{L} - \frac{kq}{\sqrt{5}L} - \frac{kq}{\sqrt{5}L}$

$= \frac{2kq}{L}\left(1 - \frac{1}{\sqrt{5}}\right).$

11. The potential energy of a particle in a force field is : $U = \frac{A}{r^2} - \frac{B}{r}$, where A and B are positive constants and r is the distance of particle from the centre of the field. For stable equilibrium the distance of the particle is **[AIPMT 2012]**

(1) B/A (2) B/2A

(3) 2A/B (4) A/B

Sol. **(3) :** For Stable equilibrium, $F = -\frac{dU}{dr} = 0$

we get $r = 2A/B$.

12. Four point charges –Q,–q, 2q and 2Q are placed, one at each corner of the square. The relation between Q and q for which the potential at the centre of the square is zero is **[AIPMT 2012]**

(1) $\frac{1}{q}$ (2) $Q = -q$

(3) $Q \; -\frac{1}{q}$ (4) $Q = q$

Sol. **(2) :** Potential V at centre of the square

$$= \frac{-kQ}{r} - \frac{kq}{r} + \frac{k2Q}{r} + \frac{k2q}{r} = 0; \text{ So } Q = -q.$$

13. A, B and C, are three points in a uniform electric field. The electric potential is **[AIPMT 2013]**

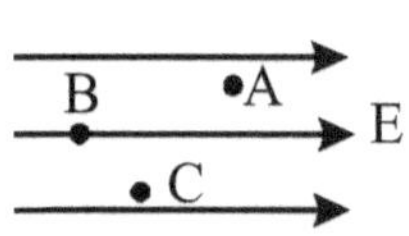

(1) Maximum at A

(2) Maximum at B

(3) Maximum at C

(4) Same at all the three points A, B and C

Sol. **(2) :** In the direction of electric field, electric potential decreases.

$\therefore V_B > V_C > V_A$

14. Two thin dielectric slabs of dielectric constants K_1 and K_2 ($K_1 < K_2$) are inserted between plates of a parallel plate capacitor, as shown in the figure. The variation of electric field E between the plates with distance d as measured from plate P is correctly shown by **[AIPMT 2014]**

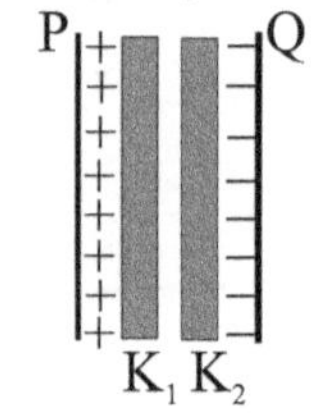

(1)

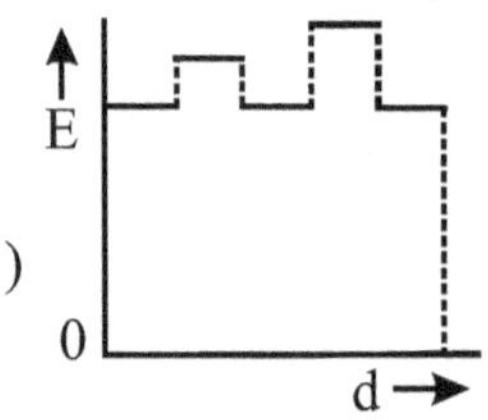

(2)

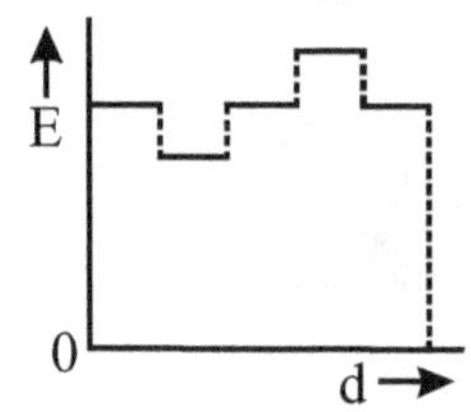

(3)

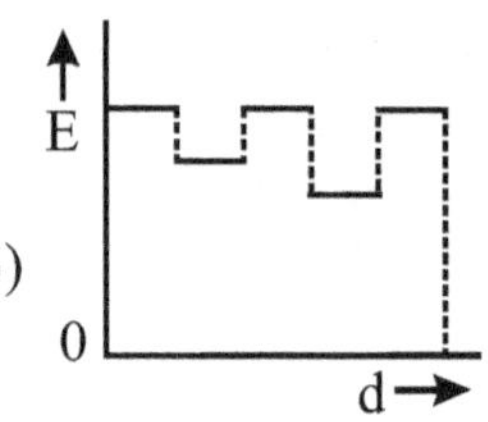

(4)

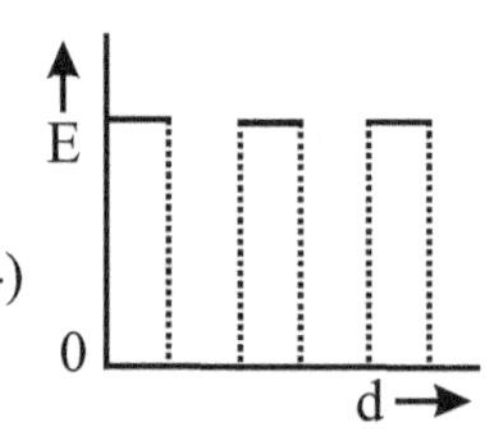

Sol. **(3) :** Electric field, $E \propto \frac{1}{K}$

As $K_1 < K_2$ so $E_1 > E_2$.

15. A conducting sphere of radius R is given a charge Q. The electric potential and the electric field at the centre of the sphere respectively are

(1) Zero and $\frac{Q}{4\pi\varepsilon_0 R^2}$ **[AIPMT 2014]**

(2) $\frac{Q}{4\pi\varepsilon_0 R}$ and Zero

(3) $\frac{Q}{4\pi\varepsilon_0 R}$ and $\frac{Q}{4\pi\varepsilon_0 R^2}$

(4) Both are zero

Sol. **(2) :** At centre, E = 0 & $V = \frac{Q}{4\pi \epsilon_0 R}$.

16. In a region, the potential is represented by V(x,y,z) = 6x – 8xy – 8y + 6yz, where V is in volts and x, y, z are in meters. The electric force experienced by a change of 2 coulomb situated at point (1,1,1) is **[AIPMT 2014]**

(1) $6\sqrt{5}$ N (2) 30 N (3) 24 N (4) $4\sqrt{35}$ N

Sol. **(4) :** $\vec{E} = -\frac{\partial V}{\partial x}\hat{i} - \frac{\partial V}{\partial y}\hat{j} - \frac{\partial V}{\partial z}\hat{k}$

$= -[(6 - 8y)\hat{i} + (-8x - 8 + 6z)\hat{j} + (6y)\hat{k}]$

At (1, 1, 1), $\vec{E} = 2\hat{i} + 10\hat{j} - 6\hat{k}$

$\Rightarrow \left(\vec{E}\right) - \sqrt{2^2 + 10^2 + 6^2} - \sqrt{140} - 4\sqrt{35}$.

17. A parallel plate air capacitor of capacitance C is connected to a cell of emf V and then disconnected from it. A dielectric slab of dielectric constant K, which can just fill the air gap of the capacitor, is now inserted in it. Which of the following is incorrect ? **[AIPMT 2015]**

(1) The potential difference between the plates decreases K times

(2) The energy stored in the capacitor decrease K times

(3) The change in energy stored is $\frac{1}{2}CV^2 \;\; \frac{1}{K} - 1$

(4) The charge on the capacitor is not conserved

Sol. **(4) :** Charge on plate will not change.

18. A parallel plate air capacitor has capacity C distance of separation between plates is d and potential difference V is applied between the plates force of attraction between the plate air capacitor is **[AIPMT 2015]**

(1) $\frac{C^2V^2}{2d^2}$ (2) $\frac{C^2V^2}{2d}$

(3) $\frac{CV^2}{2d}$ (4) $\frac{CV^2}{d}$

Sol. **(3) :** $F = \frac{Q^2}{2\varepsilon_0 A}$

$\because Q - CV$ and $C - \frac{\varepsilon_0 A}{d} \Rightarrow \varepsilon_0 A - Cd$

So $F = \frac{C^2V^2}{2Cd} = \frac{CV^2}{2d}$.

19. If potential (in volts) in a region is experessed as $V(x, y, z) = 6xy - y + 2yz$, the electric field (in N/C) at point (1,1,0) is **[AIPMT 2015]**

(1) $-6\hat{i}+9\hat{j}+\hat{k}$ (2) $-3\hat{i}+5\hat{j}+3\hat{k}$

(3) $-6\hat{i}+5\hat{j}+2\hat{k}$ (4) $-2\hat{i}+3\hat{j}+\hat{k}$

Sol. **(3) :** $\vec{E} = -\frac{\partial V}{\partial x}\hat{i} - \frac{\partial V}{\partial y}\hat{j} - \frac{\partial V}{\partial z}\hat{k}$

$\vec{E} = -(6y)\hat{i} - (6x - 1 + 2z)\hat{j} - (2y)\hat{k}$

at point (1, 1, 0)

$\vec{E} = 6\hat{i} - 5\hat{j} - 2\hat{k} = -\left(6\hat{i} + 5\hat{j} + 2\hat{k}\right)$.

20. A capacitor of 2mF is charged as shown in the diagram. When the switch S is turned to position 2, the percentage of its stored energy dissipated is **[AIPMT 2016]**

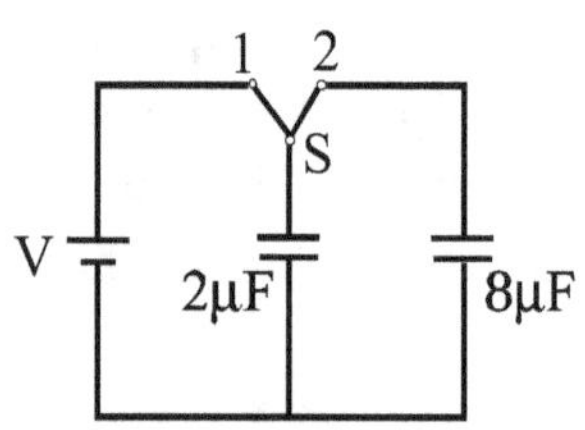

(1) 0% (2) 20% (3) 75% (4) 80%

Sol. **(4) :** Initial energy stored in the 2mF capacitor is

$= \frac{1}{2}(2\mu)V^2 = V^2\mu J$

Energy less

$= \frac{C_1C_2}{2(C_1+C_2)}(V_1 - V_2)^2 = \frac{(2\mu)(8\mu)}{2(2\mu+8\mu)}(v-0)^2$

$E_{loss} = \frac{5}{4}V^2\mu J$

$\% \text{ loss} = \frac{5/4V^2}{V^2} \times 100 = 80\%$.

21. A small signal voltage $V(t) = V_0 \sin ?\, \omega t$ is applied across an ideal capacitor C :- **[AIPMT 2016]**

(1) Current I (t), lags voltage V(t) by 90°.

(2) Over a full cycle the capacitor C does not consume any energy from the voltage source.

(3) Current I (t) is in phase with voltage V(t).

(4) Current I (t) leads voltage V(t) by 180°

Sol. **(2) :** Capacitor does not consume energy effectively over full cycles

22. A parallel-plate capacitor of area A, plateseparation d and capacitance C is filled with four dielectric materials having dielectric constants k_1,k_2, k_3 and k_4 as shown in the figure below. If a single dielectric material is to be used to have the same capacitance C in this capacitor, then its dielectric constant k is given by :- **[NEET – II (2016)]**

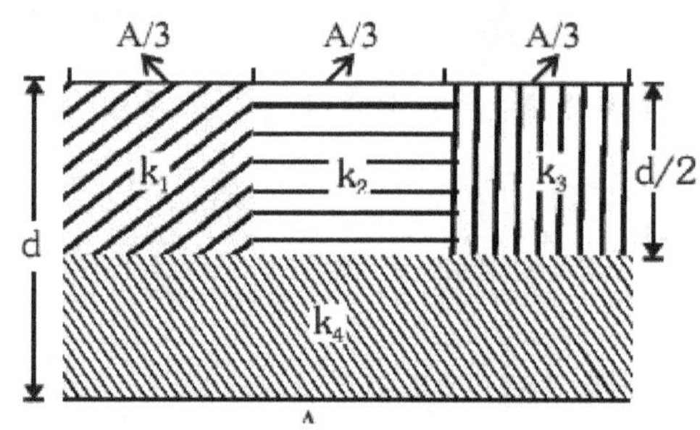

(1) $\frac{2}{k} = \frac{3}{k_1 + k_2 + k_3} + \frac{1}{k_4}$

(2) $\frac{1}{k} = \frac{1}{k_1} + \frac{1}{k_2} \quad \frac{1}{k_3} \quad \frac{3}{2k_4}$

(3) $k = k_1 + k_2 + k_3 = 3k_4$

(4) $k \quad \frac{2}{3} \quad k_1 \quad k_2 \quad k_3$

Sol. **(2) :**

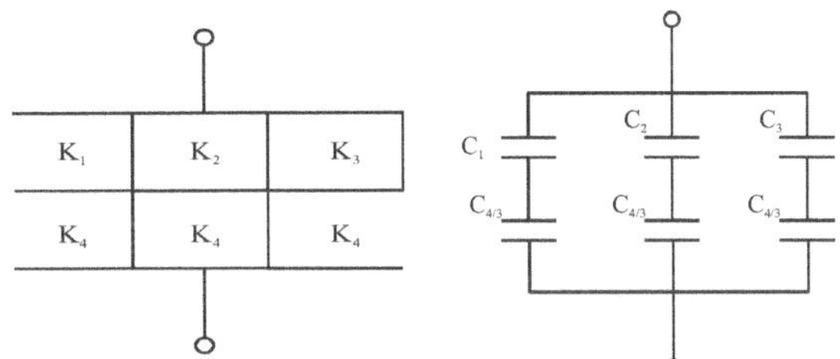

$$\frac{1}{C_1}+\frac{3}{C_4}=\frac{3d}{2k_1\varepsilon_0 A}+\frac{3d}{2k_4\varepsilon_0 A}=\frac{3d}{2\varepsilon_0 A}\left\{\frac{1}{k_1}+\frac{1}{k_4}\right\}$$

$$C_{eq}=\frac{k\varepsilon_0 A}{d}=\frac{2\varepsilon_0 A}{3d}\left\{\frac{k_1k_4}{k_2+k_4}+\frac{k_2k_4}{k_2+k_4}+\frac{k_3k_4}{k_3+k_4}\right\}$$

$$k=\frac{2}{3}\left\{\frac{k_1k_4}{k_1+k_4}+\frac{k_2k_4}{k_2+k_4}+\frac{k_3k_4}{k_3+k_4}\right\}.$$

23. The diagram below show regions of equipotentials. **[NEET – 2017]**

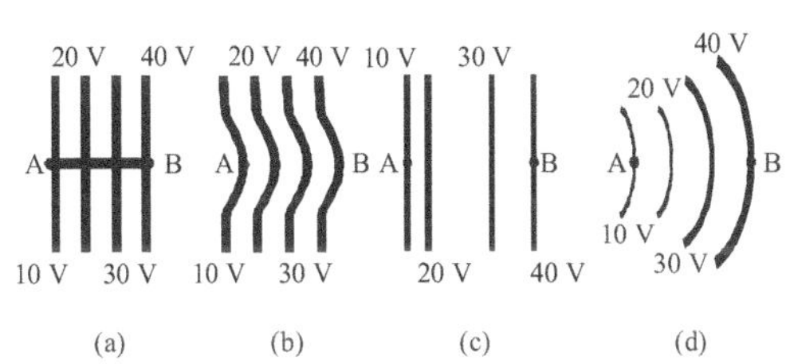

A positive charge is moved from A to B in each diagram.

(1) Maximum work is required to move q in figure (c).

(2) In all the four cases the work done is the same.

(3) Minimum work is required to move q in figure (a).

(4) Maximum work is required to move q in figure (b).

Sol. **(2) :** Work done $w=q\Delta V$

ΔV is same in all the cases so work is done will be same in all the cases.

24. A capacitor is charged by a battery. The battery is removed and another identical uncharged capacitor is connected in parallel. The total electrostatic energy of resulting system : **[NEET – 2017]**

(1) increases by a factor of 4

(2) decreases by a factor of 2

(3) remains the same

(4) increases by a factor of 2

Sol. **(2) :**

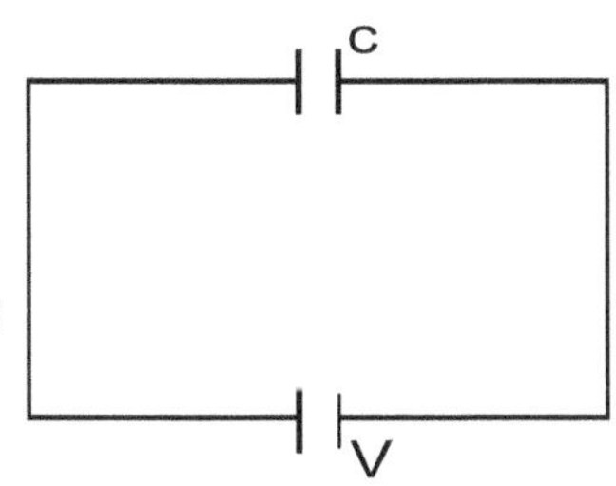

Charge on capacitor $q=CV$

When it is connected with another uncharged capacitor.

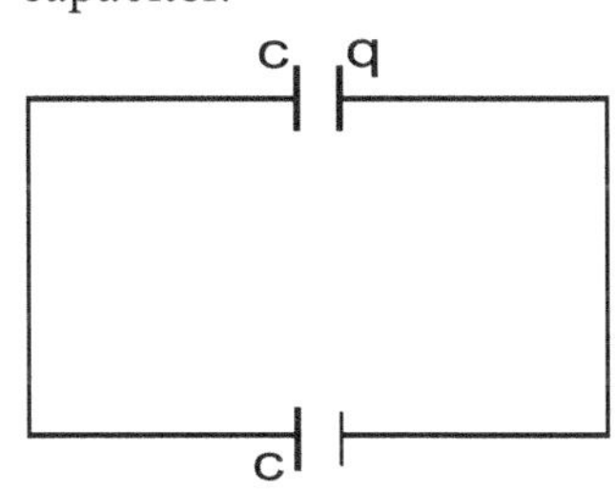

$$V_c=\frac{q_1+q_2}{C_1+C_2}=\frac{q+0}{C+C};\quad V_c=\frac{V}{2}$$

Initial energy

$$U_i=\frac{1}{2}CV^2$$

Final energy

$$U_f=\frac{1}{2}C\left(\frac{V}{2}\right)^2+\frac{1}{2}C\left(\frac{V}{2}\right)^2;\quad =\frac{CV^2}{4}$$

Loss of energy $=U_i-U_f$

$$=\frac{CV^2}{4}$$

i.e. decreases by a factor (2).

25. A carbon resistor of $(47 \pm 4.7)\ k\Omega$ is to be marked with rings of different colours for its identification. The colour code sequence will be **[NEET-2018]**

(1) Yellow - Green - Violet - Gold

(2) Yellow - Violet - Orange - Silver

(3) Violet - Yellow - Orange - Silver

(4) Green - Orange - Violet - Gold

Ans. **(2)**

26. A battery consists of veriable number 'n' of identical cell (having internal resistance 'r' each) which are connect in series. The terminals of the battery are short-circuited and the current I is measured. Which of the graphs shows the correct relationship between I and n ? **[NEET-2018]**

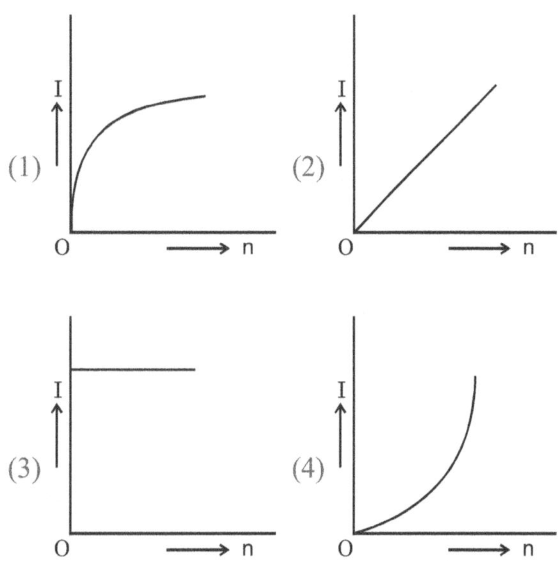

Ans. **(3)**

27. The electrostatic force between the metal plates of an isolated parallel plate capacitor C having a charge Q and area A , is **[NEET-2018]**

(1) proportional to the square root of the distance between the plates.

(2) linearly proportional to the distance between the plates.

(3) independent of the distance between the plates.

(4) inversely proportional to the distance between the plates.

Ans. **(3)**

17 Current Electricity

Note: Scan QR code with your mobile camera or QR scanner for video solutions.

1. Three resistances P, Q, R each of 2 Ω and an unknown resistance S from the four arms of a Wheatstone's bridge circuit. When a resistance of 6 Ω is connected in parallel to S the bridge gets balanced. What is the value of S ? **[AIPMT 2007]**

(1) 2 Ω (2) 3 Ω

(3) 6 Ω (4) 1 Ω

Sol. **(2) :** For balanced wheatstone bridge circuit

$$\frac{2}{2}=\frac{2}{\left(\frac{6S}{S+6}\right)} \Rightarrow S+6=3S \Rightarrow S=3\Omega$$

2. The power dissipated in the circuit shown inthe figure is 30 watt. The value of R is **[AIPMT-2007]**

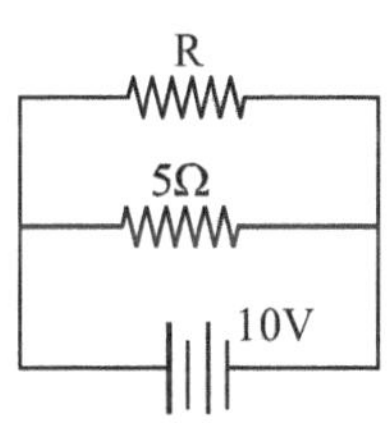

(1) 10 Ω (2) 15 Ω

(3) 10 Ω (4) 30 Ω

Sol. **(2) :**

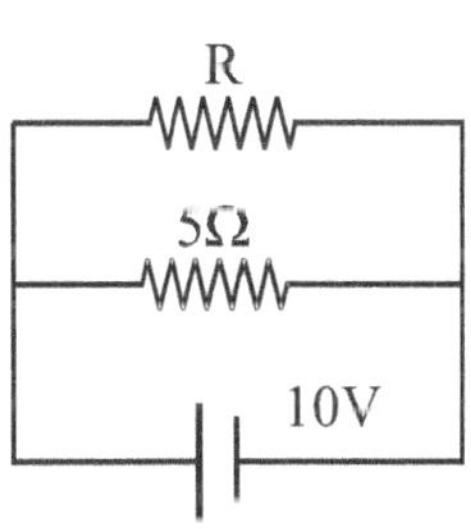

The equivalent resistance of the given circuit is

$$R_{eq}=\frac{5R}{5+R}$$

Power dissipated in the given circuit is

$$P=\frac{V^2}{R_{eq}}=30=\frac{(10)^2}{\left(\frac{5R}{5+R}\right)}$$

150 R = 100(5 + R)

150 R = 500 + 100 R

50 R = 500

$$R=\frac{500}{50}=10\Omega.$$

3. An electric kettle takes 4 A current at 220 V. How much time will it take to boil 1 kg of water from temperature 20°C ? The temperature of boiling water is 100°C **[AIPMT 2008]**

(1) 126. min (2) 4.2 min

(3) 6.3 min (4) 8.4 min

Sol. **(3) :** Power = 220 V × 4A = 880 watts. = 880 J/s.

Heat needed to raise the temperature of 1 kg water through 80° C

$= ms.\Delta T \times 4.2$ J/cal

$= 1000$ g × 1 cal/g × 80 × 4.2 J/cal.

$$\therefore \text{ time taken} = \frac{1000\times1\times80\times4.2}{880}$$

$$=\frac{336\times10^3}{880} = 382 \text{ s} = 6.3 \text{ min.}$$

4. A cell can be balanced against 110 cm and 100 cm of potentiometer wire, respectively with anbd without being short circuited threought a ristance of 10 Ω. Its internal resistance is **[AIPMT-2008]**

(1) 1.0 Ω (2) 0.5 Ω

(3) 2.0 Ω (4) zero

Sol. **(1) :** $E \propto l_1$ and $E - \dfrac{E}{R+r} \cdot r \propto l_2$

$$\Rightarrow \frac{r+R}{R} = \frac{l_1}{l_2} \Rightarrow r = \left(\frac{l_1}{l_2} - 1\right) \cdot R$$

$$= \frac{110-100}{100} \times 10 = 1\Omega$$

5. A current of 3 A flows through the 2 Ω resistor as shown in the cirucit. The power dissipated in the 5 Ω resistor is **[AIPMT-2008]**

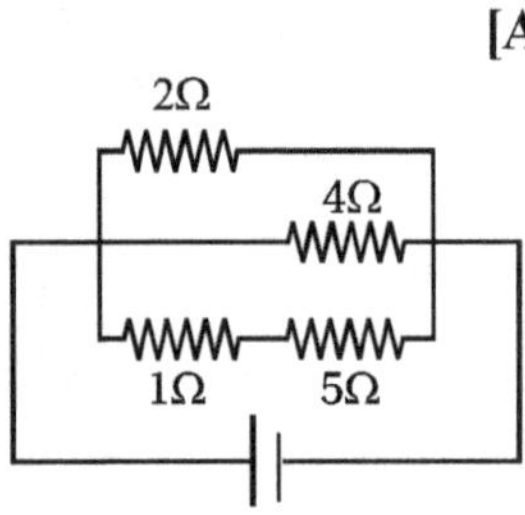

(1) 4 W (2) 2 W

(3) 1 W (4) 5 W

Sol. **(4) :** Voltage across all three branches are same, i.e., $V_1 = V_2$

$3 \times 2 = i \times (5 + 1)$

$i = 1A$

Power dissipated in 5 Ω

$P = i^2 R$

$= (1)^2 \times 5 = 5$ watt.

6. A wire of a certain material is stretched slowly by ten percent. Its new resistances and specific resistance become respectively **[AIPMT 2008]**

(1) 1.2 times, 1.1 times

(2) 1.21 times, same

(3) both remain the same

(4) 1.1 times, 1.1 times

Sol. **(2) :** $R = \dfrac{\rho l}{A}$

Now, $l = l + \dfrac{\ell}{10} = \dfrac{11l}{10}$

and therefore, $A = \dfrac{10A}{11}$

$$\text{So } R' = \frac{\rho \times \left(\frac{11l}{10}\right)}{\left(\frac{10A}{11}\right)} = \frac{\rho l}{A} \times \frac{(11)^2}{(10)^2} = 1.21R$$

Now resistance becomes 1.21 times of initial and specific resistance is the intrinsic property so remains same.

7. See the electrical circuit shown in this figure. Which of the following equations is a correct equation for it ? **[AIPMT 2009]**

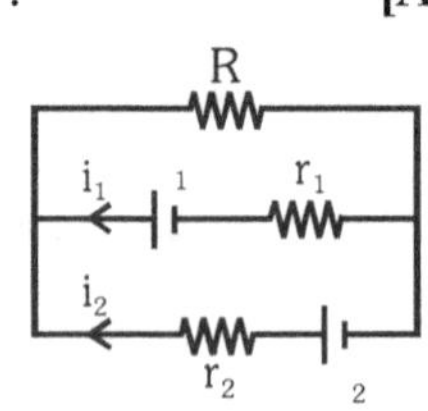

(1) $\varepsilon_1 - (i_1 + i_2)R + i_1 r_1 = 0$

(2) $\varepsilon_1 - (i_1 + i_2)R - i_1 r_1 = 0$

(3) $\varepsilon_2 - i_2 r_2 - \varepsilon_1 - i_1 r_1 = 0$

(4) $-\varepsilon_2 - (i_1 + i_2)R + i_2 r_2 = 0$

Sol. **(2) :**

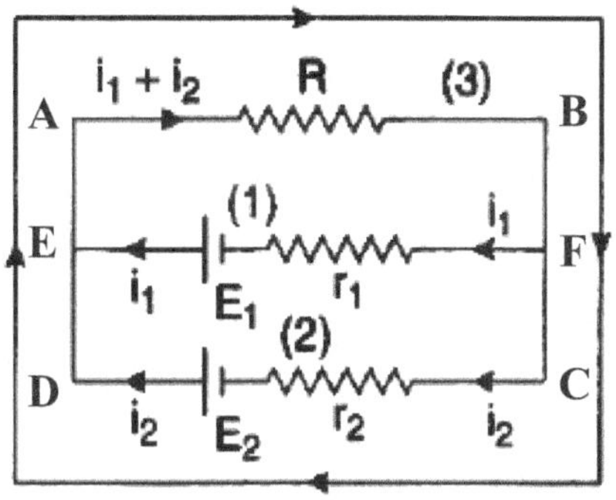

Applying Kirchoff's equation to the loop *ABFE*,

$-(i_1+i_2)R - i_1R_1 + \varepsilon_1 = 0$

$\Rightarrow (i_1+i_2)R - i_1r + \varepsilon_1 = 0$

or $\varepsilon_1 - (i_1+i_2)R - i_1r_1 = 0.$

8. A wire of resistance 12 ohms per meter is bent to form a complete circle of radius 10 cm. The resistance between its two diametrically opposite points, A and B as shown in the figure, is : **[AIPMT 2009]**

(1) 6Ω
(2) 0.6πΩ
(3) 3Ω
(4) 6πΩ

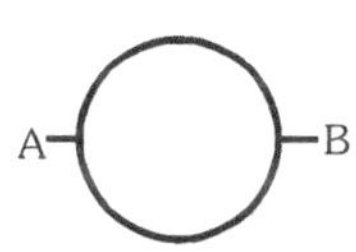

Sol. **(2) :** Total resistance of wire $= 12\Omega \times 2\pi \times 10^{-1}$

$= 2.4\pi$

Resistance of each half $= \frac{2.4\pi}{2} = 1.2\pi$

and as about diameter both parts are in parallel

Req. $= \frac{R}{2}$

Req. $= \frac{1.2\pi}{2} = 0.6\pi\Omega$.

9. A student measures the terminal potential difference (V) of a cell (of emf ε and internal resistance r) as a function of the current (I) flowing through it. The slope, and intercept, of the graph between V and I, then respectively, equal :- **[AIPMT 2009]**

(1) –ε and r (2) ε and –r
(3) –r and ε (4) r and –ε

Sol. **(2) :**

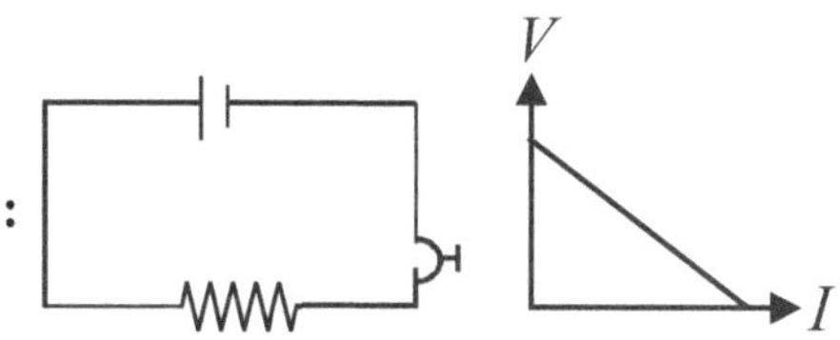

$V = \varepsilon - Ir$, comparing with $y = c - mx$

$\therefore$ Slope $= -r$, internal resistance.

V_{max} = emf ε. This is intercept on the y–axis

$\therefore$ Slope is negative

$\because$ *I* decreases as *R* increases.

10. The mean free path of electrons in a metal is 4×10^{-8} m. The electric field which can give on an average 2 eV energy to an electron in the metal will be in units V/m **[AIPMT 2009]**

(1) 5×10^{-11} (2) 8×10^{-11}
(3) 5×10^{7} (4) 8×10^{7}

Sol. **(3) :** qV = 2eV

$\Rightarrow 1.6\times10^{-19}\text{V} = 2\times1.6\times10^{-19}\text{V}$

$\Rightarrow \quad V = 2V$

$E = \frac{V}{d}$

$\Rightarrow \quad E = \frac{2V}{4\times10^{-8}} = 5\times10^{7}$.

11. A potentiometer circuit is set up as shown. The potential gradient across the potentiometer wire is k volt/cm and the ammeter present in the circuit reads 1.0 A when two-way key is switched off. The balance points, when the key between the terminals (i) 1 and 2 (ii) 1 and 3, is plugged in, are found to be at length l_1 cm l_2 cm respectively. the magnitudes, of the resistors r and X, in ohm, are then, equal, respectively, to **[AIPMT-2010]**

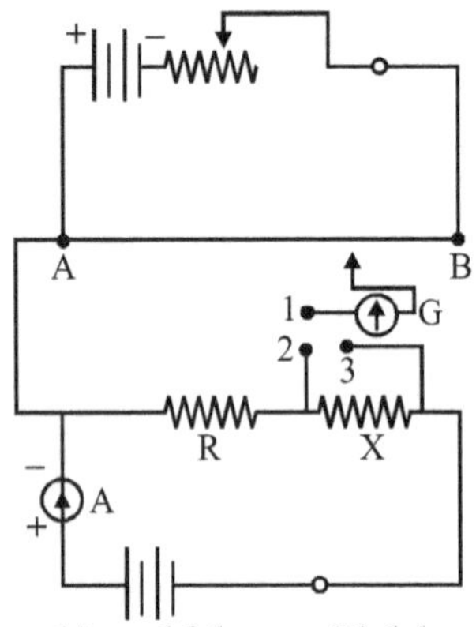

(1) $k(l_2 - l_1)$ and kl_2 (2) kl_1 and $k(l_2 - l_1)$
(3) $k(l_2 - l_1)$ and kl_1 (4) kl_1 and kl_2

Sol. **(2) :** $R = k\ell_1$ and $R + X = k\ell_2$.

12. Consider the following two statements
(A) Kirchhoff's junction law follows from the conservation of charge. **[AIPMT 2010]**
(B) Kirchhoff's loop law follows from the conservation of energy.
(1) Both (A) and (B) are wrong
(2) (A) is correct and (B) is wrong
(3) (A) is wrong and (B) is correct
(4) Both (A) and (B) are correct

Sol. **(4) :** Both (A) and (B) are correct

13. A current of 2 A flows through a 2Ω resistor when connected across a battery. The same battery supplies a current of 0.5 A when connected across a 9 Ω resistor. The internal resistance of the battery is **[AIPMT 2011]**
(1) 1/3 Ω (2) 1/4 Ω (3) 1 Ω (4) 0.5 Ω

Sol. **(1) :** $I = \dfrac{E}{R + r}$

$$2 = \frac{E}{2 + r} \quad ....(1)$$

$$0.5 = \frac{E}{9 + r} \quad ....(2)$$

(1) divided by (2)

$$4 = \frac{9 + r}{2 + r} = 8 + 4r = 9 + r \text{ or } 3r = 1$$

$$\therefore r = \frac{1}{3}\Omega.$$

14. If power dissipated in the 9Ω resistor in the ciruict shown is 36 W, the potential difference across the 2Ω resistor is **[AIPMT-2011]**

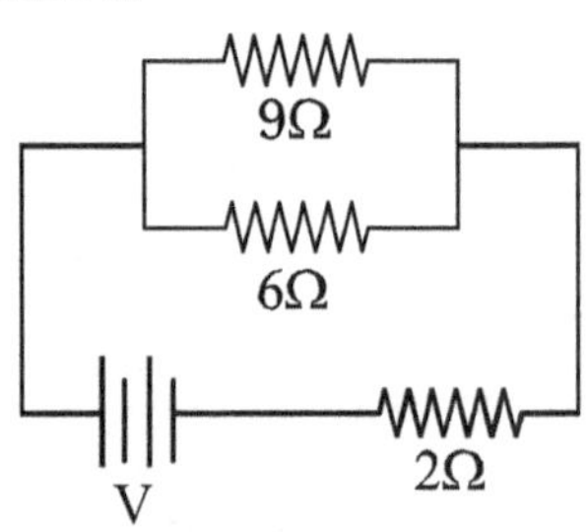

(1) 8V (2) 10 V (3) 2 V (4) 4 V

Sol. **(2) :** $\because \rho = I_g^2 R$, $P = I^2 R$

$$36 = I^2(9)$$

$$\Rightarrow I_9 = 2A$$

$\because$ In parallel $I \propto \dfrac{1}{R}$

$$\frac{I_9}{I_6} = \frac{6}{9} = \frac{2}{I_6} = \frac{6}{9}$$

$I_6 = 3A$

$\Rightarrow I_{ckt} = 2 + 3 = 5A$

$\Rightarrow V_{2\Omega} = IR = (5)(2) = 10$ volt .

15. In the circuit shown in the figure,if potential at point A is taken to be zero, the potential at point B is **[AIPMT 2011]**

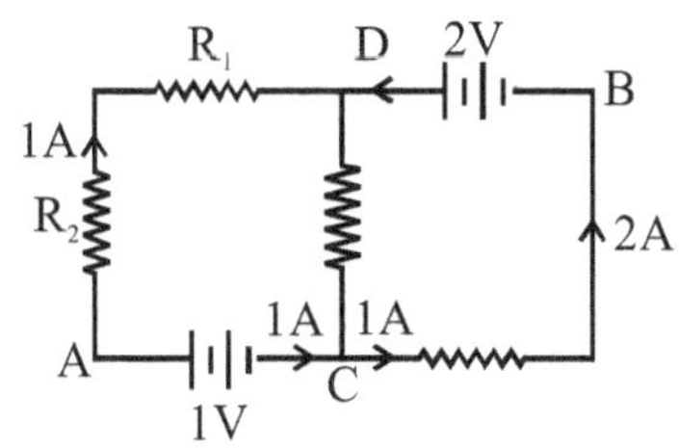

(1) –1 V (2) + 2 V (3) – 2 V (4) + 1 V

Sol. **(2) :**

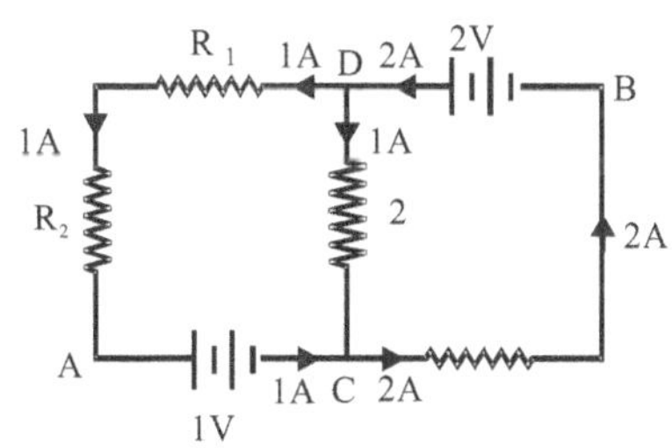

Applying Kirchhoff voltage law in the circuit as shown in the figure below.

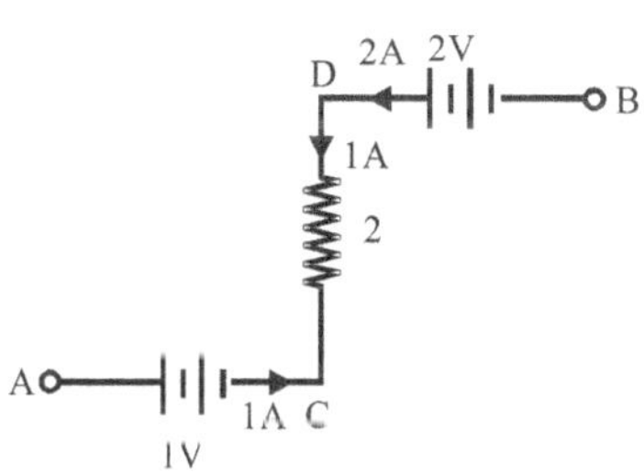

$\therefore V_A + 1 + 2(1) - 2 = V_B$

$0 + 1 = V_B$ $(\because V_A = 0\,V(\text{Given}))$

$V_B = +1V$

16. In the circuit shown the cells A and B have negligible resistances. For $V_A = 12V$, $R_1 = 500\ \Omega$ and $R = 100\ \Omega$, the galvanometer (G) shows no deflection. The value of V_B is **[AIPMT-2012]**

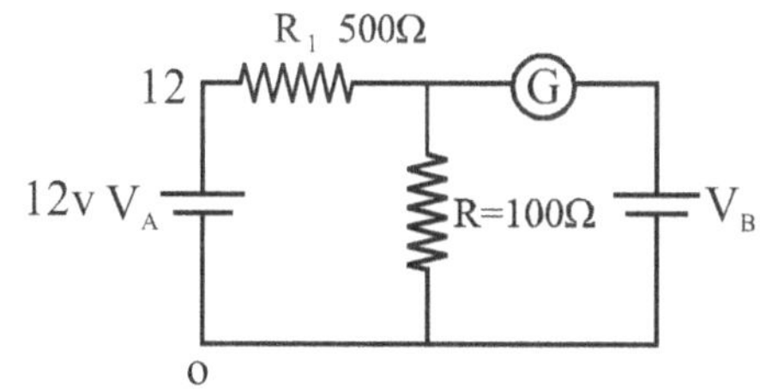

(1) 6 V (2) 4 V (3) 2 V (4) 12 V

Sol. **(3) :**

$$I = \frac{V}{Req}$$

$$I = \frac{1}{50} A$$

$$V_B = I\,R$$

$$= \frac{1}{50} \times 100 = 2\,V$$

17. A ring is made of a wire having a resistance $R_0 = 12\ \Omega$. Find the points A and B, as shown in the figure, at which a current carrying conductor should be connected so that the resistance R of the subcircuit between these points is equal to $\frac{8}{3}$ **[AIPMT-2012]**

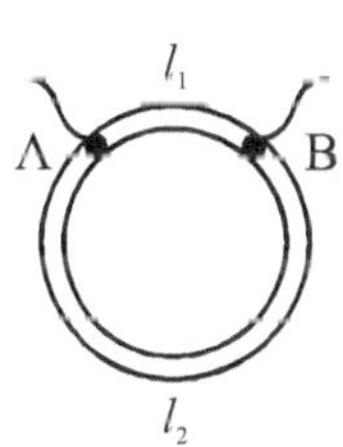

(1) $\frac{l_1}{l_2}\ \frac{1}{2}$

(2) $\frac{l_1}{l_2}\ \frac{5}{8}$

(3) $\frac{l_1}{l_2}\ \frac{1}{3}$

(4) $\frac{l_1}{l_2}\ \frac{3}{8}$

Sol. **(1) :** Since $R \propto l$.

According to problem $R_1 + R_2 = 12\Omega$ and

$$\frac{R_1 \times R_2}{R_1 + R_2} = \frac{8}{3}\Omega$$

On solving this we get $R_1 = 4\Omega$ and $R_2 = 8\Omega$

therefore the ratio $\frac{l_1}{l_2} = \frac{1}{2}$.

18. If voltage across a bulb rated 220 volt-100 watt drops by 2.5% of its rated value, the percentage of the rated value by which the power would decrease is **[AIPMT-2012]**

(1) 10% (2) 20% (3) 2.5% (4) 5%

Sol. **(4) :** Power $P = \frac{V^2}{R}$

For small variation, $\frac{\Delta P}{P} \times 100\% = \frac{2 \times \Delta V}{V} \times 100\%$

therefore power would decrease by 5 %

19. A cell having an emf ε and internal resistance r is connected across a variable external resistance R. As the resistance R is increased, the plot of potential difference V across R is given by **[AIPMT-2012]**

(1) 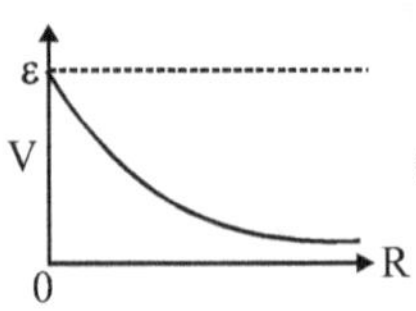

(2) 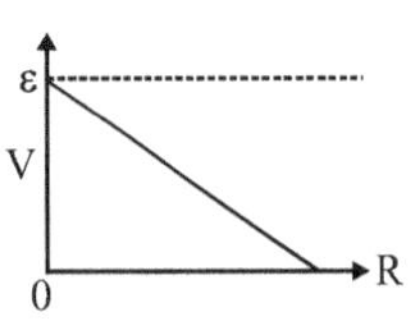

(3) 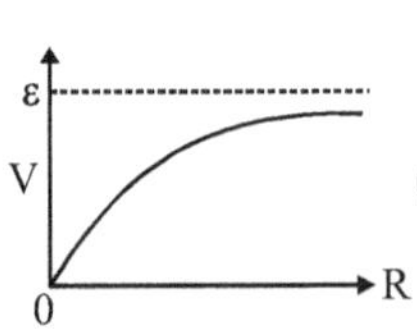

(4) 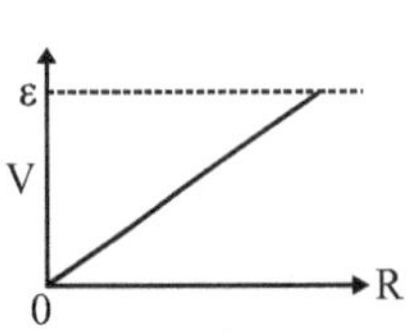

Sol. **(3) :**

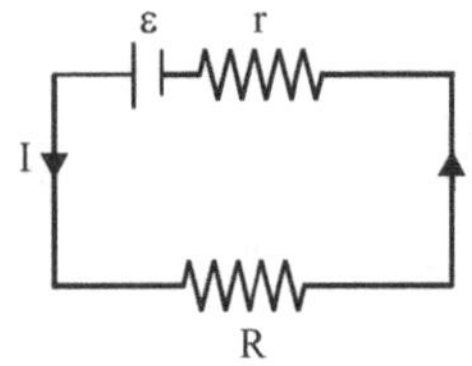

Current in the circuit, $I = \frac{\varepsilon}{R + r}$

Potential difference across R, $V = IR = \left(\frac{\varepsilon}{R + r}\right)R$

When $R = 0,\ V = 0$

$R = \infty,\ V = \varepsilon$

Hence, option (c) represents the correct graph.

20. The resistances of the four arms P, Q, R and S in a Wheatstone'sbridge are 10 ohm, 30 ohm, 30 ohm and 90 ohm, respectively. The e.m.f. and internal resistance of the cell are 7 volt and 5 ohm respectively. If the galvanometer resistance is 50 ohm, the current drawn from the cell will be **[AIPMT-2013]**

(1) 1.0 A (2) 0.2 A
(3) 0.1 A (4) 2.0 A

Sol. **(2) :** The situation is as shown in the figure.

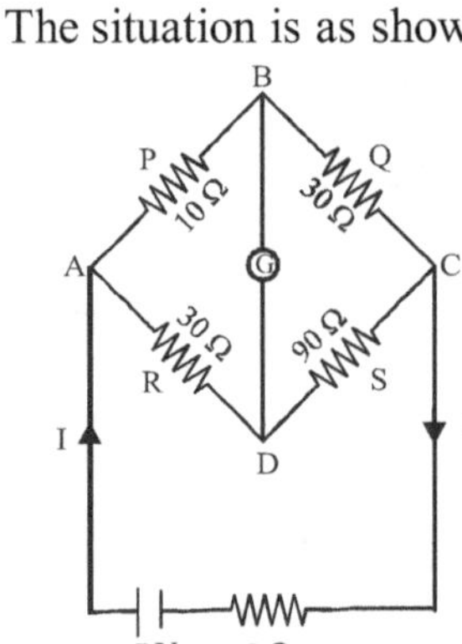

For a balanced Wheatstones's bridge

$$\frac{P}{Q} = \frac{R}{S}$$

$$\therefore \frac{10\Omega}{30\Omega} = \frac{30\Omega}{90\Omega} \text{ or } \frac{1}{3} = \frac{1}{3}$$

It is a balanced Wheatstone's bridge. Hence no current flows in the galvanometer arm. Hence, resistance 50 Ω becomes ineffective.

$\therefore$ The equivalent resistance of the circuit is

$$Req = \frac{R_1R_2}{R_1+R_2}$$

$$R_{eq} = 5\Omega + \frac{(10\Omega+30\Omega)(30\Omega+90\Omega)}{(10\Omega+30\Omega)+(30\Omega+90\Omega)}$$

$$= 5\Omega + \frac{(40\Omega)(120\Omega)}{40\Omega+120\Omega}$$

$$= 5\Omega + 30\Omega = 35\Omega$$

Current drawn from the cell is

$$I = \frac{7\text{ V}}{35\ \Omega} = \frac{1}{5}\text{A} = 0.2\text{ A}$$

21. The internal resistance of a 2.1 V cell which gives a current of 0.2 A through a resistance of 10 Ω is **[AIPMT-2013]**

(1) 0.2 Ω (2) 0.5 Ω
(3) 0.8 Ω (4) 1.0 Ω

Sol. **(2) :** $I = \frac{\varepsilon}{R+r}$

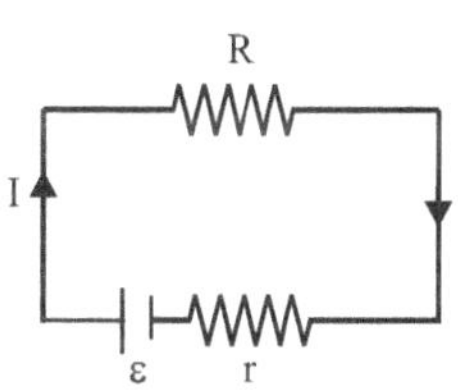

or $IR + Ir = \varepsilon$

Here, $R = 10\Omega,\ r = ?$

$\varepsilon = 2.1\text{V},\ I = 0.2\ A$

$\therefore 0.2\times10 + 0.2\times r = 2.1$

$2 + 0.2r = 2.1$

$0.2r = 0.1$ or $r = \frac{1}{2} = 0.5\Omega$.

22. A wire of a resistance 4Ω is stretched to twice its original length. The resistance of stretched wire would be **[AIPMT-2013]**

(1) 2 Ω (2) 4 Ω (3) 8 Ω (4) 16 Ω

Sol. **(4) :** Resistance of a wire,

$$R = \rho\frac{l}{A} = 4\Omega \qquad .....(i)$$

When wire is streched twice, its new length be l'. Then

$$l' = 2l$$

On stretching volume of the wire remains constant.

$\therefore lA = l'A'$ where A' is the new cross - sectional area or $A' = \frac{l}{l'}A = \frac{l}{2l}A = \frac{A}{2}$

$\therefore$ Resistance of the stretched wire is

$$R' = \rho\frac{l'}{A'} = \rho\frac{2l}{(A/2)} = 4\rho\frac{1}{A}$$

$$= 4(4\Omega) = 16\Omega \qquad \text{(Using (i))}$$

23. Two cities are 150 km apart. Electric power is sent from one city to another city through copper wires. The fall of potential per km is 8 volt and the average resistance per km is 0.5 Ω. The power loss in the wire is **[AIPMT-2014]**

(1) 19.2 W (2) 19.2 kW
(3) 19.2 J (4) 12.2 kW

Sol. **(2) :** Resistance $= (0.5\Omega/\text{km})\ (150\text{ km}) = 75\ \Omega$

Total Voltage drop

$$= (8\text{ V/km})\ (150\text{ km}) = 1200\text{ V}$$

$$\text{Power loss} = \frac{(\Delta V)^2}{R} = \frac{(1200)^2}{75}\text{W}$$

$= 19200\text{ W} = 19.2\text{ kW}$

24. The resistance in the two arms of the meter bridge are 5 Ω and R Ω, respectively. When the resistance R is shunted with an equal resistance, the new balance point is at 1.6 l_1. The resistance R is **[AIPMT-2014]**

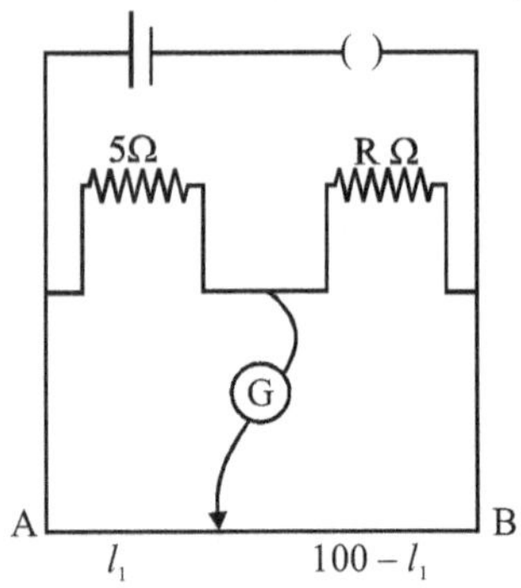

(1) 10 Ω (2) 15 Ω
(3) 20 Ω (4) 25 Ω

Sol. **(2) :** $\frac{5}{R} = \frac{\ell_1}{100 - \ell_1}$ and $\frac{5}{R/2} = \frac{1.6\ell_1}{100 - 1.6\ell_1}$

$\Rightarrow R = 15\Omega$

25. A potentiometer circuit has been set up for finding the internal resistance of a given cell. The main battery used across the potentiometer wire, has an emf of 2.0 V and a negligible internal resistance. the potentiometer wire itself is 4 m long. When the resistance, R, connected across the given cell, has values of **[AIPMT-2014]**
(i) Infinity 9 Ω
(ii) the 'balancing lengths', on the potentiometer wire are found to be 3 m and 2.85 m, respectively.
The value of internal rsistance of the cell is
(1) 0.25 Ω (2) 0.95 Ω
(3) 0.5 Ω (4) 0.75 Ω

Sol. **(3) :** Internal resistance,

$$r = \left(\frac{E - V}{V}\right)R = \left(\frac{\ell_1 - \ell_2}{\ell_2}\right)R$$

$$= \left(\frac{3 - 2.85}{2.85}\right)(9.5)\Omega = 0.5\Omega$$

26. Across a metallic conductor of non-uniform cross-section a constant potential difference is applied. The quantity which remains constant along the conductor is **[AIPMT-2015]**
(1) Current density (2) Current
(3) Drift velocity (4) Electric field

Sol. **(2) :** As all the cross sections of the conductor are considered to be in series, the current should be constant.

27. Two metal wires of identical dimensions connected in series. If σ_1 and σ_2 are the conductivities of the metal wires respectively, the effective conductivity of the combination is **[AIPMT-2015 Re]**

(1) $\frac{\ _1\ _2}{\ _1\ \ _2}$ (2) $\frac{2\ _1\ _2}{\ _1\ \ _2}$

(3) $\frac{\ _1\ \ _2}{2\ _1\ _2}$ (4) $\frac{\ _1\ \ _2}{\ _1\ _2}$

Sol. **(2) :**

$$R_{eq} = R_1 + R_2$$

$$\Rightarrow \frac{2\ell}{\sigma_{eq}A} = \frac{\ell}{\sigma_1 A} + \frac{\ell}{\sigma_2 A} \Rightarrow \sigma_{eq} = \frac{2\sigma_1\sigma_2}{\sigma_1 + \sigma_2}.$$

28. A, B and C are voltmeters of resistance R, 1.5 R amd 3 R respectively as shown inthe figure. When some potential difference is applied between X and Y, the voltmeter readings are V_A, V_B and V_C respectively, then **[AIPMT-2015]**

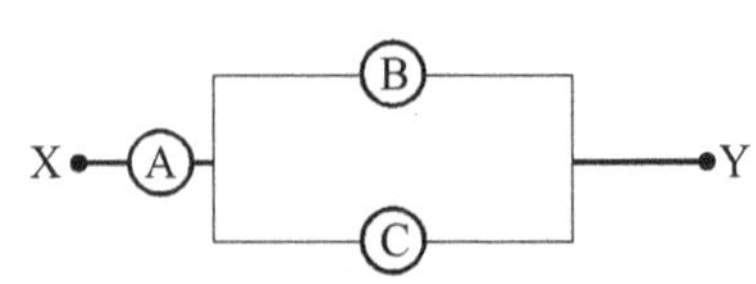

(1) $V_A = V_B = V_C$ (2) $V_A \neq V_B = V_C$
(3) $V_A = V_B \neq V_C$ (4) $V_A \neq V_B \neq V_C$

Sol. (1) ; $V_A = V_B = V_C$

29. A potentiometer wire of length L and a resistance r are connected in series with a battery of e.m.f. E_0 and a resistance r_1. An unknown e.m.f. E is balanced at a length l of the potentiometer wire. The e.m.f. E will be given by **[AIPMT-2015 Re]**

(1) $\frac{LE_0r}{(r\quad r_1)l}$ (2) $\frac{LE_0r}{lr_1}$

(3) $\frac{E_0r}{(r\quad r_1)}\ \frac{l}{L}$ (4) $\frac{E_0r}{L}$

Sol. **(3) :** Potential gradient $x = \frac{ir}{L} = \frac{E_0}{(r_1+r)}\frac{r}{L}$

$\therefore$ e.m.f. $E = xl = \frac{E_0r}{(r+r_1)}\cdot\frac{r}{L}$

30. A circuit contains an ammeter, a battery of 30 V and a resistance 40.8 ohm all connected insereis. If the ammeter has a coil of resistance 480 ohm and a shunt of 20 ohm, the reading in the ammeter will be **[AIPMT-2015 Re]**

(1) 1 A (2) 0.5 A

(3) 0.25 A (4) 2 A

Sol. **(2) :**

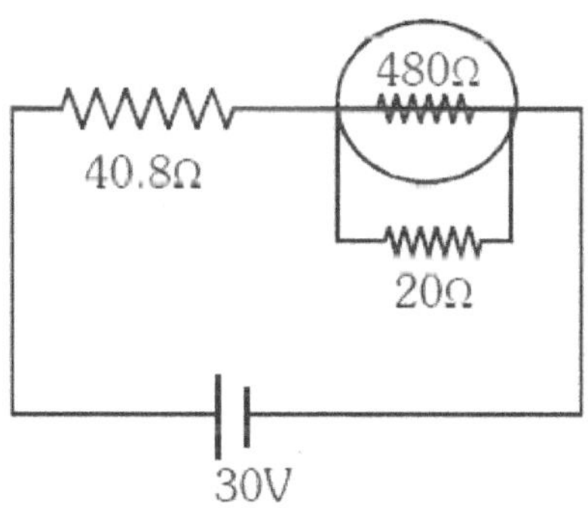

$$R_{eff} = 40.8 + \frac{480\times 20}{480+20} - 40.8 + 19.2 = 60\Omega$$

$$I = \frac{V_{eff}}{R_{eff}} = 0.5\,A$$

$$I = \frac{30}{60} = \frac{1}{2}\,A$$

31. A potentiometer wire is 100 cm long and a constant potential difference is maintained across it. Two cells are connected in series first to support one another and then in opposite direction. The balance points are obtained at 50 cm and 10 cm from the positive end of the wire in the two cases. The ratio of emf's is :- **[AIPMT 2016]**

(1) 5 : 1 (2) 5 : 4

(3) 3 : 4 (4) 3 : 2

Sol. **(4) :** $E_1 + E_2 = K(50)$

$E_1 - E_2 = K(10)$

$$\frac{E_1+E_2}{E_1-E_2} = \frac{5}{1} \Rightarrow \frac{E_2\left\{\frac{E_1}{E_2}+1\right\}}{E_2\left(\frac{E_1}{E_2}-1\right)} = \frac{5}{1}$$

$$\Rightarrow \frac{E_1}{E_2} = \frac{3}{2}.$$

32. The potential difference $(V_A - V_B)$ between the points A and B in the given figure is :- **[NEET – II (2016)]**

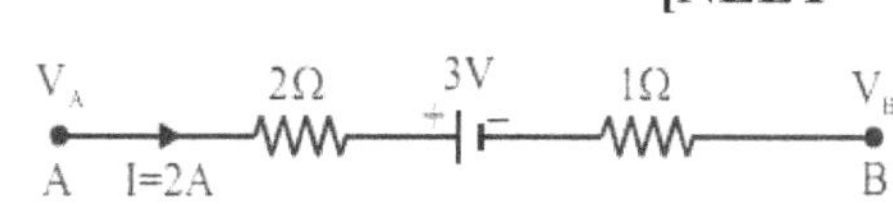

(1) + 6 V (2) + 9 V

(3) – 3 V (4) + 3 V

Sol. **(2) :**

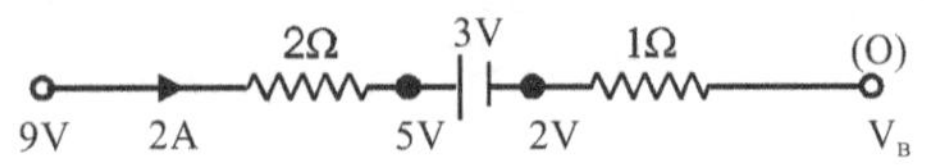

$V_A - V_B = 9 \text{ volt}$.

33. A filament bulb (500 Ω, 100 V) is to be used in a 230 V main supply. When a resistance R is connected in series, it works perfectly and the bulb consumes 500 W. The value of R is :- **[NEET – II (2016)]**

(1) 26 Ω (2) 13 Ω
(3) 230 Ω (4) 46 Ω

Sol. **(1) :**

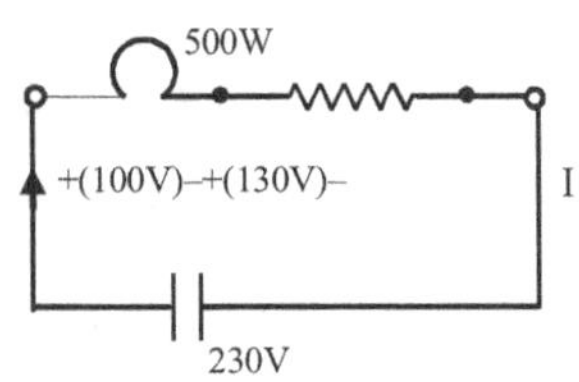

$i = \frac{500}{100} = 5A$

so $130 = 5R$

$R = 26\Omega$

34. A potentiometer is an accurated and versatile device to make electrical measurements of E.M.F. because the method involves : **[NEET – (2017)]**

(1) Cells

(2) potential gradiesnts

(3) a condition of no current flow through the galvanometer

(4) a combination of cells, galvanometer and resistance

Sol. **(3) :** Reading of potentiometer is accurate because during taking reading it does not draw any current from the circuit.

35. The resistance of a wire is 'R' ohm. If it is melted and stretched to 'n' times its original length, its new resistance will be: **[NEET – 2017]**

(1) nR (2) $\frac{R}{n}$ (3) n^2R (4) $\frac{R}{n^2}$

Sol. **(3) :**

$$\frac{R_2}{R_1} = \frac{l_2^2}{l_1^2} = \frac{n^2 l_1^2}{l_1^2} = \frac{R_2}{R_1} = n^2$$

$= R_2 = n^2 R_1$.

36. Current sensitivity of a moving coil galvanometer is 5 div/mA its voltage sensitivity (angular deflection per unit voltage applied) is 20 div/V. The resistance of the galvanometer is **[NEET-2018]**

(1) 250 Ω (2) 25 Ω
(3) 40 Ω (4) 500 Ω

18 Moving Charges and Magnetism

Note: Scan QR code with your mobile camera or QR scanner for video solutions.

1. The resistance of an ammeter is 13 Ω and its scale is graduated for a current up to 100 A. After an additional shunt has been connected to this ammeter it becomes possible to measure currents up to 750 A by this meter. The value of shunt resistance is **[AIPMT-2007]**

(1) 20 Ω (2) 2 Ω

(3) 0.2 Ω (4) 2 kΩ

Sol. **(2) :**

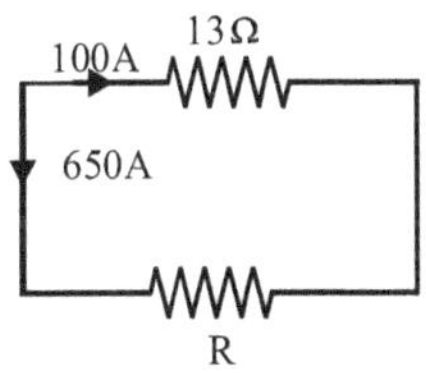

$13 \times 100 = 650 \times R \Rightarrow R = 2\Omega$

2. A particle of mass m, charge Q and kinetic energy T enters a transverse uniform magnetic field of induction $\vec{B}$. After 3 seconds the kinetic energy of the particle will be:- **[AIPMT–2008]**

(1) T (2) 4 T

(3) 3T (4) 2T

Sol. **(1) :** When a charged particle having a given K.E, *T* enters in a field of magnetic induction, which is perpendicular to its velocity, it takes a circular trajectory. It does not increase in energy, therefore *T* is the K.E.

3. A closed loop PQRS carrying a current is placed in a uniform magnetic field. If the magnetic forces on segments PS, SR and RQ are F_1, F_2 and F_3

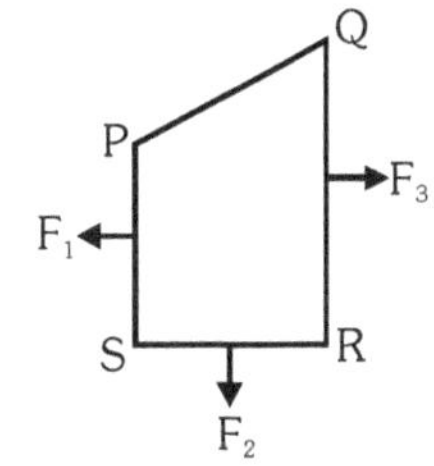

respectively and are in the plane of the paper and along the directions shown, the force on the segment QP is :- **[AIPMT–2008]**

(1) $\sqrt{(F_3 \quad F_1)^2 \quad F_2^2}$ (2) $F_3 - F_1 - F_2$

(3) $F_3 - F_1 - F_2$ (4) $\sqrt{(F_3 \quad F_1)^2 \quad F_2^2}$

Sol. **(4) :** Total force on the current carrying closed loop should be zero, if placed in uniform magnetic field.

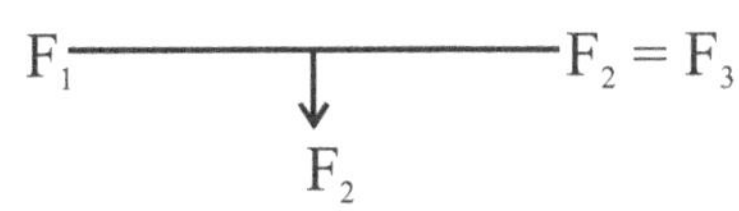

$F_{horizontal} = (F_3 - F_1)$

$F_{vertical} = F_2$

Resultant of $\vec{F_1}, \vec{F_2}$ and $\vec{F_3}$ is $\vec{F}$

Where $F = \sqrt{(F_3 - F_1)^2 + F_2^2}$

Since total force = 0, hence force on QP is equal to $\vec{F}$ in magnitude but opposite direction.

$F_{QP} = \sqrt{(F_3 - F_1)^2 + F_2^2}$.

4. A galvanometer of resistance 50 Ω is connected to a battery of 3 V along with a resistance of 2950 Ω in series. A full-scale deflection of 30 division is obtained int he galvanometer. In order to reduce this deflection to 20 divisions, the resistance in series should be **[AIPMT-2008]**

(1) 5050 Ω (2) 5550 Ω

(3) 6050 Ω (4) 4450 Ω

Sol. **(4) :** Current through galvanometer

$$I=\frac{3V}{50\Omega+2950\Omega}=10^{-3}\,A$$

Current for 30 division $=10^{-3}\,A$

Current for 30 division $=\frac{20}{30}\times10^{-3}$

$$=\frac{2}{3}\times10^{-3}\,A=\frac{3}{50+R}$$

$$\Rightarrow\ R=4450\Omega$$

5. A galvanometer having a coil resistance of 60 Ω shows full scale deflection when a current of 1.0 amp passes throughit. it canbe converted into an ammeter to read currents upto 5.0 amp by **[AIPMT 2009]**

(1) putting in series a resistane of 15 Ω

(2) putting in series a resistane of 240 Ω

(3) putting in parallel a resistane of 15 Ω

(4) putting in parallel a resistane of 240 Ω

Sol. **(3) :** $I_g=1.0A, G=60q, I=5.0\,A$

$$S=\frac{I_g}{I-I_g}G$$

$$G=\frac{1.0}{5.0-1.0}=60$$

$$=15\Omega \text{ in parallel}$$

6. Under the influence of a uniform magnetic field, a charged particle moves with constant speed v in a circle of radius R. The time period of rotation of the particle **[AIPMT 2009]**

(1) depends on R an not on v

(2) is independent of both v and R

(3) depends on both v and R

(4) depends on v and not on R

Sol. **(2) :** For the circular motion in a cyclotron,

$$qvB=\frac{mv^2}{r}\Rightarrow qB=m\omega=\frac{m\times2\pi}{T}$$

$\therefore\ T=\frac{2\pi m}{qB}$ is independent of v and r.

7. A current loop consists of two identical semicircular parts each of radius R, one lying in the x-y plane and the other in x-z plane. If the current in the loop is i. The resultant magentic field due to the two semicircular parts at their common centre is **[AIPMT 2010]**

(1) $\frac{\mu_0 i}{2\sqrt{2}R}$ (2) $\frac{\mu_0 i}{2R}$

(3) $\frac{\mu_0 i}{4R}$ (4) $\frac{\mu_0 i}{\sqrt{2}R}$

Sol. **(1) :** The loop metioned in the question must look like one as shown in the figure.

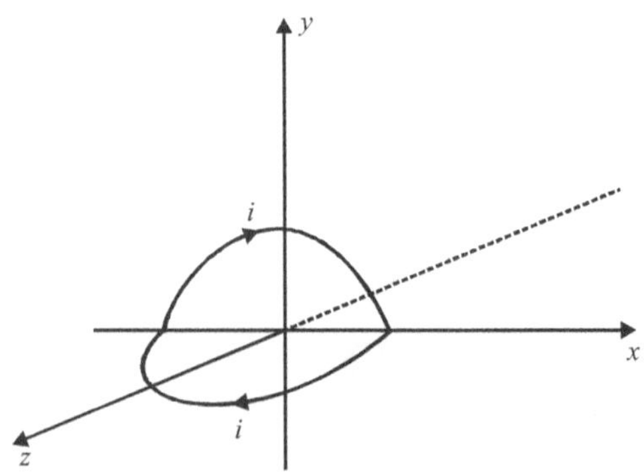

Magnetic field at the centre due to semicircular loop lying in x-y plane, $B_{xy} = \frac{1}{2}\left(\frac{\mu_0 i}{2R}\right)$ negative z direction.

Similarly field due to loop in x-z plane, $B_{xz} = \frac{1}{2}\left(\frac{\mu_0 i}{2R}\right)$ in negative y direction.

$\therefore$ Magnitude of resultant magnetic field,

$$B = \sqrt{B_{xy}^2 + B_{xz}^2} = \sqrt{\left(\frac{\mu_0 i}{4R}\right)^2 + \left(\frac{\mu_0 i}{4R}\right)^2}$$

$$= \frac{\mu_0 i}{4R}\sqrt{2} = \frac{\mu_0 i}{2\sqrt{2}R}.$$

8. Charge q uniformly spread on a thin ring of radius R. The ring rotates about its axis with a uniform frequency f Hz. THe magnitude of magnetic induction at the centre of the ring is **[AIPMT 2011]**

(1) $\frac{\mu_0 af}{2R}$ (2) $\frac{\mu_0 qf}{2R}$ (3) $\frac{\mu_0 q}{2fR}$ (4) $\frac{\mu_0 q}{2fR}$

Sol. **(2)** : The current flowing in the ring is

$I = qf$ ......(i)

The magnetic induction at the centre of the ring is

$$B = \frac{\mu_0 2\pi I}{4\pi R} = \frac{\mu_0 qf}{2R} \quad \text{(Using (i))}$$

9. A square loop, carrying a teady current I. is placed in a horizontal plane near a long straight conductor carrying a steady current I_1 at a distance d from the conductor as shown in figure. The loop will experience **[AIPMT 2011]**

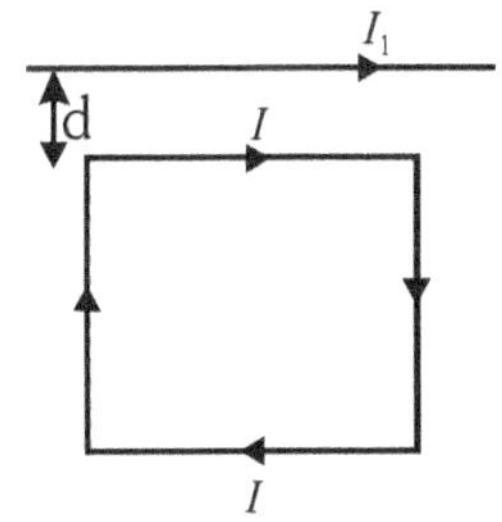

(1) a net attractive force towards the conductor

(2) a net repulsive force away from the cnductor

(3)a net torque acting upward perpendicular to the horizonal plane

(4) a net torque acting downward normal to the horizontal plane

Sol. **(2) :** A net attractive force towards the conductor.

10. A milli voltmeter of 25 milli volt range is to be converted into an ammeter of 25 ampere range. the value (in ohm) of necessary shunt will be **[AIPMT-2012]**

(1) 0.05 (2) 0.001 (3) 0.01 (4) 1

Sol. **(2) :** If the resistance of the meter is G then the full scale deflection current $i_g = \frac{25\text{mV}}{G}$ ampere

The Value of shunt required for converting it into ammeter of range 25 ampere is $S = \frac{i_g G}{i - i_g}$;

$$\text{So} \approx \frac{25\text{mV}}{25} = 0.001\Omega$$

11. A long straight wire carries a certain current and produces a magentic field 2×10^{-4} Wb m^{-2} at a perpendicular distance of 5 cm from the wire. An electron situated at 5 cm from the wire moves along perpendicular to it. The force experienced by the electron will be (charge on electron 1.6×10^{-19}C) **[AIPMT 2013]**

(1) 32. N (2) 3.2×10^{-16}N

(3) 1.6×10^{-16} N (4) zero

Sol. **(2) :** The situation is as shown in the figure.

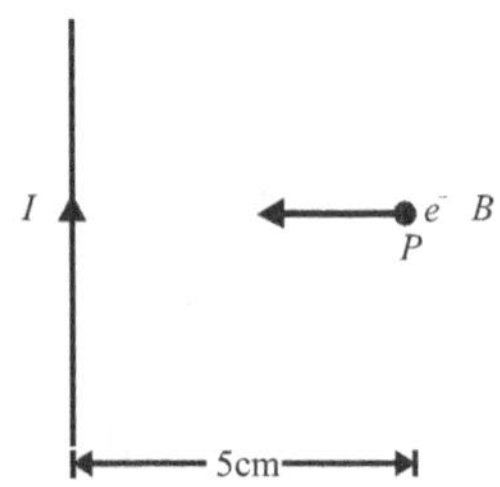

Here, $v = 10^7$ m/s, $B = 2\times10^{-4}$ Wb/m^2

The magnitude of the force experienced by the electron is

$F = evB\sin\theta$

($\because$ υ and B are perpendicular to each other)

$$= evB\sin 90$$

$$= 1.6\times10^{-19}\times10^{7}\times2\times10^{-4}\times1$$

$$= 3.2\times10^{-16}\,\text{N}$$

12. In an ammeter 0.2% of main current passes through the galvanometer. If resistance of galvanometer is G, the resistance of ammeter will be **[AIPMT-2014]**

(1) $\frac{1}{499}$G (2) $\frac{499}{500}$G

(3) $\frac{1}{500}$G (4) $\frac{500}{499}$G

Sol. **(3) :**

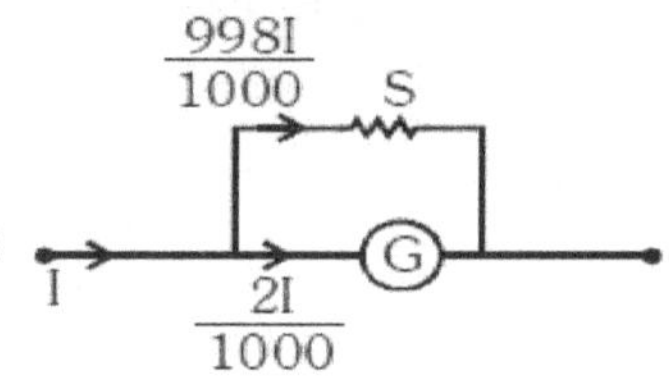

$$\left(\frac{2I}{1000}\right)G = \left(\frac{998I}{1000}\right)S \quad \Rightarrow S = \frac{G}{499}$$

Total resistance of Ammeter

$$R = \frac{SG}{S+G} = \frac{\left(\frac{G}{499}\right)F}{\left(\frac{G}{499}\right)+G} = \frac{G}{500}.$$

13. A square loop ABCD carrying a current i, is placed near and coplanar with a long straight conductor XY carrying a current I, the net force on the loop will be :- **[AIPMT-2016]**

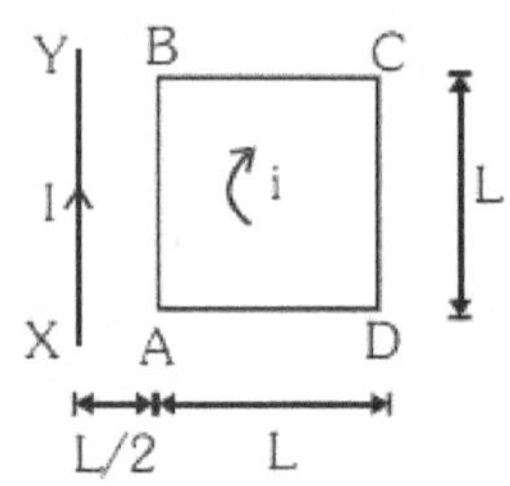

(1) $\frac{2\mu_0 Ii}{3\pi}$ (2) $\frac{\mu_0 Ii}{2\pi}$ (3) $\frac{2\mu_0 IiL}{3\pi}$ (4) $\frac{\mu_0 IiL}{2\pi}$

Sol. **(1) :**

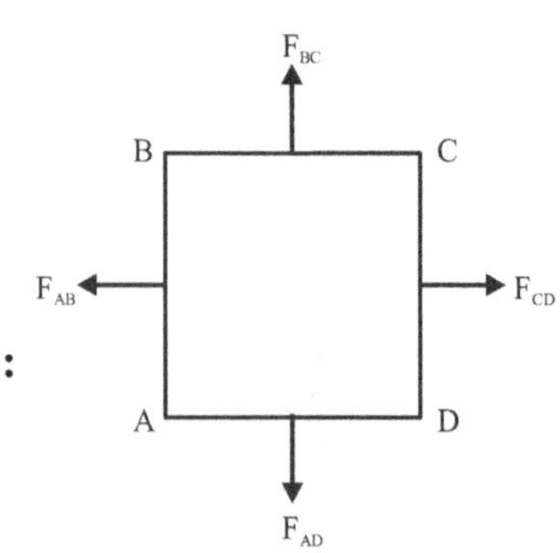

F_{BC} cancels F_{AD}

$$F_{Net} = F_{AB} - F_{CD}$$

$$= \frac{\mu_0 IiL}{2\pi\left(\frac{L}{2}\right)} - \frac{\mu_0 IiL}{2\pi\left(\frac{3L}{2}\right)} = \frac{2\mu_0 Ii}{3\pi}$$

14. A long straight wire of radius a carries a steady current I. The current is uniformly distributed over its cross-section. The ratio of the magnetic fields B and B', at radial distances $\frac{a}{2}$ and 2a respect from the axis of the wire is : **[AIPMT-2016]**

(1) $\frac{1}{4}$ (2) $\frac{1}{4}$ (3) 1 (4) 4

Sol. **(3) :** If r = radial separation

$$F = F_{inside} = \left(\frac{\mu_0 i}{2\pi R^2}\right) r = -\frac{\mu_0 i}{2\pi R^2}\left(\frac{R}{2}\right) = \frac{\mu_0 i}{2\pi R} = \frac{\mu_0 i}{2\pi R}\left(\frac{1}{2}\right)$$

$$B' = B_{outside} = \frac{\mu_0 i}{2\pi r} = \frac{\mu_0 i}{2\pi r}\left(\frac{1}{2}\right) \Rightarrow B : B' = 1 : 1$$

15. A long wire carrying a steady current is bent into a circular loop of one turn. The magnetic field at the centre of the loop is B. It is then bent into a circular coil of n turns. The magnetic field at the centre of this coil of n turns will be :-

NEET – II(2016)

(1) 2nB (2) $2n^2B$ (3) nB (4) n^2B

Sol. **(4) :**

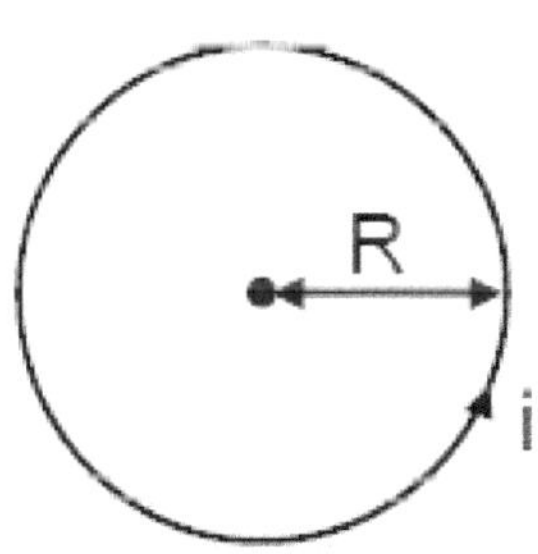

$$B = \frac{\mu_0 i}{2R} = \frac{\mu_0 i(2\pi)}{2(\ell)} = \frac{\mu_0 \pi i}{2\ell}$$

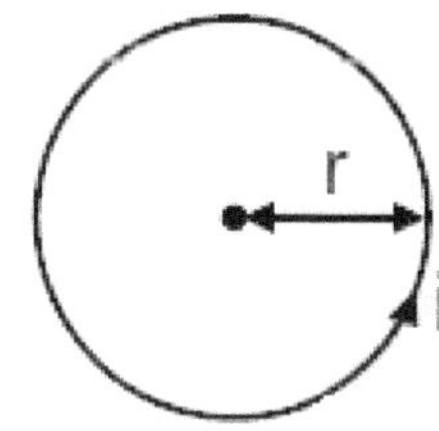

$$B' = \frac{\mu_0 ni}{2r} = \frac{\mu_0 ni}{2\left(\frac{\ell}{2n\pi}\right)} = \frac{n^2\mu_0 \pi i}{2\ell} = n^2 B$$

16. An electron is moving in a circular path under the influence of a transverse magnet ic field of 3.57×10^{-2} T. If the value of e/m is 1.76×10^{11} C/kg, the frequency of revolution of the electron is :-

NEET – II(2016)

(1) 62.8 MHz (2) 6.28 MHz
(3) 1 GHz (4) 100 MHz

Sol. **(3) :** $R = \frac{mV}{qB}$

$$\omega = \frac{V}{R} = \frac{qB}{m}$$

$$f = \frac{\omega}{2\pi} = \frac{1}{2\pi} \cdot \frac{qB}{m}$$

$$= \frac{1.76 \times 10^{11} \times 3.57 \times 10^{-2}}{(2 \times 3.14)} = 10^9 \text{ Hz} = 1 \text{ GH}_Z.$$

17. A 250 – Turn rectangular coil of length 2.1 cm and width 1.25 cm carries a current of 85 μA and subjected to a magnetic field of strength 0.85 T. Work done for rotating the coil by 180° against the torque is : **[NEET-2017]**

(1) $9.1\mu J$ (2) $4.55\mu J$

(3) $2.3\mu J$ (4) $1.15\mu J$

Sol. **(3) :** $W = MB(\cos\theta_1 - \cos\theta_2)$

When it is rotated by angle 180° then

$W = 2MB$

$W = 2(NIA)B$

$= 2\times 250\times 85\times 10^{-6}[1.25\times 2.1\times 10^{-4}]\times 85\times 10^{-2}$

$= 9.1\ \mu J$

18. An arrengement of three parallel straight wires placed perpendicular to plane of paper carrying same current 'I' along the same direction is shown in Fig. Magnitude of force per unit length on the middle wire 'B' is given by : **[NEET-2017]**

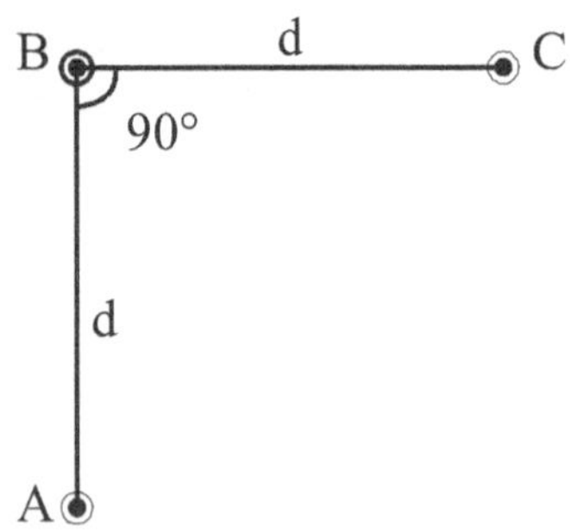

(1) $\frac{\mu_o i^2}{2\pi d}$ (2) $\frac{2\mu_o i^2}{\pi d}$ (3) $\frac{\sqrt{2}\mu_o i^2}{\pi d}$ (4) $\frac{\mu_o i^2}{\sqrt{2}\pi d}$

Sol. **(3) :** Force between BC and AB will be same in magnitude.

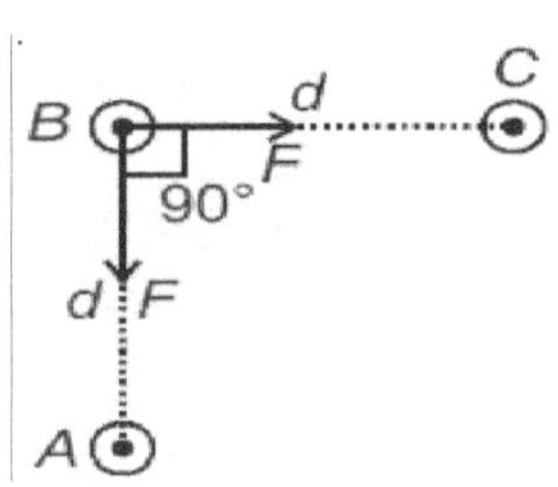

$F_{BC} = F_{BA} = \frac{\mu_0 I^2}{2\pi d}$

$F = \sqrt{2}F_{BC}$ $F = \sqrt{F_1^2 + F_2^2}$

$= \sqrt{2}\frac{\mu_0 I^2}{2\pi d}$ $\because$ $F_1 = F_2$

$F = \frac{\mu_0 I^2}{\sqrt{2}\pi d}$

19. A long solenoid of diameter 0.1 m has 2×10^4 turns per meter. At the centre of the solenoid, a coil of 100 turns and radius 0.01 m is placed with its axis coinciding with the solenoid axis. The current in the solenoid reduces at a constant rate to 0A from 4A in 0.05 s. If the resistance of the coils is $10\pi^2\Omega$, the total charge flowing through the coil during this time is : **[NEET-2017]**

(1) $32\pi\ \mu C$ (2) $16\ \mu C$

(3) $32\ \mu C$ (4) $16\pi\ \mu C$

Sol. **(3) :** $\varepsilon = -N\frac{d\phi}{dt}$

$\left|\frac{\varepsilon}{R}\right| = \frac{N}{R}\frac{d\phi}{dt}$

$dq = \frac{N}{R}d\phi$

$\Delta Q = \frac{N(\Delta\phi)}{R}$

$\Delta Q = \frac{\Delta\phi_{total}}{R}$

$= \frac{(NBA)}{R}$

$= \frac{\mu_0 n i \pi r^2}{R}$

Putting values

$= \frac{4\pi\times 10^{-7}\times 100\times 4\times\pi\times(0.01)^2}{10\pi^2}$

$\Delta Q = 32\ \mu C$.

19 Magnetism and Matter

Note: Scan QR code with your mobile camera or QR scanner for video solutions.

1. Nickel shows ferromagnetic property at room temperature. If the temperature is increased beyond Curie temperature, then it will show

(1) paramagnetism **[AIMPT 2007]**

(2) anit-ferromagnetism

(3) no magnetic property

(4) diamagnetism

Sol. **(1) :** Above curie temperature ferromagnetic material behaves as paramagnetic material.

2. Curie temperatures is the temperature above which **[AIMPT 2008]**

(1) ferromagnetic material becomes paramagnetic material

(2) paramagnetic material becomes diamangnetic material

(3) paramagnetic material becomes ferromagnetic material

(4) ferrinagnetic matgerial becomes diamagnetic material

Sol. **(1) :** Curie temperature is that temperature above which a ferromagnet becomes paramagnet.

3. A bar magnet having a magnetic moment of 2×10^4 JT^{-1} is free to rotate in a horizontal plane. A horizontal mgnetic field $B = 6 \times 10^{-4}T$ exisits in the space. The work done in taking the magnet slowly from a direction parallel to the field to a direction 60° from the field is **[AIPMT 2009]**

(1) 0.6 J (2) 12 J

(3) 6 J (4) 2 J

Sol. **(3) :** $W = MB(\cos\theta_1 - \cos\theta_2)$

$= 2\times10^4 \times 6\times10^{-4}(\cos\theta - \cos 60°)$

$= 12\times\frac{1}{2} = 6\,J$

4. If a diamagnetic substance is brought near the north or the south pole of a bar magnet, it is

(1) replelled by both the poles **[AIMPT 2009]**

(2) replelled by the north pole and attracted

(3) attracted by the north pole and repelled by the south pole

(4) attracted by both the poles

Sol. **(1) :** As diamagnetic substances have negative intensity of magnetisation, they are weekly repelled by the external field.

5. A vibration magnetometer placed in magnetic meridian has a small bar magnet. The magner executes oscillations with a time period of 2s in earth's horizontal magnetic field of 24 μT. When a horizontal field of 18 μ T is produced opposite to the earth's field by placing a current carrying wire, the new time period of magnet will be **[AIPMT 2010]**

(1) 1 s (2) 2 s (3) 3 s (4) 4 s

Sol. **(4) :** $T = 2\pi\sqrt{\frac{I}{MB_H}}$, $T' = 2\pi\sqrt{\frac{I}{M(B_H - B)}}$

$\rightarrow T' - 2T - 4s$.

6. Electromagnets are made of soil iron because soft iron has **[AIPMT 2010]**

(1) low retentivity and high coercive force

(2) high retentivit and high coercive force

(3) low retentivity and low coercive force

(4) high retentivity and low coercive force

Sol. **(3) :** Electromagnet are made of soft iron because soft iron has low retentivity and low coercive force or low coercivity. Soft iron is a soft magnetic material.

7. There are four light-weight-rod sample A, B, C, D seperately suspended by threads. A bar magnet is slowly brought near each sample and the following observations are noted **[AIPMT 2011]**

(i) A is feebly replled

(ii) B is feebly attracted

(iii) C is strongly attracted

(iv) D remains unaffected

Which one of the following is ture ?

(1) C is of dimagnetic material

(2) D is of a ferromagnetic material

(3) A is of a non - magnetic material

(4) B is of paramagnetic material

Sol. **(4) :** Diamagnetic will be feebly repelled Paramagnetic will be feebly attracted Ferromagnetic will be strongly attracted.

8. A short bar magnet of magnetic moment $0.4 J\, T^{-1}$ is place in a uniform magnetic field of 0.16 T. The magnet is stable equilibrium when the potential energy is **[AIPMT 2012]**

(1) – 0.064 J (2) zero

(3) – 00.82 J (4) 0.064 J

Sol. **(1) :** Here, Magnetic moment, $m = 0.4 J T^{-1}$

Magnetic field, B = 0.16 T

When a bar magnet of magnetic moment is placed in a uniform magnetic field, its potential energy is

$U = -\vec{M}\cdot\vec{B} = -MB\cos\theta$

For stable equilibrium, $\theta = 0°$

$\therefore U = -MB = -(0.4 J\, T^{-1})(0.16 T) = -0.064 J$.

9. A compass needle which is allowed to move in a horizontal plane is taken to a geomagnetic of pole, It **[AIPMT 2012]**

(1) will stay in east- west direction only

(2) will become rigid showing no movement

(3) Will stay in any position

(4) will stay in north -south direction only

Sol. **(3) :** Will remain in any position at geomagnetic north and south pole.

10. A magnetic needle suspended parallel to a meganetic field requires $\sqrt{3}$ J of work to turn it through 60° The torque needed to maintain the needle in this position will be **[AIPMT 2012]**

(1) $2\sqrt{3}$ J (2) 3 J

(3) $\sqrt{3}$ J (4) $\frac{3}{2}$ j

Sol. **(2) :** Work done in changing the orientation of a magnetic needle of magnetic moment M in a magnetic field B from position θ_1 to θ_2 is given by

$W = MB(\cos\theta_1 - \cos\theta_2)$

Here, $\theta_1 = 0°$, $\theta_2 = 60°$

$$= MB\left(1-\frac{1}{2}\right) = \frac{MB}{2} \quad .....(i)$$

The torque on the needle is $\vec{\tau} = \vec{M} \times \vec{B}$

In magnitude,

$$\tau = MB\sin\theta = MB\sin 60° = \frac{\sqrt{3}}{2}MB \quad ...(ii)$$

Dividing (ii) by (i), we get

$$\frac{\tau}{W} = \sqrt{3}; \quad \tau = \sqrt{3}W = \sqrt{3}\times\sqrt{3}\text{J} = 3\text{J}.$$

11. A bar magnet of length I and magnetic dipole moment M in bent in the from of an are as shown in the figure. The new magnetic dipole moment will be **[AIPMT 2013]**

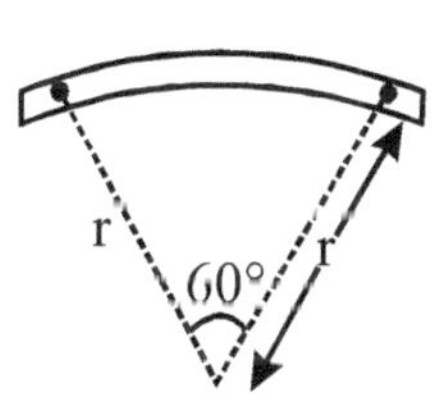

(1) M (2) 3 J

(3) $\frac{3}{}$M (4) $\frac{3}{2}$

Sol. **(3) :** Let m be strength of each pole of bar magnet of length *l*. Then

$M = m \times l \quad ....(i)$

When the bar magnet is bent in the form of an are as shown in figure

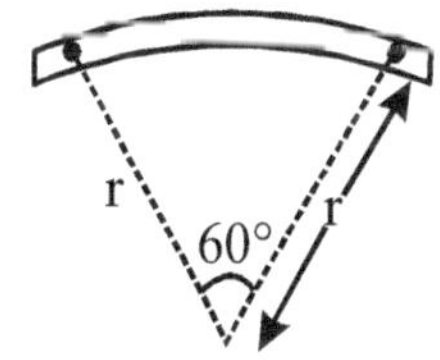

Then

$$l = \frac{\pi}{3}\times r = \frac{\pi r}{3} \text{ or } r = \frac{3l}{\pi}$$

New magnetic dipole moment

$M' = m \times 2r\sin 30°$

$$= m\times 2\times\frac{3l}{\pi}\times\frac{1}{2} = \frac{3ml}{\pi} = \frac{3M}{\pi} \text{ (Using (i))}$$

12. Following figures show the arrangement of bar magnets in ddifferent configuratins. Each magnet has magnetic dipole moment $\vec{m}$. Which configuration has highest net magnetic dipole moment ? **[AIPMT 2014]**

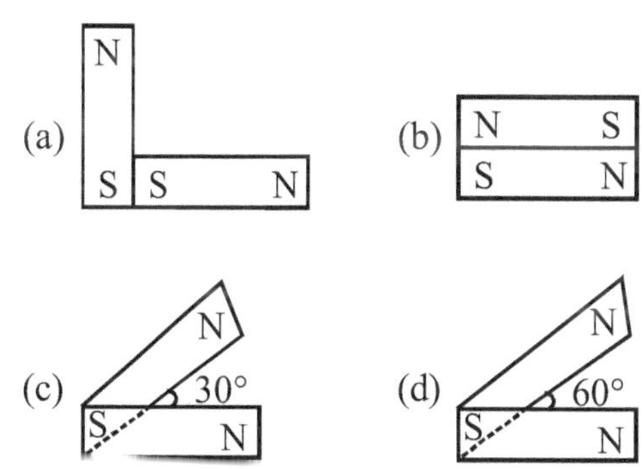

(1) (a) (2) (b) (3) (c) (4) (d)

Sol. **(3) :** Net magnetic moment

$$m_{net} = \sqrt{m_1^2 + m_2^2 + 2m_1m_2\cos\theta}.$$

13. The magnetic susceptibility is negative for :

(1) diamagnetic material only **[AIPMT 2016]**

(2) paramagnetic material only

(3) ferromagnetic material only

(4) paramagnetic and ferromagnetic materials

Sol. **(1) :** $\mu_r = 1 + x$

appropriate is diamagnetic.

14. A bar magnet is hung by a thin cotton thread in a uniform horizontal magnet ic field and is in equilibrium state. The energy required to rotate it by 60° is W. Now the torque required to keep the magnet in this new position is : **NEET – II (2016)**

(1) $\frac{\sqrt{3}W}{2}$ (2) $\frac{2W}{\sqrt{3}}$

(3) $\frac{W}{\sqrt{3}}$ (4) $\sqrt{3}\,W$

Sol. **(4) :** $W_{ext} = U_f - V_i$

$= -MB\cos 60° - (-MB)$

$= MB(1 - \cos 60°) = MB/2 = W$

$r = MB\sin 60° = MB\frac{\sqrt{3}}{2} = \sqrt{3}W$

15. If θ_1 and θ_2 be the apparent angles of dip observed in two vertical planes at right angles to each other, then the angle of dip θ is given by :

(1) $\cot^2\theta = \cot^2\theta_1 + \cot^2\theta_2$ **[NEET – 2017]**

(2) $\tan^2\theta = \tan^2\theta_1 + \tan^2\theta_2$

(3) $\cot^2\theta = \cot^2\theta_1 - \cot^2\theta_2$

(4) $\tan^2\theta = \tan^2\theta_1 - \tan^2\theta_2$

Sol. **(1) :** $\cot^2\theta = \cot^2\theta_1 + \cot^2\theta_2$

16. A thin diamagnetic rod is placed vertically between the poles of an electromagnet. When the current in the electromagnet is switched on, then the horizontal magnetic field. Hence the rod gains gravitational potential energy. The work required to do this comes from **[NEET-2018]**

(1) the lattice structure of the material of the rod

(2) The magnetic fild

(3) the current source

(4) the induced electric field due to the changing magnetic field

Ans. (3)

20 Electromagnetic Induction

Note: Scan QR code with your mobile camera or QR scanner for video solutions.

1. A long solenoid has 500 turns. When a current of 2A is passed through it, the resulting megnetic flux linked with each the turn of the solenoid is 4×10^{-3} Wb. The self-inductance of the solenoid is **[AIPMT 2008]**

(1) 2.5 H (2) 2.0 H

(3) 1.0 H (4) 4.0 H

Sol. (3) : Flux linkage = Flux through each turn × number of turns

$$\phi = 500 \times 4 \times 10^{-3} = 2\,\text{Wb}$$

$$\text{since } \phi = Li \Rightarrow L = \frac{\phi}{i} = \frac{2}{2} = 1\text{H}\ .$$

2. A rectangular, a square, a circular and an eliptical loop, all in the (x,y) plane, are moving out of a unifrorm magnetic field with a constant velocity, $\vec{V}$ $v\hat{i}$ The magnetic fieldis directed along the negative z- axis direction. The induced emf during the passage of these. loops, out of the field region, will not remain constant for **[AIPMT 2009]**

(1) the rectangular, circular and elliptical loops

(2) the circular and the elliptical loops

(3) only the elliptical loop

(4) any of the four loops

Sol. (2) : Out of the four structures, when the circular and elliptical loops come out from the field, equal are not traced in equal interval of time. So any induced in both is not constant.

3. A conducting circular loop is placed in a uniform magnetic field 0.04T with its plane perpendicular to the magnetic field. The radius of the loop starts shriking at 2 mm^1. The induced emf in the loop when the radius is 2 cm is. **[AIPMT 2009]**

(1) 3.2 π μ V (2) 4.8 π μ V

(3) 0.8 π μ V (4) 1.6 π μ V

Sol. (1) : $e = \frac{d\phi}{dt} = \frac{d}{dt}(B\pi r^2) = 2\pi r B\frac{dr}{dt}$

$$= 2 \times \pi \times 2 \times 10^{-2} \times 4 \times 10^{-2} \times 2 \times 10^{-3}$$

$$= 3.2 \times 10^{-6}\pi\text{Vol} = 3.2\ \pi\mu\text{V}\ .$$

4. A conducting circular loop is placed in a uniform magnetic field, B = 0.025 T with its plane perpendicular to the loop. The radiusof the loop is made to shrink at a constant rate of 1 mms^{-1} The induced emf when the radius is 2 cm is **[AIPMT 2010]**

(1) 2 π μ V (2) π μ V

(3) $\frac{-}{2}$ V (4) 2 μ V

Sol. (2) : $\phi = (B)(\pi r^2) \Rightarrow e = \frac{d\phi}{dt} = (B)(2\pi r)\left(\frac{dr}{dt}\right)$

$$= (0.025)(2\pi)(2 \times 10^{-2})(10^{-3}) = \pi\mu\text{V}\ .$$

5. The current in a coil varies with time as shown in the figure. The variation of induced emf with time would be **[AIPMT 2011]**

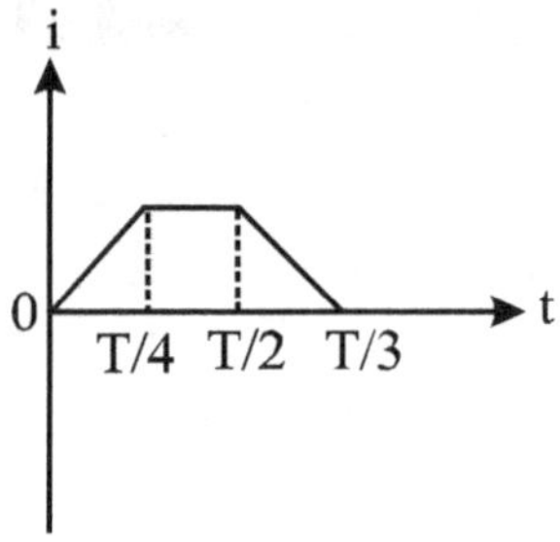

(1) 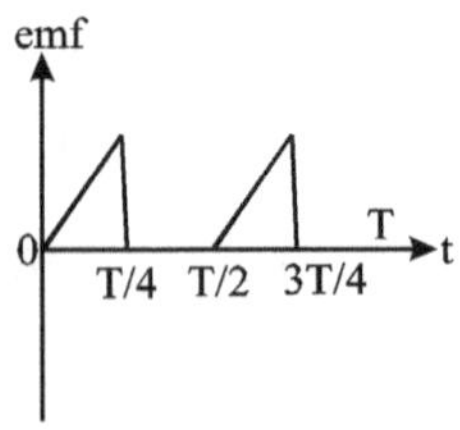

(2) 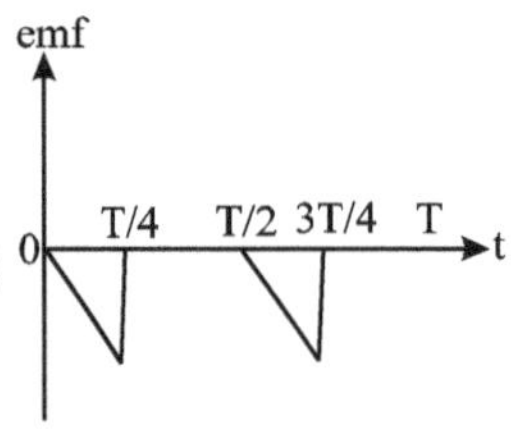

(3) 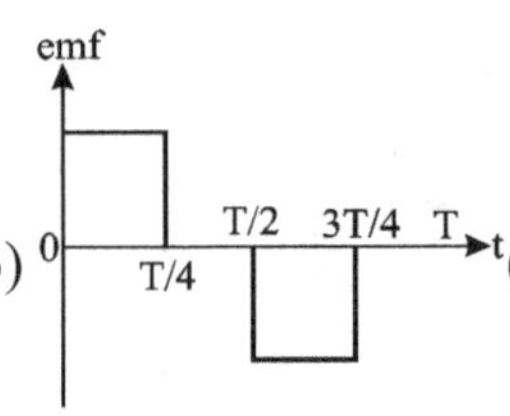

(4) 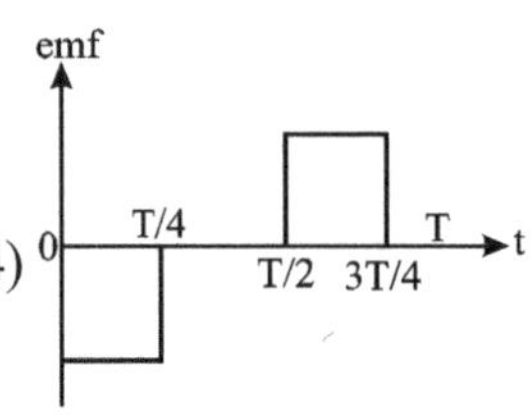

Sol. (4) : 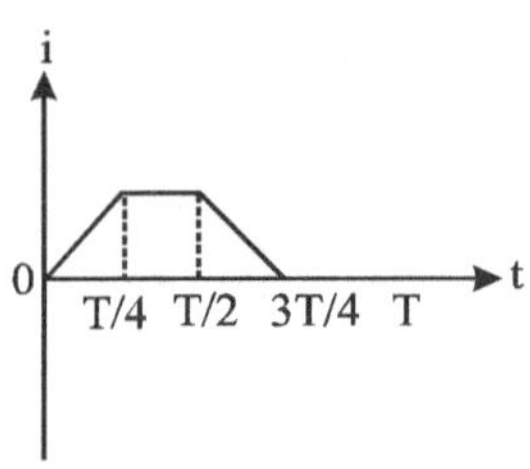

Induced emf, $e=-L\dfrac{di}{dt}$

For $0\le t\le\dfrac{T}{4}$,

$i-t$ graph is a straight line with positive constant slope.

$\therefore\ \dfrac{di}{dt}=\text{constant}$

$\Rightarrow$ e = –ve and constant For $0\le t\le\dfrac{T}{4}$

For $\dfrac{T}{4}\le t\le\dfrac{T}{2}$

i is constant $\therefore\ \dfrac{di}{dt}=0$

$\Rightarrow e=0$ For $\dfrac{T}{4}\le t\le\dfrac{T}{2}$

For $\dfrac{T}{2}\le t\le\dfrac{3T}{4}$

i–t graph is a straight line with negative constant slope.

$\therefore\ \dfrac{di}{dt}=\text{constant}$

$\Rightarrow e=+\text{ve and constant}$ For $\dfrac{T}{2}\le t\le\dfrac{3T}{4}$

For $\dfrac{3T}{4}\le t\le T$,

i is zero $\therefore\ \dfrac{di}{dt}=0$

$\Rightarrow e=0$ For $\dfrac{3T}{4}\le t\le T$

From this analysis, the variation of induced emf with time as shown in the figure below.

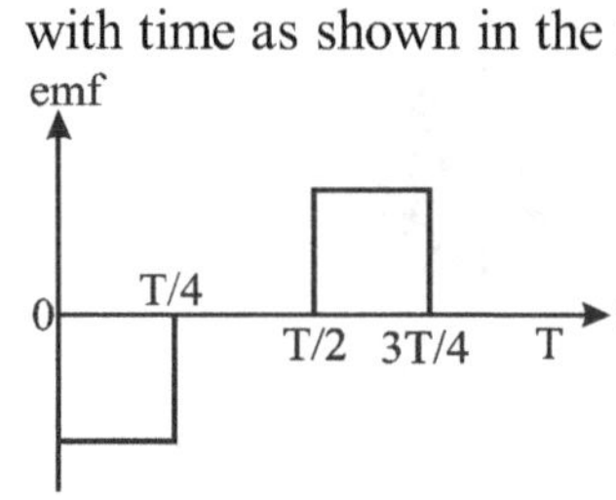

6. A coil of resistance 400 Ω is placed in a magnetic field. If the magnetic flux ϕ (wb) linked with the coil varies with time t (sec) as $\phi = 50\,t^2+4$, the current in the coil at t = 2 sec is **[AIPMT 2012]**

(1) 1 A (2) 0.5 A (3) 0.1 A (4) 2 A

Sol. (2) : $|i|=\dfrac{\varepsilon}{R}=\left|-\dfrac{d\varphi/dt}{R}\right|\left(\left|\dfrac{100\,t}{400}\right|=\left|\dfrac{200}{400}\right|=0.5\text{ A}\right.$

7. In a coil of resistane 10 Ω, the induced current developed by changing magnetic flux through it, is shown in figure as a function of time. The magnitude of change in flux through the coil in weber is **[AIPMT 2012]**

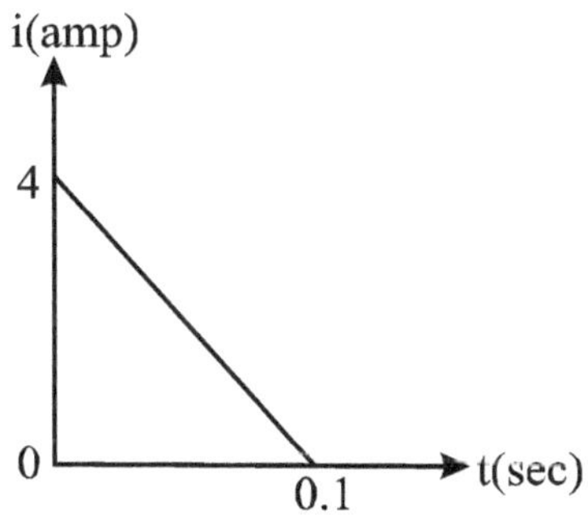

(1) 8 (2) 2 (3) 6 (4) 4

Sol. (2) : q = Area under *i-t* graph ⇒ $q = \int i\,dt$

$= \frac{1}{2} \times 4 \times 0.1 = 0.2C$; As $q = \frac{\Delta\phi}{R}$

$\therefore\ \Delta\phi = qR = (0.2C)(10\Omega) = 2$ weber.

8. A wire loop is rotated in a magnetic field. the frequency of change of direction of the induced e. m. f is **[AIPMT 2012]**

(1) Once per revolution

(2) Twice per revolution

(3) Four times per revolution

(4) Six times per revolution

Sol. (2) : Twice per revolution .

9. A thin semicircular conducting ring (PQR) of radius r is falling with its plane vertical in a horizontal magnetic field B.as shown in the figure The potential difference developed across the ring when its speed is v is **[AIMPT 2014]**

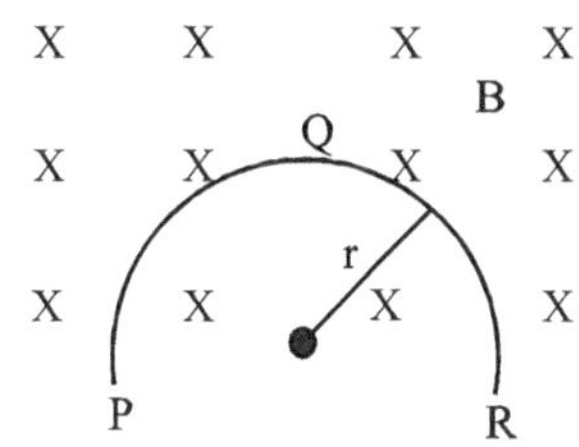

(1) Zero

(2) $Bv\pi r^2/2$ and P is at higher potential

(3) πrBv and R is at higher potential

(4) 2rBV and R is at higher potential

Sol. (4) :

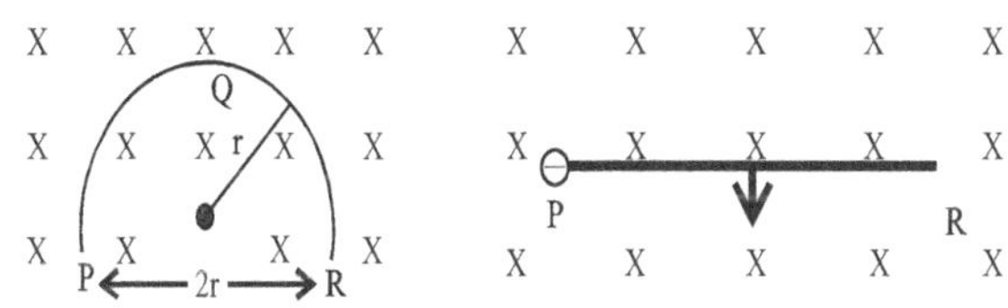

Induced emf = Bv(2r) = 2rBv

10. A conducting square frame of side a and a long straight wire carrying current I are located in the same plane as shown in the figure. The frame moves to the right with a constant velocity V. The emf induced in the frame be propertional t

[AIPMT 2015]

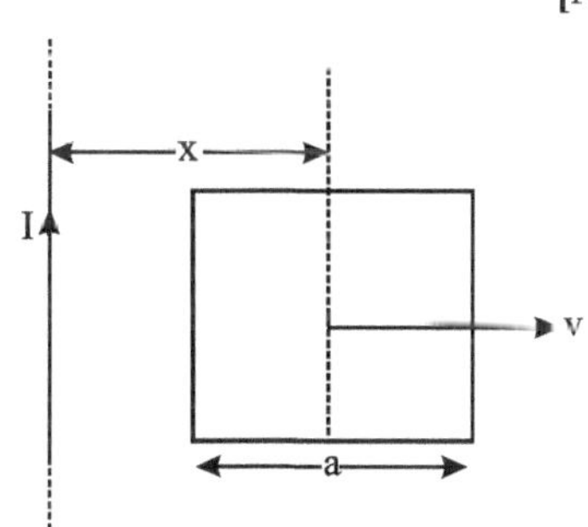

(1) $\frac{1}{x^2}$ (2) $\frac{1}{(2x-a)^2}$

(3) $\frac{1}{(2x+a)^2}$ (4) $\frac{1}{(2x-a)(2x+a)}$

Sol. (4): Apply motional emf $\Delta V \propto vL(B_2 - B_1)$

$$\propto \frac{1}{\left(x-\frac{a}{2}\right)} - \frac{1}{\left(x+\frac{a}{2}\right)}$$

$$\propto \frac{1}{(2x-a)(2x+a)}.$$

11. An electron moves on a straight line path XY as shown. The abcd is a coil adjacent to the path of electron. What will be direction of current if any, induced in the coil ? **[AIPMT 2015]**

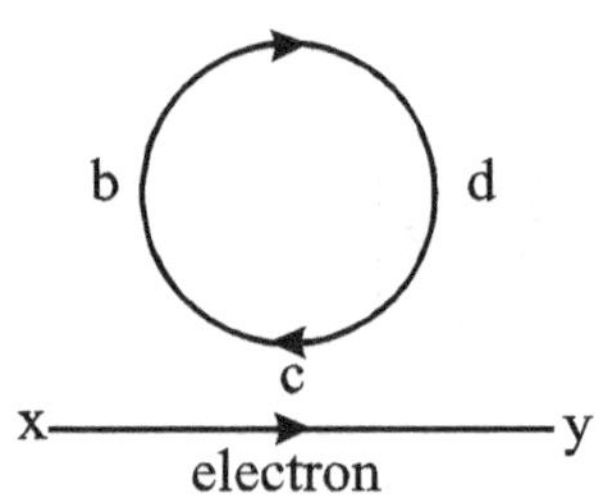

(1) No current induced

(2) abcd

(3) abcd

(4) The current will reverse its direction as the electron goes past the coil

Sol. (4) : First current develops in direction of abcd but when electron moves away, then magnetic field inside loop decreases & current changes its direction.

12. A long solenoid has 1000 turns. When a current of 4A flows through it, the magnetic flux linked with each turn of the solenoid is 4×10^{-3} Wb. The self inductance of the solenoid is :– **[AIPMT 2016]**

(1) 4H (2) 3H (3) 2H (4) 1H

Sol. (4) : $\phi_{self} = Li$

$(4 \times 10^{-3})(1000) = (L)(4)$

$L = 1$ Henry.

13. A uniform magnetic field is restricted within a region of radius r. The magnetic field changes with time at a rate $\frac{d\bar{B}}{dt}$ dB dt Loop 1 of radius R > r encloses the region r and loop 2 of radius R is outside the region of magnetic field as shown in the figure below. Then the e.m.f. generated is : **[NEET– II(2016)]**

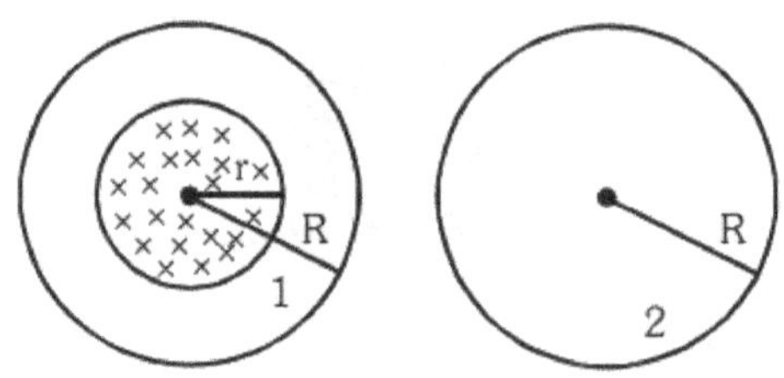

(1) $-\frac{d\bar{B}}{dt}R^2$ in loop 1 and zero in loop 2

(2) $-\frac{d\bar{B}}{dt}r^2$ in loop 1 and zero in loop 2

(3) Zero in loop 1 and zero in loop 2

(4) $-\frac{d\bar{B}}{dt}r^2$ in loop 1 and $-\frac{d\bar{B}}{dt}r^2$ in loop 2

Sol. (2) : $e = -\frac{d\phi}{dt} = -\frac{d}{dt}\{\pi r^2 B\} = -\pi r^2\frac{dB}{dt}$ in loop 1 & zero in loop 2.

14. The magnetic potential energy stored in a certain inductor is 25 mJ, when the current in the inductor is 60 mA. This inductor is of inductance

[NEET-2018]

(1) 1.389 H (2) 138.88 H

(3) 0.138 H (4) 13.89

Ans. **(4)**

21 Alternating Current

Note: Scan QR code with your mobile camera or QR scanner for video solutions.

1. The primary and secondary coils of a transformer hae 50 and 1500 turns respectively. If the magnetic flux f linked with the primary coil is given by f = f_0+4t, wher f is in webers, *t* is time in second and f_0 is a constant,the output voltage across the secondary coil is **[AIPMT 2007]**

(1) 90 V (2) 120 V (3) 220 V (4) 30 V

Sol. **(2) :** Induced emf in primary coil

$\because \phi_0$ = constant

$$E_P = \frac{d\phi}{dt} = \frac{d}{dt}(\phi_0 + 4t) = 4\text{volt}$$

Induced emf in secondary coil

$$\frac{E_S}{E_P} = \frac{N_S}{N_P} \Rightarrow \frac{E_S}{4} = \frac{1500}{50} \Rightarrow E_S = 120\,\text{volt}$$

2. A transformer is uses to light a 100 W and 110 V lamp from a 220 V mains. If the main current is 0.5 A, the Efficiency of the transformer is approximately : **[AIPMT 2007]**

(1) 30% (2) 50% (3) 90% (4) 10%

Sol. **(3) :** The efficiency of transformer

$$\eta = \frac{V_S I_S}{V_P I_P} \times 100 = \frac{100}{220 \times 0.5} \times 100 \approx 90\%.$$

3. What is the value of inductance L for which the current is a maximum in a series LCR circuit with C=10 μF and w = $1000s^{-1}$? **[AIPMT 2007]**

(1) 100 mH

(2) 1 mH

(3) cannot be calculated unless R is known

(4) 10 mH

Sol. **(1) :** Current is maximum at resonance

$$\Rightarrow \omega^2 = \frac{1}{LC} \Rightarrow L = \frac{1}{\omega^2 C} = \frac{1}{(1000)^2(10\times10^{-6})}$$

$= 0.1H = 100mH$

4. In an a.c. circuit the e.m.f. (e) and the correct (i) at any instant are given respectively by :- e = E_0 sinwt i = I_0 sin (wt –f) The average power in the circuit over one cycle of a.c. is :- **[AIPMT 2008]**

(1) $\frac{E_0 I_0}{2}$ (2) $\frac{E_0 I_0}{2}\sin\phi$ (3) $\frac{E_0 I_0}{2}\cos\phi$ (4) $E_0 I_0$

Sol. **(3) :** $e = E_0 \sin \omega t$ $\quad i = I_0 \sin(\omega t - \phi)$

$P_{av.} = E_{rms} \cdot I_{rms} \cdot \cos\phi$

$$= \frac{E_0}{\sqrt{2}} \cdot \frac{I_0}{\sqrt{2}} \cdot \cos\phi = \frac{E_0 I_0 \cos\phi}{2}$$

5. Power dissipated in an LCR series circuit connected to an a.c. source of emf e is :- **[AIPMT 2009]**

(1) $\frac{\varepsilon^2 R}{\left[R^2 + \left(L\omega - \frac{1}{C\omega}\right)^2\right]}$ (2) $\frac{\varepsilon^2\sqrt{R^2 + \left(L\omega - \frac{1}{C\omega}\right)^2}}{R}$

(3) $\frac{\varepsilon^2\left[R^2 + \left(L\omega - \frac{1}{C\omega}\right)^2\right]}{R}$ (4) $\frac{\varepsilon^2 R}{\sqrt{R^2 + \left(L\omega - \frac{1}{C\omega}\right)^2}}$

Sol. **(1) :** $P_{avg} = E_{rms} . I_{rms} \cos\phi$

$$= \varepsilon . \frac{\varepsilon}{z} . \frac{R}{z} = \frac{\varepsilon^2 R}{z^2} = \frac{\varepsilon^2 R}{R^2 + \left(\omega L - \frac{1}{\omega C}\right)^2}$$

6. In the given circuit the reading of voltmeter V_1 and V_2 are 300 V each. The reading to the voltmeter V_3 and ammeter A are respectiely **[AIPMT 2010]**

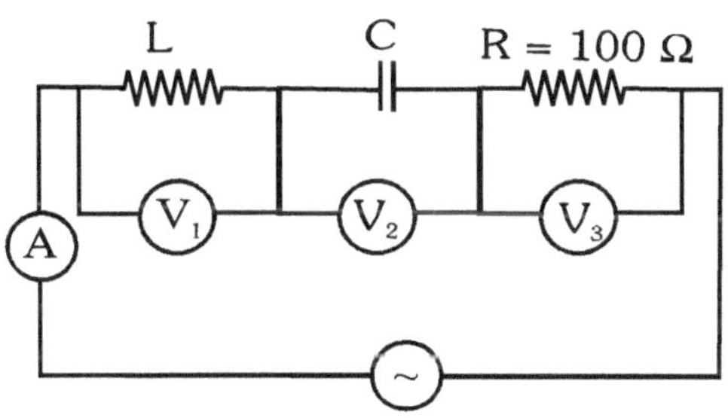

(1) 150 V, 2.2 A (2) 220 V, 2.2 A
(3) 220 V, 2.0 A (4) 100 V, 2.0 A

Sol. **(2) :** $V_3 = 220\,\text{volt},\ I = \frac{220}{100} = 2.2\,A$.

7. A 220 V input is supplied to a transformer. The output circuit draws a current of 2.0A and 440 V. If the efficiency of the transformer is 80% , the current drawn by the primary windings of the transformer is **[AIPMT 2010]**

(1) 3.6 A (2) 2.8 A (3) 2.5 A (4) 5.0 A

Sol. **(4) :** $\eta = \frac{V_S I_S}{V_P I_P} = 0.8 \Rightarrow I_P = \frac{(440)(20)}{(0.8)(200)} = 5A$.

8. An AC voltage is applied to a resistance R and an inductor L in series. If R and the inductive reatance are both equal to 3 W, the phase difference between the applied voltage and the current in the circuit is **[AIPMT 2011]**

(1) $\pi/4$ (2) $\pi/2$ (3) zero (4) $\pi/6$

Sol. **(1) :** $\tan\phi = \frac{X_L}{R} = 1,\ \phi = 45°$. [$\because$ XL = R]

9. In an AC circuit an alternating voltage e = 200 $\sqrt{2}$ sin 100 t volt is connected to a capacitor f capacity 1 mF. The rms vlaue of the current in the circuit is **[AIPMT 2011]**

(1) 100 mA (2) 200 mA (3) 20 mA (4) 10 mA

Sol. **(3) :** The given equation of alternating voltage is

$e = 200\sqrt{2}\sin 100t$ ....(i)

The standard equation of alternatig voltage is

$e = e_0 \sin\omega t$

Comparing (i) and (ii), we get

$e_0 = 200\sqrt{2}$ V, $\omega = 100$ rad s^{-1}

The capacitive reactance is

$$X_C = \frac{1}{\omega C} = \frac{1}{100 \times 1 \times 10^{-6}}\Omega$$

The r.m.s. value of the current in the circuit is

$$i_{r.m.s.} = \frac{\upsilon_{r.m.s.}}{X_C} = \frac{e_0/\sqrt{2}}{1/\omega C} = \frac{(200\sqrt{2}/\sqrt{2})}{(1/100 \times 10^{-6})}$$

$$= 200 \times 100 \times 10^{-6} A = 2 \times 10^{-2} A = 20\,mA$$

10. The rms value of potential difference V shown in the figure is **[AIPMT 2011]**

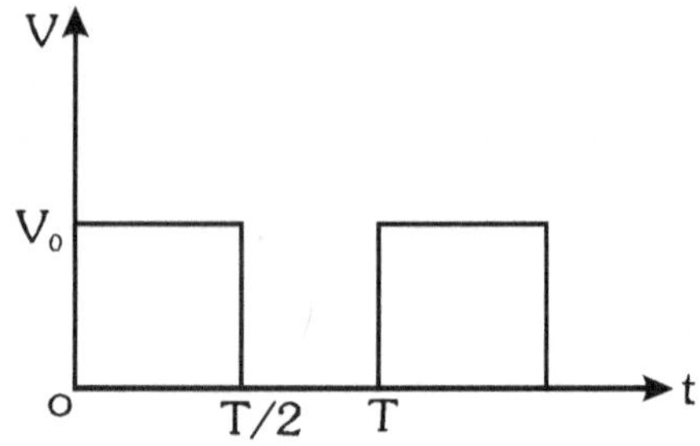

(1) V_0 (2) $\frac{V_0}{\sqrt{2}}$ (3) $\frac{V_0}{2}$ (4) $\frac{V_0}{\sqrt{3}}$

Sol. **(2) :**

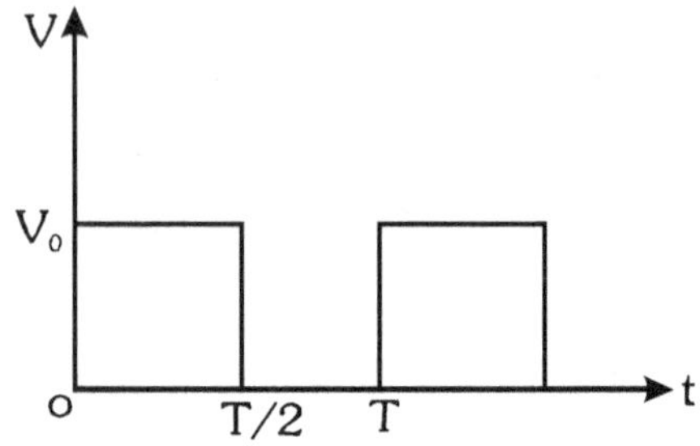

$$V = V_0 \text{ for } 0 \le t \le \frac{T}{2}$$

$$V = 0 \text{ for } \frac{T}{2} \le t \le T$$

$$V_{\text{rms}} = \left[\frac{\int_0^T V^2 dt}{\int_0^T dt}\right] = \left[\frac{\int_0^{T/2} V_0^2 dt + \int_{T/2}^T (0) dt}{\int_0^T dt}\right]^{1/2}$$

$$= \left[\frac{V_0^2}{T}[t]_0^{T/2}\right]^{1/2} = \left[\frac{V_0^2}{T}\left(\frac{T}{2}\right)\right]^{1/2} = \left[\frac{V_0^2}{2}\right]^{1/2}$$

$$V_{\text{rms}} = \frac{V_0}{\sqrt{2}}$$

11. A coil has resistance 30 Ω and inductive reactance 20 W at 50 Hz frequency. If an AC source of 200 V, 100 Hz, is connected across the coil the current in the coil will be **[AIPMT 2011]**

(1) 4.0 A (2) 8.0 A (3) $\frac{20}{\sqrt{13}}$ A (4) 2.0 A

Sol. **(1) :** Here, Resistance, R = 30 Ω

Inductive reactance , X_L = 30 Ω at 50 Hz

$$\because X_L = 2\pi \upsilon l$$

$$\therefore \frac{X_L}{X'_L} = \frac{\upsilon}{\upsilon'}$$

$$X'_L = \frac{\upsilon}{\upsilon'} \times X_L = \left(\frac{100}{50}\right) \times 20\Omega = 40\Omega$$

Impedance,

$$Z = \sqrt{R^2 + (X'_L)^2} = \sqrt{(30)^2 + (40)^2} = 50\Omega$$

Current in the coil, $I = \frac{V}{Z} = \frac{200V}{50\Omega} = 4\text{A}$.

12. In an electrical circuit R,L C and an AC voltage source are all connected in series, When L is removed from the circuit, the phase difference between the voltage and the current in the circuit is p/3. If instead, C is removed from the circuit difference the phase difference is again p/3. The power factor of the circuit is **[AIPMT 2012]**

(1) $\frac{1}{2}$ (2) $\frac{1}{\sqrt{2}}$ (3) 1 (4) $\frac{\sqrt{3}}{2}$

Sol. **(3) :** It is the condition of resonance therefore phase difference between voltage and current is zero and power factor $\cos\phi = 1$

13. The current (I) in the inductance is varying with time according to the plot shown in figure. **[AIPMT 2012]**

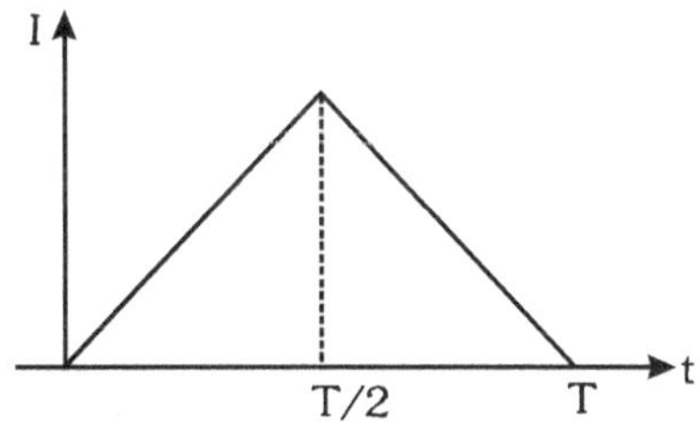

Which one fo the folowing is the correct variation of voltage with time in the coil ?

(1) 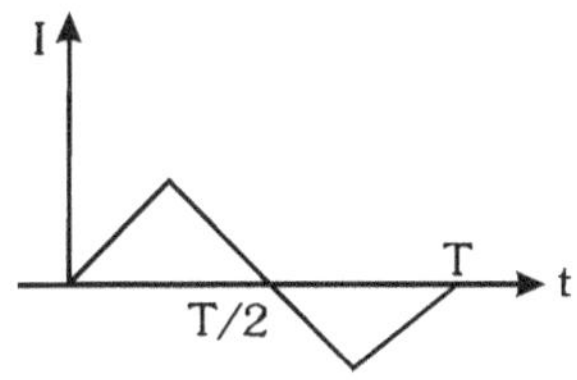

(2) 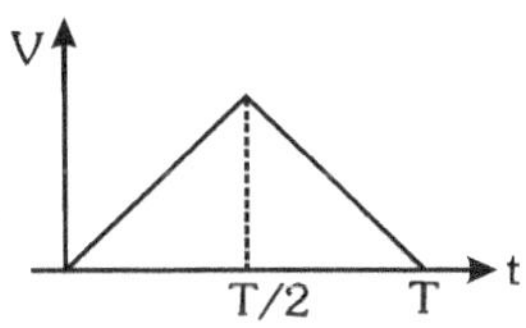

(3) 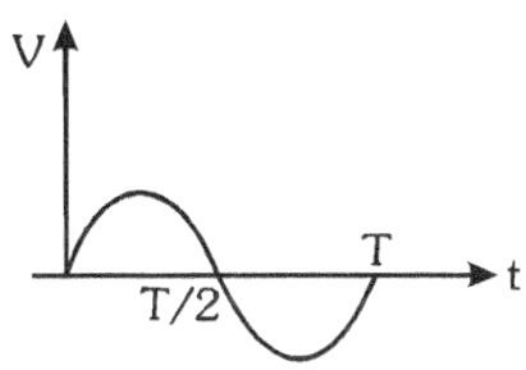

(4) 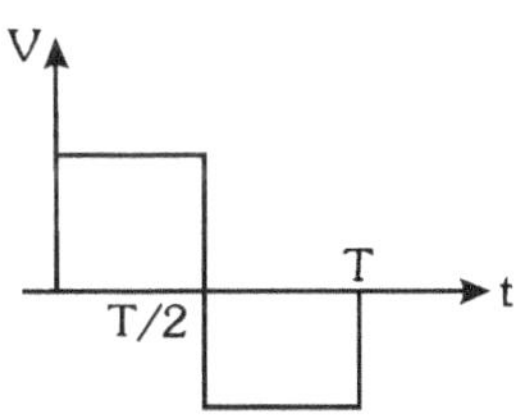

Sol. **(4) :** $|V|=\left|-L\frac{di}{dt}\right|$ therefore answer will be best represented by graph - 4 .

14. The instantanesous values of alternating current and voltages in a circuit are given as

$$i=\frac{1}{\sqrt{2}}\sin(100\pi t)\text{ampere}$$ **[AIPMT 2012]**

$$e=\frac{1}{\sqrt{2}}\sin(100\pi t+\pi/3)\text{volt}$$

The average power in watts consumed in the circuit is

(1) $\frac{1}{4}$ (2) $\frac{\sqrt{3}}{4}$ (3) $\frac{1}{2}$ (4) $\frac{1}{8}$

Sol. **(4) :** Given : $i=\frac{1}{\sqrt{2}}\sin(100\pi t)$ ampere

Compare at with $i=i_0\sin(\omega t)$, We get

$$i_0=\frac{1}{\sqrt{2}}\text{A}$$

Given ; $e=\frac{1}{\sqrt{2}}\sin\left(100\pi t+\frac{\pi}{3}\right)$volt

Compare it with, we get $e_0=\frac{1}{\sqrt{2}}\text{V},\ \phi=\frac{\pi}{3}$

$$\therefore i_{rms}=\frac{i_0}{\sqrt{2}}=\frac{\frac{1}{\sqrt{2}}}{\sqrt{2}}\text{A}=\frac{1}{2}\text{A}$$

$$e_{rms}=\frac{e_0}{\sqrt{2}}=\frac{\frac{1}{\sqrt{2}}}{\sqrt{2}}\text{V}=\frac{1}{2}\text{V}$$

Average power consumed in the circuit,

$P=i_{rms}\,e_{rms}\cos\phi$

$$=\left(\frac{1}{2}\right)\left(\frac{1}{2}\right)\cos\frac{\pi}{3}=\left(\frac{1}{2}\right)\left(\frac{1}{2}\right)\left(\frac{1}{2}\right)=\frac{1}{8}\text{W}.$$

15. A coil of self- inductance L is connected in series with a bulb B and an AC source. Brightness of the bulb decreases when **[AIPMT 2013]**

(1) Frequency of the AC source is decreased

(2) Number of turns in the coil is reduced

(3) A capactiance of reactiance $X_C = X_L$ is included in the same circuit

(4) An iron rod is in serted in the coil

Sol. **(4) :** The situation is shown in the figure

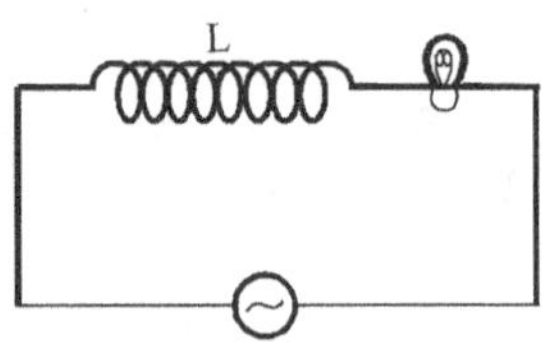

As the iron rod is inserted, the magnetic field inside the coil magnetizes the iron increasing the magnetic field inside it. Hence, the inductance of the coil increases. Consequently, the inductive reactance of the coil increases. As a result, a larger fraction of the applied AC voltage appears across the inductor, leaving less voltage across the bulb. Therefore, the brightness of the light bulb decreases.

16. A transformer having efficienty of 90% is working on 200 V and 3 kW power supply. If the current in the secondary coil is 6 A, the voltage across the secondary coil and the current in the primary coil respectively are **[AIPMT 2014]**

(1) 300 V, 15 A (2) 450 V,15 A

(3) 450 V, 135 A (4) 600 V, 15 A

Sol. **(2) :** $\eta = \dfrac{V_S I_S}{V_P I_P} \Rightarrow 0.9 = \dfrac{V_S(6)}{3\times10^3} \Rightarrow V_S = 450\,V$

As $V_P I_P = 3000$ so $I_P = \dfrac{3000}{200} A = 15\ A$

17. A resistance R draws power P when connected to an AC source. If an inductance is now placed in series with the resistances, such that the impedance of the circuit becomes Z, the power drawn will be **[AIPMT 2015]**

(1) $P\left(\dfrac{R}{Z}\right)^2$ (2) $P\sqrt{\dfrac{R}{Z}}$ (3) $P\left(\dfrac{R}{Z}\right)$ (4) P

Sol. **(1) :** $P = \dfrac{V_{rms}}{R}$ .....(i)

$P' = V_{rms}.i_{rms}.\cos\phi$

$P' = V_{rms}\left(\dfrac{V_{rms}}{Z}\right)\left(\dfrac{R}{Z}\right) = V_{rms}^2.\dfrac{R}{Z^2}$ .....(ii)

By (i) & (ii)

$P' = (P.R)\left(\dfrac{R}{Z^2}\right) = P\left(\dfrac{R}{Z}\right)^2$.

18. A series R-C circuit is connected to an alternating voltage source. Consider two situations. **[AIPMT 2015 Re]**

(a) When capacitor is air filled

(b) When capacitor is mica filled

Current through resistor is i and voltage across capacitor is V then

(1) $V_a = V_b$ (2) $V_a < V_b$

(3) $V_a > V_b$ (4) $I_a > i_b$

Sol. **(3) :** When capacitor is filled with mica then capacitance C increases so X_C decreases In case (b) $X_C \downarrow$ so voltage across capacitor decreases. so $V_a > V_b$

19. The input signal given to a CE amplifier having a voltage gain of 150 is $V_1 = 2\cos\left(15t+\frac{\pi}{3}\right)$ The corresponding output singal will be **[AIPMT 2015 Re]**

(1) $300\cos\left(15t\frac{4\pi}{3}\right)$ (2) $300\cos\left(15t\frac{\pi}{3}\right)$

(3) $75\cos\left(15t\frac{2\pi}{3}\right)$ (4) $2\cos\left(15t\frac{5\pi}{6}\right)$

Sol. **(1) :** Input signal $V_{in} = 2\cos(15t+\frac{\pi}{3})$

Voltage Gain = 150

CE amplifier gives phase difference of π between input and output signals

$$A_v = \frac{V_0}{V_{in}} \text{ so } V_0 = A_v V_{in}$$

$$\text{so } V_0 = 150\times 2\cos(15t+\frac{\pi}{3}+\pi)$$

$$V_0 = 300\cos(15t+\frac{4\pi}{3}) .$$

20. The charge flowing through a resistance R varies with time t as Q = at – bt², where a and b are positive constants. The total heat produced in R is: **[AIPMT 2016]**

(1) $\frac{a^3R}{6b}$ (2) $\frac{a^3R}{3b}$ (3) $\frac{a^3R}{2b}$ (4) $\frac{a^3R}{b}$

Sol. **(1) :** $Q = at - bt^2$

$$i = \frac{dQ}{dt} = a - 2bt \qquad i - 0\ t = \frac{a}{2b}$$

$$H = \int_0^t i^2Rbt = \frac{a^3R}{6b} \qquad \Rightarrow \int_0^t I^2Rbt$$

$$it = \int_0^{a/2b} (a-2bt)^2Rbt = a^2t + \frac{4b^2t^3}{3} - \frac{4bat^2}{2}$$

$$\text{Put } t = \frac{a}{2b} \Rightarrow H = \frac{a^3R}{6b}.$$

21. Which of the following combinations should be selected for better tuning of an L-C-R circuit used for communication ? **[NEET – 2016]**

(1) R = 15 Ω, L = 3.5 H, C = 30 μF

(2) R = 25 Ω, L = 1.5 H, C = 45 μF

(3) R = 20 Ω, L = 1.5 H, C = 35 μF

(4) R = 25 Ω, L = 2.5 H, C = 45 μF

Sol. **(1) :** Option with highest quality factor should be choosen as most appropriate answer.

$$Q = \frac{1}{R}\sqrt{\frac{L}{C}}$$

R is lower

L = is greater

22. The potential differences across the resistance, capacitance and inductance are 80 V, 40 V and 100 V respectively in an L-C-R circuit. The power factor of this circuit is :– **[NEET – 2016]**

(1) 0.8 (2) 1.0 (3) 0.4 (4) 0.5

Sol. **(1) :** Power factor

$$= \frac{R}{z} = \frac{iR}{iz} = \frac{80}{\sqrt{(80)^2+(60)^2}} = \frac{80}{100} = 0.8$$

23. Figure shows a circuit that contains three identical resistors with resistance $R=9.0\Omega$ each two identical inductors with inductance L = 2.0 mHeach, and an ideal battery with emf ε = 18 V. The current 'i' through the battery just after the witch close is,...... **[NEET – 2017]**

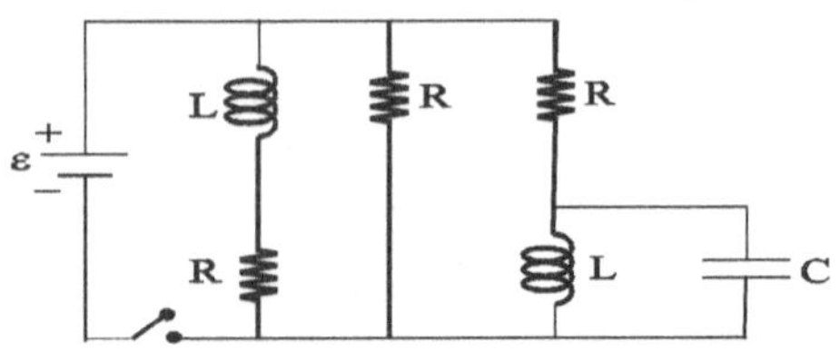

(1) 2 mA (2) 0.2 A (3) 2 A (4) 0 ampere

Sol. **(3) :**

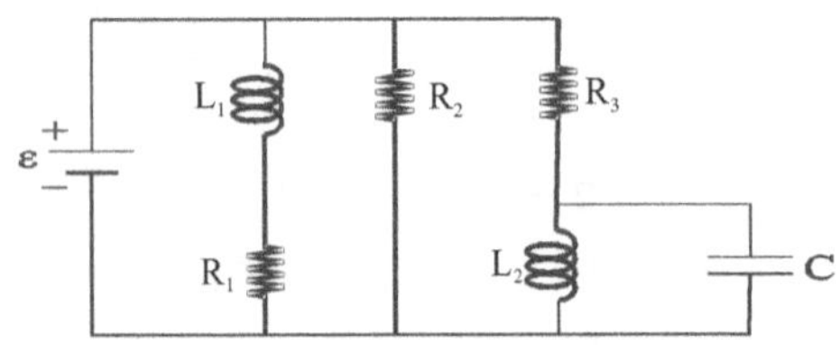

At t = 0, no current flows through R_1 and R_3

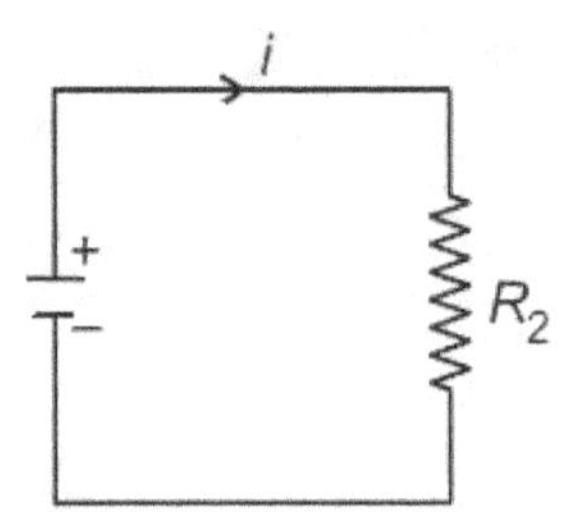

$$i=\frac{\varepsilon}{R_2}=\frac{18}{9}=2A$$

Note : Not correctly framed but the best option out of given is (3).

24. A metallic rod of mass per unit length 0.5 kg m^{-1} is lying horizontally on a smooth inclined plane which makes an angle of 30° with the horizontal. The rod is not allowed to slide down by flowing a current 0.25 T is acting on it in the vertical direction. The current flowing in the rod to keep it stationary is **[NEET-2018]**

(1) 14.76 A (2) 5.98 A

(3) 7.14 A (4) 11.32 A

Ans. **(4)** For equilibrium,

mg sin30° = I*l* Bcos30°

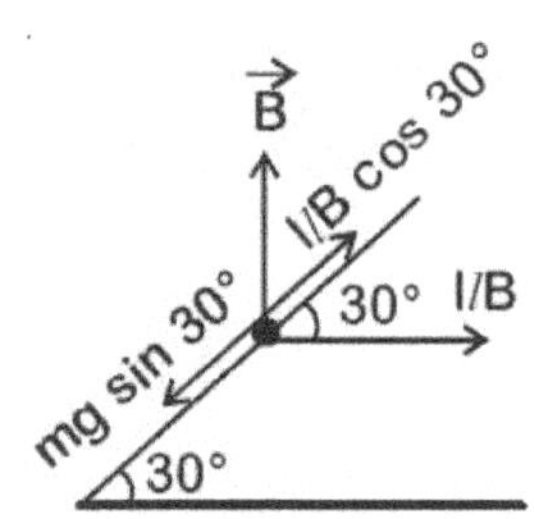

$$I=\frac{mg}{lB}\tan 30°$$

$$=\frac{0.5\times 9.8}{0.25\times\sqrt{3}}=11.32\text{ A}$$

25. An inductor 20 mH, a capacitor 100 μF and a source of The power loss in the circuit is **[NEET-2018]**

(1) 2.74 W (2) 0.43

(3) 0.79 (4) 1.13 W

Ans. **(3)** $P_{av}=\left(\frac{V_{RMS}}{Z}\right)^2 R$

$$Z=\sqrt{R^2+\left(\omega R-\frac{1}{\omega C}\right)^2}=56\,\Omega$$

$$\therefore\ P_{av}=\left(\frac{10}{(\sqrt{2})}\right)^2\times 50=0.79\text{ W}$$

22 Electromagnetic Waves

Note: Scan QR code with your mobile camera or QR scanner for video solutions.

1. The electric and magnetic field of an electromagnetic wave is **[AIPMT-2007]**

(1) in phase and parallel to each other

(2) in opposite phase and perpendicular to each other

(3) in opposite phase and parallel to each other

(4) in phase and perpendicular to each other

Sol. **(4) :** In EM waves $\vec{E}$ and $\vec{B}$ are in same phase and perpendicular to each other.

2. The velocity of electromagnetic radiation in a medium of permittivity ε_0 and permeability μ_0 is given by **[AIPMT-2008]**

(1) $\sqrt{\frac{_0}{_0}}$ (2) $\sqrt{\ _0\ _0}$ (3) $\sqrt{\frac{1}{\sqrt{\ _0\ _0}}}$ (4) $\sqrt{\frac{_0}{_0}}$

Sol. **(3) :** $C = \frac{1}{\sqrt{\mu_0\varepsilon_0}}$ = velocity of em wave through medium having permittivity (ε_0) and permeability (μ_0).

3. The electric field part of an electromagnetic wave in a medium is represented by $E_x = 0$;

$E_y = 2.5\frac{N}{C}\cos\ 2\ \ 10^6\frac{rad}{m}\ t\ \ \ 10^{-2}\frac{rad}{s}\ x$;

$E_z = 0$. The wave is : **[AIPMT 2009]**

(1) Moving along – x direction with frequency 10^6 Hz and wave length 200 m.

(2) Moving along y direction with frequency $2\pi \times 10^6$ Hz and wave length 200 m.

(3) Moving along x direction with frequency 10^6 Hz and wave length 100 m.

(4) Moving along x direction with frequency 10^6 Hz and wave length 200 m.

Sol. **(4) :** As the coefficient of x is negative, it is moving along +ve x-axis and equating the equation

$$E_y = 2.5\cos[(2\pi \times 10^6)]t - (\pi \times 10^{-2})x]$$

With $y = A\cos(\omega t - kx)$

$\omega = 2\pi \times 106$

$$\Rightarrow f = \frac{\omega}{2\pi} = 10^6 Hz$$

$k = \pi \times 10^{-2}$

$$\Rightarrow \lambda = \frac{2\pi}{k} = \frac{2\pi}{\pi \times 10^{-2}} = 200\ m.$$

4. Which of the following statement is false for the properties of electromagnetic waves? **[AIPMT-2010]**

(1) Both electric and magnetic field vectors attain the maxima and minima at the same place and the same time

(2)The energy in electromagnetic wave is divided equally between and magnetic vectors(3) Both electric and magnetic field vectors are parallel to each other and perpendicular to the direction of propagation of wave

(4) These waves do not required any material medium for propagation

Sol. **(3) :** In an electormagnetic wave Both electric and magnetic vectors are perpendicular to each other as well as perpendicular to the direction of propagation of wave.

5. The electric and the magnetic field, associated with an electromagnetic wave, propagating along the +z-axis, can be represented by **[AIPMT-2011]**

(1) $[E \;\; E_0\hat{k}, B \;\; B_0\hat{i}]$ (2) $[E \;\; E_0\hat{j}, B \;\; B_0\hat{j}]$

(3) $[E \;\; E_0\hat{j}, B \;\; B_0\hat{k}]$ (4) $[E \;\; E_0\hat{i}, B \;\; B_0\hat{j}]$

Sol. **(4) :** $\hat{v} = \hat{E} \times \hat{B}$ or (direction of propagation of waves is $\hat{E} \times \hat{B}$

6. The decreasing order of wavelength of infrared microwave, ultraviolet and gamma rays is **[AIPMT-2011]**

(1) gamm rays, ultraviolet, infrared, microwaves

(2) microwaves, gamm rays, infrared, ultraviolet

(3) infrared, microwaves, ultraviolet, gamm rays

(4) microwaves, infrared, ultraviolet, gamm rays

Sol. **(4) :** The decreasing order of wavelength of the given electromagnetic waves is as follows :

$\lambda_{\text{Microwave}} > \lambda_{\text{Infrared}} > \lambda_{\text{Ultraviolet}} > \lambda_{\text{Gamm rays}}$

7. The electric field associated with an electromagnetic wave in vacuum is given by $\vec{E} \;\; \hat{i}\,40\cos(kz \;\; 6 \;\; 10^8 t)$, where E, z and t are in volt/m, metre and second respectively. The value of wave vector k is **[AIPMT-2012]**

(1) 2 m^{-1} (2) 0.5 m^{-1}

(3) 6 m^{-1} (4) 3 m^{-1}

Sol. **(1) :** Equation of Electromagnetic wave is E = E0 cos (kz – ωt) and speed of EM wave $V = \frac{\omega}{k}$

By comparing $k = \omega/v = \frac{6\times10^8}{3\times10^8} = 2\ m^{-1}$ is the wave vector.

8. The ratio of amplitude of magnetic field to the amplitude of electric field for an electromagnetic wave propagating in vacuum is equal to **[AIPMT-2012]**

(1) the speed of light in vacuum

(2) reciprocal of speed of light in vacuum

(3) the ratio of magnetic permeability to the electric susceptibility of vacuum

(4) unity

Sol. **(2) :** The amplitude of magnetic field and electric field for an electromagnetic wave propagating in vacuum are ralated as

$$E_0 = B_0 c$$

Where c is the speed of light in vacuum.

$$\therefore \frac{B_0}{E_0} = \frac{1}{c}$$

9. Light with an energy flux of $25 \times 10^4\ W\ m^{-2}$ falls on a perfectly reflecting surface at normal incidence. If the surface area is 15 cm^2, the average force exerted on the surface is **[AIPMT-2014]**

(1) 1.25×10^{-6} N (2) 2.50×10^{-6} N

(3) 1.20×10^{-6} N (4) 3.0×10^{-6} N

Sol. **(2) :** Average force $F_{av} = \frac{\Delta p}{\Delta t} = \frac{2IA}{c}$

$$= \frac{2\times 25\times 10^4 \times 15\times 10^{-4}}{3\times 10^8}$$

$$= 2.50\times 10^{-6} \text{ N}$$

10. A radiation of energy 'E' falls normally on a perfectly reflecting surface. The momentum transferred to the surface is (C = velocity of light) **[AIPMT-2015]**

(1) $\frac{E}{C}$ (2) $\frac{2E}{C}$

(3) $\frac{2E}{C^2}$ (4) $\frac{E}{C^2}$

Sol. **(2) :** P = momentum $= \frac{E}{C}$

so, change in momentum $= \frac{2E}{C}$

11. The energy of the electromagnetic waves is of the order of 15 keV. To which part of the spectrum does it belong ? **[AIPMT-2015 Re]**

(1) γ-rays (2) X-rays

(3) Infrared rays (4) Ultraviolet rays

Sol. **(2) :** Wavelength of the ray $\lambda = \frac{hc}{E}$

$$= 0.826\,\text{Å}$$

since $\lambda < 100\,\text{Å}$

so it is X - ray.

12. Out of the following options which one canb e used to produce a propagating electromagnetic wave ? **[AIPMT 2016]**

(1) A charge moving at constant velocity

(2) A stationary charge

(3) A chargeless particle

(4) An accelerating charge

Sol. **(4) :** An accelerating charge

13. A 100 Ω resistance and a capacitor of 100 Ω reactance are connected in series across a 220 V source. When the capacitor is 50% charged, the peak value of the displacement current is :- **[AIPMT 2016]**

(1) 4.4 A (2) $11\sqrt{2}$ A

(3) 2.2 A (4) 11 A

Sol. **(3) :** $z = \sqrt{R^2 + X_c^2}$

$$= \sqrt{(100)^2 + (100)^2}$$

$$= 100\sqrt{2}$$

$$i_{max} = \frac{V_{max}}{z} = \frac{220\sqrt{2}}{100\sqrt{2}} = 2.2.$$

14. In an electromagnetic wave in free space the root mean square value of the electric field is $E_{rms} = 6V/m$. The peak value of the magnetic field is : **[NEET - 2017]**

(1) 1.41×10^{-8} T (2) 2.83×10^{-8}

(3) 0.70×10^{-8} T (4) 4.23×10^{-8} T

Sol. **(2) :** $\frac{E_{rms}}{B_{rms}} = c$

$$B_{rms} = \frac{E_{rms}}{c} = \frac{6}{3\times10^{8}}$$

$$B_{rms} = \frac{B_0}{\sqrt{2}};\quad B_0 = \sqrt{2}\times B_{rms}$$

$$= \sqrt{2}\times2\times10^{-8}$$

$$= 2.83\times10^{-8}\,\text{T}\cdot$$

15. An electron falls from rest through a vertical distance h in a uniform and vertically upward directed electric field E. The direction of electric field is now reversed, keeping its magnitude the same. A proton is allowed to fall from rest in it through the same vertical distance h. The time of fall of the electron, in comparison to the time of fall the proton is **[NEET-2018]**

(1) 10 times greater (2) 5 times greater

(3) smaller (4) equal

Ans. (3)

16. An em wave is propagating in a medium with a velocity $\overline{V} - V\hat{i}$. The instantaneous oscillating electric field of this em wave is along +y axis. Then the direction of oscillating magnetic field of the em wave will be along **[NEET-2018]**

(1) -y direction (2) +z direction

(3) -z direction (4) -x direvtion

Ans. (2)

23 Ray Optics and Optical Instruments

Note: Scan QR code with your mobile camera or QR scanner for video solutions.

1. The frequency of a light wave in a material is 2×10^{14} Hz and wavelength is 5000 Å. The refractive index of material will be **[AIPMT-2007]**

(1) 1.40 (2) 1.50 (3) 3.00 (4) 1.33

Sol. : (3) Refractive index $\mu = \frac{c}{v} = \frac{c}{f\lambda}$

$$= \frac{3\times10^{8}}{2\times10^{14}\times5000\times10^{-10}} = 3$$

2. A small coin is resting on the bottom of a beaker filled with a liquid. A ray of light from the coin travels up to the surface of the liquid and moves along its surface (see figure) **[AIPMT-2007]**

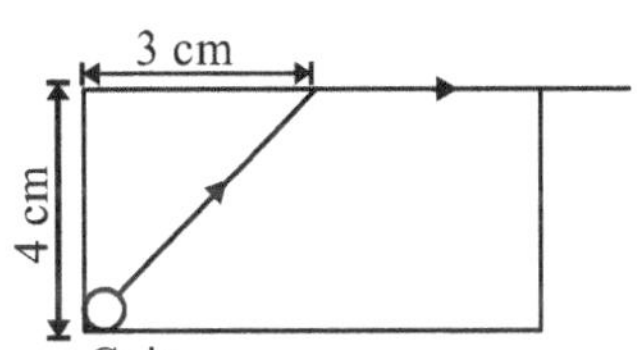

How fast is the light travelling in the liquid?

(1) 1.8×10^{8} m/s (2) 2.4×10^{8} m/s

(3) 3.0×10^{8} m/s (4) 1.2×10^{8} m/s

Sol. : **(1)**

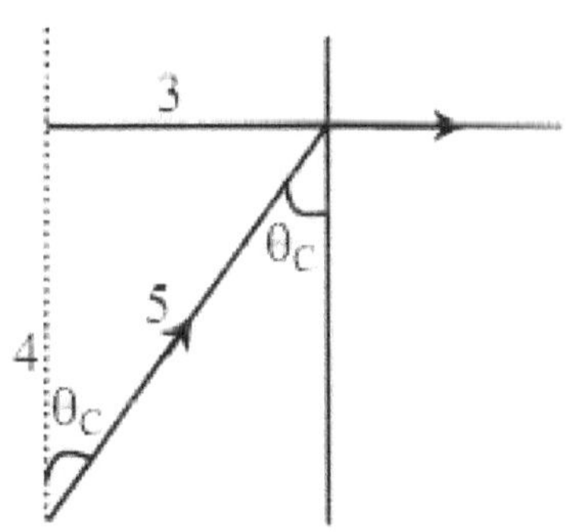

$$\frac{1}{\mu} = \sin\theta_C = \frac{3}{5} \Rightarrow \mu\frac{5}{3}$$

$$\Rightarrow v = \frac{c}{\mu} = \frac{3\times10^{8}}{5/3} = \frac{9}{5}\times10^{8}$$

$$= 1.8\times10^{8}\,ms^{-1}$$

3. Two thin lenses of focal length f_1 and f_2 are in contact and coaxial. The power of the combination is **[AIPMT-2008]**

(1) $\sqrt{\frac{f_1}{f_2}}$ (2) $\sqrt{\frac{f_2}{f_1}}$ (3) $\frac{f_1+f_2}{f_1f_2}$ (4) $\frac{f_1+f_2}{f_1f_2}$

Sol. : (4) $P = P_1 + P_2 = \frac{1}{f_1} + \frac{1}{f_2}$

$$P = \frac{f_1+f_2}{f_1.f_2}$$

4. A boy is trying to start a fire by focusing sunlight on a piece of paper using an equiconvex lens of focal length 10 cm. The diameter of the sun is 1.39×10^{9} m and its mean distance from the earth is 1.5×10^{11} m. What is the diameter of the sun's image on the paper ? **[AIPMT-2008]**

(1) 9.2×10^{-4} m (2) 6.5×10^{-4} m

(3) 6.5×10^{-5} m (4) 12.4×10^{-4} m

Sol. : (1)

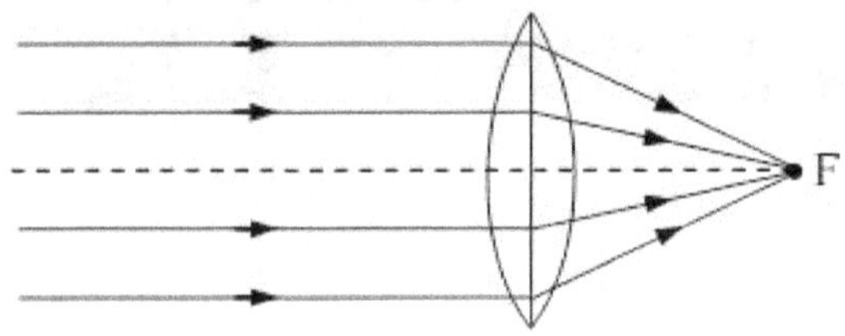

$u = 1.5\times10^{11}$m

$\upsilon = f = 10\text{cm} = 0.1\text{m}$

$$\frac{\upsilon}{u} = \frac{h_i}{h_0}$$

$$\Rightarrow \frac{0.1}{1.5\times10^{11}} = \frac{h_i}{1.39\times10^{9}}$$

$$h_i = \frac{1.39\times10^{8}}{1.5\times10^{11}} = 9.2\times10^{-4}\text{m}$$

5. A ray of light travelling in a transparent medium of refractive index μ falls, on a surface separating the medium from air at an angle of incidence of 45°. For which of the following value of μ the ray can undergo total internal reflection ? **[AIPMT-2010]**

(1) $\mu = 1.33$ (2) $\mu = 1.40$

(3) $\mu = 1.50$ (4) $\mu = 1.25$

Sol. : **(3)** For TIR $45 \geq \theta_c \Rightarrow \sin 45 \geq \sin\theta_c$

$$\Rightarrow \frac{1}{\sqrt{2}} \geq \frac{1}{\mu} \Rightarrow \mu \geq \sqrt{2}$$

6. Which of the following is not due to total internal reflection? **[AIPMT-2011]**

(1) Difference between apparent and real depth of a pond

(2) Mirage on ht summer days

(3) Brilliance of diamond

(4) Working of optical fibre

Sol. : **(1)**

Difference b/w apparent lengnt and real depth

7. A biconvex lens has a radius of curvature of magnitude 20 cm. Which one of the following options describes best the image formed of an object of height 2 cm placed 30 cm from the lens? **[AIPMT-2011]**

(1) Virtual, upright, height= 0.5 cm

(2) Real, inverted, height = 4 cm

(3) Real, inverted, height = 1 cm

(4) Virtual, upright, height = 1 cm

Sol. : **(2)** Focal length of the lens

$$\frac{1}{f} = (1.5-1)\left(\frac{1}{20} - \frac{1}{-20}\right) = \frac{1}{20}$$

f = 20 cm

From lens formula

$$\frac{1}{v} - \frac{1}{u} = \frac{1}{f}$$

$$\frac{1}{v} - \frac{1}{-30} = \frac{1}{20}$$

v = 60 cm

$$\frac{I}{0} = m = \frac{v}{u} = \frac{60}{-30} = -I$$

$$I = -2(0) = -2\times2 = -4\text{cm}$$

So image will be real inverted and of size 4 cm.

8. A thin prism of angle 15° made of glass of refractive index $\mu_1 = 1.5$ is combined with anotherprism of glass of refractive index $\mu_2 = 1.75$. the combination of the prism produces dispersion without deeviation . The angle of the second prism should be **[AIPMT-2011]**

(1) 7° (2) 10° (3) 12° (4) 5°

Sol. : **(2)** For dispersion without deviation

$$\delta_1 + \delta_2 = 0 \; ; \; (\mu_1 - 1)A_1 + (\mu_2 - 1)A_2 = 0$$

$$A_2 = -\frac{(\mu_1 - 1)A_1}{(\mu_2 - 1)}$$

Substiting the given values, we get

$$A_2 = -\frac{(1.5 - 1)15°}{(1.75 - 1)} = -10°$$

-ve sign shows that two prisms must be joined in opposition.

9. A coverging beam of rays is incident on a diverging lens. Having passed through the lens the rays intersect at a point 15 cm from the lens on the opposite side.If the lens is removed the point where the rays will move 5 cm closer to the lens. The focal length of the lens is **[AIPMT-2011]**

(1) –10 cm (2) 20 cm

(3) –30 cm (4) 5 cm

Sol. : **(3)** Here, $\upsilon = +15\text{cm}$,

$u = +(15 - 5) = +10\text{cm}$

According to lens formula

$$\frac{1}{\upsilon} - \frac{1}{u} = \frac{1}{f} \Rightarrow \frac{1}{50} - \frac{1}{10} = \frac{1}{f} \Rightarrow f = -30\text{cm}$$

10. When a biconvex lens of glass having refractive index 1.47 is dipped in a liquid, it acts as a plane sheet of glass. This implies that the liquid must have refractivel index **[AIPMT-2012]**

(1) less than that of glass

(2) equal to that of glass

(3) less than one

(4) greater than that of glass

Sol. : **(2)** According to lens maker's formula

$$\frac{1}{f} = \left(\frac{\mu_g}{\mu_L} - 1\right)\left(\frac{1}{R_1} - \frac{1}{R_2}\right)$$

Where μ_g is the refractive index of the material of the lens and μ_L is the refractive index of the liquid in which lens is dipped.

As the biconvex lens dipped in a liquid acts as a plane sheet of glass, therefore

$$f = \infty \Rightarrow \frac{1}{f} = 0$$

$$\therefore \frac{\mu_g}{\mu_L} - 1 = 0 \text{ or } \mu_g = \mu_L .$$

11. A ray of light is incident at an angle of incidence, *i* on one face of a prism of angle A (assumed to be small) and emerges normally from the opposite face. If the refractive index of the prism is μ, the angle of incidence *i*, is nearly equal to **[AIPMT-2012]**

(1) $\frac{A}{2\mu}$ (2) μA (3) $\frac{\mu A}{2}$ (4) $\frac{A}{\mu}$

Sol. : **(2)**

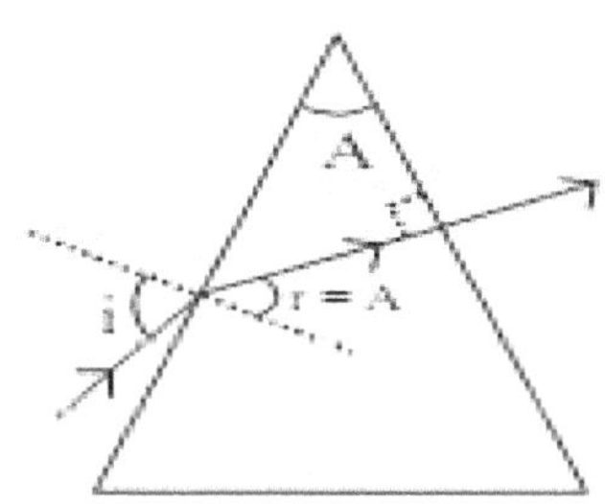

$$\mu = \sin\frac{\sin i}{\sin r} = \frac{\sin i}{\sin A} = \frac{i}{A} \text{(for small angle)}$$

$\sin\theta \approx \theta \rightarrow i = \mu A$

12. A concave mirror of focal length f_1 is placed at a distance of d from a convex lens of focal length f_2. A beam of light coming from infinity and falling on this convex lens-concave mirror combination returns to infinity. The distance d must equal

[AIPMT-2012]

(1) $-2f_1 + f_2$ (2) $f_1 + f_2$ (3) $-f_1 + f_2$ (4) $2f_1 + f_2$

Sol. : (4)

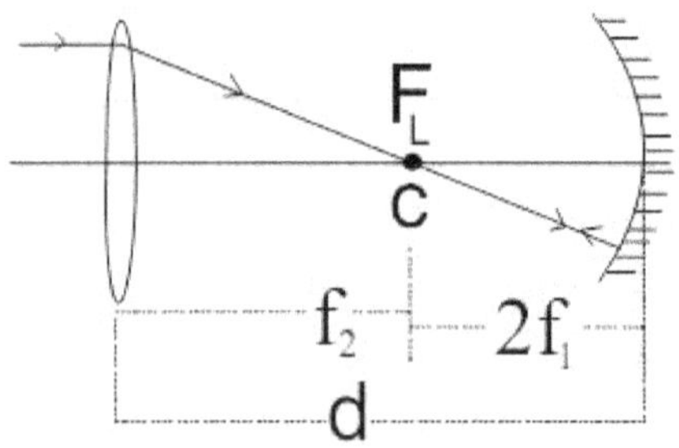

13. The magnifying power of a telescope is 9. When it is adjusted for parallel rays the distance between the objective and eyepiece is 20 cm. The focal lengths of lenses are **[AIPMT-2012]**

(1) 11cm, 9 cm (2) 10 cm, 10 cm

(3) 15 cm, 5 cm (4) 18 cm, 2 cm

Sol. : (4) $L = f_o + f_e = 20\text{cm}$ and $M = \frac{f_o}{f_e} = 9$

On solving, $f_o = 18\text{cm}$ $f_e = 2\text{cm}$

14. For the angle of minimum deviation of a prism to be equal to its refracting angle, the prism must be made of a material whose refractive index

(1) lies between $\sqrt{2}$ and 1 **[AIPMT-2012]**

(2) lies btween 2 and $\sqrt{2}$

(3) is less than 1

(4) is greater than 2

Sol. : (2) As $\mu = \dfrac{\sin\left(\frac{A+\delta_m}{2}\right)}{\sin\left(\frac{A}{2}\right)}$

$$\mu = \frac{\sin\left(\frac{A+A}{2}\right)}{\sin\left(\frac{A}{2}\right)} = \frac{\sin A}{\sin\left(\frac{A}{2}\right)} \quad (\because \delta_m = A(\text{Given}))$$

$$= \frac{2\sin\left(\frac{A}{2}\right)\cos\left(\frac{A}{2}\right)}{\sin\left(\frac{A}{2}\right)} = 2\cos\left(\frac{A}{2}\right)$$

As $\delta = i + e - A$

At minimum deviation, $\delta = \delta_m, i = e$

$\therefore \delta_m = 2i - A$

$i = \frac{\delta_m + A}{2} = \frac{A+A}{2} = A\,(\delta_m = A(\text{given}))$

$i_{min} = 0° \Rightarrow A_{min} = 0°$

Then, $\mu_{max} = \frac{\pi}{2} \Rightarrow A_{max} = \frac{\pi}{2}$

Then $\mu_{min} = 2\cos 45° = 2 \times \frac{1}{\sqrt{2}} = \sqrt{2}$

15. A rod of length 10 cm lies along the principal axis of a convace mirror of focal length 10 cm in such a way that its end closer to the pole is 20 cm away from the mirro. The length of the image is **[AIPMT-2012]**

(1) 10 cm (2) 15 cm

(3) 2.5 cm (4) 5 cm

Sol. : **(4)**

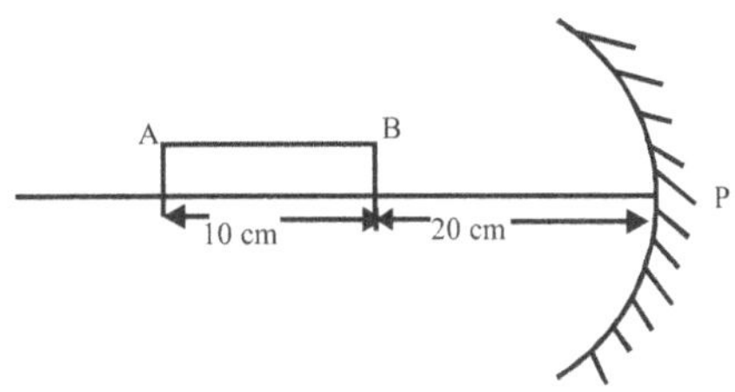

Here, $f = -10$ cm

For end A, $u_A = -20$ cm

Image position of end A,

$$\frac{1}{\upsilon_A} + \frac{1}{u_A} = \frac{1}{f}$$

$$\frac{1}{\upsilon_A} + \frac{1}{-20} = \frac{1}{(10)} \text{ or } \frac{1}{\upsilon_A} + \frac{1}{-10} + \frac{1}{20} = -\frac{1}{20}$$

$\upsilon_A = -20$ cm

For end B, $u_B = -30$ cm

Image position of end B,

$$\frac{1}{\upsilon_A} + \frac{1}{u_B} = \frac{1}{f}$$

$$\frac{1}{\upsilon_B} + \frac{1}{(-30)} = \frac{1}{(-10)} \text{ or } \frac{1}{\upsilon_B} + \frac{1}{(-30)} = \frac{1}{(-10)}$$

$\upsilon_B = -15$ cm

Length of the image

$|\upsilon_A| - |\upsilon_B| = 20\text{cm} - 15\text{cm} = 5\text{cm}$

16. A plane convex lens fits exactly into a planoconave lens. Their plane surfaces are parallel to each other. If lenses are made of different materials of refractive indices μ_1 and μ_2 and R is the radius of curvature of the curved surface of the lenses, then the focal length of the combination is **[AIPMT-2013]**

(1) $\frac{R}{2(\mu_1 + \mu_2)}$ (2) $\frac{R}{2(\mu_1 - \mu_2)}$

(3) $\frac{R}{(\mu_1 - \mu_2)}$ (4) $\frac{R}{(\mu_1 + \mu_2)}$

Sol. : **(3)** The Combination of two lenses 1 and 2 is as show in figure.

$$\therefore \frac{1}{f} = \frac{1}{f_1} + \frac{1}{f_2}$$

According to lens maker's formula

$$\frac{1}{f_1} = (\mu_1 - 1)\left(\frac{1}{\infty} - \frac{1}{R}\right) = \frac{(\mu_1 - 10}{R}$$

$$\frac{1}{f_2} = (\mu_2 - 1)\left(\frac{1}{-R} - \frac{1}{\infty}\right)$$

$$= (\mu_2 - 1)\left(-\frac{1}{R}\right) = -\frac{(\mu_2 - 1)}{R}$$

$$\therefore \frac{1}{f} = \frac{(\mu_1 - 1)}{R} - \frac{(\mu_2 - 1)}{R}$$

$$\frac{1}{f} = \frac{(\mu_1 - \mu_2)}{R}$$

$$f - \frac{R}{(\mu_1 - \mu_2)}$$

17. For a normal eye, the cornea of eye provides a converging power of 40 D and the least converging power of the eye lens behind the cornea is 20 D. Using this information, the distance between the retina and the cornea eye lens can be estimated to be **[AIPMT-2013]**

(1) 5 cm (2) 2.5 cm

(3) 1.67 cm (4) 1.5 cm

Sol. : **(3)** Converging power of cornea, $P_c = +40D$

Least converging power of eye lens, $P_e = +20D$

Power of the eye–lens, $P = P_c - P_e$

$= 40D + 20D = 60D$

Power of the eye lens

$$P = \frac{1}{\text{Focal length of the eye lens(f)}}$$

$$f = \frac{1}{P} = \frac{1}{60D} = \frac{1}{60}m = \frac{100}{60}cm = \frac{5}{3}cm$$

Distance between the retina and cornea-eye lens = Focal length of the eye lens

$$\frac{5}{3}cm = 1.67cm$$

18. If the focal length of objective lens is increased, then magnifying power of **[AIPMT-2014]**

(1) Microscope will increase but that of telescope decrease

(2) Microscope and telescope both will increase

(3) Microscope and telescope both will decrease

(4) Microscope will decrease but that of telescope will increase

Sol. : **(2)** Magnifying power of Microscope $= \frac{LD}{f_0 f_e} \propto \frac{1}{f_0}$

Magnifying power of Telescope $= \frac{f_0}{f_e} \propto f_0$

19. The angle of a prism is A. One of its refracting surfaces is silvered. Light rays falling at an angle of incidence 2 A on the first surfaces returns back through the same path after suffering reflection at the silvered surface. The refractive index μ of the prism **[AIPMT-2014]**

(1) 2 sin A (2) 2 cos A

(3) $\frac{1}{2}\cos A$ (4) tan A

Sol. : **(2)**

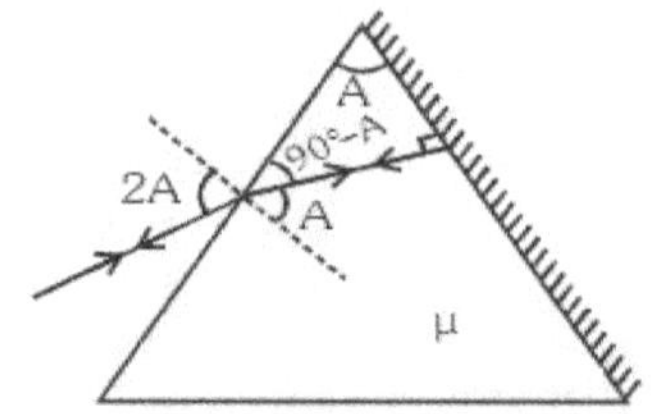

By Snell's law

(1) Sin 2A = (μ) Sin A 2sin A cos A = μ sin A μ = 2cosA ⇒ μ = 2 cos A

20. The refracting angle of a prism is A and refractive index of the material of the prism is cot (A/2). The angle of minimum deviation is **[AIPMT-2015]**

(1) 180° – 3A (2) 180° – 2A

(3) 90° – A (4) 180° + 2A

Sol. : **(2)** $\mu = \frac{\sin\frac{A+\delta}{2}}{\sin\frac{A}{2}} = \cot\frac{A}{2}$

$$\sin\frac{A+\delta}{2} = \cos\frac{A}{2}$$

$$\frac{A+\delta}{2} = \frac{\pi}{2} - \frac{A}{2}$$

$$\delta = \pi - 2A = 180° - 2A$$

21. Two identical thin planoconvex glass lenses (refractive index 1.5) each having radius of curvature of 20 cm are placed with their convex surface in contact at the centre. the intervening space is filled with oil of refractive index 1.7. The focal length of the combination is **[AIPMT-2015]**

(1) –20 cm (2) –25 cm

(3) –50 cm (4) 50 cm

Sol. : **(3)** $\frac{1}{f}=(\mu-1)\left(\frac{1}{R_1}-\frac{1}{R_2}\right)$

$$=\left(\frac{3}{2}-1\right)\times\left(\frac{1}{20}\right)=\frac{1}{40}$$

$$(1,7-1)\times\left(\frac{-1}{20}-\frac{1}{20}\right)=-\frac{7}{20}$$

$$\frac{1}{f_{eq}}=\frac{1}{f_1}+\frac{1}{f_2}+\frac{1}{f_3}$$

$$\frac{10+10-28}{400}=\frac{20-28}{400}$$

$$=\frac{-8}{400}=-\frac{2}{100}=-\frac{1}{50}$$

$$\frac{1}{f_{eq}}=\frac{1}{f_1}+\frac{1}{f_2}+\frac{1}{f_3}$$

$$=\frac{10+10-28}{400}=-\frac{2}{100}=-\frac{1}{50}$$

$f_{eq}=-50$ cm

22. In an astronomical telescope in normal adjustment a straight black line of length L is drawn on inside pat of objective lens. The length of this image is I. The magnification of the telescope is

[AIPMT-2015 Re]

(1) $\frac{L}{I}$ (2) $\frac{L}{I}+1$ (3) $\frac{L}{I}-1$ (4) $\frac{L+I}{L-I}$

Sol. : **(1)**

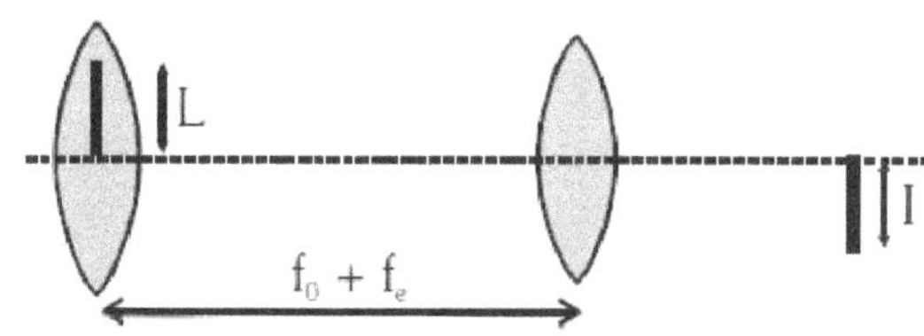

Magnification of telescope,

$$M=\frac{f_0}{f_e}$$

Here $\frac{f_e}{f_e+u}=\frac{I}{L}$

$$\Rightarrow \frac{f_e}{f_e-(f_0+f_e)}=-\frac{I}{L} \Rightarrow \frac{f_e}{f_0}=\frac{I}{L}$$

Therefore $M=\frac{L}{I}$

23. A beam of light consisting of red, green and blue colour is incident on a right angled prism. The refractive index of the material of the prism for the above red, green and blue wavelengths are 1.39, 1.44 and 1.47, respectively

[AIPMT-2015 Re]

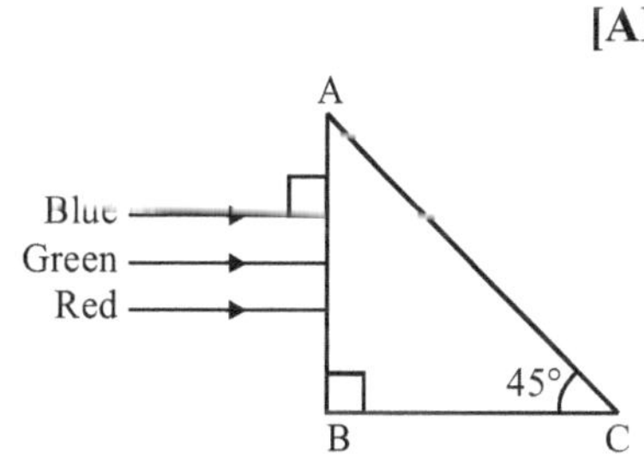

The prism will

(1) separate the red colour apart from the green and blue colours

(2) separate the blue colour apart from the red and green colours

(3) separate all the coloured from one another

(4) not separate the three colours at all

Sol. : **(1)** $\mu = \frac{1}{\sin i_c} = \frac{1}{\sin 45°} = \sqrt{2} = 1.414$

$\because (\mu_{red} = 1.39) < \mu, \mu_v > \mu; \mu_g > \mu$

only red colour do not suffer total internal reflection.

24. The angle of incidence for a ray of light at are fracting surface of a prism is 45° The angle of prism is 60°. If the ray suffers minimum deviation through the prism, the angle of minimum deviation and refractive index of the material of the prism respectively, are : **[AIPMT 2016]**

(1) $45°, \frac{1}{\sqrt{2}}$ (2) $30°, \sqrt{2}$

(3) $40°, \sqrt{2}$ (4) $30°, \frac{1}{\sqrt{2}}$

Sol. : **(2)** Give A = 60 and i = e = 60

$\delta_{min} = i + e - A = 45 + 45 - 60 = 30$

$$\mu = \frac{\sin\left(\frac{\delta_m + A}{2}\right)}{\sin\left(\frac{A}{2}\right)} = \sqrt{2}$$

25. A astronomical telescope has objective and eyepiece of focal lengths 40 cm and 4 cm respectively. To view an object 200 cm away from the objective, the lenses must be separated by a distance :- **[AIPMT 2016]**

(1) 37.3 cm (2) 46.0 cm

(3) 50.0 cm (4) 54.0 cm

Sol. : **(4)** Tube length = $V_0 + f_e$

for objective $\frac{1}{V_0} - \frac{1}{u_0} = \frac{1}{f}$

put $u_0 = -200$ and $f = 40 cm$ we get $v_0 = 50 cm$

$\Rightarrow L = 54$ cm

26 Match the corresponding entries of **column1** with **coloumn-2** (Where m is the magnification produced by the mirror) :-

Column-1	**Column-2**
(A) $m = -2$	(a) Convex mirror
(B) $m = -\frac{1}{2}$	(b) Concave mirror
(C) $m = +2$	(c) Real image
(D) $m = +\frac{1}{2}$	(d) Virtual image

[AIPMT 2016]

(1) A → b and c, B → b and c, C → b and d, D → a and d.

(2) A → a and c, B → a and d, C → a and b, D → c and d

(3) A → a and d, B → b and c, C → b and d, D → b and c

(4) A → c and d, B → b and d, C → b and c, D → a and d

Sol. : (1)

(A) m = –2, So image is magnified and inverted. Which is possible only for concave mirror. since image is i inverted so it will be real.

(B) $M = -\frac{1}{2}$, so image is inverted and diminished. since image is inverted, so it will be real, and the mirror will be concave.

(C) M = +2, image is magnified so the mirror will be concave. Image is erect so it will be virtual.

(D) $m = +\frac{1}{2}$, image is erect so image will be virtual. Image is virtual and diminished, so the mirror should be convex.

Ans. will be (1)

27. Two identical glass ($\mu_g = 3/2$) equiconvex lenses of focal length f each are kept in contact. The space between the two lenses is fi lled with water ($\mu_w = 4/3$). Th e focal length of the combination is : **[NEET – II(2016)]**

(1) 4f/3 (2) 3f/4

(3) f/3 (4) f

Sol. : (2)

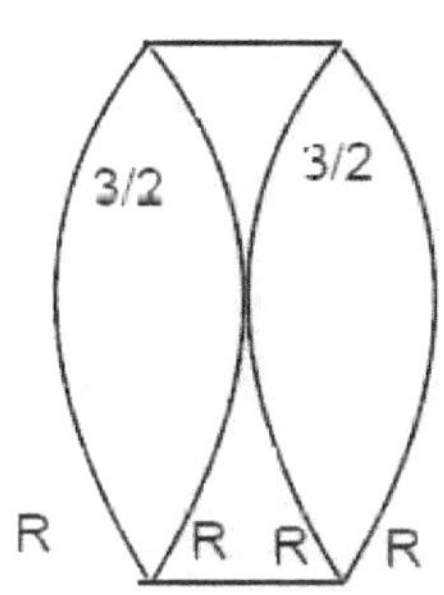

$$\frac{1}{f} = \left(\frac{3}{2} - 1\right)\frac{2}{R} = \frac{1}{R}$$

$$\frac{1}{f'} = \left(\frac{4}{3} - 1\right)\left\{-\frac{2}{R}\right\} = -\frac{2}{3R}$$

$$\text{So } \frac{1}{f_{eq}} = \frac{1}{f} - \frac{2}{3f} + \frac{1}{f} = \frac{3-2+3}{f} = \frac{4}{3f}$$

$$f_{eq} = \frac{3f}{4}$$

28. An air bubble in a glass slab with refractive index 1.5 (near normal incidence) is 5 cm deep when viewed from one surface and 3 cm deep when viewed from the opposite face. The thickness (in cm) of the slab is :- **[NEET – II(2016)]**

(1) 12 (2) 16

(3) 8 (4) 10

Sol : (1)

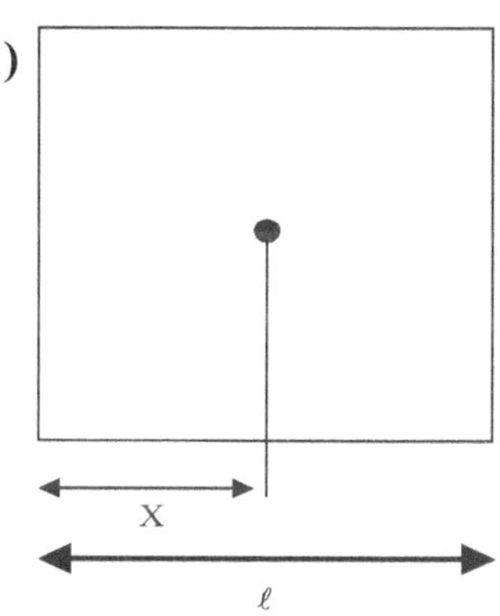

$$\frac{x}{\mu} + \frac{(\ell - x)}{\mu} = 3 + 5$$

$$\frac{\ell}{\mu} = 8; \qquad \ell = 8 \times \frac{3}{2} = 12\,\text{cm}$$

29. A person can see clearly objects only when they lie between 50 cm and 400 cm from his eyes. In order to increase the maximum distance of distinct vision to infinity, the type and power of the correcting lens the person has to use, will be :-

(1) concave, – 0.2 diopter **[NEET – II(2016)]**

(2) convex, + 0.15 diopter

(3) convex, + 2.25 diopter

(4) concave, – 0.25 diopter

Sol. : **(4)** $\frac{1}{v}-\frac{1}{u}=\frac{1}{f} \Rightarrow \frac{1}{-4m}-\frac{1}{\infty}=\frac{1}{f}$

$\Rightarrow f=-4m \Rightarrow power=\frac{1}{f}=\frac{1}{-4}=-0.25D$

30. A thin prism having refracting angle 10° is made of glass of refractive index 1.42. This prism is combined with another thin prism of glass of refractive index 1.7. This combination produces dispersion without deviation. The refracting angle of second prism should be : **[NEET – (2017)]**

(1) 4° (2) 6°

(3) 8° (4)10°

Sol. : **(2)** $(\mu-1)A+(\mu'-1)A'=0$

$|(\mu-1)A|=|(\mu'-1)A'|$

$(1.42-1)\times 10°=(1.7-1)A'$

$4.2=0.7A'$

$A'=6°$

31. A beam cf light from a source L is incident normally on a plane mirror fixed at a certain distance x from the source. The beam is reflected back as a spot on a is rotated through a small angle θ, the spot of the light is found to move through a distance y on the scale. The angle θ is given by :

(1) $\frac{y}{2x}$ (2) $\frac{y}{x}$

(3) $\frac{x}{2y}$ (4) $\frac{x}{y}$

Sol. : **(1)** When mirror is rotated by θ angle reflected ray will be rotated by 2θ.

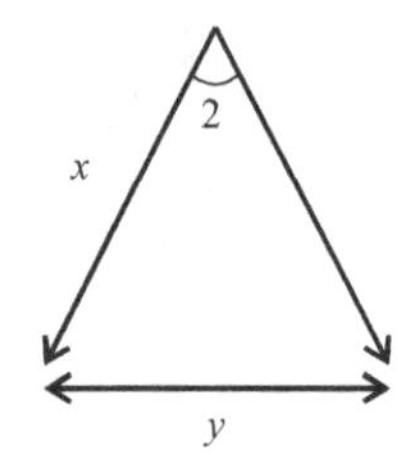

$\frac{y}{x}=2\theta$ $\theta=\frac{y}{2x}$.

32. An astronomical refracting telescope will have large angular magnification and high angular resolution, when it has an objective lens of

[NEET-2018]

(1) large focal length and large diameter

(2) large focal length and small diameter

(3) small focal length and large diameter

(4) small focal length and small diameter

Ans. **(1)** For telescope, angular magnification $= \frac{f_0}{f_E}$

So, focal length of objective lens should be large.

Angular resolution $= \frac{D}{1.22\lambda}$ should be large.

So, objective should have large focal length (f_0) and large diameter D.

33. An object is placed at a distance of 40 cm from a concave mirror of focal length 15 cm. If the object is displaced through a distance of 20 cm towards the mirror, the displacement of the image will be **[NEET-2018]**

(1) 30 cm towards the mirror

(2) 36 cm away from the mirror

(3) 30 cm away from the mirror

(4) 36 cm towards the mirror

Ans. **(2)**

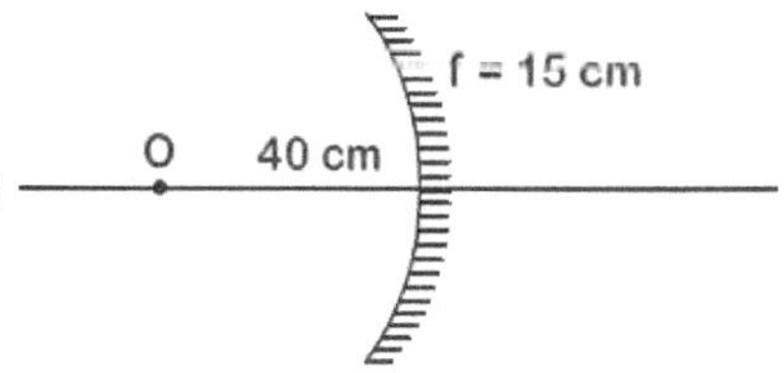

$$\frac{1}{f} = \frac{1}{v_1} + \frac{1}{u}$$

$$\Rightarrow -\frac{1}{15} = \frac{1}{v_1} - \frac{1}{40} \qquad \Rightarrow \frac{1}{v_1} = \frac{1}{-15} + \frac{1}{40}$$

$v_1 = -24$ cm

When object is displaced by 20 cm towards mirror.

Now,

$u_2 = -20$

$$\frac{1}{f} = \frac{1}{v_2} + \frac{1}{u_2}$$

$$\Rightarrow -\frac{1}{15} = \frac{1}{v_2} - \frac{1}{20} \qquad \Rightarrow \frac{1}{v_2} = \frac{1}{20} - \frac{1}{15}$$

$v_2 = -60$ cm

So, image shifts away from mirror by

$= 60 - 24 = 36$ cm.

24 Wave Optics

Note: Scan QR code with your mobile camera or QR scanner for video solutions.

1. Two periodic waves of intensities I_1 and I_2 pass through a region at the same time in the same direction. the sum of the maximum and minimum intensities is **[AIPMT-2008]**

(1) $I_1 + I_2$ (2) $(\sqrt{I_1}+\sqrt{I_2})^2$

(3) $(\sqrt{I_1}-\sqrt{I_2})^2$ (4) $2(I_1 + I_2)$

Sol. **(4) :** $I = I_1 + I_2 + 2\sqrt{I_1 I_2}\cos\phi$

$$I_{max} = \left(\sqrt{I_1}+\sqrt{I_2}\right)^2$$

$$I_{min} = \left(\sqrt{I_1}-\sqrt{I_2}\right)^2$$

$$I_{max} + I_{min}$$

$$= \left(\sqrt{I_1}+\sqrt{I_2}\right)^2 + \left(\sqrt{I_1}-\sqrt{I_2}\right)^2$$

$$= \left(I_1 + I_2 + 2\sqrt{I_1 I_2}\right) + \left(I_1 + I_2 - 2\sqrt{I_1 I_2}\right)$$

$$= 2(I_1 + I_2).$$

2. A lens having focal length and aperture of diameter d forms an image of intensity I. Aperture of diameter $\frac{d}{2}$ in central region of the lens is convered by a black paper. Focal length of lens and intensity of image now will be respectively **[AIPMT-2010]**

(1) f and $\frac{1}{4}$ (2) $\frac{3f}{4}$ and $\frac{I}{2}$

(3) f and $\frac{3I}{4}$ (4) $\frac{f}{2}$ and $\frac{I}{2}$

Sol. **(3) :**

f' = f & Intensity $\propto$ Area so $I' = I - \frac{I}{4} = \frac{3I}{4}$

3. In Young's double-slit experiment, the slits are 2 mm apart and are illuminated by photons of two wavelengths λ_1= 12000 Å and λ_2= 10000 Å. At what minimum distance from the common central beigth fringe on the screen 2 m from the slit will a bright fringe from one interference pattern coincide with a bright fringe from the other? **[AIPMT-2013]**

(1) 8 mm (2) 6 mm (3) 4 mm (4) 3 mm

Sol. **(2) :** let n_1 bright fringe of λ_1 coincides with n_2 bright fringe of λ_2. Then

$$\frac{n_1\lambda_1 D}{d} = \frac{n_2\lambda_2 D}{d} \text{ or } n_1\lambda_1 = n_2\lambda_2$$

$$\frac{n_1}{n_2} = \frac{\lambda_2}{\lambda_1} = \frac{10000}{12000} = \frac{5}{6}$$

Let x be given distance.

$$\therefore x = \frac{n_1\lambda_1 D}{d}$$

Here, $n_1 = 5, D = 2\text{m}, d = 2\text{mm} = 2\times10^{-3}\text{m}$

$\lambda_1 = 12000\,\text{Å} = 12000 \times 10^{-10}\text{m} = 12 \times 10^{-7}\text{m}$

$$x = \frac{5\times2\times10^{-7}\text{m}\times2\text{m}}{2\times10^{-3}\text{m}} = 6\times10^{-3}\text{m} = 6 \text{ mm}.$$

4. A parallel beam of fast moving electrons is incident normally ona narrow slit. A fluoresent screen is placed at a large distance from the slit. If the speed of the electorns is increased, which of the following statement is correct ? **[AIPMT-2013]**

(1) Diffraction pattern is not observed on the screen in the case of electrons

(2) The angular width of the central maximum of the diffraction pattern will increase

(3) The angular width of the central maximum will decrease

(4) The angular width of the central maximum will be unaffected

Sol. **(3) :** de Broglie wavelength of an electron

$$\lambda = \frac{h}{p} = \frac{h}{m\upsilon}$$

Where m is the mass and υ is the speed of the electron respectively.

If speed υ of electron is increased, momentum p(= mυ) will increase. hence, wavelength λ will decrease.

Angular width of the central maximum is

$$\theta_0 = \frac{2\lambda}{a}$$

Where a is the width of slit.

If λ decreases, θ_0 will decrease.

Therefore, the correct statement is (a).

5. A beam of light of λ = 600 nm from a distant source falls ona single slit 1 mm wide and the resulting diffraction pattern is observed on a screen 2 m away. The distance between first dark fringes on either side of the cnetral bright fringe is **[AIPMT-2014]**

(1) 1.2 cm (2) 1.2 mm

(3) 2.4 cm (4) 2.4 mm

Sol. **(4) :** Width of central bright fringe

$$= \frac{2\lambda D}{\lambda} = \frac{2 \times 600 \times 10^{-6} \times 2}{1 \times 10^{-3}} \text{m}$$

$$= 2.4 \times 10^{-3} \text{m}$$

$$= 2.4 \text{mm}$$

6. In the Young's double-slit experiment,the intensity of light at a point on the screen where the path difference is λ is K, (λ being the wavelength of light used). The intensity at a point where the path difference is $\frac{\lambda}{4}$ will be **[AIPMT-2014]**

(1) K (2) $\frac{K}{4}$ (3) $\frac{K}{2}$ (4) zero

Sol. **(3) :** For path difference λ, phase difference $= 2\pi$ rad For path difference $\frac{\lambda}{4}$, phase difference $\frac{\pi}{2}$ rad As $K = 4I_0$ so intensity at given point where path difference is $\frac{\lambda}{4}$

$$K' = 4I_0 \cos^2\left(\frac{\pi}{4}\right) = 2I_0 = \frac{K}{2}.$$

7. In a double-slit experiment, the two slits are 1 mm apart and the screen is placed 1 m away. A monochromatic light of wavelength 500 nm is used. What will be width of each slit for obtaining ten maxima of double slit within the central maxima of single-slit pattern ? **[AIPMT-2015]**

(1) 0.2 mm (2) 0.1 mm

(3) 0.5 mm (4) 0.02 mm

Sol. **(1) :** $d = 1mm$

$D = 1mm$ $\quad$ $\text{Width} = 2\left(\frac{\lambda}{a}\right)D$

$A = 500 \times 10^{-9}$ $\quad$ $10\frac{D\lambda}{d} = 2\frac{D\lambda}{a}$

$a = \frac{d}{5} = \frac{1}{5} = 0.2mm$

8. For a parallel beam of monochromatic light of a wavelength, 'λ' diffraction is produced by a single slit whose wideh 'a' is of the order of the wavelength of the light. If 'D' is the distance of the screen from the slit, the width of the central maxima will be **[AIPMT-2015]**

(1) $\frac{2D\lambda}{a}$ (2) $\frac{D\lambda}{a}$ (3) $\frac{Da}{\lambda}$ (4) $\frac{2Da}{\lambda}$

Sol. **(1) :** Central maxima $= 2 \times \beta$

$\beta = \frac{\lambda D}{a}$

9. At the first minima adjacent to the central maxima of a single-slit diffraction pattern the phase difference between the Huygens wavelet from the mid-point of the slit is **[AIPMT-2015 Re]**

(1) $\frac{\pi}{8}$ radian (2) $\frac{\pi}{4}$ radian

(3) 2 π radian (4) π radian

Sol. **(4) :**

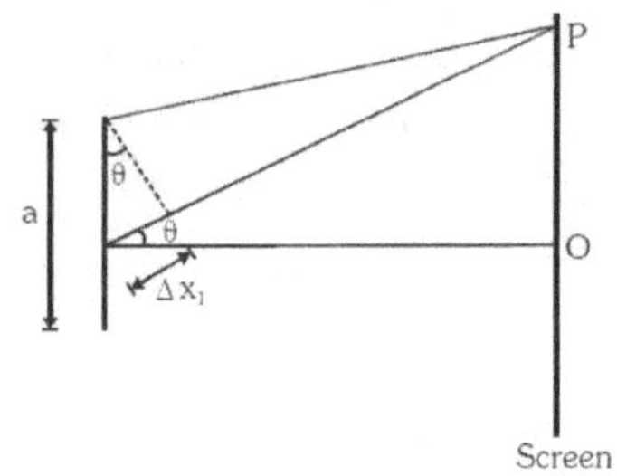

For first minima at P, a $\sin\theta = \lambda$

So phase difference $\Delta\phi_1 = \frac{\Delta x_1}{\lambda} \times 2\pi$

$= \frac{(a/2)\sin\theta}{\lambda} \times 2\pi$

$\Delta\phi_1 = \frac{\lambda}{2\lambda} \times 2\pi = \pi$ radian

10. Two slits is Young's experiment have widths in the ratio 1 : 25.the ratio of intensity at the maxima and minima in the interference patter $\frac{I_{max}}{I_{min}}$ is **[AIPMT-2015 Re]**

(1) $\frac{4}{9}$ (2) $\frac{9}{4}$ (3) $\frac{121}{49}$ (4) $\frac{49}{121}$

Sol. **(2) :** $\frac{I_1}{I_2} = \frac{W_1}{W_2} = \frac{1}{25} \Rightarrow \frac{I_2}{I_1} = \frac{25}{1}$

$$\frac{I_{max}}{I_{min}} = \frac{\left(\sqrt{I_2} + \sqrt{I_1}\right)^2}{\left(\sqrt{I_2} - \sqrt{I_1}\right)^2} = \left(\frac{\sqrt{\frac{I_2}{I_1}} + 1}{\sqrt{\frac{I_2}{I_1}} - 1}\right)^2$$

$$= \left(\frac{5+1}{5-1}\right)^2 = \left(\frac{6}{4}\right)^2 = \frac{9}{4}$$

11. In a diffraction pattern due to a single slit of width 'a', the first minimum is observed at an angle 30° when light of wavelength 5000 Å is incident on the slit. The first secondary maximum is observed at an angle of : **[AIPMT 2016]**

(1) $\sin^{-1}\left(\frac{1}{4}\right)$ (2) $\sin^{-1}\left(\frac{2}{3}\right)$

(3) $\sin^{-1}\left(\frac{1}{2}\right)$ (4) $\sin^{-1}\left(\frac{3}{4}\right)$

Sol. **(4) :** Path difference between the extreme rays at first minima $= a\sin\theta = \lambda$

$a\sin(30°) = \lambda \Rightarrow a = 2\lambda$

Path difference between the extreme rays at first secondary maxima $= a\sin\theta' = \frac{3\lambda}{2}$

$$(2\lambda)\sin\theta' = \frac{3\lambda}{2}$$

$$\Rightarrow \theta' = \sin^{-1}\left(\frac{3}{4}\right)$$

12. The intensity at the maximum in a Young's double slit experiment is I_0. Distance between two slits is d = 5 λ, where λ is the wavelength of light used in the experiment. What will be the intensity in front of one of the slits on the screen placed at a distance D = 10 d ? **[AIPMT 2016]**

(1) I_0 (2) $\frac{I_0}{4}$ (3) $\frac{3}{4}I_0$ (4) $\frac{I_0}{2}$

Sol. **(4) :** $I = I_{max}\cos^2\left(\frac{\pi y}{\beta}\right) \Rightarrow \beta = \frac{D\lambda}{d} = 10\lambda$

y for a position in front of a slit

$$\frac{\beta}{2} = \left(\frac{5\lambda}{2}\right) = 2.5\lambda \Rightarrow I = I_0\cos^2\left(\frac{\pi(2.5\lambda)}{10\lambda}\right)$$

$$= I_0\cos^2\left(\frac{\pi}{4}\right) = \frac{I_0}{2}$$

13. The interference pattern is obtained with two coherent light sources of intensity ratio n. In the interference pattern, the ratio $\frac{I_{max} - I_{min}}{I_{max} + I_{min}}$ will be: **[NEET – II(2016)]**

(1) $\frac{\sqrt{n}}{(n+1)^2}$ (2) $\frac{2\sqrt{n}}{(n+1)^2}$ (3) $\frac{\sqrt{n}}{n+1}$ (4) $\frac{2\sqrt{n}}{n+1}$

Sol. **(4) :**

$$I_{max} = \left(\sqrt{I_1} + \sqrt{I_2}\right)^2 = \left(\sqrt{nI_1} + \sqrt{I}\right)^2 = \left(\sqrt{n}+1\right)^2 I$$

$$I_{min} = \left(\sqrt{n} - 1\right)^2 I$$

$$\frac{I_{max} - I_{min}}{I_{max} + I_{min}} = \frac{n+1+2\sqrt{n}-n-1+2\sqrt{n}}{(n+1+2\sqrt{n})+(n+1-2\sqrt{n})} = \frac{4\sqrt{n}}{2(n+1)}$$

$$\Rightarrow \frac{2\sqrt{n}}{(n+1)}.$$

14. A linear aperture whose width is 0.02 cm is placed immediately in front of a lens of focal length 60 cm. The aperture is illuminated normally by a parallel beam of wavelength 5 × 10^{-5} cm. The distance of

the first dark band of the diffraction pattern from the centre of the screen is :- **[NEET – II(2016)]**

(1) 0.20 cm (2) 0.15 cm

(3) 0.10 cm (4) 0.25 cm

Sol. **(2) :** Position of I[st] minima

$$y = \frac{\lambda D}{a} = \frac{(5\times10^{-8})(0.6)}{0.02\times10^{-2}}$$

$$y = 0.15\,\text{cm}.$$

15.Q Young's double slit experiment is first performed in air and then in a medium other than air. It is found that 8th bright fringe in the medium lies where 5th dark fringe lies in air. The refractive index of the medium is nearly : **[NEET – 2017]**

(1) 1.25 (2) 1.59 (3) 1.69 (4) 1.78

Sol. **(4) :** $X_1 = X_{5\text{th dark}} = (2 \times 5 - 1)\dfrac{\lambda D}{2d}$

$X_2 = X_{8\text{th bright}} = 8\dfrac{\lambda D}{\mu d}$; $X_1 = X_2$

$\dfrac{9}{2}\dfrac{\lambda D}{d} = 8\dfrac{\lambda D}{\mu d}$

$\mu = \dfrac{16}{9} = 1.78$.

16. The ratio of resolving powers of an optical microscope for two wave lengths λ_1=4000Å and λ_2=6000Å is : **[NEET – 2017]**

(1) 8 : 27 (2) 9 : 4

(3) 3 : 2 (4) 16 : 81

Sol. **(3) :** Resolving power $\propto \dfrac{1}{\lambda}$

$\dfrac{R_1}{R_2} = \dfrac{\lambda_2}{\lambda_1}$

$= \dfrac{6000\,\text{Å}}{4000\,\text{Å}} = \dfrac{3}{2}$.

17. Two polaroids P_1 and P_2 are placed with their axist perpendicular to each other. Unpolarised light I_0 is incident on P_1 . A third polaroid P_3 is kept in between P_1 and P_2 such that its axis makes an angle 45° with that of P_1 .The intensity of transmitted light through P_2 is : **[NEET – 2017]**

(1) $\dfrac{I_0}{2}$ (2) $\dfrac{I_0}{4}$ (3) $\dfrac{I_0}{8}$ (4) $\dfrac{I_0}{16}$

Sol. **(3) :**

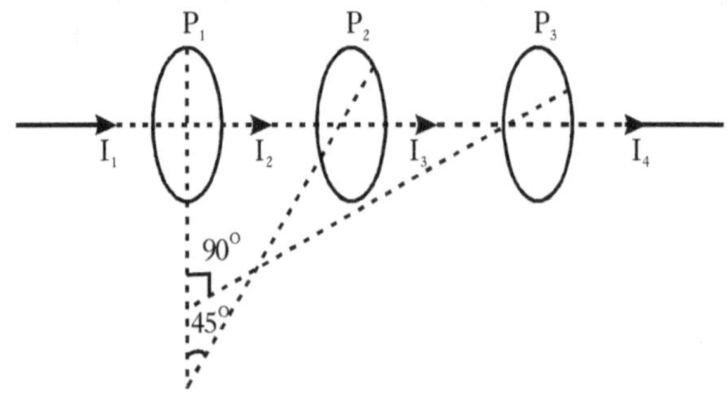

$I_2 = \dfrac{I_0}{2}\cos^2 45°$

$= \dfrac{I_0}{2} \times \dfrac{1}{2}$ $= \dfrac{I_0}{4}$

$I_3 = \dfrac{I_0}{4}\cos^2 45°$ $I_3 = \dfrac{I_0}{8}$.

18. Unpolarised light is incident from air on a plane surface of a material of refractive index 'μ'. At a particular angle of incidence 'i' it is found that the reflected and refracted rays are perpendicular to each other. Which of the following options is correct for this situation ? **[NEET-2018]**

(1) $i = \sin^{-1}\left(\dfrac{1}{\mu}\right)$

(2) Reflected light is polarized with its electric vector perpendicular to the plane of incidence

(3) Reflected light is polarized with its electric vector parallel to the plane incidence

(4) $i = \tan^{-1}\left(\dfrac{1}{\mu}\right)$

Ans. **(2)** When reflected light rays and refracted rays are perpendicular, reflected light is polarised with electric field vector perpendicular to the plane of incidence.

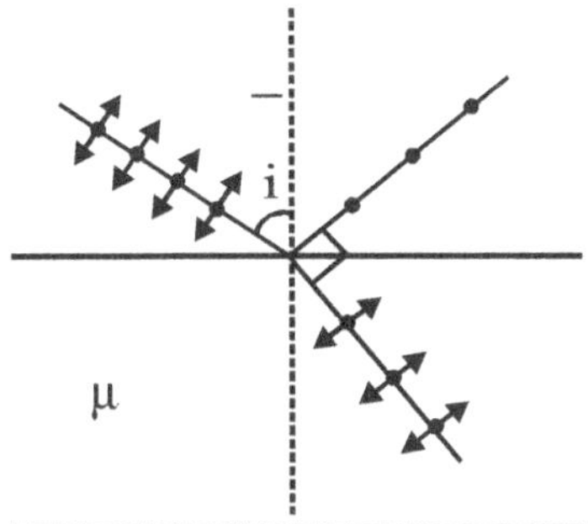

Also, tan i = μ (Brewster angle)

19. In young's double slit experiment the separation d between the slits is 2 mm, the wavelength λ of the light used is 5896 Å and distance D between the screen and slits is 100 cm. It is found that the angular width of the fringes is 0.20°. To increase the fringe angular width to 0.21° (with same λ and D) the separation between the slits needs to be changed to **[NEET-2018]**

(1) 2.1 mm (2) 1.9

(3) 1.8 (4) 1.7 mm

Ans. **(2)** Angular width $= \frac{\lambda}{d}$

$$0.20° = \frac{\lambda}{2mm} \quad ....(i)$$

$$0.21° = \frac{\lambda}{d} \quad ....(ii)$$

Dividing we get, $\frac{0.20}{0.21} = \frac{d}{2\text{ mm}}$

∴ d = 1.9 mm

20. The refractive index of the material of a prism is $\sqrt{2}$ and the angle of the prism is 30°. One of the two refracting surface of the prism is made a mirror inward by silver coating. A beam of monochromatic light entering the prism from the other face will retrace its path (after reflection from the silvered surface) if its angle of incidence on the prism is **[NEET-2018]**

(1) 30° (2) 45°

(3) 60° (4) zero

Ans. **(2)** For retracing its path, light ray should be normally incident on silvered face.

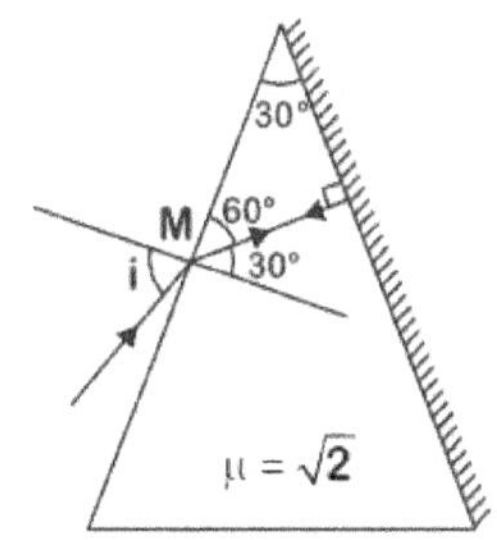

Applying Snell's law at M,

$$\frac{\sin i}{\sin 30°} = \frac{\sqrt{2}}{1}$$

$$\Rightarrow \sin i = \sqrt{2} \times \frac{1}{2}$$

$$\sin i = \frac{1}{\sqrt{2}} \text{ i.e. } i = 45°$$

25 Dual Nature of Radiation and Matter

Note: Scan QR code with your mobile camera or QR scanner for video solutions.

1. Monochromatic light of frequency 6.0×10^{14} Hz is produced by a laser. The power emitted is 2×10^{-3} W. The number of photons emitted, on the average, by the source per second is : **[AIPMT 2007]**

(1) 5×10^{15} (2) 5×10^{16}

(3) 5×10^{17} (4) 5×10^{14}

Sol : **(1)** $n = \frac{P}{h\nu} = \frac{2\times10^{-3}}{6.62\times10^{-34}\times6\times10^{14}} = 5\times10^{15}$

2. A 5 watt source emits monochromatic light of wavelength 5000 Å. When placed 0.5 m away, it liberates photoelectrons from a photosensitive metallic surface. When the source is moved to a distance of 1.0 m, the number of photo electrons liberated will be reduced by a factor of : **[AIPMT 2007]**

(1) 4 (2) 8

(3) 16 (4) 2

Sol : **(1)** For a light source of power P watt, the intensity at a distance d is given by

$$I = \frac{P}{4\pi d^2}$$

where we assume light to spread out uniformly in all directions i.e. it is a spherical source.

$$\therefore I \propto \frac{1}{d^2} \text{ or, } \frac{I_1}{I_2} = \frac{d_2^2}{d_1^2}$$

$$\text{or, } \frac{I_1}{I_2} = \left(\frac{1}{0.5}\right)^2 \text{ or, } \frac{I_1}{I_2} = 4 \text{ or, } I_2 = \frac{I_1}{4}.$$

In a photoelectric emission, the number of photoelectrons liberated per second from a photosensitive metallic surface is proportional to the intensity of the light. When a intenstiy of source is reduced by a factor of four, the number of photoelectrons is also reduced by a factor of four, the number of photoeletrons is also reduced by a factor of 4.

3. The work function of a surface of a photosensitive material is 6.2 eV. The wavelength of the incident radiation for which the stopping potential is 5V lies in the :- **[AIPMT 2008]**

(1) Ultraviolet region (2) Visible region

(3) Infrarted region (4) X-ray region

Sol : **(1)** $E_{incident} = W + K_{max}; K_{max} = eV_0$

$h\nu = h\nu_0 + eV_0$; stopping potential $= V_0$

$$\frac{hc}{\lambda} = 6.2e + 5e$$

$$\lambda = \frac{h\times c}{11.2\times1.6\times10^{-19}} \quad \frac{6.63\times10^{-34}\times3\times10^{8}}{11.2\times1.6\times10^{-19}}$$

$= 1.1\times10^{-7}$ m

Hence the wavelenght of ultraviolet region.

4. In the phenomenton of electric discharge through gases at low pressure, the coloured glow in the tube appears as a result of **[AIPMT 2008]**

(1) exciation of elecotrons in the atoms

(2) collision between the atoms of the gas

(3) collisions between the charged particles emitted from the cathode and the atoms of the gas

(4) collision between different electrons of the atoms of the gas

Sol : **(3)** In the phenomenon of electric dischatge tube through gases at low pressure, the coloured glow in the tube appears as a result of collisons between the charged particles emitted from cathode and the atoms of the gas.

5. A particle of mass 1 mg the same wavelength as an electron moving with a velocity of 3×10^6 ms^{-1}. The velocity of the particle is **[AIPMT 2008]**

(1) 2.7×10^{-18} ms^{-1} (2) 9×10^{-2} ms^{-1}

(3) 3×10^{-31} ms^{-1} (4) 2.7×10^{-21} ms^{-1}

Sol : **(4)** de-Broglie wavelength associated with electron moving with velocity V,

$$\text{So, } \lambda_c = \frac{h}{9.1 \times 10^{-31} \times 3 \times 10^6}$$

Wavelength of particle of mass 1 mg moving with velocity V,

$$\lambda_c = \frac{h}{10^{-3} \times v}$$

As given, $\lambda_c = \lambda_p$

$$\Rightarrow \frac{h}{10^{-3} \times v} = \frac{h}{9.1 \times 10^{-31} \times 10^6}$$

$$v = \frac{27.3 \times 10^{-25}}{10^{-3}} \text{ m/s} = 2.73 \times 10^{-21} \text{ m/s}$$

6. The number of photo electrons emitted for light of a frequency ν (higher than the threshold frequency ν_0) is proportional to :- **[AIPMT 2009]**

(1) $\nu - \nu_0$

(2) Threshold frequency (ν_0)

(3) Intensity of light

(4) Frequency of ligh (ν)

Sol : **(3)** No. of photoelectrons emitted is independent of frequency but depends on intensity.

7. The figure shows a plot of phot current versus anode potential for a photo sensitive surface for three different radiations. Which one of the following is a correct statement ? **[AIPMT 2009]**

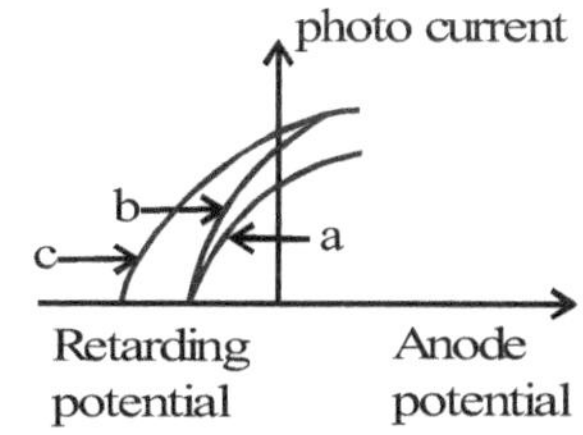

(1) curves (a) and (b) represent incident radiations of different frequencies and different intensities

(2) curves (a) and (b) represent incident radiations of same frequency but of different intensities

(3) curves (b) and (c) represent incident radiations of different frequencies and different intensities

(4) curves (b) and (c) represent incident radiations of same frequency having same intensity

Sol : **(2)** As a and b have same stopping potential and greater stopping potential, then $V_c = V_a = V_b$ as b and c have same saturation current and a has lesser value. So, $I_a < I_b = I_c$

8. Monochromatic light of wavelength 667 nm is produced by a helium neon laser. The power emitted is 9 mW. The number of photons arriving per sec. on the average at a target irradiated by this beam is : **[AIPMT 2009]**

(1) 9×10^{17} (2) 3×10^{16}

(3) 9×10^{15} (4) 3×10^{19}

Sol : **(2)** NO. of photons $= \dfrac{E}{(hc/\lambda)}$

$$= \frac{9 \times 10^{-3} \times 6.67 \times 10^{-7}}{6.6 \times 10^{-34} \times 3 \times 10^8} = 3 \times 10^{16}$$

9. A source S_1 is producing 10^{15} photons/s of wavelength 5000Å Another source S_2 is producing 1.02×10^{15} photons per second of wavelength 5100 Å. Then (power of S_2)/(power of S_1) is equal to **[AIPMT-2010]**

(1) 1.00 (2) 1.02 (3) 1.04 (4) 0.98

Sol : **(1)** $$\frac{\text{Power of } S_2}{\text{Power of } S_1} = \frac{n_2\left(\frac{hc}{\lambda_2}\right)}{n_1\left(\frac{hc}{\lambda_1}\right)} = \frac{n_2\lambda_1}{n_1\lambda_2} = 1.$$

10. The potential difference that must be applied to stop the fastest photoelectorns emitted by a nickel surface, having work function 5.01 eV, when ultraviolet light of 200 nm falls on it, must be **[AIPMT-2010]**

(1) 2.4 V (2) –1.2 V

(3) –2.4 V (4) 1.2 V

Sol : **(2)** $hv = \phi_0 + eV_0$ where

$$hv = \frac{12400}{2000} = 6.2 \text{ ev}$$

$$\Rightarrow V_0 = 6.2 - 5.01 = 1.19 \approx 1.20 \text{ V.}$$

11. Photoelectric emission occurs only when the incident light has more than a certain minimum **[AIPMT-2011]**

(1) wavelength (2) intensity

(3) frequency (4) power

Sol : **(3)** Photoelctron emission take place when certain minimum "frequency" light fall on metal surface.

12. In the Davisson and Germer experiment, the volocity of electrons emitted from the electron gun can be increased by **[AIPMT-2011]**

(1) increasing th filament current

(2) decreasing the filament current

(3) decreasing the potential difference between the anode and filament

(4) increasing the potential difference between the anode and filament

Sol : **(4)** Velocity of electon emitted from the electron gun can be increased by potential difference between the anode and filament.

13. Light of two different frequencies whose photons have energies 1eV and 2.5 eV respectively illuminate a metallic surface whose work function is 0.5 eV successively. Ratio of its maximum speeds of emitted electrons will be **[AIPMT-2011]**

(1) 1 : 2 (2) 1 :1

(3) 1 : 5 (4) 1 : 4

Sol : **(1)** $$V_{max} = \sqrt{\frac{2}{m}K.E_{max}}$$

$$V_{max} = \sqrt{\frac{2}{m}(E_{Ph} - W)}$$

$$V_{max} = \sqrt{\frac{E_{Ph_1} - W}{E_{Ph_2} - W}} = \sqrt{\frac{1-0.5}{2.5-0.5}}$$

$$\frac{V_1}{V_2} = \frac{1}{2}.$$

14. Electrons used in an electron microscope are acceleerated by a voltage of 25 kV. If the voltage is increased to 100 kV then the de-Broglie wavelength associated with the electrons would **[AIPMT-2011]**

(1) decrease by 2 times

(2) decrease by 4 times

(3) increase by 4 times

(4) increase by 2 times

Sol : **(1)** $\lambda = \frac{h}{\sqrt{2mq\Delta V}} \propto \frac{1}{\sqrt{\Delta V}}$

$$\frac{\lambda_1}{\lambda_2} = \sqrt{\frac{\Delta V_1}{\Delta V_2}} = \sqrt{\frac{25}{100}} = \frac{1}{2} \quad \lambda_2 = \frac{\lambda_1}{2}.$$

15. In photoelectric emission process from a metal of work function 1.8 eV, the kinetic energy of most energetic electron is 0.5 eV The corresponding stopping potential is **[AIPMT-2011]**

(1) 1.3 V (2) 0.5 V

(3) 5 V (4) 1.8 V

Sol : **(2)** $K.E._{max} = eV_0$

$$V_0 = \frac{K.E._{max}}{e} = \frac{0.5 \text{ eV}}{e}; \qquad V_0 = 0.5 \text{ volt.}$$

16. The threshold frequency for a photosensitive metal is 3.3 $\times 10^{14}$ 3 Hz. If light of frequency 8.2 $\times$ 1014 Hz is incidenton this metal, the cut off voltage for the photoelectric emission is nearly **[AIPMT-2011]**

(1) 2 V (2) 3 V

(3) 5 V (4) 1 V

Sol : **(1)** According to Einstein's potoelectric equation

$$eV_0 = h\upsilon - h\upsilon_0$$

Where, υ = Incident frequency

υ_0 = Thershold frequency

V_0 = Cut-off or stopping potential or

$$V_0 = \frac{h}{e}(\upsilon - \upsilon_0)$$

Substituting the given values, we get

$$V_0 = \frac{6.63\times10^{-34}(8.2\times10^{14} - 3.3\times10^{14})}{1.6\times10^{-19}} \approx 2\text{ V.}$$

17. A 200 W sodium street lamp emits yelllow light of wavelength 0.6 μm. Assuming it to be 25% efficient in converting electrical energy to light the number of photons of yellow light it emits per seconds is **[AIPMT-2011]**

(1) 3 $\times 10^{19}$ (2) 1.5 $\times 10^{20}$

(3) 6 $\times 10^{18}$ (4) 62 $\times 10^{20}$

Sol : **(2)** Energy of a photon,

$$= \frac{(6.6\times10^{-34}\text{ J s})(3\times10^{8}\text{ ms}^{-1})}{0.6\times10^{-6}\text{m}}$$

$$= 33\times10^{-20} J$$

Number of photon emitted per second is

$$N = \frac{\frac{25}{100}P}{E} = \frac{\frac{25}{100}\times200\text{ W}}{33\times10^{-20}\text{ J}} = 1.5\times10^{20}$$

18. Monochromatic radiation emitted when electron on hydrogen atom jumps from first excited to the ground state irradiates a photosensitive material The stopping potential is measured to be 3.57 V. The threshold frequency of the material is **[AIPMT-2012]**

(1) 2.5×10^{15}Hz (2) 4×10^{15}Hz
(3) 5×10^{15} Hz (4) 1.6×10^{15}Hz

Sol : **(4)** Energy released from emmition of electron is $E = (-3.4) - (-13.6) = 10.2$ eV.

From photo-electric equation, work function

$\phi = E - eV_0 = h\upsilon_0$

On Solving this $\upsilon_0 = 1.6 \times 10^{15}$ Hz.

19. If the momentum of an electron is changed by p, then the de- Broglie wavelength associated with it changes by 0.5% The initial momentum of electron will be **[AIPMT-2012]**

(1) 200 p (2) 400 p (3) $\frac{p}{200}$ (4) 100 p

Sol : **(1)** de Broglie wavelength associated with an electron is

$$\lambda = \frac{h}{p} \text{ or } P = \frac{h}{\lambda}$$

$$\therefore \frac{\Delta P}{P} = -\frac{\Delta\lambda}{\lambda}$$

$$\frac{P}{P_{initial}} = \frac{0.5}{100} \Rightarrow P_{initial} = 200P$$

20. Two radiations of photon energies 1 eV and 2.5 eV successively illuminate a photosensitive metallic surface of work function 0.5 eV . The ratio of the maximum speeds of the emitted electrons is **[AIPMT-2012]**

(1) 1 : 4 (2) 1 : 2
(3) 1 :1 (4) 1 : 5

Sol : **(2)** According to Einstein's photoelectric equation

$$\frac{1}{2}m\upsilon_{max}^2 = h\upsilon - \phi_0$$

Where $\frac{1}{2}m\upsilon_{max}^2$ is the maximum kinetic energy of the emitted electrons, $h\upsilon$ is the incident energy and ϕ_0 is the work function of the metal.

$$\frac{1}{2}m\upsilon_{max_1}^2 = 1eV - 0.5eV = 0.5eV \quad ...(i)$$

and $\frac{1}{2}m\upsilon_{max_2}^2 = 2.5eV - 0.5ev = 2eV$ ..(ii)

Divide (i) and (ii), we get

$$\frac{\upsilon_{max_1}^2}{\upsilon_{max_2}^2} = \frac{0.5}{2}$$

$$\frac{\upsilon_{max_1}^2}{\upsilon_{max_2}^2} = \sqrt{\frac{0.5}{2}} = \frac{1}{2} \Rightarrow 1 : 2$$

21. For photoelectric emission from certain metal the cut - off frequency is v. If radiation of frequency 2v impinges on the metal plate, the maximum possible velocity of emittted electron will be (m is the electron mass.) **[AIPMT-2013]**

(1) $\sqrt{\frac{hv}{(2m)}}$ (2) $\sqrt{\frac{hv}{m}}$

(3) $\sqrt{\frac{2hv}{m}}$ (4) $2\sqrt{\frac{hv}{m}}$

Sol : **(3)** Work function, $\phi = hv$

According to Einstein's photoelectric equation

$$\frac{1}{2}m\upsilon_{max}^2 = h(2\upsilon) - h\upsilon \Rightarrow \frac{1}{2}m\upsilon_{max}^2 = h\upsilon$$

$$h\upsilon_{max}^2 = \frac{2h\upsilon}{m} \Rightarrow \upsilon_{max} = \sqrt{\frac{2h\upsilon}{m}}$$

22. The wavelength λ_e of an electron and λ_p of a photon of same energy E are related by **[AIPMT-2013]**

(1) $\lambda_p \propto \lambda_e^2$ (2) $\lambda_p \propto \lambda_e$

(3) $\lambda_p \propto \sqrt{\lambda_e}$ (4) $\lambda_p \propto \frac{1}{\sqrt{\lambda_e}}$

Sol : **(1)** Wavelength of an electron of energy E is

$$\lambda_e = \frac{h}{\sqrt{2m_e E}} \qquad ...(i)$$

Wavelength of a photon of same energy E is

$$\lambda_e = \frac{hc}{E} \quad \text{or} \quad E = \frac{hc}{\lambda_p} \qquad ...(ii)$$

Squaring both sides of Eq. (i), we get

$$\lambda_e^2 = \frac{h_2}{2m_e E} \quad \text{or} \quad E = \frac{h^2}{2m_e\lambda_e^2} \qquad ...(iii)$$

Equation (ii) and (iii), we get

$$\frac{hc}{\lambda_p} = \frac{h^2}{2m_e\lambda_e^2}$$

$$\lambda_p = \frac{2m_e c}{h}\lambda_e^2 \; ; \qquad \lambda_p = \lambda_e^2$$

23. When the energy of the incident radiation is increased by 20%, the kinetic energy of the photoelectrons emitted from a metal surface increased from 0.5 eV to 0.8 eV. The work function of the metal is **[AIPMT-2014]**

(1) 0.65 eV (2) 1.0 eV

(3) 1.3 eV (4) 1.5 eV

Sol : **(2)** By using $h\nu = \phi_0 + 0.5$ ....(i)

and $1.2h\nu = \phi_0 + 0.8$ ....(ii)

Therefore $\phi_0 = 1.0\,\text{eV}$

24. If the kinetic energy of the particle is increased to 16 times its previous value, the percentage change in the de-Broglie wavelength of the particle is **[AIPMT-2014]**

(1) 25 (2) 75

(3) 60 (4) 50

Sol : **(2)** de Broglic wavelength

$$\lambda = \frac{h}{\sqrt{2mK}} \qquad ...(i)$$

Where m is the mass and K is the kinetic energy of the particle.

When kinetic energy of the particle is increased to 16 times, then its de Broglie wavelength becomes.

$$\lambda' = \frac{h}{\sqrt{2m(16K)}} = \frac{1}{4}\frac{\lambda}{\sqrt{2mK}} = \frac{\lambda}{4} \text{ (using(i))}$$

% change in the de Broglie wavelength

$$= \frac{\lambda - \lambda'}{\lambda} \times 100 = \left(1 - \frac{\lambda'}{\lambda}\right) \times 100$$

$$= \left(1 - \frac{1}{4}\right) \times 100 = 75\%$$

25. Which of the following figures represent the variation of particle momentum and the associated be-Broglie wavelength ? **[AIPMT-2015]**

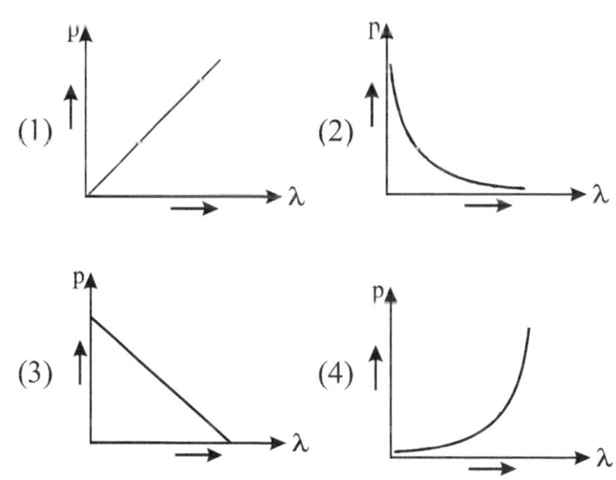

Sol : **(2)** $\lambda = \frac{h}{p}$

$\lambda \propto \frac{1}{p}$

26. A certain metallic surface is illuminated with monochromatic light of wavelenth λ, the stopping potential for photoelectric current for this light is $3V_0$. If the same surface is illuminated with light of wavelength 2λ, the stopping potential is V_0. The threshold wavelength for this surface for photoelectric effect is **[AIPMT-2015]**

(1) 6λ (2) 4λ

(3) $\frac{\lambda}{4}$ (4) $\frac{\lambda}{6}$

Sol : **(2)** $3eV_0 + \phi = \frac{hc}{\lambda}$

$eV_0 + \phi = \frac{hc}{2\lambda}$

Equation 2×3 – equation 1

$2\phi = \frac{hc}{\lambda}\left(\frac{3}{2} - 1\right) = \frac{hc}{2\lambda}$

$\phi = \frac{hc}{\lambda\pi = 4\lambda}$

27. Light of wavelength 500 nm is incidenton a metal with work function 2.28 eV. The de Broglie wavelength of the emitted electron is

[AIPMT-2015]

(1) ≤ 2.8×10^{-12} m (2) < 2.8×10^{-10} m

(3) < 2.8×10^{-9} m (4) ≥ 2.8×10^{-9} m

Sol : **(4)** Energy of photon $(E) = \frac{12400}{5000} = 2.48$ eV

Work function $(\phi) = 2.28$ eV

According to elenstein equation

$E = \phi_0 + (K.E.)_{max}$

$\Rightarrow 2.48 = 2.28 + (K.E.)_{max}$

$\Rightarrow (K.E.)_{max} = 0.20$ eV

For electron $\lambda = \frac{h}{\sqrt{2mE}} \Rightarrow \lambda \approx 28\AA$

So $\lambda \geq 2.8 \times 10^{-9}$ m

28. A photelectric surface is illuminated successively by monochromatic light of wavelength λ and $\frac{\lambda}{2}$. If the maximum kinetic energy of the emitted photoelectrons in the second case is 3 times than in the first case. The work functions of the suface of the material is

(h = Plank's constant, c = speed of light)

[AIPMT-2015]

(1) $\frac{hc}{3\lambda}$ (2) $\frac{hc}{2\lambda}$ (3) $\frac{hc}{\lambda}$ (4) $\frac{2hc}{\lambda}$

Sol : **(2)** $KE_1 = \frac{hc}{\lambda} - \phi$

$KE_2 = \frac{hc}{\lambda/2} - \phi = \frac{2hc}{\lambda} - \phi$

$KE_2 = 3KE_1$

$\Rightarrow 2\phi = \frac{hc}{\lambda} \Rightarrow \phi = \frac{hc}{2\lambda}$.

29. An electron of mass m with an initial velocity $\vec{V} = V_0\hat{i}(V_0 > 0)$ enters an electric field $\vec{E} = -E_0\hat{i}(E_0 > \text{constant})$ at t = 0. If λ_0 is its de-Broglie wavelength initially, then its de-Broglie wavelength at time t is **[NEET-2018]**

(1) $\lambda_0 t$ (2) $\lambda_0\left(1 + \frac{eE_0 t}{mV_0}\right)$

(3) $\frac{\lambda_0}{\left(1 + \frac{eE_0}{mV_0}t\right)}$ (4) λ_0

Ans. **(3)** Initial de-Broglie wavelength

$$\lambda_0 = \frac{h}{mv_0} \qquad ....(i)$$

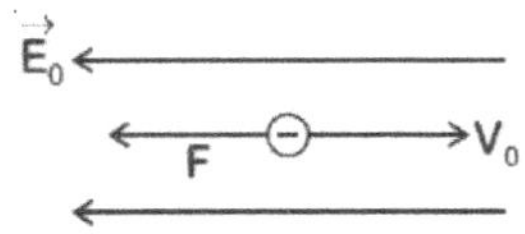

Acceleration of electron

$$a = \frac{eE_0}{m}$$

Velocity after time 't'

$$V = \left(V_0 + \frac{eE_0}{m}t\right)$$

So,

$$\lambda = \frac{h}{mV} = \frac{h}{m\left(V_0 + \frac{eE_0}{m}t\right)}$$

$$= \frac{h}{mV_0\left[1 + \frac{eE_0}{mV_0}t\right]} = \frac{\lambda_0}{\left[1 + \frac{eE_0}{mV_0}t\right]} \qquad ....(ii)$$

Divide (ii) by (i)

$$\lambda = \frac{\lambda_0}{\left[1 + \frac{eE_0}{mV_0}t\right]}$$

30. For a radioactive material, half-life is 10 minutes. If initially there are 600 number of nuclei, the time taken (in minutes) for the disintegration of 450 nuclei is **[NEET-2018]**

(1) 30 (2) 10

(3) 20 (4) 15

Ans. **(3)** Number of nuclei remaining = 600 – 450 = 150

$$\frac{N}{N_0} = \left(\frac{1}{2}\right)^n \Rightarrow \frac{150}{600} = \left(\frac{1}{2}\right)^{\frac{t}{t_{1/2}}}$$

$$\Rightarrow \left(\frac{1}{2}\right)^2 = \left(\frac{1}{2}\right)^{\frac{t}{t_{1/2}}}$$

$t = 2t_{1/2} = 2 \times 10 = 2$ minute

31. When the light of frequency $2v_0$ (where v_0 is threshold frequency), is incident on a metal plate, the maximum velocity of electrons emitted is v_1. When the frequency of the incident radiation is increased to $5v_0$, the maximum velocity of electrons emitted from the same plate is v_2. The ratio of v_1 to v_2 is **[NEET-2018]**

(1) 4 : 1 (2) 1 : 4

(3) 1 : 2 (4) 2 : 1

Ans. **(3)** $E = W_0 + \frac{1}{2}mv^2$

$$h(2\nu_0) = h\nu_0 + \frac{1}{2}mv_1^2$$

$$h\nu_0 = \frac{1}{2}mv_1^2 \qquad ....(i)$$

$$h(5\nu_0) = h\nu_0 + \frac{1}{2}mv_2^2$$

$$4h\nu_0 = \frac{1}{2}mv_2^2 \qquad .....(ii)$$

Divide (i) by (ii)

$$\frac{1}{4} = \frac{v_1^2}{v_2^2} \Rightarrow \frac{1}{4} = \frac{v_1^2}{v_2^2}$$

32. The power radiated by a black body is P and it radiates maximum energy at wavelength λ_0. If the temperature of the black body is now changed so that it radiates maximum energy at wavelength $\frac{3}{4}\lambda_0$, the power radiated by it becomes nP. The value of n is **[NEET-2018]**

(1) $\frac{256}{81}$ (2) $\frac{4}{3}$

(3) $\frac{3}{4}$ (4) $\frac{81}{256}$

Ans. **(1)** We know,

$\lambda_{max} T$ = constant (Wien's law)

So, $\lambda_{max_1} T_1 = \lambda_{max_2} T_2$

$$\Rightarrow \lambda_0 T = \frac{3\lambda_0}{4} T' \qquad \Rightarrow T' = \frac{4}{3} T$$

So, $\frac{P_2}{P_1} = \left(\frac{T'}{T}\right)^4 = \left(\frac{4}{3}\right)^4 = \frac{256}{81}$

26 Atoms

Note: Scan QR code with your mobile camera or QR scanner for video solutions.

1. The total energy of electron in the gound state of hydrogen atomis is –13.6 eV. The kinetic energy of an electron in the first excited state is **[AIPMT 2007]**

(1) 3.4 eV (2) 1.7 eV

(3) 6.8 eV (4) 13.6 eV

Sol : **(1)** Totel energy in first excited state

$$= -\frac{13.4}{4} = -3.4 \text{ eV}$$

K.E. in first excited stare = – totel energy in that state = – (–3.4) = 3.4 eV

2. The ground state energy of hydrogen atom is – 13.6eV. When its electron is in the first excited state, its excitation energy is **[AIPMT 2008]**

(1) 3.4 eV (2) 6.8 eV

(3) 10.2 eV (4) zero

Sol : **(1)** Since E0 = – 13.6 eV ; Energy in the excited state

$$= -\frac{13.4}{4} = -3.4$$

Δ E – Excitation energy

= Energy needed to raise the electron from round state to higher level

$$= -3.4 + 13.6 = 10.2 \text{ eV}$$

3. In a Rutherford scattering experiment when a projectile of charge Z_1 and mass M_1 approaches a target nucleus of charge Z_2 and mass M_2, the distance of closest approach is r_0, the energy of the projectile is **[AIPMT 2009]**

(1) directly proportional to $M_1 \times M_2$

(2) directly proportional to $Z_1 Z_2$

(3) inversely proportional to Z_1

(4) directly proportional to mass M_1

Sol : **(2)** Energy $= \frac{1}{4\pi\varepsilon_0}\frac{Z_1 Z_2}{r_0}$

4. The ionization energy of the electron in the hydrogen atomin its ground state is 13.6 eV, The atoms are excited to higher energy levels to emit radiations of 6 wavelengths. Maximum wavelength of emitted radiation corresponds to the transition between **[AIPMT 2009]**

(1) n = 3 to n = 2 states

(2) n = 3 to n = 1 states

(3) n = 2 to n = 1 states

(4) n = 4 to n = 3 states

Sol : **(4)** $\frac{n(n-1)}{2} = 6$

$\rightarrow n = 4$

For maximum wavelength energy difference nctween states should be minimum because

$$\lambda = \frac{hc}{\Delta E}$$

So, transition state in n – 4 to n – 3

5. The energy of a hydrogen atom in the ground state is –13.6 eV. The energy of a He^+ ion in the first excited state will be **[AIMPT 2010]**

(1) – 13.6 eV (2) –27.2 eV
(3) – 54.4 eV (4) – 6.8 eV

Sol : **(1)** $E_n = -13.6\left(\frac{Z^2}{n^2}\right) = (-13.6)\left(\frac{4}{4}\right) = -13.6$

6. An alpha nucleus of energy $\frac{1}{2}mv^2$ bombards a heavy nuclear target of charge Ze.Then the distance of closest approach for the alpha nucleus will be proportional to **[AIPMT 2010]**

(1) $\frac{1}{Ze}$ (2) v^2 (3) $\frac{1}{m}$ (2) $\frac{1}{v^4}$

Sol : (3) $\frac{1}{2}mv^2 \frac{(Ze)(2e)}{4\pi\varepsilon_0 d_{min}}$ then $d_{min} \propto \frac{1}{m}$

7. The wavelength of the first line of Lyman series for hydrogen atom is equal to that of the second line of Blamer series for a hydrogen -like ion. The atomic number Z of hydrogen like ion is **[AIPMT 2011]**

(1) 4 (2) 1
(3) 2 (4) 3

Sol : **(3)** $\frac{1}{\lambda} = RZ^2\left(\frac{1}{n_1^2} - \frac{1}{n_2^2}\right)$

$$R(1)^2\left(\frac{1}{2^2} - \frac{1}{2^2}\right) = RZ^2\left(\frac{1}{2^2} - \frac{1}{4^2}\right) = \; Z = 2$$

8. An electron in the hydrogen atom jumps from excited state *n* to the ground state. The wave length so emiited illuminates photo -sensitive material having work function 2.75 eV. If the stopping potential of the photoelectron is 10 V, the value of n is **[AIPMT 2011]**

(1) 3 (2) 4
(3) 5 (4) 2

Sol : **(2)** Here, Stopping potential, $V_0 = 10V$

Work function, $W = 2.75$ eV

According to Einstein's photoelectric equation

$eV_0 = h\upsilon - W$

or $h\upsilon = eV_0 + W$

$= 10 \text{ eV} + 2.75 \text{ eV} = 12.75 \text{ eV}$ ...(i)

When an electron in the hydrogen atom makes a transition from excited state n to the ground state $(n = 1)$, then the frequency (υ) of the emitted photon is given by

$h\upsilon = E_n - E_1$

$$h\upsilon = -\frac{13.6}{n^2} - \left(\frac{13.6}{1^2}\right)$$

$$\left[\because \text{ For hydrogen atom, } E_n = -\frac{13.6}{n^2}\text{eV}\right]$$

According to given problem

$$-\frac{13.6}{n^2} + 13.6 = 12.75 \quad \text{(using (i))}$$

$$\frac{13.6}{n^2} = 0.85 \Rightarrow n^2 = \frac{13.6}{0.85} = 16$$

or $n = 4$

9. Out of the following which one is not possible energy for photon to be emitted by hydrogen atom according to Bohr's atomic model ? **[AIPMT 2011]**

(1) 1.9 eV (2) 11.1 eV
(3) 13.6 eV (4) 0.65 eV

Sol : (4) The energy of nth ordit of hydrogen atom is given as

$$E_n = -\frac{13.6}{n^2} eV$$

$$\therefore E_1 = -13.6\,eV$$

$$E_2 = -\frac{13.6}{2^2} = -3.4\,eV$$

$$E_3 = -\frac{13.6}{3^2} = -1.5\,eV$$

$$E_4 = -\frac{13.6}{4^2} = -0.85\,eV$$

$$\therefore\ E_3 - E_2 = -1.5 - (-3.4) = 1.9eV$$

$$E_4 - E_3 = -0.85 - (-1.5) = 0.65eV$$

10. An electrons of a stationary hydrogen atom passes from the fitth energy level to the ground level. The velocity that the atom aquired as a result of photon emission will be **[AIPMT 2012]**

(1) $\frac{24\,m}{25\,hR}$ (2) $\frac{24\,hR}{25\,m}$ (3) $\frac{25\,hR}{24\,m}$ (4) $\frac{25\,m}{24\,hR}$

(m is the mass of the electron, R Rydberg constant and h, Planck's constant)

Sol : **(2)** According to Rydberg formula

$$\frac{1}{\lambda} = R\left[\frac{1}{n_f^2} - \frac{1}{n_i^2}\right]$$

Here, $n_f = 1$, $n_i = 5$

$$\frac{1}{\lambda} = R\left[\frac{1}{r^2} - \frac{1}{5^2}\right] = R\left[\frac{1}{1} - \frac{1}{25}\right] = \frac{24}{25}R$$

According to conservation of linear momentum, we get

Momentum of photon = Momentum of atom

$$\frac{1}{\lambda} - m\upsilon \text{ or } \upsilon = \frac{h}{m\lambda} = \frac{h}{m}\left(\frac{24R}{25}\right) = \frac{24hR}{25m}$$

11. Electron in hydrogen atom first jumps from third excited state to second excited state and then from second excited state to frist excited state. The ration of wavelengths $\lambda_1 : \lambda_2$ emitted in two cases is **[AIPMT 2012]**

(1) 7/5 (2) 27/20 (3) 27/5 (4) 20/7

Sol : **(4)** Wavelength observed from transition of n_i

to n_f is $\lambda = \frac{1}{\left[\frac{1}{n_f^2} - \frac{1}{n_i^2}\right]}$

For $\lambda_1,\ n_i = 4,\ n_f = 3$

For $\lambda_{2,} n_i = 4, n_f = 2$

we get $\lambda : n_i = 20:7$

12. The transition from the state n = 3 ton = 1 in a hydrogen- like atom results in ultraviolet radiation.Infrared radiation will be obtained in the transition froms **[AIPMT 2012]**

(1) $2 \rightarrow 1$ (2) $3 \rightarrow 2$

(3) $4 \rightarrow 2$ (4) $4 \rightarrow 3$

Sol : **(4)**

$4 \rightarrow 3$

13. Hydrogen atom in ground state is excited by a monochromatic radiation of l = 975Å. Number of spectral lines in the resulting specturum emitted will be **[AIPMT 2014]**

(1) 3 (2) 2 (3) 6 (4) 10

Sol : **(3) 6**

14. Consider 3rd orbit of He^+(Helium) using non-relativistic approach the speed of electron in this orbit will be (given K = 9 ×109 constant Z = 2 and h (Plank's constant) = 6.6×10^{-34} Js)

[AIPMT 2015]

(1) 2.92×10^6 m/s (2) 1.46×10^6 m/s

(3) 0.73×10^6 m/s (4) 3.0×10^8 m/s

Sol : **(2)** $k\dfrac{q_1q_2}{r^2} = \dfrac{mv^2}{r}$

$$k\frac{(e)(2e)}{r} = mv^2 \quad ...(i)$$

$$mvr = \frac{nh}{2\pi}; \quad mvr = \frac{3h}{2\pi}$$

$$r = \frac{3h}{2\pi mv} \quad ...(ii)$$

by (i) & (ii)

$$k\frac{2e^2}{\left(\dfrac{3h}{2\pi mv}\right)} = mv^2$$

$$v = \frac{4\pi Ke^2 mv}{3h} = mv^2 \;;\; v = \frac{4\pi Ke^2}{3h} = 1.46\times10^6 \text{ m/s}$$

15. Two particles of masses m_1,m_2 move with initial velocities u_1 and u_2. On collision ,one of the particles get excited to higher level. after absorbing energy e. If final velocities of particles be v_1 and v_2 then we must have **[AIPMT 2015]**

(1) $m_1u_1^2 + m_2u_2^2 - \varepsilon = m_1v_1^2 + m_2v_2^2$

(2) $\frac{1}{2}m_1u_1 + \frac{1}{2}m_2u_2^2 = \frac{1}{2}m_1v_1^2 + \frac{1}{2}m_2v_2^2 - \varepsilon$

(3) $\frac{1}{2}m_1u_1^2 + \frac{1}{2}m_2u_2^2 - \varepsilon = \frac{1}{2}m_1v_1^2 + \frac{1}{2}m_2v_2^2$

(4) $\frac{1}{2}m_1^2u_1^2 + \frac{1}{2}m_2^2u_2^2 + \varepsilon = \frac{1}{2}m_1^2v_1^2 + \frac{1}{2}m_2^2v_2^2$

Sol : **(3)** Apply conservation of mechanical energy.

$$\frac{1}{2}m_1u_1^2 + \frac{1}{2}m_2u_2^2 - \varepsilon = \frac{1}{2}m_1v_1^2 + \frac{1}{2}m_2v_2^2$$

16. In the spectrum of hydrogen the ratio of th longest wavelength in the Lyman series to the longest wavelength in the Blamer series is : **[AIPMT 2015 Re]**

(1) $\frac{5}{27}$ (2) $\frac{4}{9}$ (3) $\frac{9}{4}$ (4) $\frac{27}{5}$

Sol : **(1)** For Lyman series

$$\left(\frac{1}{\lambda_{max}}\right)_L = R(1)^2\left[\frac{1}{(1)^2} - \frac{1}{(2)^2}\right]$$

$$\left(\frac{1}{\lambda_{max}}\right)_L = \frac{4}{3R}$$

For Balmer series

$$\left(\frac{1}{\lambda_{max}}\right)_B = R(1)^2\left[\frac{1}{(1)^2} - \frac{1}{(3)^2}\right]$$

$$\left(\frac{1}{\lambda_{max}}\right)_B = \frac{36}{5R}$$

$$\frac{(\lambda_{max})_L}{(\lambda_{max})_B} = \frac{4}{3R}\times\frac{5R}{36} = \frac{5}{27}.$$

17. An electron of mass m and a photon have same energy E. The ratio of de-Broglie wavelengths associated with them is : **[AIPMT 2016]**

(1) $\frac{1}{c}\left(\frac{E}{2m}\right)^{1/2}$ (2) $\left(\frac{E}{2m}\right)^{1/2}$

(3) $c(2cM)^{1/2}$ (4) $\frac{1}{xc}\left(\frac{2m}{E}\right)^{1/2}$

Sol : **(1)** $\lambda_{electron} = \dfrac{h}{\sqrt{2ME}}$ ...(i)

For λ_{photon}

$$E = hv = \frac{hc}{\lambda_{photon}} \quad ...(ii)$$

From these two ratio obtained by dividing these (2)

$$\lambda_1 : \lambda_2 = \frac{1}{c}\left[\frac{E}{2M}\right]^{1/2}$$

18. If an electron in a hydrogen atom jumps from the 3rd orbit to the 2nd orbit, it emits a photon of wavelength λ. When it jumps from the 4th orbit to the 3rd orbit, the corresponding wavelength of the photon will be :- **[NEET – II(2016)]**

(1) $\frac{20}{7}\lambda$ (2) $\frac{20}{13}\lambda$

(3) $\frac{16}{25}\lambda$ (4) $\frac{9}{16}\lambda$

Sol : **(1)** $\frac{1}{\lambda} = \text{Re}\left(\frac{1}{2^2} - \frac{1}{3^2}\right)$

$$\frac{1}{\lambda'} = \text{Re}\left(\frac{1}{3^2} - \frac{1}{4^2}\right)$$

Dividing $\frac{1}{\lambda'} = \frac{20}{7}\lambda$.

19. The ratio of wavelengths of the last line of Balmer series and the last line of Lyman series is : **[NEET – 2017]**

(1) 2 (2) 1 (3) 4 (4) 0.5

Sol : **(3)** For last Balmer serise

$$\frac{1}{\lambda_b} = R\left[\frac{1}{2^2} - \frac{1}{\infty^2}\right]$$

$$\frac{1}{\lambda_b} = \frac{4}{R}$$

For last Lyman serise

$$\frac{1}{\lambda_1} = R\left[\frac{1}{1^2} - \frac{1}{\infty^2}\right]$$

$$\frac{1}{\lambda_1} = \frac{1}{R}$$

$$\frac{\lambda_b}{\lambda_1} = \frac{\frac{4}{R}}{\frac{1}{R}}$$

$$\frac{\lambda_b}{\lambda_1} = 4$$

20. The ratio of kinetic energy to the total energy of an electron in a Bohr orbit of the hydrogen atom, is **[NEET-2018]**

(1) 2 : –1 (2) 1 : –1

(3) 1 : 1 (4) 1 : –2

Ans. **(2)** KE = – (Total energy)

So, Kinetic energy : total energy = 1 : –1

27 Nuclei

Note: Scan QR code with your mobile camera or QR scanner for video solutions.

1. Two radioactive subsatnces A and B have decay constants 5λ and λ respectively. At $t = 0$ they have the same number f nuclei, The ratio of number of nuclei of A and those of B will be $\left(\frac{1}{e}\right)^2$ after a time interval **[AIPMT 2007]**

(1) $\frac{1}{4\lambda}$ (2) 4λ

(3) 2λ (4) $\frac{1}{2\lambda}$

Sol : (4) $\frac{N_A}{N_B} = \frac{N_0 e^{-\lambda_A t}}{N_0 e^{-\lambda_B t}} = \frac{e^{-5\lambda t}}{e^{-\lambda t}}$

$\Rightarrow \frac{1}{e^{4\lambda t}} = \frac{1}{e^2} \Rightarrow t = \frac{1}{2\lambda}$.

2. In radioactive decay process, the negatively charged emitted β - particles are **[AIPMT 2007]**

(1) the electrons persent inside the nucleus

(2) the electrons produced as a result of the decay of neutrons inside the nucleus

(3) the electrons proudced as a result of collisoins between atoms

(4) the electrons orbiting around the nucleus

Sol : (2) the electrons produced as a result of the decay of neutrons inside the nucleus

3. A nuclues ${}^{A}_{Z}X$ has mass represented by M (A, Z). If M_p and M_n denote the mass of proton and neutron respectively and BE the binding energy (in MeV), then : **[AIPMT 2007]**

(1) $BE = [M(A, Z) - ZM_p - (A - Z)Mn]c^2$

(2) $BE = [ZM_p + (A - Z)M_n - M(A, Z)]c^2$

(3) $BE = [ZM_p + AM_n - M(A, Z)]c^2$

(4) $BE = M(A, Z) - ZM_p - (A - Z)M_n$

Sol : (2) $BE = [ZM_p + (A - Z)M_n - M(A, Z)]c^2$

4. If the nucleus ${}^{27}_{23}$ A1 has nuclear radiusof about 3.6 fm, then ${}^{125}_{52}$ Te would haveits radius approximately as **[AIPMT 2008]**

(1) 6.0 fm (2) 9.6 fm

(3) 12.0 fm (4) 4.8 fm

Sol : (1) $\because R = R_0 A^{1/3}$

$\therefore \frac{R_{Te}}{R_{Al}} = \left(\frac{125}{27}\right)^{1/3} = \left(\frac{5^3}{3^3}\right)^{1/3} = \frac{5}{3}$

$\Rightarrow R_{Te} = \left(\frac{5}{3}\right)(3.6) = 6$ fm

5. Two radiaoactive materials X_1 and X_2 have decay constants 5λ and λ respectiely. If initially they have the same number of nuclei, than the ratio of the number o nuclei of X_1 to that of X_2 will be $\frac{1}{e}$ after a time. **[AIPMT 2008]**

(1) λ (2) $\frac{1}{\lambda}$

(3) $\frac{1}{4\lambda}$ (4) $\frac{e}{\lambda}$

Sol : (3) $X_1 = N_0 e^{-5\lambda t}$

$X_2 = N_0 e^{\lambda t}$

$\frac{X_1}{X_2} = e^{-5\lambda t + \lambda t}$; $\frac{1}{e} = e^{-4\lambda t}$

$e^{-1} = e^{-4\lambda t} \Rightarrow t = \frac{1}{4\lambda}$

6. If M (A, Z), M_p and M_n denote the masses of the nucleus $^A_Z X$, proton and neturon respectively in units of u(1u = 931. 5 MeV/C^2) and BE represents its binding energy in MeV, then **[AIPMT 2008]**

(1) $M(A, Z) = ZM_p + (A - Z)M_n - BE/C^2$

(2) $M(A, Z) = ZM_p + (A - Z)M_n - BE$

(3) $M(A, Z) = ZM_p + (A - Z)M_n - BE$

(4) $M(A, Z) = ZM_p + (A - Z)M_n - BE/C^2$

Sol : (1) Mass degect

$\Delta m = ZM_p + (A - Z)M_n - M(A, Z)$

Binding energy $= \Delta m C^2$

$BE = [ZM_p + (A - Z)M_n - M(A, Z)].C^2$

$M(A, Z) = ZM_p + (A - Z)M_n - \frac{BE}{C^2}$.

7. In the nuclear decay given below

$^A_Z X \rightarrow {}_{Z+1}{}^A Y \rightarrow {}^{A-4}_{Z-1} B^* \rightarrow {}^{A-4}_{Z-1} B$,

the partiales emitted in the sequence are **[AIPMT 2009]**

(1) β, α, γ (2) γ, β, α

(3) β, γ, α (4) α, β, γ

Sol : (1) ${}_Z X^A \xrightarrow{\beta} {}_{Z+1} Y^A \xrightarrow{\alpha} {}_{Z-1} B^{A-4} \xrightarrow{\gamma} {}_{Z-1} B^{A-4}$

8. The mass of a $^7_3$ Li nucleus is 0.042u less than the sum of the masses of all its nucleons. The binding energy per nucleon of $^7_3$ Li nucleus is nearly **[AIPMT 2010]**

(1) 46 Mev (2) 5.6 MeV

(3) 3.9 Mev (4) 23 MeV

Sol : (2) $\frac{BE}{nucleon} = \frac{0.042 \times 931}{7} = 5.6\,MeV$

9. The activity of a radioactive sample is measured as N_o counts per ninute at t = 0 and N_o/e counts per minute at t = 5 min. The time (in minute) at which the activity reduces to half its value is **[AIPMT 2010]**

(1) $\log_e 2/5$ (2) $\frac{5}{\log_2 2}$

(3) $5 \log_{10} 2$ (4) $5 \log_e 2$

Sol : (4) $N = N_0 e^{-\lambda t} \Rightarrow \frac{N_0}{e} = N_0 e^{-\lambda(5)} \Rightarrow \lambda = \frac{1}{5}$

Now $\frac{N_0}{2} - N_0 e^{-\lambda(t)} \Rightarrow t - \frac{1}{\lambda} \ell n 2 = 5 \ell n 2$

$= 5 \log 2$

10. The half- life of a radioactive isotope X is 50 years. It decays to another element Y which is stable The two elements X and Y were found to be in the ratio of 1 : 15 in a sample of a given rock The age of the rock was estimated to be **[AIPMT 2011]**

(1) 200 yr (2) 250 yr (3) 1 µg (4) 150 yr

Sol : (1) $X \rightarrow Y$

$X : Y = 1 : 15$

$A.P. = \frac{1}{16} = \frac{1}{2^n}$

No. of half life $n = 4$

$t = nT_{1/2} = 4 \times 50 = 200$ yr.

11. The power obtained in a reactor using U^{235} disintegration is 1000 kW. The mass decay of U^{235} per hour is **[AIPMT 2011]**

(1) 20 μg (2) 40 μg (3) 1 μg (4) 10 μg

Sol : (2) $E = Pt = mc^2$

$m = \frac{Pt}{c^2} = \frac{10^6 \times 3600}{(3 \times 10^8)^2}$ $m = 40\ \mu g$

12. A radioactive nucleus of mass M emits a photon of frequency v and the nucleus recoils. The recoil energy will be **[AIPMT 2011]**

(1) $h^2v^2/2MC^2$ (2) zero (3) hv (4) $Mc^2 - hv$

Sol : (1)

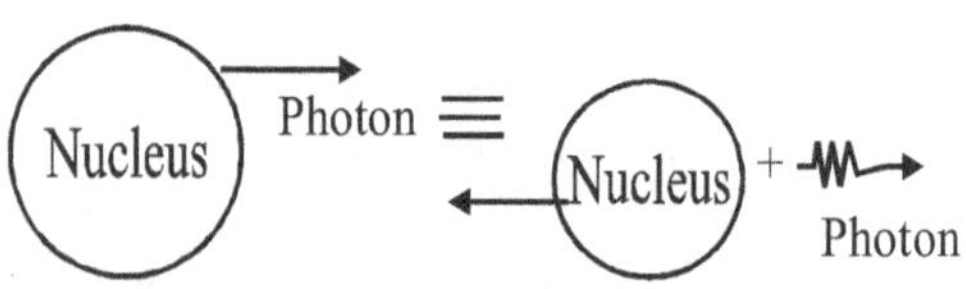

$F_{ex} = \frac{dP}{dt} = 0 \Rightarrow dP = 0 \Rightarrow P = \text{constant}$

$\boxed{\vec{P_i} = \vec{P_f}}$

$0 = \vec{P}_{Nu} + \vec{P}_{Ph}$ $\left|\vec{P}_{Nu}\right| = \left|\vec{P}_{Ph}\right| = \frac{h}{\lambda} = \frac{hv}{c}$

Recoil K.E. of nucleus $K.E_{Nu} = \frac{P_{Nu}^2}{2M_{Nu}}$

$K.E_{Nu} = \frac{(hv/c)^2}{2M} = \frac{h^2v^2}{2Mc^2}$

13. A nucleus ${}^{m}_{n}X$ emits one α - particle and two β- particles. The resulting nucleus is **[AIPMT 2011]**

(1) ${}^{m-6}_{n}Z$ (2) ${}^{m-4}_{n}Z$

(3) ${}^{m-4}_{n-2}Y$ (4) ${}^{m-6}_{n-4}Z$

Sol : (2) ${}_{n}X^{m} \xrightarrow{1\alpha} {}_{n-2}Y^{m-4} \xrightarrow{2\beta^-} {}_{n}Z^{m-4}$

α emission decreases mass no. by 4 and atomic no. by 2 and β^- emission increases atomic number by one but leaves mass no. unchanged.

14. Fusion reaction takes place at high temperature because **[AIPMT 2011]**

(1) atoms get ionised at high temperature

(2) kinetic energy is high enough to overcome the coulomb repulsion between nuclei

(3) molecules break up at high temperatrue

(4) nuclei break up at high temperature.

Sol : (2) Thermal K.E. ≥ Electrostatic P.E.

15. Two radioactive nuclei P and Q, in a given sample decay into a stable nucleus are $4N_0$ and that of Q are N_0 Half-life of P (for conversion to R) is 1 min whereas that of Q is 2 min. Initially there are no nuclei of P and Q ar equal. the number o nuclei of R present in the sample would be : **[AIPMT 2011]**

(1) $3\ N_0$ (2) $\frac{9N_0}{2}$

(3) $\frac{5N_0}{2}$ (4) $2\ N_0$

Sol : (2)

	p	Q
No. of nuclei, at t=0	$4N_0$	N_0
Half-life	1 min	2min
No. of nuclei after time t	N_P	N_Q

Let afrer t min the number of nuclei of P and Q are equal.

$$\therefore\ N_P = 4N_0\left(\frac{1}{2}\right)^{t/2} \text{ and } N_Q = N_0\left(\frac{1}{2}\right)^{1/2}$$

As $N_P = N_Q$

$$\therefore\ 4N_0\left(\frac{1}{2}\right)^{t/1} = N_0\left(\frac{1}{2}\right)^{t/2}$$

$$\frac{4}{2^{t/2}} = \frac{1}{2^{t/2}} \text{ or } 4 = \frac{2^t}{2^{t/2}} \text{ or } 4 = 2^{t/2} \text{ or } 2^2 = 2^{t/2}$$

$$\text{or } \frac{t}{2} = 2 \text{ or } t = 4 \text{ min}$$

After 4 minutes, both P and Q have equal number of nuclei.

$\therefore$ Number of nuclei of R

$$= \left(4N_0 - \frac{N_0}{4}\right) + \left(N_0 - \frac{N_0}{4}\right)$$

$$= \frac{15N_0}{4} + \frac{3N_0}{4} = \frac{9N_0}{2}$$

16. If the nucle ar radius of ^{27} A1 is 3.6 Fermi, the approximate nuclear radius of 64Cu in Fermi is **[AIPMT 2012]**

(1) 3.6 (2) 2.4 (3) 1.2 (4) 4.8

Sol : (2) Nuclear radius, $R = R_0 A^{1/3}$

Where R_0 is a constant and A is the mass number

$$\therefore \frac{R_{Al}}{R_{Cu}} = \frac{(27)^{1/3}}{(64)^{1/3}} = \frac{3}{4} \text{ or}$$

$$R_{Cu} = \frac{4}{3} \times R_{Al} = \frac{4}{3} \times 3.6 \text{ fermi} = 4.8 \text{ fermi}$$

17. A mixture consists of two radioactive materials A_1 and A_2 with half-lives of 20s and 10 s respectively. Initially the mixture has 40g of A_1 and 160 g of A_2. The amount of the two in the mixture will become equal after. **[AIPMT 2012]**

(1) 40 s (2) 20 s

(3) 60 s (4) 80 s

Sol : (1)For A, $40g \xrightarrow{20s} 20g \xrightarrow{20s} 10g$

For B, $160g \xrightarrow{10s} 80g \xrightarrow{10s} 40g$

$\xrightarrow{10s} 20g \xrightarrow{10s} 10g$

18. The half-life of a radioactive nucleus is 50 days The time interval $(t_2 - t_1)$ between the time t_2 when $\frac{2}{3}$ of it has decayed and the time t_1 when $\frac{1}{3}$ of it had decayed is **[AIPMT 2012]**

(1) 30 days (2) 50 days

(3) 60 days (4) 15 days

Sol : (2)According to radioactive decay law

$$N = N_0 e^{-\lambda t}$$

Where N_0 = Number of radioactive nuclei at time $t = 0$

$N = 0$ Numberof radioactive nuclei left undecayed at any time t

λ = decay constant

At time $t_2, \frac{2}{3}$ of the sample had decayed

$$\therefore\ N = \frac{1}{3}N_0$$

$$\therefore\ \frac{1}{3}N_0 = N_0 e^{-\lambda t_2} \quad ...(i)$$

At time $t_1, \frac{1}{3}$ of the sample had decayed,

$$\therefore\ N = \frac{2}{3}N_0$$

$$\therefore \frac{3}{2}N_0 = N_0 e^{-\lambda t_1} \quad ...(ii)$$

Divide (i) by (ii), we get

$$\frac{1}{2} = \frac{e^{-\lambda t_2}}{e^{-\lambda t_1}}$$

$$\frac{1}{2} = e^{-\lambda(t_2 - t_1)}$$

$$\lambda(t_2 - t_1) = \text{In}2$$

$$t_2 - t_1 = \frac{\text{In}2}{\lambda} = \frac{\text{In}2}{\left(\frac{\text{In}2}{T_{1/2}}\right)} \qquad \left(\because \lambda = \frac{\text{In}2}{T_{1/2}}\right)$$

$$= T_{1/2} = 50 \text{ days}$$

19. A certain mass of hydrogen is changed to helium by the process of fusion .The mass defect in fusion reaction is 0.02866 u. The energy liberated per u is (given 1 u = 931 MeV.) **[AIPMT 2013]**

(1) 2.67 MeV (2) 26.7 MeV
(3) 6.675 MeV (4) 13.35 MeV

Sol : (3) As ${}_1^2H + {}_1^2H \rightarrow {}_2^4He$

Here, $\Delta M = 0.02866$ u

$\therefore$ The energy liberated per u is

$$= \frac{\Delta M \times 931}{4}\text{Mev} = \frac{0.02866 \times 931}{4}\text{meV}$$

$$= \frac{26.7}{4}\text{MeV} = 6.675\text{MeV}$$

20. The half- life of a radioactive isotope 'X' is 20 years. It decays to another element 'Y' which is stable. The two elements 'X' and 'Y' were found to be in the ratio 1 : 7 in a sample of a given rock The age of the rock is estimated to be **[AIPMT 2013]**

(1) 40 years (2) 60 years
(3) 80 years (4) 100 years

Sol : (2)

	X	→	Y
Intial number of atoms,	N_0		0
Number of atoms after time t	N		$N_0 - N$

As per question

$$\frac{N}{N_0 - N} = \frac{1}{7} \Rightarrow 7N = N_0 - N$$

$$8N = N_0 \Rightarrow \frac{N}{N_0} = \frac{1}{8}$$

As $\frac{N}{N_0} = \left(\frac{1}{2}\right)^n$ where n is the no. of half lives

$$\therefore \frac{1}{8} = \left(\frac{1}{2}\right)^n; \qquad \left(\frac{1}{2}\right)^3 = \left(\frac{1}{2}\right)^n$$

$$\therefore n = 3; \qquad n = \frac{t}{T_{t/2}}$$

or $t = nT_{1/2} = 3 \times 20\text{years} = 60$ years

21. The binding energy per nucleon of ${}_3^7Li$ and ${}_2^4He$ nuclei are 5.60 MeV and 7.06 MeV, respectively. In the nuclear reaction ${}_3^7Li + {}_1^1H \rightarrow {}_2^4He^+$,the value of energy Q released is **[AIPMT 2014]**

(1) 19.6 MeV (2) –2.4 MeV
(3) 8.4 MeV (4) 17.3 MeV

Sol : (4) BE of ${}_2He^4 = 4 \times 7.06 = 28.24\text{MeV}$

BE of ${}_3^7Li = 7 \times 5.60 = 39.20\text{MeV}$

$${}_3^7Li + {}_1^1H \rightarrow {}_2He^4 + {}_2He^4 + Q$$

9.20 28.24×2

$Q = 56.48 - 39.20 = 17.28\text{MeV} \approx$ 17.03 Mev

22. A radio isotope X with a half-life 1.4×10^9 years of Y which is stable. A sample of the rock from a cave was found to contain X and Y in the ratio 1 : 7. The age of the rock is **[AIPMT 2014]**

(1) 1.96×10^9 years (2) 3.92×10^9 years

(3) 4.20×10^9 years (4) 8.40×10^9 years

Sol : (3) As $\frac{N_x}{N_y} = \frac{1}{7} \Rightarrow \frac{N_x}{N_x + N_y} = \frac{1}{8} = \left(\frac{1}{2}\right)^3$

So $t = 3T_{1/2} = 3 \times 1.4 \times 10^9$ yrs

$= 4.2 \times 10^9$ yrs.

23. If radius of the $^{27}_{13}Al$ nucleus is taken to be R_{Al} then the radius of $^{125}_{53}$ Te nucleus is nearly **[AIPMT 2015]**

(1) $\left(\frac{53}{13}\right)^{1/3} R_{Al}$ (2) $\frac{5}{3} R_{Al}$

(3) $\frac{3}{5} R_{Al}$ (4) $\left(\frac{13}{53}\right)^{1/3} R_{Al}$

Sol : (2) $\frac{R_{TE}}{R_{Al}} = \left(\frac{A_{TE}}{R_{Al}}\right)^{1/3} = \left(\frac{125}{27}\right)^{1/3}$

$R_{TE} = \frac{5}{3} R_{Al}$

24. When an α-particle of mass 'm' moving with velocity 'v' bombards on a heavy nucleus of charge 'Ze', its distance of closest approach from the nucleus depends on m as : **[AIPMT 2016]**

(1) $\frac{1}{m}$ (2) $\frac{1}{\sqrt{m}}$ (3) $\frac{1}{m^2}$ (4) m

Sol : (1) At closest approach

KE gets converted to PE

$\frac{1}{2} mV^2 = \frac{k(2e)(ze)}{r} \Rightarrow m \propto \frac{1}{r}$ or $r \propto \frac{1}{m}$

25. The half-life of a radioactive substance is 30 minutes. The time (in minutes) taken between 40% decay and 85% decay of the same radioactive substance is :- **[NEET -II(2016)]**

(1) 45 (2) 60 (3) 15 (4) 30

Sol : (2) $N_1 = 0.6\ N_0$

$N_2 = 0.15\ N_0$

$\frac{N_1}{N_2} = \left(\frac{1}{2}\right)^2$ So two half life period has passed

So time taken = $2t_{1/2} = 2 \times 30 = 60$ minutes

26. Radioactive material 'A' has decay constant '8λ' and material 'B' has decay constant 'λ'. Initially they have same number of nuclei. After what time, the ratio of number of nuclie of material 'B' to that 'A' will be $\frac{1}{e}$? **[NEET - (2017)]**

(1) $\frac{1}{\lambda}$ (2) $\frac{1}{7\lambda}$ (3) $\frac{1}{8\lambda}$ (4) $\frac{1}{9\lambda}$

Sol : (2) No option is correct

It we take $\frac{N_A}{N_B} = \frac{1}{e}$

Then $\frac{N_A}{N_B} = \frac{e^{-8\lambda t}}{e^{-\lambda t}}$

$\frac{1}{e} = e^{-7\lambda t}$ $-1 = -7\lambda t$

$t = \frac{1}{7\lambda}$

28 Semiconductors Electronics

Note: Scan QR code with your mobile camera or QR scanner for video solutions.

1. In the following circuit, the output Y for all possible inputs A and B is expressed by the truth table :- **[AIPMT 2007]**

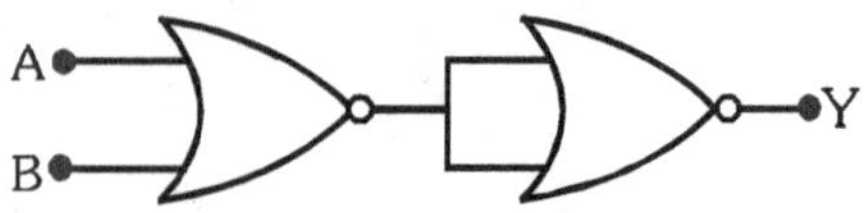

(1)

A	B	Y
0	0	0
0	1	1
1	0	1
1	1	1

(2)

A	B	Y
0	0	0
0	1	0
1	0	0
1	1	1

(3)

A	B	Y
0	0	1
0	1	1
1	0	1
1	1	0

(4)

A	B	Y
0	0	1
0	1	0
1	0	0
1	1	0

Sol : **(1)** For given logic circuit

$$Y = \overline{\overline{A+B}} = A + B \Rightarrow \text{OR gate}$$

2. A common emitter amplifier has a voltage gain of 50, an input impedane of 100 Ω and an output impedance of 200 Ω. The power gain of the amplifier is **[AIPMT 2007]**

(1) 500 (2) 1000

(3) 1250 (4) 100

Sol : **(3)** Voltage gain $= (\beta)\left(\frac{R_0}{R_i}\right) = 50$

$$\Rightarrow \beta = \frac{(50)(100)}{(200)} = 25$$

Power gain $= (\beta^2)\left(\frac{R_0}{R_i}\right) = (25)^2\left(\frac{200}{100}\right)$

$$= 625 \times 2 = 1250$$

3. For a cubic crystal structure which one of the following relations indicating the cell characteristic is correct ? **[AIPMT 2007]**

(1) $a \neq b \neq c$ and $\alpha \neq \beta$ and $\gamma \neq 90°$

(2) $a \neq b \neq c$ and $\alpha = \beta = \gamma = 90°$

(3) $a = b = c$ and $\alpha \neq \beta \neq \gamma = 90°$

(4) $a = b = c$ and $\alpha = \beta = \gamma = 90°$

Sol : **(4)** For cubic crystal structure

$$a = b = c \ \& \ \alpha = \beta = \gamma = 90°$$

4. In the energy band diagram of a material shown below, the open circles and filled circles denote holes and electrons respectively. The material is a/an **[AIPMT 2007]**

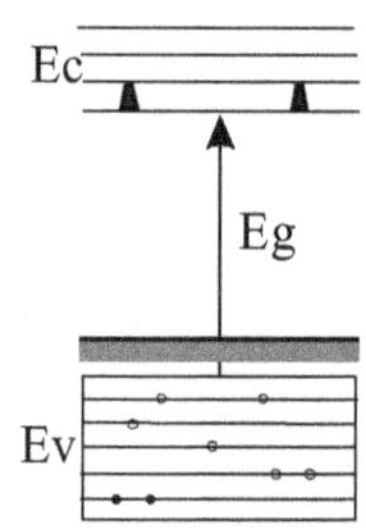

(1) p-type semiconductor

(2) insulator

(3) metal

(4) n - type semiconductor

Sol : **(1)** p-type semiconductor

5. The voltage gain of an amplifier with 9% negative feedback is 10. The voltage gain without feedback will be **[AIPMT 2008]**

(1) 90 (2) 10

(3) 1.25 (4) 100

Sol : **(4)** Voltage gain $=\dfrac{A_V}{1+\beta.A_V}$

Where $\beta=\dfrac{9}{100}=0.09$, Voltage gain = 10

$\Rightarrow 10=\dfrac{A_V}{1+\dfrac{9}{100}.A_V}$ $\qquad A_V=\dfrac{10}{0.1}=100$

6. A p-n photodiode is made of a material with a band gap of 2.0 eV. The minimum frequency of the radiation that can be absorbed by the material in nearly **[AIPMT 2008]**

(1) 10×10^{14} Hz (2) 5×10^{14} Hz
(3) 1×10^{14} Hz (4) 20×10^{14} Hz

Sol : **(2)** Frequency corresponding to 2eV is given by E = hv

$\Rightarrow 2\times1.6\times10^{-19}=66\times10^{-34}\times v$

$v=\dfrac{3.2\times10^{-19}}{6.6\times10^{-34}}=5\times10^{14}\text{Hz}$.

7. The circuit is equivalent to

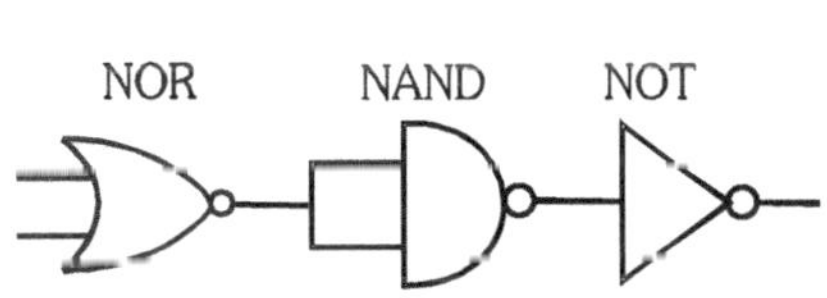

is equilvalent to:- **[AIPMT 2008]**

(1) NOR gate (2) OR gate
(3) AND gate (4) NAND gate

Sol : **(1)** The output is the output of NOR gate hence the combination will act as a NOR gate.

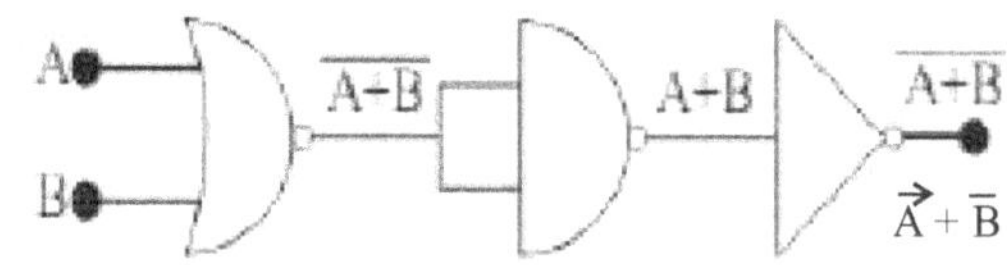

8. A p-n photodiode is fabricated from a semiconductor with a band gap of 2.5 eV. It can detect a signal of wavelength :- **[AIPMT 2009]**

(1) 4000 Å (2) 6000 Å
(3) 4000nm (4) 6000 nm

Sol : **(1)** $\lambda_{max}=\dfrac{hc}{eV}$

$\dfrac{1242\text{evÅ}}{2.5\text{eV}}=4960\text{Å}\approx 4000^{3}$

9. A transistor is operated in common-emitter configuration at V_c = 2V such that a change in the base current from 100 μA to 200 μA produces a change in the collector current from 5 mA to 10 mA. The current gain is : **[AIPMT 2009]**

(1) 50 (2) 75 (3) 100 (4) 150

Sol : **(1)** $\Delta I_B = 100\ \mu A$

$\Delta I_C = 5$ mA

$\beta=\dfrac{\Delta I_C}{\Delta I_B}=\dfrac{5\times10^{-3}}{100\times10^{-6}}=50$

10. The number of beta particles emitted by a radio-active substance is twice the number of alpha particles emitted by it. The resulting daughter is an **[AIPMT 2009]**

(1) isobar of parent (2) isomer of parent

(3) isotone of parent (4) isotone of parent

Sol : **(4)** $_{Z}X^{A} \xrightarrow{\alpha} {}_{Z-2}Y^{A-4} \xrightarrow{2\beta} {}_{Z}P^{A-4}$

As the resulting daughter and parent nucleus has same atomic number. So they are isotone.

11. Sodium has body centred packing. Distance between two nearest atoms is 3.7 Å. The lattice parameter is **[AIPMT 2009]**

(1) 6.8 Å (2) 4.3 Å

(3) 3.0 Å (4) 8.6 Å

Sol : **(2)** $\frac{\sqrt{3a}}{2} = 3.7\text{Å}$

$\Rightarrow a = \frac{2 \times 3.7}{\sqrt{3}} = 4.3\text{Å}$

12. Which one of the following statement is false ? **[AIPMT 2010]**

(1) The resistance of intrinsic semiconductor decreases with increase of temperature

(2) Pure Si doped with trivalent impurities gives a p-type semiconductor

(3) Mojority carriers in a n-type semiconductor are holes

(4) Minority carriers in a p-type semiconductor are electrons

Sol : **(2)** Electric and magnetic field vectors are perpendicular to each other in electromagnetic wave.

13. Which one of the following bonds produces a solid that reflects light in the visible region and whose electrical conductivity decreases with temperature and has high melting point ? **[AIPMT 2010]**

(1) metallic bonding

(2) van der Waals' bonding

(3) ionic bonding

(4) covalent bonding

Sol : **(1)** metallic bonding.

14. The device that can act as a complete electronic circuit is **[AIPMT 2010]**

(1) Junction diode (2) Integrated circuit

(3) Junction transistor (4) Zener diode

Sol : **(2)** Integrated circuit

15. To get an output Y=1 from the circuit shown below, then input must be : **[AIPMT 2010]**

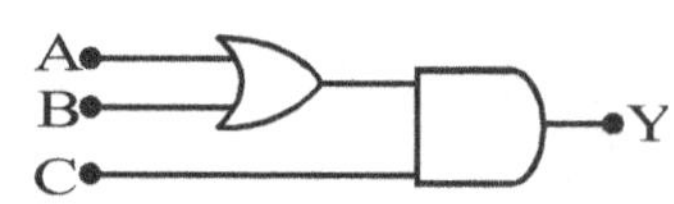

	A	B	C
(1)	1	0	0
(2)	0	1	0
(3)	0	0	1
(4)	1	0	1

Sol : **(4)** $Y = (A + B).C$

16. A transistor is operated in common emitter configuration at Vc = 2V such that a change in the base current from 100μA to 300 μA produces a change in the collector current from 10 mA to 20 mA.The current gain is **[AIPMT 2011]**

(1) 75 (2) 100

(3) 25 (4) 50

Sol : **(4)** $\beta = \frac{\Delta I_C}{\Delta I_B} = \frac{(20-10)\times 10^{-3}}{(300-100)\times 10^{-6}} = 50$

17. In forward biasing of the p-n junction **[AIPMT 2011]**

(1) the positive terminal of the battery is connected to n-side and the depletion region becomes thin

(2) the positive terminal of the battery is connected to p-side and the depletion region becomes thick

(3) the positive terminal of the battery is connected to p- side and the depletion region become thin

(4) the positive terminal of the battery is connected to p-side and the depletion region becomes thick

Sol : **(3)** In FB width of depletion layer is decreased.

18. The symbolic representation of four logic gates are given below :

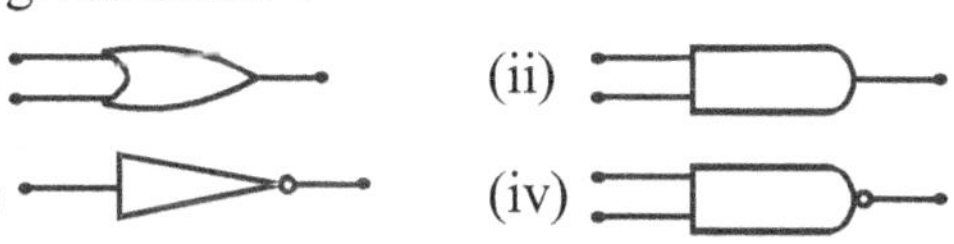

The logic symbols for AND, NAND and NOT gates are respectively :- **[AIPMT 2011]**

(1) (iii), (ii), (i) (2) (iii), (ii), (iv)

(3) (ii), (iv), (iii) (4) (ii), (iii), (iv)

Sol : **(3)** From theory

19. If a small amount of antimony is added to germanium crystal **[AIPMT 2011]**

(1) the antimony becomes an acceptor atom

(2) there will be more free electrons than holes in the semiconductor

(3) its resistances is increased

(4) it becomes a p-type semiconductor

Sol : **(2)** By addition of pertavalent impurity only n-type of semiconductor are constructed.

20. In the following figure, the diodes, which are forward biased, are **[AIPMT 2011]**

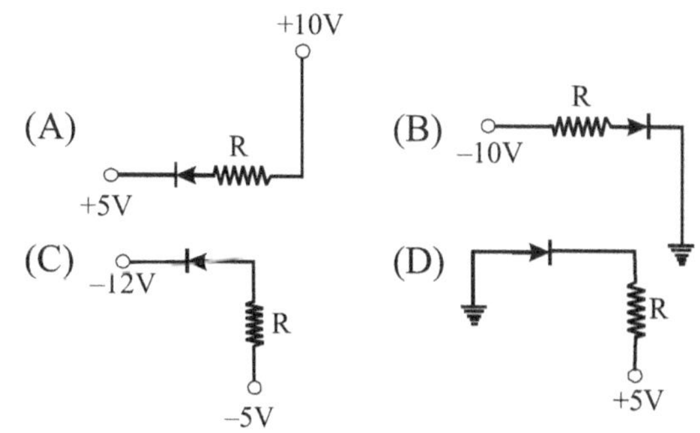

(1) (C) only (2) (C) and (A)

(3) (B) and (D) (4) (A), (B),and (D)

Sol : **(2)** p-n junction is paid to be forward biased when p side is at high potential than n side. It is for circuit (A) and (C).

21. Pure Si at 500 K has equal number of electron (n_e and hole (n_h) concentrations of 1.5×10^{16} m^{-3} Doping by indium increases nh to 4.5×10^{22} m^{-3} The doped semiconductor is of **[AIPMT 2011]**

(1) n - type with electron concentration $n_e = 5 \times 10^{22}$ m^{-3}

(2) p - type with electron concentration $n_e = 2.5 \times 10^{10}$ m^{-3}

(3) n - type with electron concentration $n_e = 2.5 \times 10^{23}$ m^{-3}

(4) p - type with electron concentration $n_e = 5 \times 10^{9}$ m^{-3}

Sol : **(4)** p-type semiconductor is obtained when Si or Ge is doped with a trivalent impurity like aluminium (Al), boron (B), indium (In) etc,

Here, $n_i = 1.5\times 10^{16} m^{-3}$

$n_i = 4.5\times 10^{22} m^{-3}$

As $n_e n_h = n_i^2$

$$n_e = \frac{n_i^2}{n_h} = \frac{\left(1.5\times 10^{16} m^{-3}\right)^2}{4.5\times 10^{22} m^{-3}} = 5\times 10^{9} m^{-3}.$$

22. A Zener diope, having breakdown voltage equal to 15 V, is used in a voltage regulator circuit shown in the figure. The current through the diode is **[AIPMT 2011]**

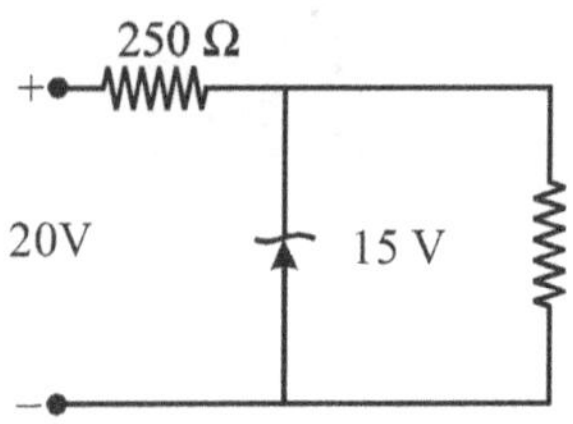

(1) 10 mA (2) 15 mA
(3) 20 mA (4) 5 mA

Sol : **(4)**

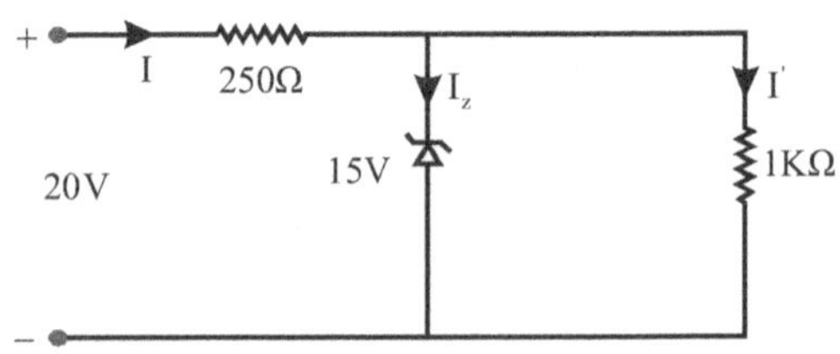

The voltage drop across $1\ k\Omega = V_z = 15\ V$

The current through $1\ k\Omega$ is

$$I' = \frac{15\ V}{1\times10^3\ \Omega} = 15\times10^{-3}\ A = 15mA$$

The voltage drop across

$250\ \Omega = 20\ V - 15\ V$

The current through $250\ \Omega$ is

$$I = \frac{5\ V}{250\ \Omega} = 0.02A = 20mA = 5V$$

The current through the zener diode is

$I_z = I - I' = (20-15)mA = 5mA$

23. Two ideal diodes are connected to a battery as shown in the curcuit. The current supplied by battery is **[AIPMT 2012]**

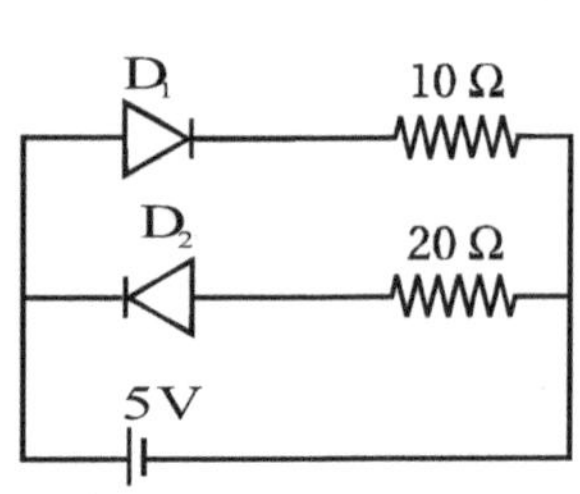

(1) 0.5 A (2) 0.75 A
(3) zero (4) 0.25 A

Sol : **(1)** Current will flow only in diode D_1 therefore current supplied by the battery is 0.5 A Since D_1 is forward bias and D_2 is reverse bias.

24. In a CE transistor amplifier, the audio signal voltage across the collector resistance is 1 kΩ and the current amplification of the transistor is 100, the input signal voltage is **[AIPMT 2012]**

(1) 10 mV (2) 0.1 V
(3) 1.0 V (4) 1 mV

Sol : **(1)** Voltage amplification

$$\frac{V_o}{V_i} = \text{Current gain} \times \frac{R_o}{R_i}$$

25. C and Si both have same lattice structure, having 4 bonding electrons in each. However, C is insulator whereas Si is intrinsic semiconductor. This is because **[AIPMT 2012]**

(1) The four bonding electrons in the case of C lie in the third orbit, whereas for Si they lie in the fourth orbit

(2) In case of C the valance bond is not completely filled at absolute zero temperature

(3) In case of C the conduction band is partly filled even at absolute zero temperature

(4) The four bonding electrons in the case of C lie in the second orbit, whereas in the case of Si they lie in the third orbit

Sol : **(4)** The four bonding electrons in the case of C lie in the second orbit, whereas in the case of Si they lie in the third.

26. Transfer characteristics [Output voltage (V_0) vs. Input voltage (V_i)] for a base biased transistor in CE configuration is as shown in the figure. For using transistor as a switch, it is used **[AIPMT 2012]**

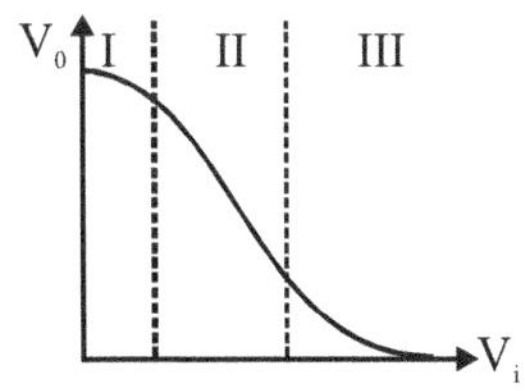

(1) in region I

(2) in region III

(3) both in regions (I) and in (III)

(4) in region II

Sol : **(3)** For using transistor as a switch, it is used in cut off state and saturation state only.

27. The figure shows a logic circuit with two imputs A and B and the output C. The voltage wave forms across A, B and C are as given. the logic circuit gate is **[AIPMT 2012]**

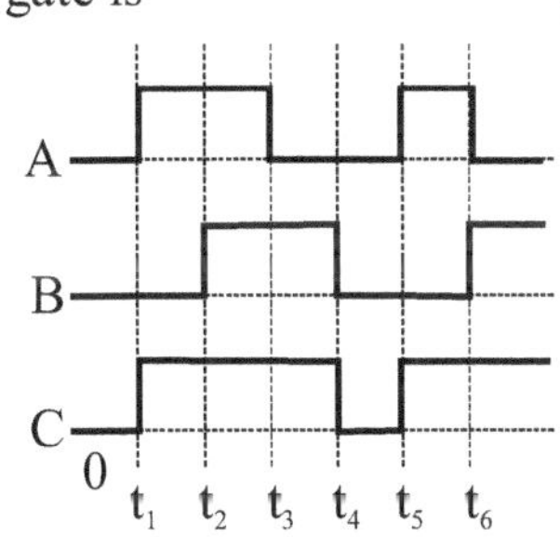

(1) NAND (2) OR gate

(3) NOR gate (4) AND gate

Sol : **(2)** The logic of the OR gate is if any of the input in one then output is one.

28. The input resistance of a silicon transistor is 100 Ω. Base current is changed by 40 μA which results in a change in collector current by 2 mA. This transistor is used as a common-emitter amplifier with a load as a common-emitter amplifier with a load resistance of 4kΩ. The voltage gain of the amplifier is **[AIPMT 2012]**

(1) 2000 (2) 3000

(3) 4000 (4) 1000

Sol : **(1)** Here,

Input resistance, $R_i = 100\ \Omega$

change in base current, $\Delta I_B = 40\ \mu A$

Change in collector current, $\Delta I_C = 2\ mA$

Load resistance, $R_L = 4\ k\Omega = 4\times10^3\ \Omega$

Current gain, $\beta = \frac{\Delta I_C}{\Delta I_B} = \frac{2mA}{40\mu A}$

$$= \frac{2\times10^{-3}A}{40\times10^{-6}A} = 50$$

Voltage gain of the amplifier is

$$A_V = \beta\frac{R_L}{R_i} = 50\times\frac{4\times10^3}{100} = 2000$$

29. To get an output Y = I in given circuit which of the following input will be correct **[AIPMT 2012]**

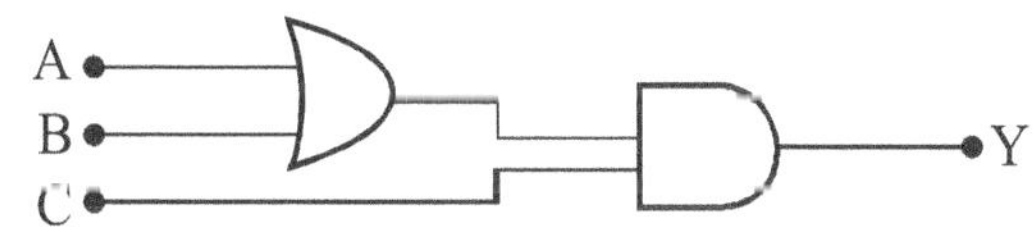

	A	B	C		A	B	C
(1)	1	0	0	(2)	1	0	1
(3)	1	1	0	(4)	0	1	0

Sol : (2) 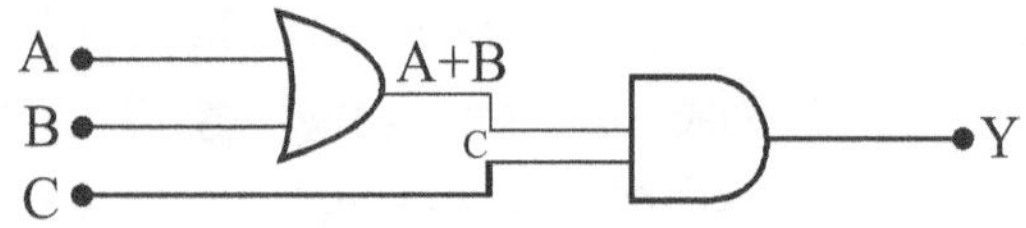

The Boolean expression of the given circuit is $Y = (A + B).C$

The table truth of the given inputs is as shown in the table.

	Inputs		Output
A	B	C	Y=(A+B).C
1	0	0	0
1	0	1	1
1	1	0	0
0	1	0	0

Form the above truth table it is clear that $y = 1$

when $A = 1$, $B = 0$ and $C = 1$ $\begin{bmatrix} 1 & 0 & 1 \\ A & B & C \end{bmatrix}$

30. In a n-type semiconductor, which of the following statement is true? **[AIPMT 2013]**

(1) Electrons are majority carriers and trivalent atoms are dopant

(2) Electrons are minority carriers and pentavalent atoms are dopants

(3) Holes are minority carriers and pentavalent atoms are dopants

(4) Holes are majority carriers and trivalent atoms are dopants

Sol : **(3)** In n-type semiconductor, electrons are majority change carriers and holes are minority charge carriers and pentavalent atoms are dopants.

31. In a common emitter (CE) amplifier having a voltage gain G, the transistor used has transconductance 0.03 mho and current gain 25. If the above transistor is replaced with another one with transconductance 0.02 mho and current gain 20, the voltage gain will be **[AIPMT 2013]**

(1) $\frac{2}{3}G$ (2) 1.5 G

(3) $\frac{1}{3}G$ (4) $\frac{5}{4}G$

Sol : **(1)** Voltage gain = Current gain × Resitance gain

$$A_\upsilon = \beta \times \frac{R_{out}}{R_{in}}$$

Transconductance, $g_m = \frac{\beta}{R_{in}}$ or $R_{in} = \frac{\beta}{g_m}$

$$A_\upsilon = g_m R_{out}$$

For second case, $A_\upsilon = G$, $g_m = 0.03$ mho or $\beta = 25$

$\therefore G = 0.03R_{out}$ ...(i)

For secound case, $A_\upsilon = G'$, $g_m = 0.02$, $\beta = 20$

$\therefore G' = 0.02R_{out}$ ...(ii)

Divide (ii) bt (i), we get

$$\frac{G'}{G} = \frac{2}{3} \text{ or } G' = \frac{2}{3}G$$

32. The output (X) of the logic circuit shown in figure will be **[AIPMT 2013]**

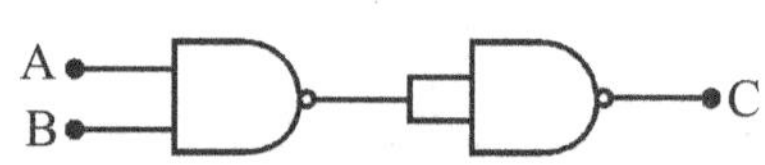

(1) $X = \overline{\overline{A}} \cdot \overline{\overline{B}}$ (2) $X = \overline{A \cdot B}$

(3) $X = A \cdot B$ (4) $X = \overline{A + B}$

Sol : (3) 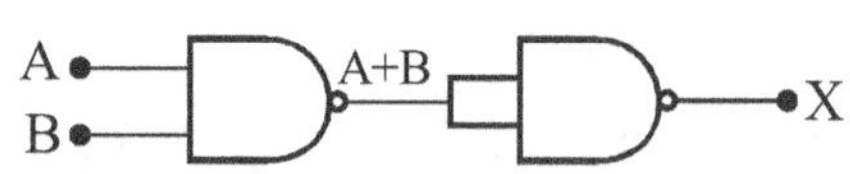

The output of the given logic circuit is

$$X = \overline{\overline{A.B}} = A.B$$

33. The given graph represent V–I characteristic for a semiconductor device.

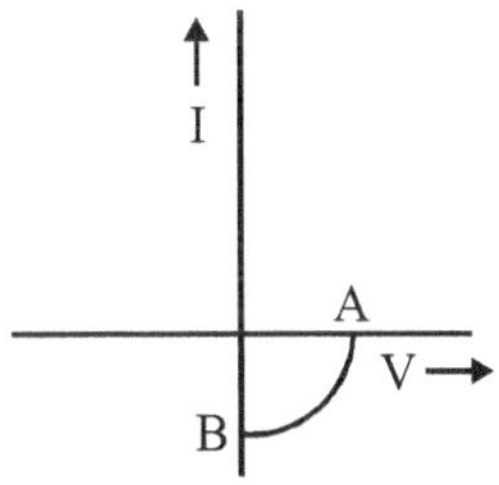

Which of the following statement is correct?

[AIPMT 2014]

(1) It is V-I characteristic for solar cell where point A represents open circuit voltage and point B short circuit current

(2) It is for a solar cell and points A and B represent open ciruit voltage and current, respectively

(3) It is for a photodiode and points A and B represent open circuit voltage and current, resppectively

(4) It is for and LED and points A and B represents open circuit voltage and short circuit current respectively

Sol : **(1)**

34. The barrier potential of a p-n juction depends on **[AIPMT 2014]**

(i) Type of semiconductor material

(ii) Amount of doping

(iii) Temperature

Which one of the following is correct?

(1) (i) and (ii) only (2) (ii) only

(3) (ii) and (iii) only (4) (i), (ii) and (iii)

Sol : **(4)**

35. Which logic gate is represented by the following combination of logic gates? **[AIPMT 2015]**

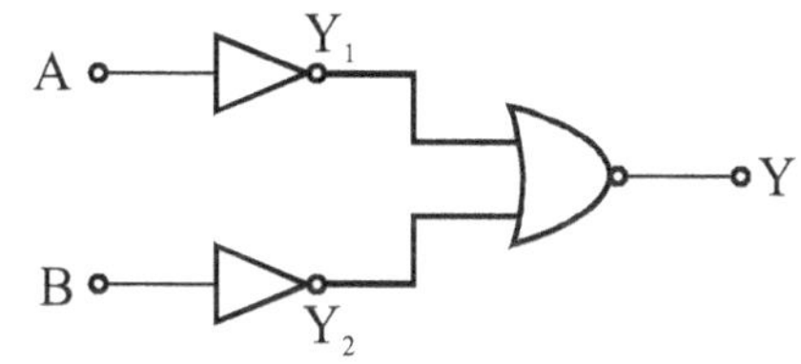

(1) OR (2) NAND

(3) AND (4) NOR

Sol : **(3)** AND

36. If in a p-n junction, a square input signal of 10 V is applied, as shown **[AIPMT 2015]**

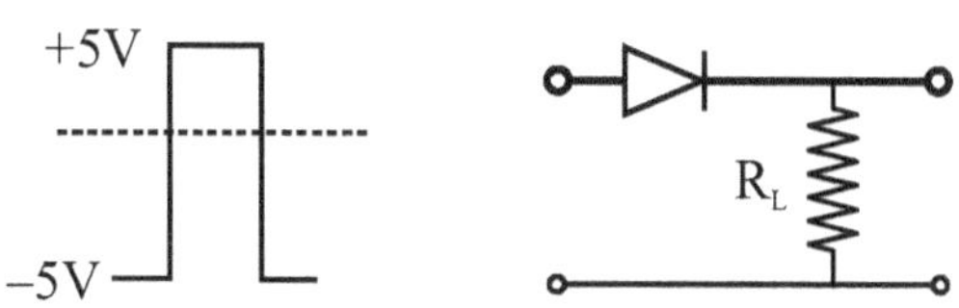

then the output across R_L will be

(1) 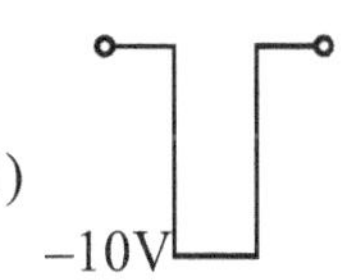

(2) 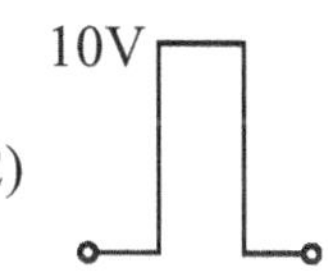

(3) 

(4) 

Sol : **(3)** The diode will work in forward bios only hence answer 2.

37. In the given figure, a diode D is connected to an external resistance R = 100 Ω and an emf of 3.5 V. If the barrier potential developed across the diode is 0.5 V, the current in the circuit will be **[AIPMT 2015 Re]**

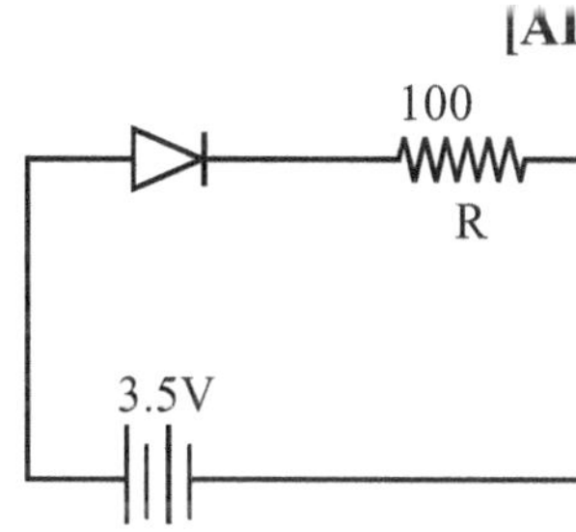

(1) 35 mA (2) 30 mA

(3) 40 mA (4) 20 mA

Sol : **(2)**

Potential difference on $R = 3.5 - 0.5 = 3.0$ Volte

Current in circuit $i = \frac{V}{R} = \frac{3}{100} = 30\text{mA}$

38. Consider the junction diode as ideal. The value of current flowing through AB is : **[AIPMT 2016]**

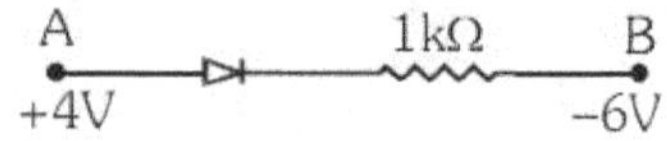

(1) 0 A (2) 10^{-2}A
(3) 10^{-1} A (4) 10^{-3} A

Sol : **(2)** For diode as ideal

$$i=\frac{\Delta V}{R}=\frac{4-(-6)}{10^3}=10^{-2}\text{ A}$$

39. A npn transistor is connected in common emitter configuration in a given amplifier. A load resistance of 800 Ω is connected in the collector circuit and the voltage drop across it is 0.8 V. If the current amplification factor is 0.96 and the input resistance of the circuit is 192 Ω, the voltage gain and the power gain of the amplifier will respectively be : **[AIPMT 2016]**

(1) 4, 3.84 (2) 3.69, 3.84
(3) 4, 4 (4) 4, 3.69

Sol : **(1)** Voltage gain = [current gain] [resistance gain]$[.96]\frac{800}{192}$

power gain = [current gain] [resistance gain]

$[.96][4]=3.84$

40. To get output 1 for the following circuit, the correct choice for the input is **[AIPMT 2016]**

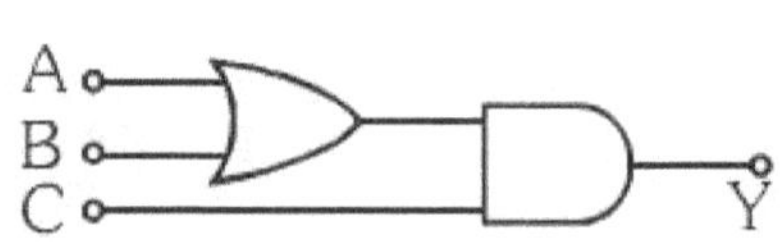

(1) A = 0, B = 1, C = 0
(2) A = 1, B = 0, C = 0
(3) A = 1, B = 1, C = 0
(4) A = 1, B = 0, C = 1

Sol : **(4)**

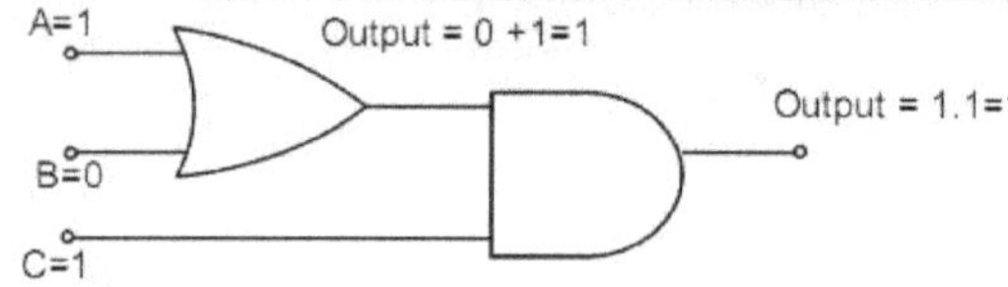

41. For CE transistor amplifier, the audio signal voltage across the collector resistance of 2 k Ω is 4 V. If the current amplification factor of the transistor is 100 and the base resistance is 1 k Ω, then the input signal voltage is :- **[NEET–II(2016)]**

(1) 30 mV (2) 15 mV (3) 10 mV (4) 20 mV

Sol : **(4)** $A_V=\beta\frac{R_{out}}{R_{in}}$

$$A_V=100\times\frac{2k\Omega}{1k\Omega}\Rightarrow A_V=200$$

$$A_V=\frac{(V_{out})_{Ac}}{(V_m)_{Ac}}=200 \quad (V_{in})_{AC}=\frac{4}{200}=200\text{mV}$$

42. The given circuit has two ideal diodes connected as shown in the figure below. The current flowing through the resistance R_1 will be :- **[NEET–II(2016)]**

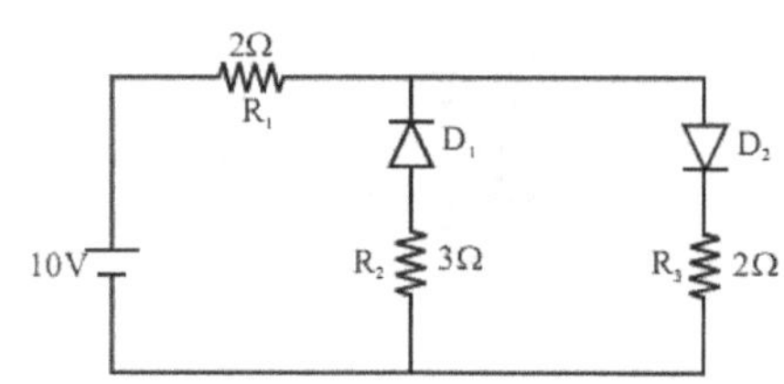

(1) 1.43 A (2) 3.13 A
(3) 2.5 A (4) 10.0 A

Sol : **(3)** The diode D_1 will be be in reverse bias , so it will block the current and diode D_1 will be in forward bias, so it will pass the current

$$i=\frac{10}{2+2}=2.5\text{A} .$$

43. What is the output Y in the following circuit, when **[NEET – II(2016)]**

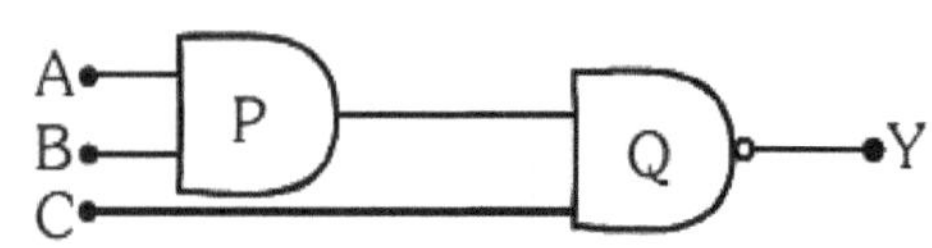

all the three inputs A,B,C are first 0 and then 1 ?

(1) 1,0 (2) 1,1 (3) 0,1 (4) 0,0

Sol : (1) 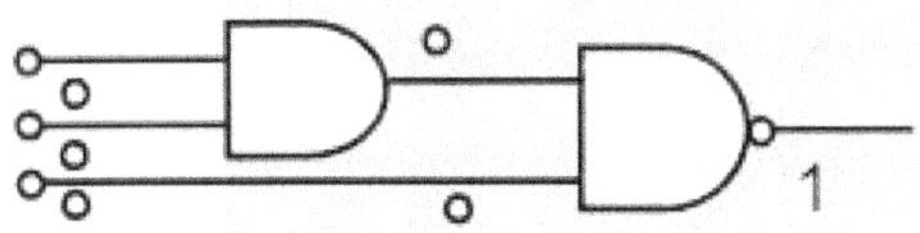

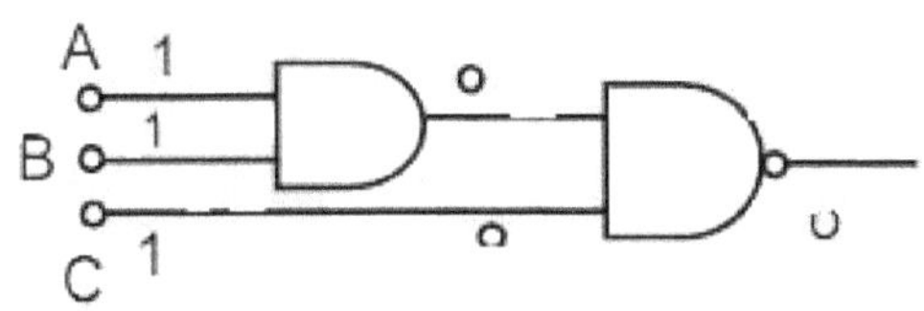

44. In a common emitter transistor amplifier the audio signal voltage across the collector is 3 v. The resistance of collector 3 kΩ. If current gain is 100 and the base resistance is 2 kΩ , the voltage and power gain of the amplifier is :

[NEET – 2017]

(1) 200 and 1000 (2) 15 and 200

(3) 150 and 15000 (4) 20 and 2000

Sol : **(3)** Current gain $(\beta) = 100$

Voltage gain $(A_V) = \beta \frac{R_c}{R_b}$

$= 100\left(\frac{3}{2}\right) = 150$

power gain $= A_V\beta$

$= 150(100) = 15000.$

45. Which one of the following represents forward bias diode ? **[NEET – 2017]**

(1) 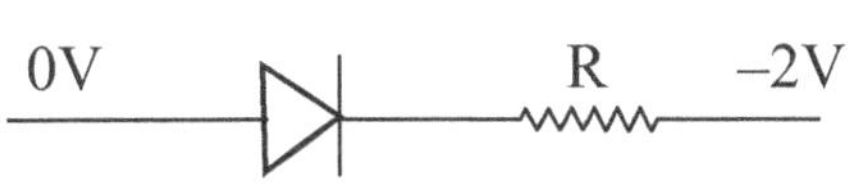

(2) 

(3) 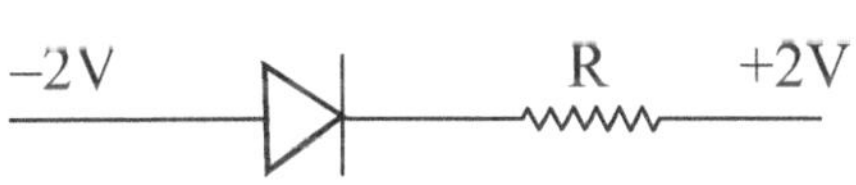

(4) 

Sol : **(1)** In forward bias, p-type semiconductor is at higher potential w.r.t. n -type semiconductor.

46. The given electrical network is equivalent to :

[NEET – 2017]

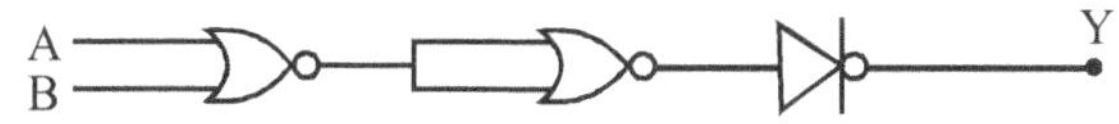

(1) AND gate (2) OR gate

(3) NOR gate (4) NOT gate

Sol : **(3)** $Y = \overline{A + B}$

47. In the circuit shown in the figure, the input voltage V_i is 20 V, $V_{BE} = 0$ and $V_{CE} = 0$. The values of I_B, I_C and β are given by **[NEET-2018]**

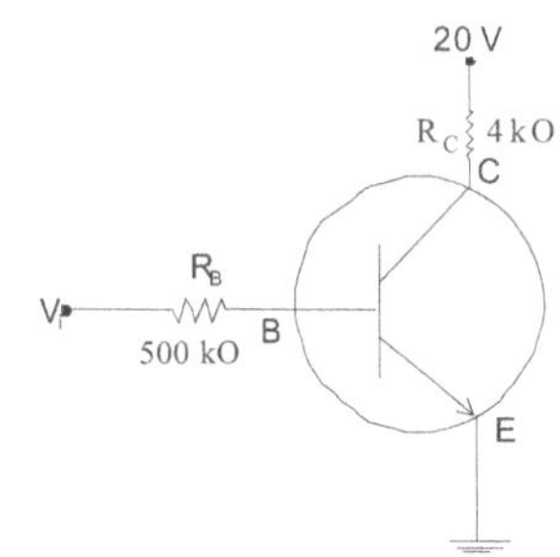

(1) $I_B = 20\ \mu A$, $I_C = 5$ mA, $\beta = 250$

(2) $I_B = 25\ \mu A$, $I_C = 5$ mA, $\beta = 200$

(3) $I_B = 40\ \mu A$, $I_C = 10$ mA, $\beta = 250$

(4) $I_B = 40\ \mu A$, $I_C = 5$ mA, $\beta = 125$

Ans. **(4)** $V_{BE} = 0$; $V_{CE} = 0$; $V_b = 0$

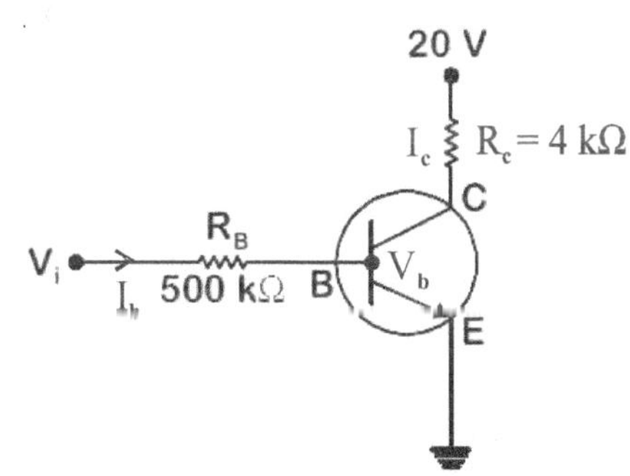

$I_C = \frac{(20-0)}{4\times10^3}$

$I_C = 5 \times 10^{-3} = 5$ mA

$V_i = V_{BE} + I_B R_B$

$20 - 0 + I_B R_B$

$20 = I_B \times 500 \times 10^3$

$I_B = \frac{20}{500\times10^3} = 40\ \mu A$

$\beta = \frac{I_c}{I_b} = \frac{25\times10^{-3}}{40\times10^{-6}} = 125$

48. In a p-n junction diode, change in temperature due to heating **[NEET-2018]**

(1) does not affect resistance of p-n junction

(2) affects only forward resistance

(3) affects only reverse resistance

(4) affects the overall V - I characteristics of p-n junction

Ans. **(4)** Due to heating, number of electron-hole pairs will increase, so overall resistance of diode will change.

Due to which forward biasing and reversed biasing both are changed.

49. In the combination of the following gates the output Y can be written in terms of inputs A and B as **[NEET-2018]**

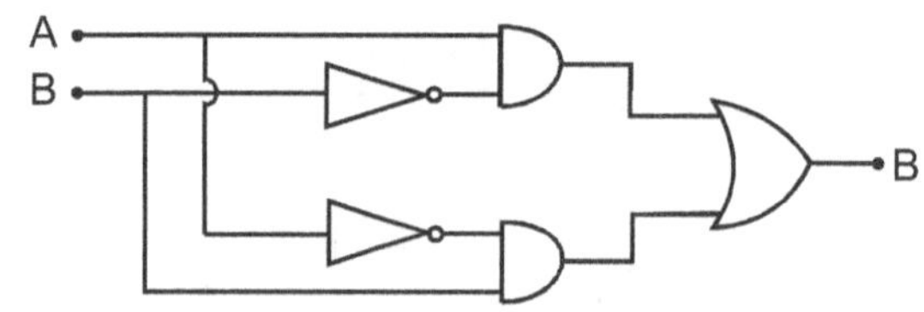

(1) $\overline{A \cdot B} + A \cdot B$ (2) $A \cdot \overline{B} + \overline{A} \cdot B$

(3) $\overline{A \cdot B}$ (4) $\overline{A + B}$

Ans. **(2)**

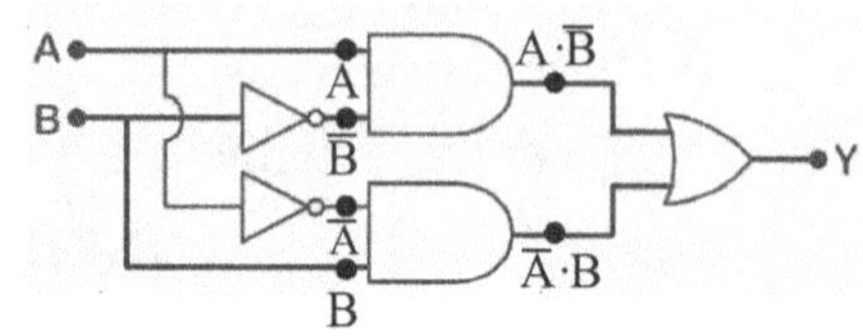

$Y = (A \cdot \overline{B} + \overline{A} \cdot B)$

www.ingramcontent.com/pod-product-compliance
Lightning Source LLC
Chambersburg PA
CBHW080242170726
48282CB00031B/1175
* 9 7 8 8 1 9 3 9 2 7 4 1 0 *